Freedom Music

Freedom Music

Wales, Emancipation and Jazz 1850–1950

Jen Wilson

University of Wales Press
2019

© Jen Wilson, 2019

All rights reserved. No part of this book may be reproduced in any material form (including photocopying or storing it in any medium by electronic means and whether or not transiently or incidentally to some other use of this publication) without the written permission of the copyright owner except in accordance with the provisions of the Copyright, Designs and Patents Act 1988. Applications for the copyright owner's written permission to reproduce any part of this publication should be addressed to The University of Wales Press, University Registry, King Edward VII Avenue, Cardiff CF10 3NS
www.uwp.co.uk

British Library Cataloguing-in-Publication Data
A catalogue record for this book is available from the British Library.

ISBN   978-1-78683-407-2
e-ISBN 978-1-78683-408-9

The right of Jen Wilson to be identified as author of this work has been asserted by her in accordance with sections 77 and 79 of the Copyright, Designs and Patents Act 1988.

The publisher acknowledges the financial support of the Welsh Books Council.

Typeset by Eira Fenn Gaunt, Pentyrch
Printed by CPI Antony Rowe, Melksham

For Haulwen my mother who played piano,
Bill my father who played ukulele
and brother John who played drums.

Without the following two people this book would not have been written:
Dr Ursula Masson (1945–2008) who kick-started my discovery of education, and my husband Mike, a well-read man. Thank you for the support and encouragement. Sons Rhydderch, Meredydd and Owain still talk to me, and grandson Marty.

Contents

Dedication	v
Foreword	ix
Preface	xiii
Acknowledgements	xvii
Illustrations	xxiii
Introduction	1
1 The Life, Times and Music of Swansea Abolitionist Jessie Donaldson (1799–1889)	13
2 Doing the Plantation Walkaround Skedaddle	51
3 The Fisk Jubilee Singers in Wales, Freed Slaves and their Songs	83
4 Ragtime and the Cake Walk: On Stage and in the Workhouse	111
5 The First World War: Ragtime Trenches and Suffragettes	129
6 Café Society: The Jazz Age	153
7 Cutting a Rug to the Second World War: Jews and 'Negro Morals'	183
8 Fair Treatment for the 'Fair Sex'?	223
Conclusion	253
Notes	259
Bibliography	295
Index	305

Foreword

Deirdre Beddoe, Emeritus Professor of Women's History at the University of South Wales
I am delighted to be invited to provide a short foreword to *Freedom Music*. I cannot claim to be an expert on jazz or indeed on any type of music. My expertise lies in the history of women in Wales and this book makes an important contribution to both women's history and to the history of popular culture in Wales. It demolishes the popular conception that all Welsh music was chapel based and dominated by male voice choirs. And it also shows the importance of women performers in the development of jazz and in other areas of popular musical entertainment. *Freedom Music* brings to our attention for the first time the part played by Welsh women both in the USA and in Wales in the anti-slavery movement. This book makes a key contribution not only to the history of music but to the history of Wales. Clearly American music, be it jazz or Negro minstrel performances, was a diversion and a delight to the Welsh urban working class. To me personally, it explains my father's delight in performing the Charleston well into his later years!

Sir Deian Hopkin, Former Vice-Chancellor of London South Bank University and retired President of the National Library of Wales
In recent years, there has been increased interest in the history of jazz in Wales as a new generation of accomplished and innovative Welsh musicians, both women and men, make their mark in Britain and internationally. While we await a comprehensive account of jazz from Harry Parry and Dill Jones to the present day, we now have an enthralling and original account of the role of women in the early days of jazz in Wales. Jen Wilson, herself an accomplished jazz pianist and performer,

who has directed the notable Jazz Heritage Wales multimedia resource centre, examines how jazz is rooted in the culture and even politics of Wales. Long before the American Original Dixieland Jazz Band's 1919 tour, often claimed as the starting point for jazz in Britain, there were earlier roots, carefully traced by Jen Wilson, from abolitionist songs and Negro minstrelsy performances in the nineteenth century to the influential tours by the ex-slave Fisk Jubilee Singers over a thirty-year period to 1907. She also shows how dance, fashion and popular culture, in which women were prominent, shaped the response of Wales to jazz. This is a major contribution to the historiography of Welsh jazz, and Welsh music generally, as well as to a richer appreciation of popular culture in Wales and the central role of women in it.

Kim Collis, County Archivist, West Glamorgan County Archives, City and County of Swansea

I am delighted to be invited to contribute a few words here as a foreword. There is a growing recognition amongst historians that the hitherto mainstream historical narrative of industrial development and post-industrial decline often overlooks and ignores the importance of other narratives within the story of mass migration and urbanisation in nineteenth and twentieth century Wales. In particular, two sets of voices are now more frequently encountered in recent accounts, those of women and those of immigrants to Wales. I am pleased that Jen Wilson is adding to our body of knowledge on both counts in this book. Challenging as it is to locate the archives and printed sources for this rebalancing of our modern history, it represents a necessary reinterpretation of the history of Wales. The eminent historian Christopher Hill once wrote, 'History has to be rewritten in every generation, because although the past does not change, the present does; each generation asks new questions of the past and finds new areas of sympathy as it re-lives different aspects of the experiences of its predecessors.'[1]

In today's multicultural society, it is crucial that we recognise the diverse world we live in, not just as a phenomenon of the past few decades, but as a continuation of human experience in Wales over several centuries, a natural product of our human instinct to seek out, absorb and integrate new experiences which is the catalyst for our continuing cultural growth as a nation.

1   Christopher Hill, *The World Turned Upside Down: Radical Ideas During the English Revolution* (London: Penguin Books, 1972), p. 15

Preface

When and how did jazz come to Wales? The research for this book began in 1980 when Ursula Masson, with an MA in History, set up the Swansea Women's History Group, and in 1998 the Women's Archive of Wales/ Archif Menywod Cymru. Ursula was keen to experience what she described as a 'new way of working' to discover the lost voices of women in Wales. Gail Allen and I joined the group. Some work was later combined with Women in Jazz, now incorporated into Jazz Heritage Wales. Ursula Masson said to me, 'You are a jazz pianist, what's the Welsh story?' I didn't know. 'Then find out', she said.

Over the following decades, I amassed materials on the history of jazz, much of which is housed in Jazz Heritage Wales. I recorded oral interviews and collected books, audio tapes and videos, trawled through microfiche and old newspapers, wrote and published articles, presented papers at conferences and gave talks to local history groups about jazz and its cultural history and politics, as well as developing exhibitions, giving performances and composing jazz music. However, this is my first full-length publication.

I make no apologies for being fascinated by the minutiae of people's lives, which form the core content of this book, as I am primarily a local historian rather than a political theorist. There is more research still to be done on the history of jazz in Wales, and so I hope that this book will inspire others.

This book uses the raw material of social and cultural history drawing on contemporary accounts using vernacular expressions, for example, 'coon', 'nigger minstrelsy' and 'negro morals'. Following active political campaigning against racial discrimination, such racist and offensive terms are no longer acceptable in the public media.

As a historian, I would not wish to whitewash any terminology used in its historical context. That was the time. That was how people were referred to. And, although in my lifetime I have seen important changes in the increased respect given to African and African American musicians, many people in the USA and Britain still have ingrained racist attitudes which have sadly become more publicly evident over the period of my writing this book.

As a female jazz pianist, I identify with the struggles of women jazz musicians against sexism. My perspective is that of a white Welsh feminist jazz musician and historian, and so this book is written unashamedly from a feminist viewpoint. I make no apologies for that, as feminism has given me the impetus to put back those lost stories where they belong.

The Swansea poet David Hughes has written of his poem *Rescuers*, 'It is also dedicated to the many local historians who contribute every day to a greater understanding of the history of extraordinary "ordinary people". The following poem celebrates you.'

Rescuers
In praise of local historians.
For ER, JW and RC

'*The past [is] not a millstone but a life raft*' – Paul Durcan

They pester neighbours,
note their memories,
translate family ramblings;
prowl around archives,
blow dust off registers,
get tangled in the internet.

They climb the branches of family trees,
root out parents,
uncover children;
haunt cemeteries,
scrape lichen, gouge out moss,
reveal '*The Beloved Wife*'.

They discover where the pilgrims walked,
where the washing was done,
and the stone quarried;
where the Welfare stood,
where the dances were held
and the bands that played.

They list the servants at Ty Mawr,
the names of those who went to war
and those who stayed.

They know where the trains ran,
and when they stopped.
They mark the last mine.

They wander purposefully,
wondering why?
Why there? Why then?

They nudge councils,
needle developers,
make planners revise plans.

They throw us a rope from the past,
reminding us who we are –
they make life rafts.

David Hughes (2016, unpublished)

Acknowledgements

This book has been a slow burn. I had a distrust for academia prompted by my escape from school in 1960 aged sixteen (they kept the piano locked to discourage me from corrupting young minds), which resulted in honing my piano skills in jazz clubs. The return-to-learn process began in 1980 when Ursula Masson, MA (later Dr), encouraged me to join the Swansea Women's History Group she had recently set up. I joined, together with Gail Allen, BA. Through the Group I learned how to ask questions and discuss the answers. With them, various research and filming projects took me to the Public Record Office (now National Archives), Kew, London, the National Library of Wales, Aberystwyth, and a variety of universities, conferences and archives. Filming and research skills were developed at West Glamorgan Video and Film Workshop, Swansea, and Chapter Arts Centre, Cardiff. A parallel life entailed working with community music and integrated music projects, poets, writers, dancers and painters. All the while the unanswered question dawdled, prompted by Ursula asking 'What's the jazz story in Wales?' I began answering it in 1986 when I set up the Women's Jazz Archive from a spare bedroom. I am indebted to Ursula Masson, Gail Allen and Swansea Women's History Group for setting me on the road to discovery.

I am very grateful for the early support and encouragement received from South West Wales Media and to Jonathan Roberts, Editor of the *South Wales Evening Post*, for permission to use text, quotes and adverts from the *Cambrian* and *South Wales Daily Post*; local newspapers are an invaluable contribution to our knowledge and understanding of our cultural heritage.

Without our libraries and archives keeping safe the minutiae of our lives, our understanding of our past would be lost in the fog. Particular thanks are owed to Marilyn Jones, Local Studies librarian at Swansea

Central Library, for her guidance and support during my years of tracing threads of stories, and to the staff of the glorious old Swansea Reference Library, who were patience personified; this building is now the Alex Building, University of Wales Trinity St David.

My thanks for their early help and support go to the National Jazz Archive at Loughton Library, Loughton, Essex, started by trumpeter Digby Fairweather, and especially to archivist David Nathan. The complete run of the *Melody Maker* is held here.

I would like to thank University of Wales Trinity Saint David (UWTSD) for their support in housing the multimedia collections of Jazz Heritage Wales, now incorporating Women's Jazz Archive and Women in Jazz, for providing a safe haven for research and access to the archive's resources. UWTSD staff who realised the potential in the Jazz Heritage Wales archives and collections, and that a book could eventually emerge, need to be thanked profusely. These are Vice Chancellor Professor Medwin Hughes; former Vice Chancellor Professor David Warner; Pro-Vice Chancellor Professor Mike Phillips, Research, Innovation, Enterprise and Commercialisation; Professor Ian Walsh, Dean of Faculty of Art and Design/Swansea College of Art; Gill Fildes, Archives and Records Manager; and Senior Research Fellow Dr Catriona Ryan. For technical help with reimaging, a grateful thanks goes to Garry Bartlett. The UWTSD Library staff have been particularly encouraging and supportive, Alison Harding, Executive Head of Library and Learning Resources, and Mari Thomas Deputy Head Librarian at the Townhill Campus Library and her staff in which Jazz Heritage Wales resides in a pleasant and convivial atmosphere. A move to a new campus is planned for 2019.

I would like to thank Deb Checkland, Chair of Jazz Heritage Wales Board of Trustees, Patrons Dame Cleo Laine, Paula Gardiner, composer/double bass player, pianist and composer Huw Warren, together with the Trustees and Advisers for the encouragement of my research work, and the support I received during the running of various projects, from which live performances, published articles, conference papers and exhibitions emerged, eventually leading to this book. Adviser, friend and colleague Silva Huws is due a very large, special thank you, as

Silva encouraged me to start work on this book. I am indebted to her for her attention to planning, detail and formulating of chapters, for proofreading and sharing gallons of tea and many packets of biscuits during discussions. I am indebted to Trustee and Treasurer Gail Allen's continued encouragement and support, and many laughs, during the writing of this book. Catherine Tackley, Trustee/Adviser, is thanked profusely for advising from a distance and being available.

Val Feld (1947–2001), AM, our first Chair of Trustees, is still much missed for her early work in inaugurating the Board of Trustees, as is Trustee Ursula Masson (1945–2008) who was there from the beginning and taught me how to undertake research work with Swansea Women's History Group. I would like to thank Jazz Heritage Wales Trustee, academic and saxophonist Daniel G. Williams for encouraging me to submit a paper for his groundbreaking international conference in March 2007, 'Transatlantic Exchange: African Americans and the Celtic Nations', seeds of which appear in chapter 1, 'The Life, Times and Music of Swansea Abolitionist Jessie Donaldson (1799–1889)'.

For many discussions on how jazz functions within business and financial infrastructures, and how it continues to survive, despite the jobsworths and jazz police, a salute to trumpeter Chris Hodgkins, formerly Director of Jazz Services Ltd UK.

Warm thanks are given to good friends Margot Morgan and Elissa Evans, supreme vocalists and 'Divas', who worked with me over many projects interpreting old sheet music and bringing it to the public, particularly for the schools touring project 'Before Freedom'. Margot runs the Brynmill Community Choir, which now gives public performances of the songs of the Fisk Jubilee Singers (see chapter 3). Elissa is a fine artist in her own right and undertakes commissions in jazz and other prints. The gifted vocalist Christian Rae brought the fugitive slave Willis to life for 'Before Freedom', enabling thousands of schoolchildren to think about attitudes to slavery and join in the singing of abolitionist songs and plantation melodies while they learned about Wales's forgotten history. Thanks too, go to Deborah Glenister, who wrote band charts and supported the concept of, and performed for, 'Before Freedom' and also ran workshops for the Women in Jazz Allstars, the first all-woman swing band in Swansea since the Second World War. All these projects helped to formulate the story of how jazz came to Wales.

My much missed friend Nigel Jenkins (1949–2014) writer, poet, historian, blues harmonica player, activist and co-editor of *The Welsh Academy Encyclopaedia of Wales* (University of Wales Press, 2008), gave me insights into Welsh history while we were touring Wales with the Salubrious Rhythm Company, together with poet and guitarist John Barnie, the best of travelling companions. Both helped me to form ideas for this book.

Thanks are also due to Emeritus Professor of Women's History Deirdre Beddoe for her early encouragement, lively discussions on feminist history, and subsequent acceptance of my chapter, 'Redefining the Sixties Myth: Letters Home to Swansea', in Deirdre Beddoe (ed.), *Changing Times, Welsh Women Writing on the 1950s and 1960s* (Honno, 2003), from which ideas for this book flowed. Thanks also go to jazz pianist Professor Sir Deian Hopkin, former President, National Library of Wales, Aberystwyth, Honorary Professor (History) at Essex University, and Emeritus Professor UEL and LSBU, for discussions on jazz and Welsh history, threads of which appear in this book. Kim Collis, City Archivist at West Glamorgan Archive Services, keeps our records safe and has supported and encouraged my work over many years, thank you. Formerly Professor of Adult and Continuing Education at Swansea University, Dr Hywel Francis, founder of the South Wales Miners' Library, former MP for Aberavon and Trustee of the Paul Robeson Wales Trust, is also due my thanks for giving an early home to the Women's Jazz Archive at DACE Swansea University from 1992–6, and for his encouragement and stimulating discussions on Wales, feminism and the Miners' Strike, 1984–5, which encouraged research for this book. I would like to thank Dr. Rainer E. Lotz, jazz historian, record collector and contributor to radio and television programmes whom I met at a conference, for his early support for my research into African American music in Wales. Patron Paula Gardiner, bass player, composer and arranger, and Head of Jazz Studies at Cardiff's Royal Welsh College of Music and Drama, consented to an oral history interview and became an early inspiration to uncover the hidden story of jazz in Wales. The interviews I did for the Jazz Heritage Wales Oral History Collection (1986–2008) have helped me understand and interpret theories on feminist cultural history and provided ideas for the book, together with an anxious realisation that primary sources were fast disappearing. Therefore my grateful thanks go to the following women, some of whom are sadly no longer with us, for their oral histories: Cheryl Alleyne, Beryl Bryden, Elaine Delmar, Monique Ennis, Blanche Finlay, Patti Flynn, Li Harding, Uzo Iwobi, Carol Anne Jones, Paula King, Crissie Lee, Margaret Morris, Ottilie Patterson, Marcia Pendlebury, Marjorie Scott, Kathy Stobart, Barbara Thompson, Jackie Tracey, Humie Webbe and Sally White.

Many enjoyable discussions have taken place on the minutiae of jazz since 1991 with jazz photographer and long-term volunteer at Jazz Heritage Wales Derek Gabriel. Derek's attention to detail plus the organisation and cataloguing of the shelves helped me in researching parts of this book, and grateful thanks go to him for allowing me to pick clean his encyclopaedic brain. I am grateful too for the support and encouragement of many musicians who have been willing to listen, debate and dissect arguments on what jazz is and its role within history, culture and politics, Cris Haines, trumpeter, composer and arranger, in particular, for throwing into the mix that the 1613 ap Huw harp manuscripts contained flattened thirds, fifths and sevenths. Ergo – When Was Jazz? (See Introduction.) Gary Phillips's wide knowledge of jazz, blues and the folk tradition, and his encouragement of me, together with his enthusiasm for generating performance in people who did not know they could, is to be applauded. Guitarist Brian Breeze's philosophical take on music and his support during various projects is much appreciated. Guitarist and founder of the Dodgy Jammers Richard Williams, aka Blod, showed me how integrated musicians of mixed ability could work together, leading me to re-assess what jazz is. The pleasure of discussing the minutiae of jazz and historical opinion through writing, first on blue airmail paper, typed letters, then emails, has been undertaken over fifty years with guitarist and flautist A. D. M. Glass (Steve), Professor Emeritus of Botany, University of British Columbia, Canada; nothing is wasted.

Every effort has been made to trace the owners of copyright material, and the publishers will be pleased to correct any omissions brought to their attention. I am grateful that Brown University Library Sheet Music Collection, Providence, RI, permitted us to use 'Everybody Loves a "Jass" Band'. Many thanks go to Special Collections Library, Fisk University, Nashville, TN, for permission to use illustrations from their archives. I am indebted to genealogist Patricia Donaldson-Mills, Ohio, for permission to use material from her *Donaldson Family History* (1978) regarding the life and times of Jessie Donaldson. Some sections of this book have appeared in shorter published articles, and I am grateful to *Planet: The Welsh Internationalist* for allowing me to draw on articles '1956 'n' All That' (2002), 'Devil's Music' (1998/9), and 'Doing the Walkaround Skedaddle' (2006). My thanks go to John F. Blair Publishing (*www.blairpub.com*) for their support and their permission to quote from *Before Freedom: When I Can Just Remember* (1989), edited by Belinda Hurmence, and *Mighty Rough Times, I Tell You* (2000), edited by Andrea Sutcliffe.

I would like to thank Time Inc. for permission to reproduce texts, quotes and images from the *Melody Maker*, '©Time Inc. (UK) Ltd'; their support has been much appreciated. David M. Rubenstein Rare Book and Manuscript Library, Duke University, gave permission to quote from 'Everything is Peaches Down in Georgia'. I am grateful to Mel Bay Publications, Inc., for permission to quote from Jerry Silverman, 'The Marching Song of the First Arkansas (Negro) Regiment', in *Ballads and Songs of the Civil War* (Mel Bay Publications, 1993). Thanks also to the *Guardian* for permission to publish from Clare Deniz's obituary by Val Wilmer, 3 January 2003.

Finally, for permission to use his poem 'Rescuers' at the beginning of this book, my appreciation and thanks go to poet and writer David Hughes.

List of Illustrations

Figure 1	'Abolitionists Beware', 1836 (Pat Donaldson Family History, Ohio, 1978)
Figure 2	Jessie Donaldson (1799–1889) (Hilary Edmiston Collection, Donaldson Family Archive Collection)
Figure 3	'Uncle Tom's Cabin' advertisement, 1878 (SWW Media)
Figure 4	The Harry Collins Minstrels, date unknown (Cynon Valley Museum and Gallery, Aberdare)
Figure 5	The Mandolin Band, Tregaron, c.1880 (Jazz Heritage Wales Collection)
Figure 6a	The Fisk Jubilee Singers, 1882 (Fisk University Special Collections Library, Nashville, TN)
Figure 6b	The Fisk Jubilee Singers, 1881–2 (Fisk University Special Collections Library, Nashville, TN)
Figure 7	'Weird Slave Songs', 1874 (SWW Media)
Figure 8	'Troubled In Mind', *Negro Spirituals, or The Songs of the Jubilee Singers* (undated, out of copyright)
Figure 9	'In Dahomey', 1903 (Brown University Library African American Sheet Music Collection, Providence, RI)
Figure 10	'In Dahomey', trio of dancers (Williams, Walker, Walker) 1903 (out of copyright)
Figure 11	Johnson and Dean, 'In Society', 1905 (Harvard Theatre Collection, Houghton Library, Harvard University)
Figure 12	'Everybody Loves A "Jass" Band', 1917 (Brown University Library, African American Sheet Music Collection)
Figure 13	'Gramophone' advertisement, Oxford Music Stores, Swansea, 1919 (SWW Media)

Figure 14	'Munition Girls Concert Party' advertisement, 1917 (SWW Media)
Figure 15	'Thanks', Royal Theatre advertisement, 1918 (SWW Media)
Figure 16	Record sleeve for Snell and Sons, established 1900 (Jazz Heritage Wales Record Collection)
Figure 17	'Buy A Jazz Band' advertisement, 1919 (SWW Media)
Figure 18	'Jazz it' advertisement, 1922 (SWW Media)
Figure 19	Advertisement cartoon, 'At Carlton Café', 1915 (SWW Media)
Figure 20	Jazz Dance advertisement, 1919 (SWW Media)
Figure 21	'The Links between the Hwyl and the Negro Spiritual', 1934, *Melody Maker* (©Time Inc. (UK) Ltd)
Figure 22	Margaret Morris in a shop window, 1947 (Jazz Heritage Wales Collection)
Figure 23	Ivy Benson, Vienna, 1947 (Jazz Heritage Wales Collection, donated by Diana Lusher and Richard Arnatt from Sheila Tracy Collection)
Figure 24	Maria Jane Williams (1795–1873) (St Fagans National Museum of History, Wales)
Figure 25	Song collecting, Llandysul, 1911 (St Fagans National Museum of History, Wales)
Figure 26	Spike Hughes (*Second Movement – Continuing the Autobiography* (London: Museum Press, 1951))

Introduction

THE PURPOSE OF THIS book is to reclaim the history and culture for Wales of a music that eventually emerged as jazz in the 1920s, whose tendrils and roots extend back to slave songs and abolition campaign songs and Swansea's long forgotten connection with Cincinnati, Ohio. The main themes of this book are: firstly, the strong links between emerging African American music in the USA and the development of jazz in mainstream popular culture in Wales; secondly, the emancipation and contribution of Welsh women to the music and its social-cultural heritage, thirdly, a historical appraisal as the music journeyed towards the Second World War and within living memory. The jazz story will be set amongst the politics, sociocultural and feminist history of the time whence the music emerged, which begs the question, 'When Was Jazz?' echoing the historian Gwyn Alf Williams's 1985 question 'When Was Wales?'[1]

Feminist historians emerging during the 1970s and 1980s in Wales, such as Ursula Masson, Deirdre Beddoe, Angela John and Jane Aaron, inspired this initial research and encouraged my development of oral history projects on jazz and its predominantly working-class popular culture, a reclamation of our story in Wales from the perspective of women's experience. Professor Deirdre Beddoe reinterprets Welsh history; her many books and television programmes examine women's lives in Wales and place women at the heart of the story of Wales where they belong, and not 'hidden from history'.

Although not in the remit of this book, the Welsh have their own particular improvisational roots and our musical traditions can be traced from written descriptions left behind by others. An example is Giraldus Cambrensis/Gerald of Wales, born 1146 in Manorbier, Pembrokeshire. In his writings in *The Description of Wales*, completed in 1193–4, there are tantalising glimpses of the ordinary people of Wales going about their business, keeping open house and offering refreshment to travellers, with young women providing entertainment on the harp. Giraldus wrote:

> Guests who arrive early in the day are entertained until nightfall by girls who play to them on the harp . . . and in every Welsh court or family the menfolk consider playing on the harp to be the greatest of all accomplishments. When they play their instruments they charm and delight the ear with the sweetness of their music. They play quickly and in subtle harmony. Their fingering is so rapid that they produce this harmony out of discord . . . Whether they are playing in fourths or fifths, they always begin with B-flat and then come back to it at the end, so that the whole melody is rounded off sweetly and merrily . . . They play grace notes with great abandon, above the heavier bourdon of the bass strings, and so produce a gay and lilting melody . . . The Welsh play three instruments, the harp, the pipe and the *crwth* [a stringed instrument]. When they come together to make music, the Welsh sing their traditional songs, not in unison, as is done elsewhere, but in parts, in many modes and modulations. When a choir gathers to sing, which happens often in this country, you will hear as many different parts and voices as there are performers, all joining together in the end to produce a single organic harmony and melody in the soft sweetness of B-flat[.][2]

Wales continued to produce innovators prepared to experiment and expand on voicings and stylistic interpretations. Research work undertaken by trumpeter, composer and arranger Cris Haines of Llanelli points to the 1613 ap Huw Welsh harp manuscripts discovered in about 1738. The manuscripts, which ap Huw copied from medieval manuscripts, now reside in the British Museum under their title of 'Musica neu Beroriaeth'. Osian Ellis in his book *The Story of the Harp in Wales* maintains that ap Huw was:

> the last of the harpers to have played this ancient harp music of medieval times, for there is no trace of this style in later Welsh music... ap Huw gives the names and titles of pieces he had written elsewhere ... this, of course, was written in Welsh, but he uses the Elizabethan term for writing or making a mark: *pricio* – to prick.[3]

Cris Haines writes:

> Nobody really knows the correct tunings of the scales mentioned in the ap Huw manuscripts of early Welsh harp music. In 1995 I was commissioned for Swansea's UK Year of Literature and Writing to write a Jazz Suite for Harp, Trumpet and Double Bass loosely based on these sets of chord sequences or *clymau cytgerdd* and the scales as interpreted by Osian Ellis in his book, *The Story of the Harp in Wales*. With the *bragod gywair* and *isgywair* or *tro tant* corresponding with the mixolydian and dorian modes respectively, scales used by jazz musicians on dominant and minor seventh chords and Ellis saying 'The melodies were improvised on the small harp over strict patterns of chords,' it is easy to imagine a similarity between early Welsh music and the modern jazz idiom. Of course the rhythmic patterns, whatever they might have been, would bear no similarity to those of today, but as for harmony, Osian Ellis goes on to say '... the chords and harmonies in the *bragod gywair* and *gogywair* come as a shock at first hearing, with their added sixths and major and minor sevenths.' Ellis's interpretation of the *gogywair* is actually the same as the so-called jazz melodic minor, i.e. a

major scale with a minor third. There are many definitions of what jazz actually is, was or might be in the future and many more heated discussions about it to come, I am sure. Improvising over patterns of chords and discords, using perhaps a variety of related scales is surely one definition whether in the 21st or 17th century. Ellis mentions that the most 'perplexing' part of ap Huw's manuscripts were keys and scales citing ap Huw's instructions of *Lleddf gwtwair Gwyddyl*, with '*lledd*' given as the old meaning of awry, oblique, askew, warped, and the tunings containing the flattened 3rds, 5ths and 7ths. These tunings would not perplex the jazz musician, as they are fundamental to the blues scale. Harp stringing could also be adjusted by pegs in the string-holes to make a '. . . buzzing effect, which added a percussive sound for dancing'. Melodies were improvised over 'strict patterns of chords. . . and rules were formulated so as to consolidate certain customs and practices which were already operative.' Ellis states that the alternating chords of this 17th-century music would be 'in dispute with one another . . . creating a degree of dissonance and discomfort'.[4]

An apt description of jazz music, as analysed by Cris Haines.

The process of untangling jazz from its myths and legends can begin by questioning one's own process of understanding. Books in the Jazz Heritage Wales library rarely mention Wales or women performers in Wales. The common perception of Wales in these books, if mentioned at all by jazz historians, was that the people of Wales only sang in choirs or chapels, therefore jazz in Wales was non-existent and not requiring investigation. This book will begin to address the neglect. Back to those questions, 'When and how did Jazz come to Wales?' By tracing the story backwards after those initial questions, there was a story to be told far older than the familiar one of the London story – 1920s supper clubs, hot music, swing music, the Second World War, and bebop arriving in Ronnie Scott's and other London clubs. This is a story of an industrial south Wales and its early forms of jazz music, shaped by the urban conurbation of the industrial revolution and Swansea's emergence as a popular seaside resort combining successfully with its heavy industry of shipping and coal exporting. As Swansea is my hometown, I wished to discover how jazz had developed within its particular environment and why the contribution Wales had made was neglected in the literary canon. These activities developed and strengthened the links of transatlantic cultural exchange, and examples of newspaper articles and published programmes reflect this geographical identity. There is a historically important body of work reflecting the rich cultural heritage of people living and working within Cardiff Bay, housed at Butetown History and Arts Centre, Cardiff (with a question mark over its future and currently being relocated). BHAC, a unique resource, is referred to in the text and bibliography, and additionally supports this research. The historical data at BHAC relates to the specific area of Butetown, rather than the cultural mainstream of Cardiff and wider Wales. This book will reflect popular culture in south Wales within its wider context.

Jazz, the etymology of which is obscure, developed out of music from the United States, made predominantly by African Americans, during the early twentieth century. Musical elements that contributed to its formation were a combination of spiritual and gospel music in the 1840s, ragtime during the 1890s, plus traditional European jigs and reels integrated through immigration. The latter, for example Appalachian music, rooted in West Virginia during the early 1800s, with its strong Celtic traditions, arrived in the US with the pioneer settlers skilled in heavy industry: coal, iron and agriculture. These dates are acknowledged within jazz history by, for example, Oliver[5] and Dahl[6] as being those of an evolutionary fusion of cultures and styles which eventually determined the sound of jazz music.

Hobsbawm discusses jazz, referring to its birth as the music of 'protest and rebellion', when enslaved African people retained memories of lost heritage through song, dance and the rhythmic beating of drums. He writes: 'At its best the democratic protest of jazz merely means that this music stakes a claim to a serious participation in the arts for people who would, but for it, be mostly debarred from such participation; and its appeal for such people is therefore strong.'[7] Historians, academics and men of the cloth dismissed an African American disenfranchised people and their music, and confined them, and it, to hell. Black music represented savagery, moral depravity and uncontrolled sexuality, expressed through freedom of movement and extemporisation, in opposition to the control and repressions of white, Christianised and acceptable music in society. These dichotomies were entrenched in public perceptions for centuries, linked with beliefs in the superiority of the white race, held by imperialists and slave-owners. Slowly, stealthily, intellectual discussion and debate began with the publication of W. E. B. Du Bois's *The Souls of Black Folk*, published at the same time as *In Dahomey* was touring Britain (see chapter 4). Du Bois wrote:

> Before each chapter, as now printed, stands a bar of the Sorrow Songs – some echo of haunting melody from the only American music, which welled up from black souls in the dark past . . . It has been neglected, it has been, and is, half despised, and above all it has been persistently mistaken and misunderstood; but notwithstanding, it still remains as the singular spiritual heritage of the nation and the greatest gift of the Negro people.[8]

Du Bois referred to their life behind 'the veil', and to the 'double consciousness' of the black experience. Stuart Hall writes in the *Guardian*:

> [Du Bois] came to understand how emancipated slaves who, as Levering Lewis observes, had come 'singing, praying and aspiring out of slavery', had so swiftly fallen into poverty, degradation and indifference as a result of their marginalisation. Du Bois aimed to show instead the spiritual depth and complexity of life behind 'the veil'.[9]

Du Bois's statue in the grounds of Fisk University, Nashville, Tennessee, which he had attended from 1885–8 and from where the Fisk Jubilee Singers had set off on their tour (see chapter 3), portrays Du Bois holding out two large books, indicating an invitation to come inside and get educated.

Evelyn Brooks Higginbotham debates the complexity of racial and gender meanings of black churchwomen. She writes:

> The cynical era of Jim Crow and the optimistic woman's era stood entangled one with the other . . . The complexity of the racial and gender meanings of the age suggests both the multiple consciousness of multiple positionings of black women, and also the complexity of the black church itself – an institution overwhelmingly female in membership.[10]

African American women vocalists brought up within the church tradition were regarded as deviant if they crossed over into secular music. Deviancy had multiple outlets. Swansea experienced a 'Real Wild Men of Africa Negro Entertainment', by the Edmond's Late Wombell's Royal Windsor Exhibition and Castle Menagerie, which also toured Pontardawe, Ystalyfera and Morriston in 1861.[11] The 'Negro Entertainment' was in native costume with a full musical programme. The Welsh were witnessing African Americans corralled on stage as 'Wild Men' singing and dancing, which may have evoked forms of pity and sympathy, together with wonder and excitement. The 'corralled slaves' were no doubt grateful for the money they earned entertaining the crowds, preferable to fighting in the Civil War raging back home. Welsh entrepreneurs and performers adapted aspects of African American music, a new hybrid of blackface and clowning for local consumption, distasteful though we might find it now, a tradition that lingered in Wales long into the twentieth century at carnivals and fetes (see chapter 2).

Yet, in addition to these formative elements, there can also be found West African rhythms and harmonies, maintained through strong oral and musical traditions despite a 300-year history of African enslavement in the US. A significant feature of these rhythms and harmonies was the tribal talking drum and the drum's ability to communicate language within a society denied freedom of expression; it could be argued a dilemma familiar to Wales with its loss of language and identity. Early blues music, which focused on the times of release from slavery, was a significant element in the formation of jazz music. Jazz continues to survive through its ability to take what is best from other forms of music, and adapt, develop and perform it to suit the requirements of the time.

Daniel G. Williams, in his book *Black Skin, Blue Books*, discusses 'Welshness' within transatlantic exchanges and explores 'how sociohistorical forces converge to shape particular notions of identity in different periods, and how they influence the formal and aesthetic representations of those identities in written texts'.[12] Forces did converge rather unexpectedly in south Wales, to the mutual benefit of Welsh people and African Americans, from as early as the 1870s, eventually becoming part of the cafe culture mainstream during the first Jazz Age in Wales, from 1919 (see chapter 6).

Chapter 1, 'The Life, Times and Music of Abolitionist Jessie Donaldson (1799–1889)', was inspired by the simple expedient of asking just the one question 'What was happening in Wales before 1900?' and discovering an obituary that showed Welsh women abolitionists were active in international politics in Cincinnati, Ohio. They offered refuge to runaway slaves by establishing safe houses on the banks of the mighty Ohio River in Cincinnati, glorified by the Fisk Jubilee Singers (see chapter 3) as the River Jordan. Stephen Collins Foster was living in Cincinnati at the same time, writing his plantation melodies and sentimental ballads, inspired by 'slave songs', and sympathetic to the abolitionist cause. One might ask what this has to do with jazz? It has everything to do with early jazz's incubation and is just one part of the untold story of why choirs of freed slaves came to Wales in the 1870s, bringing their 'slave songs' or early gospel music with them. Abolitionist campaign songs helped the cause by encouraging people into meetings. Foster, later known as the 'Father of American music', penned melodies that pulled at the heart-strings and became universally popular, composing campaign and plantation melodies, minstrel songs and socio-dramatic parlour songs. Songs such as 'Oh! Susanna' and 'Old Folks at Home' were published and made it over the Atlantic for people in Wales to buy. That great champion of Wales, Paul Robeson, recorded many of Foster's songs.

Chapter 2, 'Doing the Plantation Walkaround Skedaddle', unravels the intricacies of cross-cultural exchanges in the Welsh version of Negro minstrelsy, which included the added attraction of the harmonium. Jazz did not appear out of a vacuum but, as Parsonage points out, slowly took shape from 'the musical antecedents of the genre, including the complex evolutionary pattern of events in the history of American culture and music in Britain'.[13] Sheet music was very popular, featuring music hall favourites, comic songs and glees. Abolitionist campaign songs were being sung in America and Wales at the same time as Negro minstrelsy was being performed in Welsh halls and theatres. These exchanges coincided with the performances of 'real Negros' or 'coloured' performers, from which Welsh performers took inspiration, adapting the music for inclusion into their own take on popular culture.

Chapter 3, 'The Fisk Jubilee Singers in Wales, Freed Slaves and their Songs', traces their journeys, visits to Wales and their influences on Welsh audiences. They performed their 'weird slave songs' and plantation melodies, competing with minstrelsy shows and blackface 'extravaganzas' in the variety halls and on theatre stages. The Fisk Jubilee Singers, a choir of freed slaves, undertook fundraising tours for their campus building at Fisk University for the 'Education of Freed Slaves and their Children' in Nashville, Tennessee, inaugurated in 1866 after the end of the American Civil War. In 1907, aware of the large amounts of money previously donated by the poor of Wales to their building fund, the Fisk Jubilee Trio returned the goodwill by donating fees from their concerts to 'the poor of Swansea' via the YMCA. The Fisk Jubilee Singers (and later the Trio) were the first to come and perform in Wales with a particular political and sociocultural message, again prompting the Welsh to think about issues such as anti-slavery, conditions in the home and at work, and the Welsh's own particular place in politics and society. Audiences bought the choir's Jubilee songbooks[14] and returned to their chapels and village halls to learn to sing the rousing melodies of hope and redemption and the heart-rending slave songs calling for universal freedom.

Chapter 4, 'Ragtime and the Cake Walk: On Stage and in the Workhouse', explores ragtime and its dance variant, the cake walk. The spectacular 1903 African American production of *In Dahomey* (the west African country now called Benin), with its excitement, brashness, send-ups and put-downs, left behind a legacy in the mindset of Wales. Ragtime was heavily featured in the show which toured Britain, arriving in Swansea in 1905. It was written and composed by Will Marion Cook, an African American violinist eager to showcase his own people's story. The show featured a melange of minstrelsy, vaudeville, comic opera and musical comedy familiar to Welsh audiences from attending music hall variety shows and extravaganzas. It made stars of Aida Overton Walker, Rhoda King, Birdie Williams and Ida Gigas, working alongside the big names of Bert Williams and George Walker. Writer Rudyard Kipling commented at the time that it presented 'a savage and lustful dance, quite proper in Ashanti, but shocking on the boards of a London Hall'.[15] There is debate that *In Dahomey* presented a satire on the 'Back to Africa' movement by the American Colonization Society, as well as a statement on contemporary African American experience. This new music initially had to fight with bizarre variety acts for space on the boards. Theatres, too, had to compete successfully one with another to book the new music and dance shows; innovative theatres needed to install the latest in decor, lighting and scenic attractions in order to house the big productions coming through. This chapter also examines how ragtime music and cake walk dances were regularly performed for the Swansea Workhouse inmates as part of their cultural enlightenment. For example, Jennie Lewis played ragtime piano for the Georgians Concert Party there. For the 1922 Christmas festivities, the Workhouse dining hall was decorated in the manner of an Old Kentucky Plantation, with the Empire Theatre minstrel troupe, the White Eyed Coons, performing a full show for the inmates. For a decade, the Workhouse was a hotbed of style and innovation. The cake walk was a huge hit with Swansea audiences, despite the Great Welsh Revival of 1904–5, which engulfed the churches and chapels at the time. The Revival movement coincided with the rising popularity of socialism and labour politics, and was accompanied by rousing, uplifting hymns and choral singing in order to cleanse the soul and unite communities. Those not attending Revival meetings, however, thronged to *In Dahomey*, eager to see how the cake walk was done and possibly colluding with the African Americans on stage in debunking English Victorian values and colonial imperialism. Parsonage writes 'in retrospect, the portrayals of supposedly stereotypical Negroes in *In Dahomey* take on a very different slant compared to earlier, particularly blackface, minstrel shows'.[16] Sheet music became easier to buy, through such music chains as Duck, Son and Pinker Ltd, encouraging locals to learn to play some of the songs heard on stage.

Chapter 5, 'The First World War: Ragtime Trenches and Suffragettes', examines ways in which the war propelled women into politics and on to the public stage. The flowering of early jazz managed to raise its head and open its mouth despite the usual fare of weekly theatre melodramas, which often portrayed women in a bad light, such as *Can a Woman be Good?* and *The Bad Girl in the Family*. Women's bands and combos had a significant presence in theatre pits, accompanying silent films, a subject which is not covered by the terms of reference for this book, but surely needs investigating. They were also popular on the variety stage, competing with Negro minstrelsy troupes and melanges. Women also became prominent in the new format of revues.

Chapter 6, 'Café Society: The Jazz Age', shows the innovative emergence of south Wales café society, with its women entrepreneurs producing and directing floor shows inspired by visiting African American musicians, touring on the theatre circuit. Initially the cafés opened sporadically during 1915, offering support and comfort for bereaved women and those missing loved ones during the First World War. The cafés flourished throughout the war and on into the 1920s, a decade before Dylan Thomas and his crowd frequented the Kardomah and talked literary matters. Ragtime and remnants of minstrelsy were part of the burgeoning Welsh café culture, and these entered the mainstream of the first jazz age. African American combos and revues toured the cafés, fitting in afternoon floor shows before their evening performances at the big theatres. They left hints and traces of their cultural heritage for the Welsh to decipher, embrace and edit to their own requirements.

Chapter 7, 'Cutting a Rug to the Second World War: Jews and "Negro Morals"', follows the women jazz musicians securing a niche market that encouraged other art forms to become fashionable, with women running jazz dance courses and performing exhibition dance shows. Pianos proliferated in the parlours of the working classes through the new easy terms of hire purchase. Welsh dance trends were so exciting that two women journalists from the *South Wales Daily Post*, Joan and Viola, were sent out just to cover the fashions – this against a background of racial mudslinging. When early women jazz musicians raised their heads above the parapet the ladders were kicked away; women were required to know their place in the male hierarchy and demarcation lines were drawn with regard to a professional career. Some women, such as Ivy Benson, refused to play the game and marched off to join ENSA, becoming pioneers in their field, keeping up high spirits and morale during the Second World War.

Chapter 8, 'Fair Treatment for the "Fair Sex"?' describes the explosion of cultural dynamism and women jazz musicians' forays and successes in the business. Women were perceived as an increasing threat by the male jazz patriarchy, and had to fight for their right to perform jazz. Spike Hughes, a regular journalist and record reviewer for the *Melody Maker* writing as 'Anon', led the onslaught, aided and abetted by fellow journalists. Women were 'allowed space' within the *Melody Maker* columns to fight back, continuing to manage their careers regardless of these misogynistic attitudes.

Therefore, it now seems timely to think again about Gwyn Alf Williams's question 'When Was Wales?' and ask 'When Was Jazz?' I hope readers will enjoy these stories of how 'Freedom Music' came to Wales. Hopefully, this book will stimulate further debate . . . it is certainly not the definitive version.

Chapter One

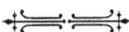

The Life, Times and Music of Swansea Abolitionist Jessie Donaldson (1799–1889)

I WAS EAGER TO KNOW just when exactly jazz began in Wales. My parents told stories of going to London on honeymoon for a week in 1934 to see the big bands. They'd danced the Charleston, and my father said he had seen Louis Armstrong and his Band performing in Swansea in the 1930s. These were stories within living memory. But what music was popular in Wales in 1900 before the Charleston, and when did jazz start? Was it called ragtime then? 'When Was Jazz?' I trawled slowly backwards into history. While researching the history of slave songs in Wales on reference library microfiche machines, my eye was caught by an unusual item, an obituary of a woman. The fact that it was given a headline 'Death of Mrs Donaldson of Swansea – Record of a Remarkable Life' invited me to read and ask 'Who?' The obituary in *The Cambrian* of September 1889 had an intriguing few lines:

> In America Mrs Donaldson united with her husband and his family in support of the Abolitionist movement. She was well acquainted with Lloyd Garrison, Fred. Douglass, Ellen Craft and many of the other leaders. The house where she and her husband lived was on the banks of the Ohio,

opposite to the slave holding state of Kentucky and at times it was used by fugitives as one of the stations of what was termed the 'underground railway' by which they travelled to the free land of Canada.[1]

This sounded like quite a story. The reference was filed away, but not forgotten, until a grant from the Swansea Citizenship Millennium Award enabled me to discover more about her for my 'Roots 2000' project. Jessie Donaldson's life is undocumented and she left no papers. For three years she existed with just a surname in the Women's Jazz Archive in Swansea. As I was to discover, she also existed with just an initial 'J.' in Cincinnati Museum Center Library and Archives, Ohio. To know her and the music that surrounded her, we have to begin with her obituary and work backwards with the people and politics of her time mentioned in her obituary, adding a little more information to that question 'When Was Jazz?'

Mrs Donaldson, then Jessie Heineken, was well aware of the extent of Britain's trade in human misery. As an abolitionist, she was a member of Swansea's Anti-Slavery Society, the largest and most committed in Wales.[2] Wales contributed its part to slavery by manufacturing and exporting metal goods to Africa, shipping African slave labour to the West Indies, and importing sugar, tobacco and rum for Britain. This was known as the 'triangular trade'. These lucrative trade routes financed the industrial revolution and fuelled heavy industry in south Wales, allowing the slave trade to be economically viable.

An example of the 'metal goods' was discovered in 2004 by four local men researching a walk for the *Guide to the Landore Copper Works Site*. A rubble bank had recently collapsed, and an object was picked up and inspected:

> It was a Token used by Slave Traders to buy goods and slaves in West Africa, known as a 'Manilla' horseshoe . . . A drawing of the White Rock Copper Works still exists and, what is more important, the drawing identifies the various buildings. On the site is a building clearly marked as 'The Manilla House'.[3]

Bristol was the major port operating the triangular trade, and its most profitable years were from 1698 to the 1740s. It was from Bristol that Jessie's father, Samuel Heineken, arrived in Swansea. Samuel Heineken had practised as a lawyer in London and Bristol before moving to a three-storey terrace house in Dynevor Place in Swansea; he had married Jennet in 1790. Jessie was born in 1799, and she and her elder sister Mary Ann and brother Sam grew up in a family active in local and national politics.

The 'Welsh Mam' is a familiar stereotype we have embraced within popular culture. Some women, usually middle-class, had the opportunity to step outside that stifling tradition of home, chapel and community, and Jessie grabbed her opportunities with both hands. The abolitionist movement not only stirred local debates on economics and racism, it challenged traditional perceptions of the woman's role in local and national public life. The abolitionist movement also precipitated women into international politics on a grand scale; Jessie was one of those women.

Opposition to the slave trade was strong in Wales, especially in Swansea, where the meetings and organised opposition centred around the Unitarian and Quaker communities. Abolitionists, whether members of the Anti-Slavery Society or individuals from the sympathetic Quaker or Unitarian backgrounds, were publicly denounced by Aedanus Burke, a member of the South Carolina House of Representatives from 1778 to 1779, as 'spies, traitors and suppliers of the enemy'.[4] Abolitionists and staunch Unitarians like the Swansea Heineken family were tarred with the same brush. The Swansea Unitarian congregation to which the Heineken family belonged was originally 'gathered together' between 1633 and 1648 by preacher Ambrose Martyn and founded before the Great Ejection in 1662, which created Nonconformity. Preacher Martyn joined with the Rev. Stephen Hughes and the Rev. Daniel Higgs, and their houses were licensed for religious services under the Declaration of Indulgence of 1672. The first Unitarian Chapel was built in High Street, Swansea, in 1689 under the ministry of Daniel Higgs, but it needed the Dissenters Chapel Act of 1844 to enable Unitarians to hold chapels and trust money, which were originally for Orthodox purposes. The Heineken family would have known Richard Awbrey, minister from 1814–36, and George Browne Brock, 1837–54.[5]

Jessie, during her 20s, opened a school for 'young Ladies and Gentlemen' at 32 Wind Street, Swansea.[6] Later the school advertised for boarders and became a prep school. Jessie remained single and committed herself to the school, while elder sister Mary Ann married Richard Perkins Jnr of Penmaen, Monmouth.[7] The descendants of Mary Ann continue to live in Swansea today.[8]

When Jessie was 21 and campaigning alongside her father with the Anti-Slavery Society, her aunt Anna Margaretta Donaldson (her father's sister), together with her uncle Francis and their seven adult children, emigrated in 1822 from Penmaen Farm, Perfunnor, near Rhayader, to Cincinnati, Ohio. They were pioneers who would make their mark in world events. The *Cambrian* reported the family's safe arrival in America:

> The numerous friends of Francis Donaldson, Esq. late of Perfunnor, near Rhayader, Radnorshire, will learn with pleasure that he arrived safely with his family at Philadelphia, and pursued his journey to the vicinity of the rising town of Cincinnati, which is situate about five hundred miles up the great Ohio, and where his sons had previously purchased a large tract of land from the Government of the United States.[9]

There is a description of the Donaldsons' Cincinnati by a Welshman, D. Williams, who published an account of his journey home from Mexico to Wales in 1829. Of Cincinnati he wrote:

> We went by steamboat from Louis Ville to Cincinnati, one hundred and fifty miles for six shillings. Cincinnati is a beautiful town in the State of Ohio, consisting of over twenty thousand people; a lively place with every sign of prosperity . . . Craftsmen earn from four shillings to six shillings per day. Many Welsh people in this town are members in English churches, and they hold a prayer meeting in Welsh every

Sunday evening, and also once a week, and sometimes they have a sermon in Welsh. It seems strange that there is not more communication between places like this and Wales. It is a great pity that a way cannot be found to send *Seren, Gomer, Lleuad yr Oes* and other publications to them, this would be a great help in keeping the language alive amongst the children; this is one reason why the Welsh language like the Irish language finishes with those born in Wales.[10]

Jessie must have waited anxiously for the letters to arrive from Cincinnati relating her aunt's campaigns and adventures. Perhaps Jessie told her pupils in her classes all about the goings on in America. Once established in Cincinnati, the Donaldson family ran the prosperous family business C. (Christian) Donaldson and Co., 'Importers & Dealers in Hardware and Cutlery, Steel, Brass Ware and Saddlery', at 24 Main Street, Cincinnati. They built a home on the banks of the Ohio River and called it 'Frandon', after the man of the house and head of the family, Francis Donaldson. Francis Donaldson died just two years after his arrival in Cincinnati, and the death was noted back home in Wales.[11] 'Frandon', the family home, was described as 'part of the picturesque waterfront at New Richmond, in later years known as the St Charles Hotel patronized by many river captains on their trips up and down the Ohio'.[12] 'Frandon' was the first of the three Welsh safe houses for fugitive slaves operating on the 'underground railroad' freedom passage. Runaways were helped from safe house to safe house, and 'Frandon' became part of the chain. Reaching the river, runaways looked and listened for the signs.[13]

The Ohio River, wider and faster flowing than the river Thames, was the scene of myths, legends and factual events. It was known through song as the River Jordan, familiar from spiritual and gospel songbooks; the river that separated slavery from freedom. The far south bank was Kentucky, the slave-holding and plantation state; the opposite bank on the north side was Cincinnati, Ohio, and freedom. Spirituals, known at the time as slave songs, carried messages and signs on how to reach and cross the Ohio River – the River Jordan – and salvation: songs such as 'Deep River', 'Down by the River', 'In the River of Jordan', 'Oh Wasn't That a Wide River', 'Steal Away', 'Show Me the Way', 'There's a Meeting Here Tonight', 'We Shall Walk Through the Valley', and many more. They were signposts through song. Booker T. Washington, writing in *Up From Slavery* about the day freedom was nearly come, says of the music:

> It was a momentous and eventful day to all upon our plantation. We had been expecting it. Freedom was in the air, and had been for months. Deserting soldiers returning to their homes were to be seen every day . . . The news and mutterings of great events were swiftly carried from one plantation to another . . . As the great day drew nearer, there was more singing in the slave quarters than usual. It was bolder, had more ring, and lasted later into the night. Most of the verses of the plantation songs had some reference to freedom. True, they had sung those same verses before, but they had been careful to explain that the 'freedom' in these songs referred to the next world, and had no connection with life in this world. Now they gradually threw off the mask, and were not afraid to let it be known that the 'freedom' in their songs meant freedom of the body in this world.[14]

While Jessie's aunt Anna Margaretta, uncle Francis and seven cousins were establishing themselves and their business in Cincinnati and getting involved in the 1820s anti-slavery and abolitionist movements, similar meetings were taking place in Swansea. The anti-slavery movement appealed to the radical ideas of the Heineken family, supported by their Nonconformist allegiance of Unitarianism. A series of anti-slavery meetings were held in 1823 at Swansea Town Hall, near Swansea Castle in High Street, which prominent families such as the Heinekens of Dynevor Place attended. The local press reported that topics under discussion were, apart from various petitions, the West Indies question, the sugar plantations, and the involvement of the Welsh slave-owning Caernarvon family, the Pennants of Penrhyn Castle. Meetings like these were political hot potatoes locally.[15]

The level of Welsh anti-slavery sentiment can be gauged from the diary kept by Thomas Clarkson (1760–1846), the prominent abolitionist who had undertaken a tour of Wales in 1824. Clarkson had shocked society when, in 1789, his survey of a slave ship was published, with detailed drawings illustrating how the human cargo, 'black cattle', was stowed. Clarkson wrote and organised tirelessly. He reached Swansea on 12 July 1824 after visiting Chepstow, Abergavenny, Newport, Cardiff, Cowbridge, Pyle and Neath Abbey. His diary entry reads: 'Proceeded onto Swansea. In the evening met the Swansea committee with friends, 24 in number, at the town hall . . . Received £24 in hand. They made resolution to send another £25 or £50.'[16] Swansea was the only town that had actually collected money in advance, which suggests Swansea had a more committed following than any other town in Wales. South Wales also had its slave-owning connections, such as the eminent Swansea geologist De la Beche, whose family owned plantations and slaves in Jamaica, and Thomas Eaton, who reputedly freed his slaves then returned to Swansea in 1780 to build Brynymor, today known as Stella Maris, the Ursuline convent, and now a care home. Both De la Beche and Eaton have roads named after them in Swansea.

Thomas Clarkson's diary states he stayed with Thomas Biggs, then dined at Robert Eaton's. He wrote letters to Dr William Edwards and Joseph Price. He then rode on to Carmarthen, St David's (where he dined with the Bishop), Milford, Haverfordwest, Llandovery, Brecon, Kington, Aberystwyth, Newtown, Leighton Hall Chester, Ruthin, Bala, Dolgelly, 'Bethgelert' (Beddgelert), etc. At Caernarvon, Clarkson encountered problems, as there were only six present at the meeting. This may have been because the Pennants of Penrhyn Castle were employers of large numbers of local people, who may have been warned off by their employers from getting involved in politics. Although they admitted that slavery would eventually fall and that ministers condemned it, Clarkson commented on his fraught visit:

This opinion is constantly urged against us as a reason for (them) not joining us, the idea being Government must and will do it and yet it is of great importance to our cause to know that this idea pervades all England and Wales. The Rev. Sam Williams refused to act or to have anything to do with a committee unless the vicar would gain. Both very shy of acting lest they should interfere with government. Captain Parry of the navy, a magistrate and gentleman of fortune in the town (Caernarvon) is one of these. He states that to his knowledge the slaves are better off than British labourers. Wm. Pennant, the heir of Lord Penrhyn,[17] a man of £50,000 per annum, is quite against us in consequence of being a very large West Indian proprietor. Mr Robert the Surgeon thought it practicable to form a committee in the town consisting of respectable tradesmen, but not one gentleman would give support. If such a committee were formed, it would cause the town to be divided. In this awkward situation I know not how to act. Rev. Trevor and magistrate, desirous of promoting the cause, he offered himself and the curate to be a committee for the distribution of our books and to plead our cause. Gentlemen would not follow a committee of tradesmen, but a committee of respectable tradesmen would follow the committee of gentlemen. Eight respectable tradesmen with one gentleman Lieutenant Boultber of the navy formed a committee. (There was a debate on what to do, I didn't want to make enemies of the vicar and curate). I thought it was better to let matters stand – but we must never lose sight of proffered services.

It was obvious from the Clarkson diary that each town visited must have been a political minefield to negotiate. From the above arguments it can be seen that Swansea had indeed one of the largest and most committed of the anti-slavery societies operating in Wales at this time. Clarkson noted that he had travelled 3,000 miles and was absent from home nearly a year.

While Thomas Clarkson continued on his tour of Wales, Jessie's aunt Anna Margaretta, a feisty, determined and outspoken Welsh widow of 57, continued harbouring runaway slaves. Slaves would travel northward by night, covering an average of about seventeen miles. They were guided by the stars – the Plough, Big Dipper, the Drinking Gourd – perhaps singing the 'message song' or slave song 'Follow the Drinking Gourd' (traditional):

> *Chorus*
> Follow the drinking gourd
> Follow the drinking gourd
> For the old man is a waitin' for to carry you to freedom
> Follow the drinking gourd.
>
> When the sun comes up
> And the first quail calls
> Follow the drinking gourd . . .
> The river bank will make a mighty good road
> Dead trees to show you the way
> Left foot, pig foot, travelling on
> Follow the drinking gourd
> For the old man is a waitin' for to carry you to freedom
>
> The river ends between two hills
> Follow the drinking gourd
> But there's another river on the other side
> Follow the drinking gourd.
>
> For the old man is a waitin' for to carry you to freedom
> Follow the drinking gourd.[18]

Runaways followed signs, such as moss that grew only on the north side of dead trees. The best time to travel would be spring, when the quail sang, or winter, when the Ohio froze over. Owners of safe houses hung quilts on their washing lines, some with directions worked into the design (now exhibited at historic Old Washington, Kentucky), or they sometimes hung them on the north side of the house. Slaves were hidden behind cupboards, in lofts and cellars. Sometimes pepper was scattered to confuse the pursuing dogs. Some 30,000 slaves escaped through Cincinnati.

Another traditional river song about escape is 'Roll, Jordan, Roll', performed by freed slaves, the Fisk Jubilee Singers (see chapter 3), who gave many concerts in Swansea:

> Roll, Jordan, roll,
> Roll, Jordan, roll,
> I want to go to heaven when I die,
> To hear Jordan roll.[19]

The river was an important icon. For those unfortunate African Americans south of the Ohio River the ultimate goal was to reach its banks, whether overland or following the river's tributaries. Some slaves worked the riverboats, relishing the relative freedom of movement they gained as they travelled the Ohio and Mississippi Rivers, but able to come ashore only to load or unload cargo:[20]

> Ah, yes! There is a fairer zone,
> Where sin and sorrow are unknown;
> Where weary souls find peaceful rest,
> And all that love the Lord are blest.
>
> *Chorus*
> 'Tis just across the river,
> The narrow, narrow river,
> 'Tis just across the river,
> Upon the other shore.[21]

With Jessie still busy teaching in Swansea and reading the letters from her aunt, Anna Margaretta was involved in one of the most significant abolitionist campaigns, known as the Cincinnati Riots of 1836. The local press reported that the Donaldson family and others supported

James G. Birney, publisher of *The Philanthropist*, the anti-slavery newspaper. Anna Margaretta's sons William and Christian Donaldson were on the original committee of the South West Ohio Anti-Slavery Society. James G. Birney could not publish *The Philanthropist* in his home state of Kentucky but had to cross over to the Cincinnati side of the river, having been promised financial help by the Donaldsons:

> They kept their word faithfully, even some of the pro-slavery men being manly enough to insist that the mob from another State should not molest him while in New Richmond, Cincinnati. The paper was removed to Cincinnati, under the advice and counsels of the Donaldsons, to give it a wider field for circulation and influence, and there published some three months, when July 14th, the press-room was broken open, the press and materials defaced and destroyed. July 23rd a meeting of citizens was convened at the lower market house to decide whether they would permit the publication and circulation of abolition papers in the city. At this meeting a committee was appointed, who opened a correspondence with the conductors of *The Philanthropist* – the executive committee of the Ohio Anti-Slavery Society, of which William Donaldson was a member – requesting them to discontinue its publication.[22]

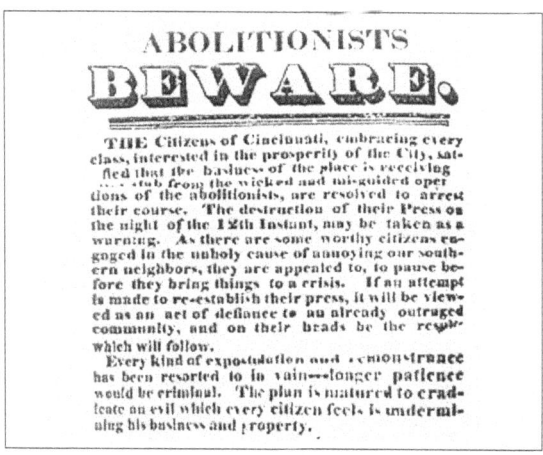

Figure 1: 'Abolitionists Beware', 1836 (Pat Donaldson Family History, Ohio, 1978)

The request by 'citizens' to the abolitionists to shut down *The Philanthropist* was ignored, and it continued to be published. The abolitionists received warnings with placards nailed at street corners or on trees:

> ABOLITIONISTS BEWARE!
>
> The Citizens of Cincinnati, embracing every class, interested in the prosperity of the City, satisfied that the business of the place is receiving a vital stab from the wicked and misguided operations of the abolitionists are resolved to arrest their course. The destruction of their Press on the night of the 12th instant, may be taken as a warning.[23]

Anna Margaretta Donaldson

> took an active part in the anti-slavery agitation . . . and by her means, voice, and great social influence largely contributed to swell the increasing volume of unrelenting opposition to negro slavery in America. Many a poor despised slave she assisted to his or her freedom, and in her the downtrodden black man found a friend. The Donaldsons – herself, her sons and families – were among the leaders in the abolition movement in Cincinnati and Clermont County. Their lives and property were often saved by their heroic conduct or high position in society from the minions of the accursed slave dynasty, then all-powerful in church and state. Her action at the time the mob destroyed *The Philanthropist*, published by the lamented James G. Birney, on July 30, 1836, is worthy of recognition in Ohio's annals.[24]

The unrest had started in January 1836 when

> 'a meeting of 500 anti-abolitionists, led by Mayor Samuel Davies, William Burke the postmaster and Methodist minister and former U.S. Senator Jacob Burnet, took place in Cincinnati. Birney was again warned to keep his paper out of the City or suffer the consequences. By April, circulation was doing well and Birney was fed up with the arduous commute' (by boat up the river).[25]

The 'worthy' mayor called a meeting of citizens opposed to Abolition on the 22 January 1936, after three issues of *The Philanthropist* had been published. More than fifty attended including judges and men of the cloth. It was resolved to suppress any paper 'which might be established for the purpose of discussing the slavery question'. The Anti-Slavery Society continued the story: 'a band of men, amounting to thirty or forty in number, made an assault on the premises of Mr Pugh the printer, scaled a high wall, mounted the roof of the press office and destroyed the press.'

It is some measure of the stamina and fortitude of the Donaldson family, being owners of a major business in the city, that they continued with their abolitionist campaign. They were given another public warning through the press on 26 July 1836: 'The abolitionists in Cincinnati, the Birneys, the Donaldsons etc. have doubtless received their last warning'.[26]

Then appeared a resolution, purporting to be from the Cincinnati Union Society of Colored Persons, appearing to side with the 'worthy mayor' and his mob, and urging the abolitionists to lay off. However, this press notice provoked one of the most astonishing acts of bravery from the Cincinnati Union Society of Colored Persons; this apparent collusion with the mayor and the mob had been a sham perpetrated by the authorities to undermine the growing abolitionist movement, and the CUSCP quickly responded with a disclaimer:

> We, the undersigned, members of the Cincinnati Union Society of Colored Persons, having seen, with regret, our name affixed to a publication, purporting to be the proceeding of a meeting of the Union Society held on August 1st at 12 o'clock, in which proceeding, the motives, principles, and characters of the friends of abolitions are impugned and denounced: – We do hereby declare that our names were used (by Dennis Hill, the President of our Society) without our knowledge or consent.[27]

The Cincinnati mob, which included the 'worthy mayor, judges and men of the cloth', attacked on the night of Saturday 30 July 1836:

> Very soon after dark a concourse of citizens assembled at the corner of Main and Seventh streets in this city, and upon a short consultation, broke open the printing office of *The Philanthropist*, the abolition paper, scattered the type into the streets, tore down the presses, and completely dismantled the office. It was owned by A. Pugh, a peaceable and orderly printer, who published *The Philanthropist* for the Anti-Slavery Society of Ohio. From the printing office the crowd went to the house of A. Pugh, where they supposed there were other printing materials, but found none, nor offered any violence. Then to the Messrs. Donaldsons', where ladies only were at home.[28]

Anna Margaretta defended her home against the mob, challenging them to search her house. The mob backed off, but attacked the homes of 'Blacks in Church Alley', and guns were fired. Riots continued throughout the night. The Anti-Slavery Society and the 'worthy Mayor' issued resolutions and proclamations to each other through the press. The Ohio Anti-Slavery Society issued a resolution:

> That it is with deep regret and shame, that we have to acknowledge that our city, heretofore so distinguished for its public order, has recently presented a scene of unlicensed violence; and that private property has been destroyed, and personal security endangered, and domestic peace invaded, by an unrestrained mob.

The mayor and his cohorts replied: 'that the discretion, prudence and energy of our worthy Mayor, and the city authorities generally, during the late excitement, are worthy of all praise'.[29] Throughout all these disturbances Anna Margaretta continued to shield and nurture fugitive slaves at 'Frandon'.

These momentous events must have been conveyed via letter to Jessie in Swansea and discussed at length via print across the ocean. A legacy of Anna Margaretta and Francis's family was the financial assistance given to the Cincinnati Colored Orphan Asylum, set up in 1844–5. Prominent white founders 'included Salmon P. Chase, who did the legal work, and Christian Donaldson, who raised the money as founding Treasurer'.[30] William and Christian Donaldson were also board members. The orphanage remained in existence until 1967, when 'the land was taken for Interstate 71. Throughout its history the asylum cared for both orphans and children whose parents could not physically or economically care for them.'[31] It is to be regretted that the Donaldson family's philanthropic work has gone unrecognised.

Jessie continued to teach at her school in Swansea's Wind Street but events in 1840 were to turn her life in a new direction. Anna Margaretta's eldest son, Francis Donaldson Jnr, possibly in respite from personal tragedy and the Cincinnati riots of 1836, made a trip to Swansea to visit the relations; he was aged 46. His wife Elizabeth and three of his five children had died. Francis and Jessie met and he must have been quite taken with this enterprising 41-year-old schoolteacher and abolitionist. After all, they had much in common and presumably had kept up a correspondence. Despite being cousins, they married (not unusual in those days) on 7 July 1840 at Bettws Church, Carmarthenshire, with Francis described as 'of "Frandon" Ohio' on church records. Jessie moved out of her parents' family home in Dynevor Place, and with her new husband set up home in a three-storey house around the corner in 9 Grove Place.

In 1844 Anna Margaretta, the tough pioneer aunt from Penmaen Farm, Rhayader, and now Jessie's mother-in-law, died in Cincinnati aged 77. She had devoted the last twenty years of her life to the anti-slavery and safe passage causes. Her obituary in the *Clermont County Press*, Cincinnati, reads: 'Anna Margaretta (Heineken) Donaldson, a lady of singularly gentle disposition, but of determined will, which never yielded where principle and the sense of right were involved. She was among the leaders in the abolition movement in Cincinnati.' The Donaldson history records:

> The death of this noble woman, so richly endowed with physical beauty, with an active mind thoroughly cultured, and a spirit fully attuned to the Father's will, severed one of the most interesting links that connected

two nations and two centuries, leaving hallowed memories of a long, useful, and blameless life to be revered, and most worthy of imitation.[32]

Anna Margaretta's family probably sent a copy of her obituary to Jessie and Francis in Swansea.

It is not clear whether Jessie gave up her school in Wind Street upon her marriage, probably not. Jessie, as a campaigner and educator, might also have been teaching poems and ballads on anti-slavery to her pupils. James discusses those poems circulating during Jessie's lifetime, such as that by Benjamin Price (1792–1854), 'Cân y Negro Bach' ('The Song of the Little Negro').[33] Jessie and Francis might also have gone to see the Original Female American Serenaders at the Assembly Rooms in 1850, or Madame Macarte's American Circus parading in 1851 along the streets, accompanied by 'fine pieces of instrumental music from the band'. If that was not to their liking, they might have investigated Mr Pelham's 'Sambo 'It-'Em-Hard' at the theatre.[34]

In Cincinnati, Thomas, Anna Margaretta's youngest son, who was only 15 years old when he left his home in Wales, would eventually build his own house on the Cincinnati riverbank, calling it 'Penmaen' (the brow of the hill) after the old family farm back in Wales. This became the second of the Donaldson safe houses on the underground railroad on the riverbank. In Swansea, Jessie and Francis were contemplating their future; perhaps Francis was homesick for Cincinnati, or maybe Swansea was too quiet. Records show that in 1854 they bought 251 acres of land in Clermont County, Cincinnati, near 'Penmaen', Thomas's house. In 1856 Jessie and Francis auctioned their household effects at 9 Grove Place and, after sixteen years of marriage in Swansea, they set sail to join their relatives in Cincinnati.[35] They stayed with Thomas (Francis's brother) and his wife Susanna, Jessie's cousins, at 'Penmaen' safe house while their own house in Clermont was being built. Jessie's new home would eventually become the third of the Welsh safe houses. Jessie, another strong-willed woman, had now embarked on a new life of adventure at the age of 57, mirroring that of her aunt Anna Margaretta twenty years earlier. For the next ten years, from 1856 to 1866, Jessie and Francis joined with the freed African Americans, abolitionists, Unitarians and Quakers, as Cincinnati had remained a hotbed of political upheaval since the riots of 1836. Stitching it all together were the work songs of African American slaves, which, in turn, inspired the sentimental ballads and plantation melodies of Stephen Collins Foster (1826–1964), sometimes referred to as the father of American music.

In 1846 Stephen Collins Foster, a young white man of 20, was in Cincinnati writing songs. The political upheavals and social unrest formed a backdrop to the music he heard at public entertainments and church socials. While getting established, Foster's day job was working as a bookkeeper for his brother's steamboat ticket sales agency in Cassilly's Row in the town, the first line of buildings along the waterfront. Foster and his brother boarded at Fourth Street, from where the brothers would walk down Broadway Hill together to the office.[36] Foster's songs, penned to tell the stories of the folk he saw around him, began to sell, contemporary ballads written in a direct and easy style that went to the heart of the story.

Dismissed down the years as discriminatory to the African American, as sentimentalising or trivialising the lives endured by slaves on their plantations, the music also went to the core of the social and political conditions of the time. Foster felt the enslaved shared the same feelings for home and family as white people did. His songs did their part in bringing slavery and its conditions to public attention, however we interpret them today. Foster's friend Charles Shiras was a leader in the abolitionist movement in Pittsburgh and had seen Garrison and Douglass speaking, so Foster would have been aware how fiery or sentimental words could inspire an audience.

O'Connell examines Stephen Collins Foster's music:

> by placing Foster and his music within the historical context of his own antebellum society, culture and history, I sought explanations for the function of sentimentality in Foster's tear-inducing parlour songs and in his blackface plantation songs; . . . [and] Foster's position on minstrelsy and how he transformed the racially denigrating

minstrel song into the refined, sentimental hybrid plantation song that sympathized with the slaves.[37]

O'Connell describes how free black river men would sing as they unloaded huge bales of cotton from the steamships, their voices carrying over the river to Foster, who was supposed to be clerking in his brother's office but was composing songs instead. Foster's time in Cincinnati coincided with Harriet Beecher Stowe's last three years there, although it is not clear if they met. O'Connell writes:

> Harriet Beecher Stowe, while living in Cincinnati, was influenced by new theories on race that came to be known as romantic racialism. Stephen Foster was undoubtedly influenced by these same theories . . . when Alexander Kinmont gave a series of lectures expounding his theories. Stowe probably attended one of the lectures or at least read about them. Kinmont's romantic racialism identified the black race with Christian virtues, thus creating more sympathy for blacks . . . But he explained in some ways they were actually superior. That is, morally and spiritually. . . . The life and times of the river, the work songs, shouts and noises, provided the 'working material' for his own music . . . Foster, it seems, never was far from the river, either in Pittsburgh or Allegheny or Cincinnati, and the river was never far from his songs.[38]

Foster died aged 37, 'with 38 cents in his pocket', having sold the copyright on his songs.[39] His songs included 'Oh! Susanna', 'Jeanie with the Light Brown Hair' (written for his wife Jane McDowell), 'Old Black Joe' and 'Old Folks At Home'. Some of these lovely songs were routinely given the variety showbiz treatment by BBC TV on their *Black and White Minstrel Show*, which ran from 1958 to 1978, with top-hatted, high-kicking showgirls (the *Television Toppers*) serving an unfortunate downgraded version of the songs' original meanings for popular appeal. The songs were performed by whites in blackface, featuring the George Mitchell Singers. Stan Stennett, Welshman, self-taught guitarist from Pencoed, Bridgend, provided the comedy songs and interludes for the show, and published his autobiography *Fully Booked* in 2010 in his mid-80s. Also in the show, baritone Dai Francis from Swansea was the announcer and one of the main soloists, appearing in the persona of the Al Jolson character. Francis Davies, tenor, another Welshman, born in Cilfynydd, performed with the *Minstrels* shows as well as other variety and comedy TV shows. Stennett and Francis toured for years with the *Black and White Minstrels* stage show, which included another fellow Welshman, Glyn Dawson.[40] Stephen Collins Foster's songs, sung by Welshmen, lived on via the BBC TV show.

Foster's 'Old Folks At Home', written in 'vernacular' in 1851 from the perspective of a slave, causes trouble and embarrassment for modern vocalists, with critics alluding to the romanticising of slavery. Foster was an abolitionist and supported the North during the Civil War; his song was a plea to performers and audiences to look about them and see how the other folk lived:

> Way down upon de Swanee Ribber,
> Far, far away,
> Dere's wha my heart is turning ebber,
> Dere's wha de old folks stay.
> All up and down de whole creation
> Sadly I roam,
> Still longing for de old plantation,
> And for de old folks at home.
>
> *Chorus*
> All de world am sad and dreary,
> Eb-rywhere I roam;
> Oh, darkeys, how my heart grows weary,
> Far from de old folks at home![41]

Stephen Collins Foster and his music are brought to life by accordionist and banjo player Ashley Ford, as a costumed interpreter in the impressive Cincinnati History Museum, where visitors can step aboard the

Queen City of the West, a replica side-wheel steamboat of the 1850s, berthed at the bustling Cincinnati public landing in the basement of this innovative museum.[42]

African Americans had been encouraged to seek employment in a flourishing Cincinnati, but in 1841 there had been a long drought, causing widespread unemployment. Unrest and poverty initiated attacks by the white unemployed on African Americans, who fought back. The African Americans, some of whom had 'escaped from enslavement only a few weeks or months previously, were rounded up and jailed for their own protection'. These events were known as the Cincinnati Race Riot of 1841. Some people justified the riot on the grounds that African Americans were 'inferior and did not deserve to be recognised or protected by the legal system'. The Ohio Anti-Slavery Society produced pamphlets counteracting this argument, portraying African Americans in a positive light.[43]

In 1850 Congress passed the Fugitive Slave Act, under which those who sheltered runaways could be fined up to $1,000 and be imprisoned for six months. Bounty hunters, or slave catchers, hired by the slave owners, would capture anyone and sell them 'down the river' (hence the expression). Freed slaves could not testify against a white person in court. Although the abolitionist movement was a bi-racial assault on slavery, there were internal conflicts between black and white on how to attain the common goal. Two of Jessie Donaldson's friends, William Lloyd Garrison and Frederick Douglass, both significant figures, disagreed on rhetorical methods. Some slave owners were Quakers, working from within, and some were among the earliest protesters, fighting against the practice of selling slaves off separately from their families.

Jessie and Francis arrived in Cincinnati in 1856 at a particularly momentous time of political upheaval, leading to the American Civil War. Cincinnati, situated on the border, needed to keep the peace with its neighbours and was as far south as one could go without leaving the North. The references in Jessie's obituary about her friends are brief enough to be tantalising. Already in Cincinnati and making plenty of noise were William Lloyd Garrison, the fiery abolitionist; Harriet Beecher

Figure 2: Jessie Donaldson (1799–1889) (Hilary Edmiston Collection, Donaldson Family Archive Collection)

Stowe, whose book *Uncle Tom's Cabin*, published in 1852, had caused a sensation; Frederick Douglass, the African American who was campaigning for freedom and women's rights, and who had a song, 'The Fugitive's Song', named for him; and freed slaves Ellen and William Craft, who published their book *Running a Thousand Miles for Freedom* in 1860; the Crafts visited Swansea in October 1858 and gave a lecture at Mount Pleasant Chapel on 'American Slavery'. Also active at the same time, not mentioned in her obituary but surely known to Jessie, were Levi Coffin and his wife Catherine, who ran the school for enslaved

African Americans which had originally been set up by the Donaldsons and their friends. The Rev. John Rankin was downriver in Ripley shouting abolitionist sermons from his pulpit. Philip Phillips, 'The Singing Pilgrim', would soon set up his business in Cincinnati selling pianos, organs and Sunday School songbooks, and he too would perform at Swansea's Mount Pleasant Chapel, in November 1876. (It cannot be a coincidence that several of Jessie's friends and a choir of freed slaves would speak or sing at Mount Pleasant Chapel, just around the corner from her previous Swansea home; she must have organised letters of introduction.) Providing the background to this cacophony of community organising and political action were the songs and shouts of the enslaved, the music of Stephen Collins Foster, and Harriet Beecher Stowe's book, all of which would endure into contemporary popular culture.

Abolitionists used the power of song not only to stir up enthusiasm for the cause but to get their points across. A prime example was Jessie's friend William Lloyd Garrison (1805–79). A wily, highly combustible personality by all accounts, he wrote new lyrics to well-known songs such as 'Auld Lang Syne' (below), in order to encourage waverers into his meetings:

> I am an abolitionist
> Then urge me not to pause;
> For joyfully do I enlist
> In Freedom's social cause.
> A nobler strife the world ne'er saw,
> The enslaved to disenthrall,
> I am a solder for the war,
> Whatever may befall!

Sung no doubt to the accompaniment of a piano, maybe a harmonium, or tambourines and hand-clapping, the song was an uplifting encouragement to join up to the anti-slavery movement. In the first issue of his newspaper *The Liberator*, in 1831, Garrison had set out his stall:

I do not wish to think, speak, or write with moderation. I am in earnest, I will not equivocate. I will not excuse. I will not retreat a single inch – AND I WILL BE HEARD. The apathy of the people is enough to make every statue leap from its pedestal and hasten the resurrection of the dead.[44]

You knew where you were with Garrison. Garrison believed in non-violence and passive resistance, and campaigned for a school for black girls. In 1833 he evaded arrest by the state of Georgia, which had put a $5,000 reward out for his capture, by attending the World Anti-Slavery Convention in London. Two years later Garrison was dragged though Boston by a rope, he was hated by so many. This volatile man not only upset the public with his anti-slavery campaigns, but also used his newspaper 'to attack the smokers, the drinkers, the military, the clergy, the government and those that were cruel to animals', which left few untouched by his views. The last fifteen years of Garrison's life were spent campaigning for the temperance movement and women's suffrage. Jessie's discussions with Mr Garrison must have been stimulating. Garrison wrote to his wife Helen in April 1853:

Cleveland April 1853

Dear Wife

I take my pencil in hand to let you know that I am well, and hope these few lines will find you enjoying the same blessing . . . The weather has been fair all the way and this morning everything is brilliant in the extreme. In the course of another hour, I shall leave for [the Convention in] Cincinnati.[45]

The Anti-Slavery Convention was on 19, 20 and 21 April 1853, three years before Jessie and Francis's arrival, and Garrison was met by A. H. Ernst and Christian Donaldson, Francis's brother. The convention was blessed by the Rev. John Rankin of Ripley, and amongst others 'C. Donaldson and Mr Garrison' were selected as officers. The Rev. Rankin (1793–1886) was described as 'a venerable looking man of sixty-five or seventy years. He resides on the summit of the high hill that rises back of the river at Ripley, Ohio, and his house has been pointed out to passengers.' The Rankin house featured on the safe-passage route for fugitives and would have been known to Jessie:

> The Rankin home stood on a 300-foot high hill that overlooked the Ohio River, where he and his sons would signal runaways in Kentucky with lanterns when it was safe for them to cross the river. Harriet Beecher Stowe immortalised Rankin's efforts to help African Americans in her book *Uncle Tom's Cabin*, with the Rankin home being the first stop in Ohio for Eliza, one of the book's main characters.[46]

William Lloyd Garrison, as chairman of the business committee at the Convention, reported on a long list of resolutions then 'enumerated many books, beginning with "Uncle Tom's Cabin"'.[47]

Another of Jessie's friends mentioned in her obituary was the freed slave Frederick Douglass (1818–95). He was an ardent abolitionist and another campaigner for women's rights. By 1851 Douglass was arguing that the Constitution could be used as a weapon against slavery. Garrison attacked Douglass through the pages of *The Liberator*, challenging this belief. Garrison felt Douglass was of the less radical school of abolitionist. Harriett Beecher Stowe, author of the controversial, dismissed, and again accepted and revered book *Uncle Tom's Cabin*, defended Douglass's views. Writing to Garrison 19 December 1853 in an endeavour to reconcile their differences, Stowe said of Douglass:

> His plans for the elevation of his own race are manly, sensible, comprehensive, he has evidently observed carefully and thought deeply and will I trust act efficiently. You speak of him as an apostate – I cannot but regard this language as unjustly severe – Why is he any more to be called an apostate for having spoken ill tempered things of former friends than they for having spoken severely and cruelly as they have of him? – Where is this work of excommunication to end – Is there but one true anti-slavery church and all others infidels? – Who shall declare

which it is? . . . There is abundant room in the anti-slavery field for him to perform a work without crossing the track or impeding the movement of his old friends, and perhaps in some future time meeting each other from opposite quarters of a victorious field you may yet shake hands together.[48]

Despite Stowe's endeavours, the two campaigners were never fully reconciled.

Frederick Douglass was initially hired by the Massachusetts Anti-Slavery Society in 1841 to talk on his life and times as a slave. Douglass had earlier escaped slavery, disguised in sailor's clothes. In his *Narrative of the Life of Frederick Douglass*, he recalls:

> I had not long been a reader of *The Liberator* before I got a pretty correct idea of the principles, measures and spirit of the anti-slavery reform. While attending an anti-slavery convention at Nantucket 11 August 1841 I felt strongly moved to speak, and was much urged to do so by Mr William C. Coffin, a gentleman who had heard me speak in the colored people's meeting at New Bedford. It was a severe cross, and I took it up reluctantly. The truth was I felt myself a slave, and the idea of speaking to white people weighed me down. I spoke but a few moments, when I felt a degree of freedom, and said what I desired with considerable ease. From that time until now, I have been engaged in pleading the cause of my brethren.[49]

Douglass idealised motherhood, as a consequence of his father, a white man, deserting the family, using these memories and emotions to later champion the cause of women's rights. Deborah E. McDowell, in her introduction to Douglass's *Narrative*, states: 'Abolitionist rhetoric regularly exploited the cultural currency of family and Motherhood in its indictments of slavery, an institution that wantonly and routinely severed slave family ties for profit.'[50]

By the newspaper accounts, Douglass's speeches at rallies and conferences were electrifying and an uncompromising legacy for feminist historians. Douglass published his newspaper *The North Star* in Rochester because of its active Female Anti-Slavery Society; the paper's banner read: 'Right is of No Sex – Truth is of No Color'. Douglass was also depicted in an illustration on the cover of the sheet music for 'The Fugitive's Song', written in 1845 by his friend Jesse Hutchinson Jnr. Douglass and his wife Ann, a freewoman, were helped to flee to Britain in 1845, where supporters purchased Douglass's freedom for $700. Jessie, at that time the Swansea schoolteacher, would surely have known of his arrival in Britain from the cousins in Cincinnati and from the Anti-Slavery Society grapevine. Williams writes of an 'eagerly anticipated' visit to Wrexham Town Hall in 1846 by Douglass, together with William Lloyd Garrison, which 1,000 attended, and analyses the impact made by the level of their debates on the anti-slavery audiences. Williams points out that:

> the anti-slavery movement can be seen to have offered the leaders of Welsh opinion a context in which they could imagine themselves to be at the heart of a global political struggle. This was particularly significant at a time when the Blue Books of 1847 had given the impression that education in Wales was in an appallingly underdeveloped state, leading to a fear that the nation was being left behind by Western 'progress'. Abolitionism thus played a role in the construction of an image of the Welsh as a highly moral, devout and essentially peaceful people who could play a valuable role in the cultural and political life of Victorian Britain.[51]

Ellen Craft was the other friend of Jessie mentioned in her obituary. Ellen's story is astonishing in its own right; Jessie must have got to know her through William Lloyd Garrison. Ellen and her husband William, runaway slaves, eventually went on to publish their own narrative in London in 1860,[52] a testament to great ingenuity, stamina, cross-dressing, race, class, feminism and gender. William Lloyd Garrison, Wendell Phillips, Theodore Parker and others helped their escape.[53] William W. Brown, another abolitionist friend, wrote to Garrison in 1849:

DEAR FRIEND GARRISON:
One of the most interesting cases of the escape of fugitives from American slavery that have ever come before the American people, has just occurred... They will be at the meeting of the Massachusetts Anti-Slavery Society, in Boston, in the latter part of this month, where I know the history of their escape will be listened to with great interest. They are very intelligent. They are young, Ellen 22, and Wm. 24 years of age. Ellen is truly a heroine.
Yours, truly,
WM. W. BROWN.

P.S. They are now hid away within 25 miles of Philadelphia, where they will remain until the 6th when they will leave me for New England. Will you please say in The Liberator that I will lecture, in connexion with them, as follows:—
At Norwich, Ct., Thursday evening, Jan. 18.
At Worcester, Mass., Friday evening, 19.
At Pawtucket, Mass., Saturday evening, 20.
At New Bedford, Mass., Sunday afternoon and evening, 28.[54]

Ellen Craft, born in 1826 to a slave mother, was fathered by a plantation owner. She was light-skinned enough to pass for white. William, born in 1824, was dark-skinned; both were from Georgia. They married through legalities available to them at the time on the plantation. Ellen and William devised their devious escape plan with Ellen disguising herself as a white, male slave-holder, wrapping a scarf around her face to disguise her lack of beard and her arm in a sling to hide her illiteracy. She walked ahead of William, her 'slave'. They managed to travel by train, steamer and ferry without being discovered, eventually reaching Boston. They were the first of Boston's fugitives to be sought under the new 1850 Fugitive Slave Act. Ellen found work as a seamstress and William as a cabinet-maker, but the Crafts were not safe in Boston. The Vigilance Committee got them to Portland, Maine, and finally to Britain, where they remained for nineteen years, campaigning at rallies and meetings. William Craft lectured on 'The Fugitive Slave' at Swansea's Mount Pleasant Chapel;[55] it is likely that Jessie, now in Cincinnati, had recommended to the Anti-Slavery Society that Swansea be added to the Crafts' itinerary. The Crafts, with their three children, returned to America in 1868. They founded the Woodville Co-operative Farm School in 1873 for the education and employment of freed men.

It is unfortunate that Jessie's life in America becomes accessible only through the published accounts of the lives of her friends. Harriet Beecher Stowe moved to Cincinnati in 1932, when she was 21; she was the daughter of the President of the Lane Theological Seminary there, Lyman Beecher. Stowe's great-grandmother had emigrated from Wales in the mid-eighteenth century.[56] Stowe married Calvin Ellis Stowe, a professor at the Seminary, in 1836, the same year as the Cincinnati riots. The Beecher Stowe house, which Jessie would have known, is now used as a community school and social-work centre. It also acts as the host house and starting point for the Secret Passages Tour, operating in conjunction with the National Underground Railroad Freedom Center, Cincinnati. Stowe wrote to Gamaliel Bailey, her editor on the anti-slavery newspaper *The National Era*, who had previously edited *The Philanthropist*, as he was interested in serialising her new story:

> Brunswick, Maine March 9 (1851)
>
> I am at present occupied upon a story which will be a much longer one than any I have ever written embracing a series of sketches which give the lights and shadows of the 'patriarchal institution' . . . Such peril and shame as now hangs over this country is worse than Roman Slavery, and I hope every woman who can write will not be silent . . . My object will be to hold up in the most graphic manner possible slavery, its reverses, changes and the negro character, which I have had ample opportunities for studying. It will be ready in two or three weeks.
> Yours, with sincere esteem H. Stowe.[57]

Uncle Tom's Cabin first appeared on 5 June 1851. Stowe expected it to run for three or four instalments; it ran for over forty.

Harriet Beecher Stowe had witnessed a slave auction in 1833, when she was aged 22. She was visiting her pupil Elizabeth Marshall Key, who lived at the Marshall Key House (now a museum) in Old Washington, Kentucky. Elizabeth's father had taken Harriet up the street to witness a slave auction on the block on the courthouse steps. It was never forgotten.[58] Beecher Stowe incorporated actual people, events, sights and sounds into her book, including real-life stories of runaways such as Josiah Henson. Slave narratives had also begun to be published. In 1876 the Swansea local press carried an article about Josiah Henson (1789–1883):

> A coloured clergyman from Canada, reputedly the inspiration for Uncle Tom; he had been lecturing to a large audience in London, talked about his appearance at the Hyde Park Exhibition in 1851 and was touring Britain. Father Henson was described as aged over 87, although 'hale and hearty, carries the marks on his body of brutal treatment he received while forty-two years spent in slavery'. Henson and his wife then had an audience with the Archbishop of Canterbury telling him he had been 'educated at the University of Adversity'.[59]

Henson's book, *A Life of Josiah Henson, Formerly a Slave, Now an inhabitant of Canada, as Narrated by Himself*, had been published in 1849, and translated into Welsh in 1877.[60] Williams discusses the importance of the Welsh translation of Henson's autobiography as a 'striking example' of the phenomenon of the popularity of *Uncle Tom's Cabin*. He writes: 'In attending a meeting of the Welsh Calvinistic Methodist Church in Paddington, London, Henson described his pleasure at hearing one of William Williams Pantycelyn's hymns sung by the congregation "in their native Welsh".'[61]

Henson's escape with his wife and children in September 1830 across the Ohio River in a small boat had inspired Beecher Stowe. Visitors to the Harriet Beecher Stowe House in Cincinnati are handed a leaflet on Josiah Henson, which reads:

When the party reached the Indiana shore, Henson packed his two youngest children into a knapsack and shouldered it. Two older children walked beside his wife. Travelling by night and hiding by day, they reached Cincinnati within two weeks. Friends helped them to Sandusky, Ohio where a sympathetic ship's captain hired Henson to help load his ship for a small wage and free passage for himself and family to Buffalo. There Henson found a ship to take them to Canada. They reached freedom on 28 October 1830. For Josiah Henson the road from slavery had taken many a turn. He summed up his faith and hopes for his people: 'We are peaceable and I believe the day is not far distant when we shall take a respectable rank among the subjects of Her Majesty, the excellent and most gracious Queen of England and Canada'.[62]

A production of *Uncle Tom's Cabin* arrived at Swansea's Star Theatre in November 1877, with the special engagement of 'Bob Height's Blacks for the Plantation Scene'; Jessie was back home in Swansea at this time, aged only 78. The production was also booked into the Theatre Royal in Temple Street 'including a host of freed slaves, Jubilee Singers and same at Princess's Theatre, London for 6 nights'.[63] Three months later the production returned to the Star, featuring George Melville as George Harris. Such was the popularity of *Uncle Tom's Cabin* on the stage that local theatre and music groups were eager to produce it. Kilvey Music Hall, Swansea, featured a production with music interpreted by the Kilvey Church Choir. The review read:

> Concert at Kilvey Music Hall, the lengthy programme consisted of a musically arranged 'service' entitled Uncle Tom the prose portion culled from Mrs. Beecher Stowe's world-renowned story, supplemented by several pieces of music arranged by Mr. James Tipton. Some of the pieces were really touching, such as the duet and chorus, the Parting, He is Gone, Steal Away.[64]

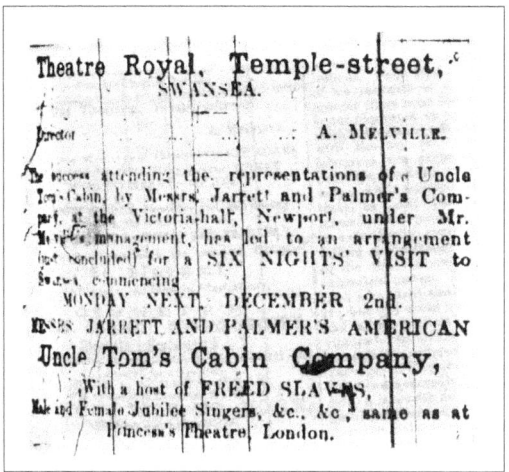

Figure 3: 'Uncle Tom's Cabin' advertisement, 1878
(SWW Media)

Uncle Tom's Cabin returned again to Swansea's Theatre Royal in November 1878, 'with a host of freed slaves and male and female Jubilee Singers'. The review reads:

> the leading characters are enacted by very clever impersonators, but what lends a distinctive and very realistic charm to the performances is the fact that the famous part of Uncle Tom, Topsy and others are taken by real negroes. This is by far the best dramatic rendering of Mrs. Beecher Stowe's celebrated story we have yet seen and the company give a sufficiently vivid but not overstrained picture of the horrors of slavery. The intelligent and pathetic rendering of Eva, the sprightly and most enjoyable playing of Topsy are especially noticeable and the scenes wherein the large crowd of some 20 or 25 negroes appear are not easily forgotten. The cotton-picking, the jubilee singing, the whistling, the major playing, the dancing, are all worthy of mention.[65]

Williams discusses the transatlantic impact of the Welsh translation by Hugh Williams of *Uncle Tom's Cabin*, published by John Cassell in London in 1853. Chapters had already appeared in Welsh newspapers: 'there were three different Welsh versions of Stowe's novel in circulation . . . the sheer number of versions of *Uncle Tom's Cabin* produced within a two-year period is remarkable . . . It is clear that Stowe's novel resonated with Welsh audiences.'[66]

Uncle Tom's Cabin continued to resonate to the end of the century. In 1899 the editor of the *South Wales Daily Post*, David Davies, penned an article for his newspaper headlined: 'In Uncle Tom's Land – At a Negro Funeral Service – Pulpit Oratory of the Blacks, by the Editor'. It is a reflection of his middle-class attitude to 'the negro' at that time. David Davies had been invited to the southern states of the United States by his friend Mr Wingfield, an ex-slave owner. Davies writes:

> A former article described the circumstances which took me into the pulpit of a coloured people's church a few miles from Newport News while a 'double event' service was going on. The truth came to me with irresistible force that in the people before me was a race widely separated from the white not merely in degree of civilisation, but also organically. It is difficult, nay, impossible, to convey to the reader an idea of the influences contributing to the impression of profound and elemental racial divergence. But the impression could not be evaded. The congregation was a monumental piece of evidence of race inferiority . . . The service ended, the people filed past the coffin to have their last look at Sam Lee . . . On the way back I could not fail to notice the extreme eagerness of the older men and women to catch the eye and exchange a word or two with Mr. Wingfield. Some would hurry to catch him up, others would wait for him to overtake them. Each old negro was 'Uncle' something, and all the old women were 'Aunts'. I commented on the fact. 'Yes,' said the ex-slave owner, 'they were most of them my property once, and some of them are in my service still. They are very respectful, as you say. It is only the younger ones that show insolence.'[67]

Jessie's ten years in America coincided with some of the most tumultuous times that she and America were to witness. Her brother

Samuel Heineken Jnr, who had followed her out to Cincinnati, became a cavalry officer during the American Civil War, fighting, naturally, on the side of the Union. Involved in the battle of Murfreesboro, Tennessee, his horse shot from under him, he escaped serious injury, was captured, nearly starved to death, but survived to write home to Swansea in 1863 from Ward 7, US General Hospital, Annapolis. Samuel's opinion of the way the war was heading at that time was dispiriting, fearing a Union defeat. However, the war was to endure another two years, which concluded when Robert E. Lee surrendered to Ulysses S. Grant on 9 April 1865. *The Cambrian* published a long account of Samuel's adventures; he survived into old age.[68] Of the fighting men, Fern Riddell, contributing editor at *History Today*, writes:

> By the end of the war 186,000 black men, both freemen and 'fugitive' slaves, had joined the Union's army forming regiments that were derided both by southerners and northerners alike. Although the abolition of slavery has become the popular perception of the war, the historical reality is much more complicated and, in many cases, much more uncomfortable and less clear cut than we might like.[69]

Marching songs were intrinsic to empowering the fighting spirit of soldiers. The Militia Act of 17 July 1862 authorised the enrolment of 'persons of the African descent in any military or naval service for which they may be found competent'. Captain Lindley Miller, a white officer of the First Arkansas Coloured Regiment penned these words for his troops, a rousing recruiting song, sung to the tune of 'John Brown's Body':

> Oh, we're the bully soldiers of the 'First of Arkansas',
> We are fighting for the Union, we are fighting for the law,
> We can hit a Rebel further than a white man ever saw,
> As we go marching on.

Chorus
Glory, glory, hallelujah,
Glory, glory, hallelujah,
Glory, glory, hallelujah,
As we go marching on.[70]

Jessie and Francis returned home to Swansea in 1866 after the end of the American Civil War. It is not known what prompted their return. Francis was an American citizen, after all, so why should he want to end his days in Swansea? Perhaps they had had enough of the war and the politics. They resided for a while in a small terraced house at 2 Phillips Parade, near the city centre. Francis died in 1873, shortly before the arrival in Swansea in 1874 of the Fisk Jubilee Singers (see chapter 3) for their very first concert in Craddock Street Music Hall, described in advertisements as performing 'strange weird slave songs'. The Fisk Jubilee Singers were freed slaves fundraising for their campus buildings for the first university inaugurated for the education of freed slaves and their children, in Nashville, Tennessee. The concert was attended by town dignitaries. Jessie, aged only 74 at the time, may have attended. In 1889 Jessie (Heineken) Donaldson died, aged 90, at Ael-y-Bryn, Sketty, Swansea. The house no longer stands.[71]

In 1836 the astute Maria Weston Chapman wrote:

> We should let no opportunity escape which can be legitimately used for the benefit of the slave. Let us have public celebrations whenever they can be made to subserve the great and glorious principles we advocate. Let us encourage the young to learn and speak those pieces, which breathe forth the sentiments of liberty, and to sing those songs which will inspire them with a love of freedom. These sentiments, early engraven upon their hearts, may change their future course and police of action, and lead them to become the benefactors, instead of the oppressors of mankind. Public opinion is now so modified on the question of slavery, that common and other schools will tolerate the rehearsal of pieces which embody the principles of freedom. If the

young are encouraged in this, much, very much, may be done to increase sympathy for the cause of the enslaved.[72]

President Abraham Lincoln issued the Emancipation Proclamation on 1 January 1863. In Britain, the Slave Emancipation Act was passed in August 1833, under the Whig government led by Lord Grey, giving all slaves in the British Empire their freedom, albeit after a set period of years.

A Postscript: The Ones that Got Away

There are several instances of runaways and freed slaves arriving in Swansea, possibly on the strength of its successful Anti-Slavery Society activities.

Willis (his owner's name) arrived in Swansea on 24 February 1833 aboard the American copper ore carrier *St. Peter*.[73] Described as 'a very fine young negro about 20 years of age', he had worked his passage as a cook and helper in the ship's galley. Willis had heard on his plantation that 'if he could but put his foot upon British ground he would then be free and requested advice upon this point'. Captain H. Mickle sent for the Portreeve, Mr T. Edward Thomas, who arrived in a horse and buggy from the Old Guildhall (now the site of the Dylan Thomas Centre), and immediately pronounced Willis a free man. Willis wisely turned down the offer of a job from the captain of the *St. Peter* for its return voyage, fearing that bounty hunters would get him and he would once again become a slave. With a written discharge from the ship, and two sovereigns from the captain, he turned towards the town, 'anxious to be free'. There is another reference to our Willis in Runaway Slaves. It reads: 'When the slave Willis boarded a steamboat in New Orleans in 1832, he wore a white shirt, brown linen pants, a blue cloth frock coat, and a black hat. He also took with him a bundle of clothing wrapped in a sheet'. The timing and description would suggest this was indeed the same fugitive slave, Willis, from New Orleans.[74] The last reference concerns an 'old Negro Man' (Willis again?)

described as a well-known Swansea character who sat on the wall in Northampton Lane waving and smiling at passers-by, and who told tales of slavery days.[75]

'Thomas Rigby, at Llanelly, Carms. Aged 51. Former African Slave.'[76] Lyn John, writing for Treftadaeth Cymuned Llanelli/Llanelli Community Heritage, states:

> Research carried out at both the Swansea and Llanelli Reference Libraries has finally revealed that Thomas Rigby was indeed, *Thomas the black barber*! He was an African slave who was born about the year of 1790, and at the age of eight, he was taken as a slave to the West Indies. After an elapse of a few years he obtained his freedom and came to England and then Llanelli and made a living as a barber or hairdresser in the town. Later he married a local woman by the name of Mary and between them they had six children.[77]

Henry 'Box' Brown lectured on 'The American Fugitive Slave' at Swansea's Goat Street Schoolroom in March 1855. He returned in November 1863, this time presenting a 'Panorama of Slavery' at the Eisteddfod Pavilion, Swansea. Brown, a slave in Virginia for thirty-three years, acquired his name through the enterprising, but extremely dangerous, escape method of packing himself into a box 'as if a container of dry goods' and shipping himself 275 miles to freedom, to the abolitionist James Miller McKim in Philadelphia. The box was small; Mr Brown was five feet eight inches tall and weighed 200 pounds. The box travelled by wagon, railroad, steamboat, wagon, railroad, ferry, railroad and finally a delivery wagon. The journey took twenty-six hours. Mr McKim 'and other members of the Philadelphia Vigilance Committee' received the box, and Mr Brown's first words on being unpacked were 'How do you do, gentlemen?' He published *The Narrative of Henry 'Box' Brown*, and toured Britain for twenty-five years.[78]

Other escapees who lectured in Swansea were James Thompson on 'His Own Experience of Slavery', at Castle Street Chapel, Swansea, in 1863,[79] and the Rev. Johnson, a 'Coloured Gentleman, once a slave in USA', who spoke at the Independent Chapel, Castle Street, Swansea.[80]

Jessie Donaldson's story was submitted to the National Underground Railroad Freedom Center's Kroger Everyday Freedom Heroes Award and Gallery.[81] Jessie Donaldson has also been incorporated into the Swansea Women's History Walk – Taith Gerdded Hanes Menywod Abertawe, inaugurated by Women's Archive of Wales, Archif Menywod Cymru, in 2014.

Jazz music does not have a beginning or an end, and it did not suddenly appear out of a vacuum. It took hundreds of years to form, encompassing people's lost history, both black and white, a voice for protest and rebellion. African Americans retained their memories through work songs. The abolitionists and anti-slavery campaigners contributed politics and passion. Musicians wrote down the sounds, songs and music. Jessie Donaldson's contribution to social change whilst in Cincinnati meant that she paved the way for African American freed slaves to perform on concert platforms in Wales. Jessie also provided a legacy of historical significance in her hometown of Swansea.

Chapter Two

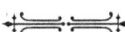

Doing the Plantation Walkaround Skedaddle

Figure 4: The Harry Collins Minstrels, date unknown
(Cynon Valley Museum and Gallery, Aberdare)

AN EARLY EXAMPLE OF THE intercultural cross-fertilisation of Welsh and American culture was the minstrel show, which, between the 1850s and the beginning of the twentieth century, was a highly popular entertainment, especially in industrial south Wales. Minstrel shows were performed in 'blackface' (using burnt cork as face-paint), mostly by white entertainers, and these musical interpretations contained banjos, percussion and dance, all part of the early soup that evolved into jazz. From at least the 1830s, troupes of 'minstrels' and 'serenaders' were performing in Wales on a regular basis. Often they were family groups, like the Oxfordshire Minstrels, who performed English folk songs at the Assembly Rooms, Swansea, or the British Minstrels, whose repertoire of overtures, songs, duets and 'glees' was offered for the enjoyment of the 'Gentry and Public', with the added attraction of a 'Miniature Organ'. European troupes toured Wales too, such as the yodelling Tyrolese Minstrels, a sister and four brothers of the Rainer family, appearing in national dress.[1]

A photograph (c.1880) exists of the all-woman Mandolin Band which emanated from the Tregaron area, Ceredigion. The musicians are pictured in staid Victorian dress and looking quite solemn, but the nine-piece band must have delighted local audiences with their variety of stringed instruments led by a formidable lady on violin. They would have performed a programme of light airs and ballads. In the 2000s Rachel Stelmach, of Women in Tune and living in Tregaron, donated this photograph of the Tregaron Mandolin Band to Jazz Heritage Wales, and told me of her 95-year-old neighbour Miss Betts, who had pointed out her mother holding her mandolin in the top row, first left.[2]

From the mid-1800s south Wales was bombarded with a variety of entertainers attracted to the areas of heavy industry, namely coalfields, tinplate and shipping, which provided the potential for large audiences. New venues were also opening up to cater for cultural appetites, be they high or low. Sometimes the general public got lucky with free entertainment, such as the American circus with forty horses parading through Swansea in 1844. Described as an 'Equestrian Cavalcade', a Grand Procession wound its way through the town, accompanied by a

Figure 5: The Mandolin Band, Tregaron, c.1880
(Jazz Heritage Wales Collection)

brass band, headed by a carriage drawn by ten 'splendid cream-coloured horses'. A special pavilion was erected in a field opposite Heathfield Terrace (now dense housing) for their ticketed performances during the week.[3]

Entertainment from America was always popular. In 1850 crowds flocked to see the Original Female American Serenaders from the St James's Assembly Rooms in London, led by Madame Cora. The Serenaders, with three banjos, three percussionists and an organ or piano, performed at Swansea's Assembly Rooms, then travelled to Neath for their next show. There is no further information for Swansea, but a playbill for an 1847 performance at the Town Hall, Birmingham, reads 'The Invitation Card of the Coloured Ladies to the Public of Birmingham'. However the Birmingham press also referred to them as 'Female Ethiopian Serenaders', implying they were white women in blackface. There is a possibility that the Original Female American Serenaders were men in drag. *The Birmingham Journal*'s description states:

> The band of Ethiopian Serenaders consists of seven females, their faces coloured to a complexion resembling that of the Bushmen, wearing short petticoats which allows a full view of legs encased in reddish brown skin tights; on various parts of their bodies there is an abundance of brass, and, as may be supposed, that material is not wanting in other respects.[4]

In 1851 another American circus toured south Wales venues at Cowbridge, Neath and Swansea, this time led by Madame Macarte and her 'splendid band'. The review stated that the 'celebrated company of equestrians were very gay as they passed along the streets, with skilful horsemanship by the ladies, and fine instrumental music'.[5]

Talent was a two-way flow, although ours was of a more traditional nature. In 1854 the press highlighted how well the Welsh were doing in America:

> It is highly gratifying to find that our fellow-countrymen in America still cherish and foster the ancient and national customs of 'Gwyllt Walia' [Wild Wales], and that they are to hold an Eisteddfod on a grand scale in the city of New York in the autumn of 1855. They offer six prizes of $300, three prizes of $250, nine of $200, six of $100 and one prize of $50 for the best essays in Welsh on Astronomy, Chemistry, Geology etc. We hope the most sanguine expectations of its promoters will be realised.

The prizes were considerable amounts of money for the time.[6]

By mid-century, the Welsh were competing for space with African American performers of what was known in the racist terminology of the time as 'Nigger minstrelsy' and 'Coon songs', together with their white imitators, who took the variety circuit by storm. This created a significant musical mix between Wales and America as Welsh audiences embraced the new form of entertainment, and local Welsh performers 'blacked up', adapting the minstrel tradition for local audiences. In fact, between 1860 and 1900 there were so many 'Negro' minstrel troupes, groups and 'melanges' (mixtures) on tour that rival companies would often be performing at various venues in Swansea in the same week, feeding a seemingly insatiable appetite among south Wales audiences for this transatlantic vogue.

Frantz Fanon dissects his arguments through ontology – the philosophy of information science – confronting the 'language of the civilizing nation'. He discusses aspects of blackness in which he states that, 'Not only must the black man be black; he must be black in relation to the white man.' Fanon asks the question:

> Do I have to be limited to the justification of a facial conformation? . . .
> I as a man of colour do not have the right to seek to know in what respect my race is superior or inferior to another race . . . In the world through which I travel, I am endlessly creating myself.[7]

Black feminist historians and theorists re-evaluate black historical, cultural and political ideologies. The African American feminist theorist Audre Lorde wrote extensively on life's civil and social injustices. She recommends that a re-evaluation be motivated by the following: 'Divide and conquer, in our world, must become define and empower.'[8]

Michael Pickering, in discussing minstrelsy in Britain, suggests that a 'two-way cultural interchange' was in progress at this time, with African Americans 'borrowing, imitating, adapting and accommodating themselves to white musical genres' and white performers in their turn adapting aspects of black music for their own purposes. Pickering describes a typical minstrel show that would entail a line of seated performers in a semi-circle with 'end men', and the Master of Ceremonies, 'Mr Interlocutor', the straight man, seated centrally. Comicalities would commence with songs, gags and 'rapid fire cross-talk . . . madcap antics and buffoonery' and skits on current affairs. At the end, all participants would take part in the 'walkaround', featuring their speciality music or comic act, a precursor of the finale in a variety show. Although there is continuing debate over his role, the white performer T. Daddy Rice seems to have been an important catalyst in introducing

Negro minstrelsy to Britain, as Pickering asserts. Rice never performed in Wales but between 1836 and 1842 his appearances at English venues with his rendition of 'Jump Jim Crow' caused a sensation. As Pickering has noted, however, it was Dan Emmet's company in 1843 that established 'the combination of banjo fiddle, tambourine and bone castanets which remained at the core of minstrelsy performance'.[9]

Pickering debates how African American entertainers were perceived by British audiences and whether audiences were witnessing a genuine form of black entertainment, 'yet their public performances always occurred within the context of the white host culture, and that context exerted a considerable shaping pressure . . . on their repertory and style of presentation'.[10]

By at least 1854 'negro delineators' (whites in blackface) were making an appearance in south Wales. In July of that year, *The Cambrian* reported that Mr Pelham would make a return visit to the town, an advertisement in the paper announcing that he would 'repeat his Sambo 'It-'Em-'Ard' at the theatre. Queues of people formed outside the theatres, music rooms, assembly rooms, drill halls, circus houses and palaces of culture, all willing to part with their hard-earned pennies. Wales's nightlife at this time was multicultural and loud, washed down with liberal doses of satirical comment aimed at the middle and upper classes, in which the working classes could collude. Popular culture was at least in part a culture of protest against Victorian values, and performers and audiences alike asserted their right to partake in, parody and develop any style of music as they wished – especially the working-class Welsh, who had particular axes to grind regarding their relationships with the English coal, copper and iron masters. Any excuse to collude with the performers on stage was grist to the mill.

Some Negro minstrel troupes, as a result, adapted their act to the Welsh vernacular, including place names, local characters' names, venues or particular local idiosyncrasies in their act, to the delight of the local audiences. *The Cambrian*, forerunner of the *South Wales Daily Post*, fuelled the flames by urging potential audiences to 'make haste' to a particular venue to catch the latest arrivals. In the heyday of these troupes, some theatres or halls would be advertising black performers, and white performers in blackface, on the same bill, which served to emphasise the cross-over between cultures on the stage.

A troupe appearing in October 1854 at the Swansea Assembly Rooms, on their first tour of Wales, were the Celebrated and Original Ethiopian Serenaders of St James's (St James's Hall, Piccadilly). The advert stressed that 'it was their first tour as they are aware that there have been persons who have assumed their original title of "Ethiopian Serenaders"'. Whether this troupe was the same as Pell's Ethiopian Serenaders, who had appeared at Buckingham Palace, is not clear. If it is the same troupe, then appearing with them was William Henry Lane, an African American (or 'Real Negro') also known as Master Juba, whom Pickering describes as an 'outstanding contemporary exponent of popular dance'. Master Juba performed the Virginny Breakdown, the Tennessee Double Shuffle and the Louisiana Toe 'n' Heel as 'authentic Nigger dances'. He was also a tambourine virtuoso, receiving top billing at Swansea along with four white minstrels. Tickets were quite expensive, at 3s., 2s. and 1s. No review of this performance was printed.[11]

By 1860 the Assembly Rooms boasted of a 'Fashionable Entertainment of Refined Negro Music', complete with a morning concert and another at 2 p.m. The large advert announced:

> The reunion of the Celebrated and Original Ethiopian Serenaders, Messrs. Pell, White, Stanwood and Germon from St. James's, singing selections from their celebrated programme, including Original Songs and Pieces brought by them from the USA, being copyright can be sung by no other artistes.

The advert suggests that a more genteel audience was expected for the morning show, as tickets were more expensive. Tickets were available from Brader's Piano and Harp Warehouse in Wind Street. Songbooks of the performance were available for purchase, and carriages could be ordered for the journey home.[12]

Welsh venues were now beginning to advertise a confusing mix of blackface, 'Refined Fashionable Negro Entertainment', as well as 'Real Wild Men of Africa'. An example of the latter was 'Edmond's Late Wombell's Royal Windsor Exhibition and Castle Menagerie', which toured Pontardawe, Ystalyfera, Morriston and Swansea in July 1861. Based at Swansea's St Helen's Road, the menagerie contained not only sixteen large carriages but also:

> The Rare and Extraordinary Zulu Kaffirs and Wild Men of Africa, the Only Men of Their Race ever brought to Alien Country, in native costume, with their manners and customs of Kaffir Life: viz the War Signal, Mode of Warfare, War Dances, Club Dances, and Songs of War and Peace etc.[13]

The troupe and its menagerie were clearly bent on exploiting mid-nineteenth-century enthusiasm for Empire and the colonisation of Africa, with all the jingoism which that entailed. Perhaps, though, with a full programme of music, the Zulus and 'Wild Men of Africa' took advantage of the opportunity provided to celebrate at least a vestige of their own culture before a white audience and pass it on to their new Welsh audiences. It was a parody and a cultural translation on their part. Entertainment was never a simple expedient.

It is possible, too, that the Welsh could sympathise somewhat with the black performers they saw corralled on stage, especially those audiences in Swansea, as during its earlier campaigning years of anti-slavery and abolitionist activity, Swansea had had the largest and most committed Anti-Slavery Society in Wales. The experience of watching corralled 'Zulus' singing and dancing on stage must have evoked forms of compassion as well as awe, especially for those old enough to remember the tumultuous years of the early anti-slavery movement. The British Empire abolished slavery with the 1833 Act of Parliament. The American Civil War (1861–5) had started just a few months earlier. Now Wales was witnessing freed African American 'real Negros', chained as 'Zulus', parodying their cultural heritage while America was being torn apart in real time. An added complication was that Wales also laboured under the yoke of English rule and law. There had been a growing demand for greater autonomy in Wales; Nonconformist consciousness and Welsh Methodism, Liberal politics and, above all, an increasing interest in preserving the Welsh language fuelled a Welsh nationalist sentiment. Eisteddfoddau, the literary, poetic and musical competitions, had seen a resurgence in Carmarthen in 1819. However, Wales had been damned in 1847 with an investigation into the state of education in the country, especially into the 'means afforded to the labouring classes of acquiring a knowledge of the English language'. The *Report of the Commissioners of Inquiry into the State of Education in Wales, 1847*, 'did not confine itself to commenting upon what was represented as Wales's woefully inadequate educational provisions, but went on to denounce Welsh people as a whole as backward and lawless, as if in an attempt to shame them into rapid Anglicization'.[14]

However, in contrast and as a result of these increased visits by black entertainers, Welsh entrepreneurs and performers began to adapt aspects of African American music for their own ends, by donning blackface and clowning on one hand, and by appropriating the 'Refined Negro' act on the other. In this way Welsh entertainers created a new hybrid for local consumption. By the mid-1860s, south Wales troupes were regularly using blackface. The Swansea Original Coloured Serenaders, for example, gave a benefit concert in March 1865 at the Music Hall. Some troupes were sufficiently professional to appear at the main venues.[15]

What the 'Refined Negro Entertainers' thought of the locals' efforts is unknown, though it could be argued that an audience who turned out at a local hall to see their neighbours performing in blackface might well have been encouraged to visit the town theatres to see African Americans perform. Certainly by this time minstrelsy was so much a part of south Wales popular culture that the combined schools annual outing was treated to a spectacular by the local Swansea East-side troupe the Kilvey Coloured Minstrels, who performed their 'Nigger part-songs' for the Kilvey Copper Works schools of Pentrechwyth,

St Thomas and Danygraig Infants at Maesteg House, the seat of the Grenfell family on Kilvey Hill. Twelve hundred schoolchildren attended this performance. The Grenfells were industrialists who owned the Upper Bank copper works in the lower Swansea valley, employing 800 at the height of production, and also owned a fleet of ships. Their philanthropic activities with the annual school outing and treat, together with benevolent activities improving and renovating their workers' cottages, helped, perhaps, to assuage guilt at their wealth built on the backs of their workers.[16]

In October 1865, the harmonium made its first appearance among the plantation 'walkarounds' performed by locals in blackface, adding a particular Welsh dimension to the genre. Anxious to instil a little decorum in minstrelsy performance, Mr Joseph Parry, a native of Merthyr, hosted a 'Celebrated Cambro-American Concert' at the Merthyr Temperance music hall. Mr Parry had emigrated to America, where he worked at the ironworks in Danville, Pennsylvania, and had returned to his roots as a local boy made good. He was known for his compositions 'The Cambrian Minstrels' and 'Comic Glees'. The Cambro-American concert, with Mr Parry at the harmonium, attracted large audiences.[17]

The following year, 1866, the CCC Christy Minstrels appeared before a large audience at Loughor Schoolroom, performing the 'Oudie Oudie', with the finale of the 'Plantation Walkaround Skeddadle accompanied by excited peals of laughter'. The review of the show ends with the comment that it was accompanied on harmonium by Mr C. D. Ace of Swansea. The harmonium was obviously becoming popular as a variant on the 'Negro Minstrelsy' genre.[18] The Christy name was synonymous with successful blackface artistes; troupes would add it to their own name, thereby causing great confusion as to who were the Original Christy Minstrels and who were local imitators. Swansea had their own troupe, the Swansea Christy Minstrels.[19]

Troupes in blackface became increasingly bizarre, with lengthy titles such as the Original and Only Christy's Eclipse Constellation Concert Company and Assemblage of Stars. This company listed George Forest 'the President', Howard Campbell 'Bones Ethiopian Comedian and Dancer', Charles Bayne, Joe Leeson and R. Macgregor, 'the MD and Solo Violinist'. Part two of the performance included a 'Grand Comical, Mimical and Musical Melange', comprising 'Songs, Burlesques, Readings, Sketches of Character, Instrumental Solos, Dances and Breakdowns'. Each evening would feature Miss Annie Manners, Miss Amy Montague and Miss Lottie Keene, followed by a 'Laughable Burlesque Extravaganza, To Conclude with the Original Plantation Walk-Round Darkies Carnival'.[20]

Another 'Original Christy's Minstrels' troupe was touring a year later, in 1868, in Swansea and Llanelli, and even *The Cambrian* newspaper was in doubt as to whether they were the original Originals, having to debate their authenticity within its pages:

> Are these, then, the real 'originals' who entertained a very fair and respectable audience at the Music Hall last night? We say no, but they bear evident signs from their talent of being a branch from the parent stem. Talent is restless and like the brood in the nest when sufficiently fledged, will go over its boundary to warble the songs of its ancestors under the same name and form . . . The whole entertainment possessed an infusion of the sublime mingled with the ridiculous but there was much refinement and rigour pervading.[21]

During 1868 Swansea audiences were treated to a combination of local talent by the Sketty (an aspiring area of Swansea) Minstrels performing their version of 'Empire and Plantation' in blackface at the Sketty Schoolroom before the Mayor and 'several leading families'. It was an eye-opening programme. Sentimental ballads such as 'Just Before the Battle Mother' were contrasted with 'Ten Little Niggers'. Mr W. H. Hilton, listed as 'Alabama Sam', got a particular mention as 'the lion of the evening with an excellent song and dance, together with his American Jig'. The 'Alabama Sam' lyrics confronted audiences with the realities of life of the African American, now delivered by an on-the-up middle-class Welshman from Sketty:

> I came over to England
> My fortune for to make,
> By golly it nearly broke their hearts,
> The fair ones to forsake.
> Among them all I was first chap,
> A regular darkey swell,
> A taxation nigger I was called
> By every yaller belle.
>
> How I came to England,
> I cross'd the Atlantic waves,
> For in North or South there is no home,
> For us poor negro slaves.
> John Bull with open heart and hand,
> Greets brothers white or black,
> So in freedom's land I'll take my stand,
> For they'll never get me back.[22]

Next on the bill was a duet, 'Banjo and Bones', by Messrs Jones and Edwards, which was 'exceedingly well performed'. Then Mr J. Edwards delighted the audience with his version of the song and dance number 'Ham Fat Pan'. This number was quite possibly the American music hall number 'De Ham Fat Man', popular during the American Civil War:

> Oh! Good-ev'n to you, white folks,
> I'm glad to see you all
> I'm right from ole Virginny,
> Which some people say will fall;
> You may talk about ole massa,
> But he am just de man,
> To make de niggers happy
> Wid de ham-fat man.

Chorus
Ham-fat, ham-fat, zig a zig a zam,
Ham-fat, ham-fat frying in de pan;
Oh! Roll into de kitchen fast, boys, as you can,
Oh! Rooksey, Cooksey, Cooksey, I'm de ham-fat man.[23]

The American vernacular witnessed in live performances on stage was obviously having a great influence upon the local members of the Sketty Minstrels, who, perhaps, had never been further in 1868 than Merthyr Tydfil. This very successful evening was brought to a close by the obligatory 'Plantation Walkaround'. It is also gratifying that the local paper saw fit to send a reporter to cover some of these performances, to our benefit.[24]

With minstrelsy in full swing on the local scene, many new groups sprang up perfecting their 'Nigger Delineations'. In 1869 the Aberavon Star Troupe of Amateur Coloured Minstrels (whites in blackface) performed songs, dances, burlesques and a plantation walkaround at the National School, accompanied by piano, harmonium, cornet, castanets and tambourines. Jokes 'on local matters were provided by the corner men and elicited much applause'. A review of the performance particularly mentions the fine 'burlesque dresses', though these were probably worn by men in drag, as blackface drag acts were popular. Again, the harmonium was a Welsh touch to suit local tastes.[25]

By 1869, however, blackface minstrelsy was undergoing a change in Wales. Appearing now to even greater acclaim were 'Real Negroes' adopting the 'white blackface' – that is, African Americans applying burnt cork in exaggerated style, mimicking and subverting in its turn the Welsh adaption of slave plantation life. One such group was Hutchinson and Tayleure's Great American Slave Troupe, who appeared at Swansea's Wind Street Grand Circus building, site of the later Star Theatre and then Rialto Cinema. The show featured Japanese Tommy, who was not Japanese at all, but a black dwarf, Thomas Dilward, known as the 'Tom Thumb of Africa'. Pickering describes Dilward as working 'as a fiddler, singer and dancer'. The local press advertised that the company contained sixteen 'Real Negroes from the Plantations of America', making twenty-six black performers in all; the African Americans had arrived in Wales only four years after the end of the American Civil War. Hutchinson and Tayleure's acts included the performers of 'Negro Life and Character' Chapman and Cushman, who were described as former members of the Original Christy's Minstrels Troupe. Chapman and Cushman were making their first appearance in Swansea, and the Cushman half of the duo was the African American singer Carlene Cushman, a member of the famous Black Swan Trio. Their programme contained sketches of 'Life in a Virginny Log House' interspersed with 'Mirth, Stirring Songs, Stories, Pump and Big Boot Dances, and Break-Down Hornpipes'. Very early forms of jazz music can now be sniffed in the air. South Wales was not short of variety in the choice of cultural nights out, as Charles Dickens was the next booked artist after Hutchinson and Tayleure's departure to continue their tour. Dickens was to give a Farewell Reading; unfortunately, there was no review of this performance.[26]

African American women, such as Carlene Cushman, were making careers on the stage on equal terms to men. However, compromises were being made, in that music from an African American heritage was adulterated and made accessible for white audiences. Women would make further concessions in how their gender was perceived, not only among their fellow performers, but from the audience viewpoint. But Cushman and others like her were earning independent livings and felt they had the right to do so. It had only been eighteen years since Sojourner Truth rose and spoke at the 1851 Women's Convention in Akron, Ohio. Her famous 'Ain't I a Woman' speech electrified the audience. Although some white women urged her to keep quiet, as she might divert attention away from the cause of emancipation, Truth said:

> Look at me! Look at my arm! I have ploughed and planted, and gathered into barns, and no man could head me! And ain't I a woman? I could work as much and eat as much as a man – when I could get it – and bear the lash as well! And ain't I a woman? I have borne thirteen children,

and seen them most all sold off to slavery, and when I cried out with my mother's grief, none but Jesus heard me! And ain't I a woman?[27]

The right not to remain silent or unseen was a powerful incentive for some African American women to carve out a career on the stage, even if they were challenging their own cultural heritage to do so. They also had to stand up to male performers for their right to a career. These pioneering black women were, in their way, advocating 'social equality for women . . . and to emerge triumphant', as bell hooks puts it.[28]

In 1869 the Music Hall also squeezed in, 'for one night only', 'The Carpet Bag Character Entertainment', pronounced as 'the most humorous and astonishing performances in the world'. There was no description of what this performance might entail, but the troupe were booked through to Brecon, Merthyr, Llanelly (sic), Tenby, Pembroke, Carmarthen and Llandeilo, so they must have been professional, at least. This performance was immediately followed by a large ensemble from Japan, the Royal Tycoons, males and females, showing off their skills in 'Topspinning, Balancing, Bamboo Butterfly Fanning, Archery, Shooting Lighted Matches from off the Top of a Man's Head, followed by the Ladies Brick Balancing and Egg Spinning . . . the performers turning somersaults on the points of sharp swords with frightful rapidity'. The programme didn't end there; it continued with an illustrated performance (lantern slides) of 'Twenty Minutes in Japan', with the troupe showing their fashions and customs, for example, 'Nepon Pom or Japanese Streamer', concluding with the 'Temple of Mikado'. It is a recognition of the popularity of the minstrelsy genre that minstrelsy continued to survive, considering such death-defying feats as those exhibited by the Japanese Tycoons were also on offer.[29]

Irish minstrelsy troupes also toured south Wales. The Irish Minstrels and Dramatic Company included two 'coloured comedians and dancers' (not named) performing 'Opera, Comedy, Farce, Songs Sentimental and Comic, Dance, Jigs, Hornpipes, and amusing Character Sketches'. Another innovative take on minstrelsy in order to stand out from the crowd was given by the Livermore Brothers troupe, described as 'the

Only Original World Renowned Court Minstrels, Titled Registered!' Advertised as 'Direct from the Crystal Palace', they were attired in the 'Unique and Picturesque Costumes of the time of George II', a 'Refined Entertainment of Negro Minstrelsy and Comicalities' with eleven performers. Advertising an extensive repertoire of 'Ballads, Quartets, Screaming Comic Burlesques and Extravaganzas, Grotesque and other Dances, all entirely original', the Livermore Brothers stressed that all the music and dancing steps had been expressly written and arranged for the company and not performed by any other troupe. Mr Leach of Cardiff had booked them at 'enormous expense' and now recommended them to Swansea's Music Hall. For some, this profusion of entertainments must have signalled the end of the traditional and revered Welsh cultural life. An incensed R. Sutherland wrote to *The Cambrian* complaining about the 'Dark Side of Swansea and its wickedness, debauchery and depraved habits of the lower orders'. However, life for the lower orders carried on as normal. For refinement, R. Sutherland might have gone to see the 'Celebrated Spanish Minstrels in their Picturesque Native Costume', as they had already appeared before the King and Queen of Portugal in Madrid, and the Empress Eugenie and the Royal Family of England at Windsor Castle. Their performance contained 'Magnificent stage arrangements with the room deliciously perfumed by Rimmel's Reversible Fountain'.[30]

The competition between troupes and companies to grab a good audience for the survival of their particular brand of minstrelsy necessitated innovative groups offering something a little different. Scotland's Birrell's New Diorama and the Royal Caledonian Minstrels had lantern slides and a lecture by Louis Richard, 'the popular Elocutionist'. The programme contained songs, droll stories, duologues, pibrochs (bagpipe music), dancers and broadsword combats.[31]

A really innovative move on behalf of women trying to edge their way on to the male-dominated minstrelsy circuit was the Blondinette Melodists. These were 'twelve ladies in number from Crystal Palace and St. George's Hall, London', described as a 'Refined, Attractive and Original Vocal and Instrumental Entertainment of Instrumentalists,

Vocalists and Dancers', performing original songs, duets and choruses plus instrumental solos, with 'superb dresses and appointments'. The Blondinette Melodists were a throwback to the minstrel genre prior to 'Negro' minstrelsy. Sadly, there was no review. However, there exists a charming illustration of them, dated 1873, advertising a performance at St George's Hall, Langham Place, London. The company comprised a pianist, a harmonium player, a drummer, five percussionists, a guitarist, harpist and fiddle player. An extra performer had been added by the time they visited Swansea. From their appearance, they were very much a white middle-class act, with absolutely no aspirations to being perceived as 'Negro delineators'.[32]

Venues also had to keep up appearances and regularly updated their premises to attract new audiences. An example is the Swansea YMCA, who planned in 1874 to upgrade their rooms and provide chess tables and a piano. Another was the work advertised for the attention of 'Music Hall Proprietors' being undertaken at the Gloucester Arms Free and Concert Hall Hotel in the Strand, Swansea. Fitting out was to include a new bar, new concert hall with stage, footlights and dressing room, with seating for 500 and 1,500 standing. Average weekly takings were 'approximately £50 per week'. Mr Barlow, the previous manager, was leaving to 'expand his time in the Dynamite Trade'. For those of a nervous disposition, there was also on offer an alternative to Swansea's more raucous cultural activities, the more sedate Temperance Hotel, which, also being refurbished for entertainments, advertised a large commercial room, coffee rooms, back parlour, kitchens, pantries, twelve bedrooms and attics, with feather beds and brass bedsteads.[33]

During 1874 there was catastrophe and unrest in America. In the south Wales local press, a long report on the Mississippi floods described Louisiana and Arkansas under water. The report went to great lengths to list the tonnage of rice, cotton, sugar and molasses lost, but gave no mention of the number of African American lives lost through working in the fields. Fresh conflict had also broken out in the southern states between 'negroes and their former taskmasters at Coushatta in Louisiana when six black leaders were captured and lynched'. This atrocity was known as the Coushatta Massacre, initiated by white supremacists. While enjoying minstrelsy and African American performance on stage, the people of south Wales were also reminded of the horrors being enacted overseas.[34]

Then another shocking report in the local press. The headline 'Capture of a Slaver' told of Captain Arthur Brooks, RN, Commander of HMS *Vulture*, who took control of a full-rigged slaver. On deck were eighty slaves, most of them children. Captain Brooks describes the slave deck below:

> measuring 102 feet by 4 foot high out of which we took one hundred and fifty human beings, helpless, naked, filthy and emaciated. Our men and officers worked with a will and fed them soup and boiled rice . . . I do not think I ever realised the horrors of the slave trade until this capture was made. Every morning we have to wash them. We went into Maygunga and bought up all the cotton stuff we could get but with this and the slaver's sails, we have made them decent. We took as prisoners thirty-seven Arabs armed. Seven slaves were already dead. We intend to land the slaves at the Seychelles and take the Arabs before the Admiralty Court. Such state on the dhow we had to set her afire. A woman slave states
>
>> I belong to Mochour tribe, live at Bessane, people come from other country with cloth, beads and guns, buy a lot to sell to Arab men, walk for four months to get to Kamilane, sell to Arab man, but he put me in dhow. Very glad to see white man. When die, body thrown in bush and that is all.[35]

African Americans performing in Wales, and perhaps reading these reports in local papers, must have been given much cause for reflection.

The local press also found space at this time to champion women's suffrage, saying 'men shrink from the idea of a woman having any career but a domestic one, but women need to find some means to earn their daily bread'.[36] Certainly, on the stage there were increasing adverts and reviews of female minstrelsy groups plying their trade. An example was Twelve Virginia Female Christys, described as 'unrivalled artistes [who] provided great Amazonian scenes of laughable combinations of oddities including burlesque, operetta, comedy and farce'.[37] Employment for women in Wales was causing increasing discussion. A report stated that Her Majesty's civil servants were jealous of 'the softer sex'. It had been found that women could do most of the work done by male clerks just as well, but the demand for female labour was presently far short of the supply – women were a good deal cheaper to employ. Males therefore regarded women as a threat and a reduction in their wage packets. For the New Year of 1878 the local press aimed an article at 'The Ladies Bless Them' listing various hints that would enhance a woman's lifestyle choices. The first on a long list was 'Never rise until you hear the breakfast bell'; advice not applicable to working-class Welsh women, as they were the ones up at dawn and ringing the bells.[38]

Occasionally a minstrelsy performance was reviewed in detail, and we can enjoy this one. Advertised as the Great CCC Christy Minstrels, the company were 'coloured artists established in 1868 and who during their fourteen years peregrinations throughout the country have won golden opinions from the London and Provincial press'. In the company were six comedians, two 'Interlocutors', a full band, singers and chorus, and burlesque. The overture was 'Joy, Joy Freedom Today', then a song, 'Skating on the Rink', a ballad, 'My Heart Resides with Thee', a comic song, 'The Spelling Bee of the CCC', another ballad, 'My Heart is Far Away', a comic song, 'St. Patrick's Day Parade', a ballad and chorus, 'Close the Shutters Willie's Dead', and the finale to part one, 'Jumbo's College'. Part two opened with a comic quartet, 'Dooral Mac Dill Darrell', then 'The Grand Triple Machine', after that the 'Challenge Dance' and 'Burlesque Tragedy and Scena'. Then came the 'Great Burlesque Skaters with the Brothers Spence', followed by the 'most comic act of Jim Crow and his Brother Sambo's first appearance on the ice and learning to skate'. (This is a prime example of African Americans subverting their own culture.) Then came an 'Old English Madrigal or Glee with the Matthews' Incomparable Choir'. The very successful evening was concluded with the 'Daddy Long Legs' by the entire company. Seats could be reserved at 3s., 2s. and 1s., the rear was 6d, children under twelve were half price. This was a true minstrelsy 'melange' of something for everybody, with the CCC Christy Minstrels enjoying good money on their tours.[39]

In 1877 the Swansea press, anxious to encourage an all-encompassing cultural enlightenment and educational enhancement for its people, urged potential customers to hasten to the Music Hall for 'The Death of Nelson' with piano and violin accompaniment, plus a programme of solos, recitations, glees, trios, duets and eight songs, conducted by Mr Silas Evans. The press stated:

> The object of these entertainments is to provide the people of Swansea with a high-class evening's amusement. If duly patronised, as they should be, they will be the means of counteracting the alluring influences of questionable and hurtful places of resort; they will prove an agreeable change from the monotony of home life; their cheapness will enable all classes to avail themselves, and will be a means of cultivating the musical ability of the town. With a view to the furtherance of these desirable objects, several ladies and gentlemen of position have consented to take part in the entertainments.[40]

Perhaps the local press were worrying about the lower orders devouring too much minstrelsy entertainment perceived as being of little educational value.

By 1878 the number of female minstrelsy groups on tour were increasing; for example, the Butterworth Female Christy Minstrel Troupe, comprising fifteen artistes, had a week's residency at the Theatre Royal. There was no review but they had to compete with *King Lear* at the Star Theatre in Wind Street, Swansea. The Boucicault *Octoroon Comic Ballet and Cure for Fidgets* was also advertised at the Star for the following week, this being a reworking of a popular play by Dion Boucicault that opened in New York in 1859, was kept on tour by various companies and said to be second in popularity only to *Uncle Tom's Cabin*. (The word octoroon means someone who is one-eighth black.) Whether this *Comic*

Ballet version retained any of the original settings of plantation life in Louisiana is not clear, as the original play contained a theatrical depiction of a slave auction. Having to compete with these offerings must have been difficult for traditional performers. Madame Edith Wynne, vocalist, had to suffer stiff competition from minstrelsy and variety. Her concert was billed as her 'Musical Treat for Wales and Things Welsh', performing a new work called 'The Bride of Neath Valley', by John Thomas (no review). Edith Wynne was regarded as one of the best vocalists in the country, touring in 1862 with Madam Patti, and also undertaking a tour of America in 1871.[41]

The Female Christy Minstrels paid a return visit under the proprietorship of Mr Andy Merrilees. The 'Armour Clad Amazons' were described as a 'talented company'. The crowds gave rapturous applause to Miss Bella Collins's ballads, including her version of 'Kiss Kiss'. Their 'Comicalities of Uproar in the Kitchen' and 'Spelling Bee Preparations' provoked roars of laughter, and the other acts of Little Jesse and Patcahoula and the Happy Ashantees with their songs and dances 'were most warmly welcomed and applauded, proving that anything the men could do, so could the women!' The company would have performed in blackface for the Happy Ashantees item.[42]

Local amateur groups continued to draw inspiration from the professional touring companies, copying and adapting to meet their own ends. We are fortunate that *The Cambrian* felt it worthwhile to cover the performance of the Mumbles Amateur Christy Minstrels, who jumped on the bandwagon and earned rave reviews for their performance of 'Carry Me Back to Old Virginny' at the Mumbles Assembly Rooms, in aid of Swansea Hospital. It was an eclectic show, with songs that included 'Empty Cradle', sung by Roger Jones; Reg Gold sang 'When You Are Seventeen, Maggie', and Fred Jones performed the comic song 'The Laughing Nigger' 'with gesticulations and cachinations in keeping with the song'. The review continued that the chorus sang 'Mother, Bear Me To The Window' and Mr D. Evans sang his own composition entitled 'Little Footsteps'. The second half opened with Mr Wall playing Welsh airs on the violin with 'variations', followed by more comic songs by Mr Crapper. Playing the banjo was Mr D. Evans, whose solos invited encores and who was described as 'a good tête à tête to Bones'. The evening concluded with a Stump Oration by Mr Crapper and the obligatory Skedaddle, complete with big drum accompaniment. It was stated that the troupe would be able to hand over a 'neat little sum' to Swansea Hospital.[43]

However distasteful we consider songs such as 'The Laughing Nigger' from a contemporary viewpoint, it is important that we include them in our history as part of the learning process of understanding the readings of popular culture in Wales at the time. Williams debates these readings and discusses the 'shifting responses of Frederick Douglass', the African American abolitionist, who toured the UK and witnessed performances and audience attitudes to minstrelsy. Williams argued that Douglass felt that the popularity of minstrelsy in the UK contributed to his successful anti-slavery speeches, quoting Douglass saying with irony: 'It is quite an advantage to be a nigger here. I find I am hardly black enough for British taste, but by keeping my hair as woolly as possible I make out to pass for at least half Negro at any rate.' Williams concludes his chapter by saying that minstrelsy 'brought African Americans to Wales during a crucial period in the nation's modern history, and laid the basis for future instances of transatlantic exchange'. These exchanges encompassed not only performers, but abolitionists, historians and writers.[44]

Among troupes making frequent appearances in south Wales on the touring circuit were the famous Sam Hague's Minstrels. Hague himself was an English clog dancer who had become a 'minstrel business manager' while in the US. Pickering describes Hague's troupe as comprising twenty-six ex-slaves enacting a portrait of life on the old plantation: 'the troupe had been freed from plantation existence only a few months before their first performance in England at the Theatre Royal in Liverpool in 1866'. Their stage costumes consisted of garments identical to those worn in their slavery days. The Welsh were to find Sam Hague's homespun attempts at entertainment not up to the local standard. Moreover, some of Hague's Minstrels found what was expected of them hard to reconcile with their new-found freedom, and Hague was forced to send home to the States those performers who wanted to return. He then employed white professionals, who donned blackface to perform with those African Americans who had opted to stay on in Britain.[45] Reynolds recalls he found the troupe a 'crude representation of real negro life', in contrast to the professional touring groups. Pickering describes Reynolds as 'disapproving' of the members of Hague's troupe who opted to stay on, as Reynolds thought 'they lived a fast and dissipated life'. This must have been owing to the culture shock of a swift exit from plantation life to the boards of venues in England and Wales.[46]

Sam Hague's troupe toured the US very successfully in the early 1880s and returned to Swansea in 1883 with their Magestic (sic) Double Company of Anglo-American Artistes at the New Theatre and Star Opera House, Wind Street. Their new show was fast, furious and, with good publicity prior to engagements, was now much more professional, slick, witty and satirical. The programme was packed with songs, clog dances, comic scenes and 'Major Burk's American Military sensation'. They sometimes even satirised and burlesqued the concert hall performances of the Fisk Jubilee Singers (see chapter 3), but not on this occasion. The entertainment profession was obviously a cut-throat business.[47]

With the profusion of 'real Negro' troupes on tour, again we can follow the fortunes of the enterprising Mumbles Amateur Christy Minstrels for their take on this intercultural interchange. Their second performance was at the Public Hall before a packed audience of 'dignitaries and chief residents of the town'. This time, the reviewer for *The Cambrian* took copious notes:

> the troupe hide their faces behind burnt cork. The Musical Director Mr E. B. Wall had not darkened his visage at this time, and presided at the piano, and the appearance of the 'niggers' was the signal for such hearty applause. Mr Graham Gold sang 'Carry Me Back To Old Virginny' in good style. Brannighan's Band, a noisy chorus with a liberal allowance

of big drum accompaniment, concluded the first part . . . Mr D. W. Evans's banjo song was also well received . . . Novello's rendition of 'The Queen' concluded the programme in good time.

We are now able to hear those voices and echoes of our past and, as Pickering says, look at the 'process of assimilation, adaption, collision, synthesis and re-assimilation [which] has operated continuously across the boundaries between black and white musical traditions and genres'.[48]

The Welsh press were continually evaluating the extent and popularity of popular music on the country's youth, anxious that there would be long-term effects on behavioural patterns, leading to moral lapses. In 1883 there was plenty of cheap, accessible and popular provision of entertainment already on offer. The press worried that there was a tendency for youth to 'stand or stroll listlessly about without having anywhere to go, or any genial occupation (within their reach) to afford them the recreation they desire and which is absolutely necessary'. The halls and assembly rooms did in fact offer plenty of cheap and varied entertainment, but nevertheless the 'local worthies' were concerned enough to have formed themselves into a committee to carry out a plan of action working with local talent, the proceeds to go towards augmenting the fund for the erection of the new Free Library buildings. Meetings were held 'with the mayor presiding', and a sub-committee appointed to carry out preliminary arrangements. The first of these entertainments would be given in 1884 in the form of a 'Vocal and Instrumental Concert'. As there was already a profusion of the same, it is not clear how this new arrangement by 'local worthies' was going to make a difference in encouraging youth from street corners. Outcome unknown.[49]

Times were changing, however, and Negro minstrelsy was itself experiencing stiff competition from the famous Bohee Brothers from the States, whose act was evolving from minstrelsy into slick revue and ragtime formulas. James and George Bohee made regular visits to Swansea from 1888 to 1897. Their 'initial bow' in Swansea was in

November 1888 at the New Theatre, Wind Street, with a full house despite stormy weather. The company performed popular ballads and comic songs, clog dances and soft-shoe shuffles, with the Bohees 'exhibiting considerable talent on banjo'. The Bohee Brothers ran a banjo studio in London called the Great American Banjo Academy, with lessons on the five-string 'Banjo given to Ladies and Gentlemen'. They were significant, in that they especially promoted the African American performers Josie Rivers, Amy Height and Carlene Cushman (the Black Swan Trio). This trio delighted Swansea audiences by satirising Tyrolean yodelling, which so amused the house it had to be repeated. Perhaps they yodelled in whiteface, subverting their own genre? Webster Sykes danced 'Plantation pastimes turning somersaults to time'. Carlene Cushman sang 'Beloved Star', and Amy Height performed a 'characteristic negro comicality with a working figure of a baby'. Josie Rivers sang 'They Can't Do It You Know'; as this song is untraceable, we are left wondering. The reviewer pointed out that those American lyrics needed revision for Wales, as 'we happen to know where women vote and also where Irishmen wear red coats'. Then the Bohee Brothers came forward 'and treated the immense audience to an exhibition of their skill on the banjo, which pleased all'. The medley included 'The Boulanger March', 'Popular Airs' and 'A Boy's Best Friend is His Mother' by James Bohee, and George Bohee played 'Home Sweet Home' with variations. The programme followed with the brothers dancing while playing the banjos, concluding with the National Anthem. Charles Reid conducted the house orchestra.[50]

The Bohee Brothers enjoyed a benefit night at the end of their week's residency. They told their audience that although reputed to be Americans they were, in fact, British subjects, having been born at St John's, New Brunswick, a fact of which 'they were both very proud'. They felt deeply the honour which had been paid them by the people of Swansea in patronising their entertainment, 'all the more agreeable when considering the excellent entertainment of a similar nature given in another place in town by the Celebrated Moore and Burgess Minstrels', sentiments which were loudly cheered. The press gave special mention to the Bohee Brothers' eighth and final performance of the week, when James Bohee was presented by the theatre manager with a gold pencil-case for his forty-fourth birthday.[51]

In 1889 the Royal Bohee Brothers returned with a new name and new show, this time comprising thirty 'coloured' principal artists working alongside the Swansea United Band, for a week's residency at the Albert Hall. Artists included Carlene Cushman ('America's Black Swan'), Rosie Rivers, Marie Roche, Fred Walton and Ike Jones. The performance portrayed 'coloured life in the religious aspect of the Old Southern States', with each evening offering a different aspect. Again, performance would entail subverting the genre with 'crank and jest and screamingly farcical episodes in the life of the Old Coloured Folks at Home', but also included classical instrumentals and vocal music. Their virtuoso banjo and dance performances straddled minstrelsy and ragtime, with ragtime (raggedy time) soon to become the basis for 'hot' and jazz music, which would evolve during the First World War.[52]

Eight years later, in 1897, Miss Amy Height, previously a star within the Bohee Brothers Company, was now touring as the star in her own show. The Swansea Empire featured her as 'The Dandy Coloured Cooness' and songs included 'Climb the Golden Gates' and 'Darling Little Dinah'.[53] Shortly after Miss Height's appearance, the Bohee Brothers made their last visit to Swansea, also at the Empire. The programme was very much slanted toward the recent North West Frontier campaigns; Britain had lost control of the Khyber Pass with great loss of life, enabling 'local tribesmen' to move from Afghanistan down to the 'fertile valleys'. The Bohee Brothers' programme paid their respects to the fallen with marching songs, accompanied on banjo: 'Soldiers of the Queen', 'Washington Post March', 'A British Toast' and 'Home Sweet Home'. One of the most popular numbers in their barrel-organ repertoire was 'I'll Meet Her When the Sun Goes Down'. Sadly, James Bohee died at the County Hotel, Ebbw Vale, while on tour.[54]

Pontardawe had its own irrepressible minstrel troupe, giving 'negro minstrel entertainment' a new 'Romanesque' outlook in December 1889. Dr F. Jones's String Band added a 'polishing touch' to the following proceedings: 'The Rocky Mountain Lion' sung by the whole troupe, jokes by the 'Safe Men', a song, 'The Hen Convocation', sung by Mr J. Gray, finishing with a

'Spurring' between the Bones and Tambo, with a 'Conclusion Crow' . . . the bones and tambourines were splendidly played by Messrs. Jones, P. Hopkin, T. Gray and Joe. Gray while the dignified Mr Johnson (Mr. Diss) in the middle, did his best to answer the crackers put to him.

The second half included 'Professor Eddishion (alias Mr T. Gray)' doing the 'imitation of the cornet . . . and a unique fight between the Professor and his instrument brought the house down'. Then followed a long item called the 'Rum'uns from Rome, or Ajax and Hercules', with Roman statues by Julius and Joe, and various comicalities; Romans in blackface was unique to Pontardawe.[55]

The 1890 Morfa Colliery disaster in Taibach, Port Talbot, which killed eighty-seven of the two hundred and fifty miners underground, prompted a flurry of fund-raising concerts by local artists. One such included Mr Tomlinson's Juvenile String and Wind Band, comprising forty youngsters aged 8 to 18. Minstrelsy troupes also performed fund-raisers for the victims' families. During the concert by 'the very amusing Negro entertainers Scully & Morrell', local performers were thanked for their voluntary contributions. There had been three previous major disasters at Morfa since 1858. With life still a hardship for most Welsh people, and local minstrelsy troupes giving charitable performances such as those for the Morfa colliery disaster, Swansea Town Council took it into its head to buy a gift for Princess Mary and the Duke of York (later King George V) on the occasion of their wedding on 6 July1893. It was a £250 Broadwood grand piano. The Town Council pronounced haughtily that it was presented 'at the expense of public festivities . . . the population will not be less loyal on that account'.[56] We are. We want it back.

There is no doubt that south Wales audiences kept many white and black minstrel troupes in highly paid employment for a substantial period. In 1890, for example, Swansea formed its own Black Snowdrop Minstrels performing for Madame Adelina Patti at her Craig-y-Nos Castle. She had recently returned from touring in Russia. Confusingly, Craig-y-Nos formed its own Christy Minstrels, whose innovative publicity included that 'they performed Plantation Scenes accompanied by the Penwyllt Black Hussars for the Plantation Walkaround'.[57]

In 1894 the prestigious Swansea Empire hosted an evening with Miss May Clarke, 'The Alabama Coon'. She was described as an expressive contralto; her main feature was the Foster song 'Way Down Upon the Swanee Ribber', the proper title being 'Old Folks At Home' (written by Stephen Collins Foster in 1851 (see chapter 1) but credited to E. P. Christy, as Christy had paid for the privilege). Foster later came to regret his generosity, dying in penury. Other very popular songs by Foster were 'Oh Susanna', 'De Camptown Races', 'Nelly Bly', 'My Old Kentucky Home', 'Old Black Joe', and many more.[58]

In March 1895 an extraordinary performance at the Empire by Mlle Texerkansas prompted the *South Wales Daily Post* to undertake a backstage interview with the star. 'We have had imitation of plantation sand dances here before but never have we had such a faithful representation by such a charming exponent.' Advertised as a 'Singer, Jig Buck and Wing Dancer', Mlle Texerkansas told her story to the Post:

> I was born in the village of Arkansas in a house through which passes the boundary line of the two states of Texas and Kansas and hence the conglomeration. My dance is an exact imitation of those on the plantations in the Southern States, absolutely correct in movement. As I had become acknowledged the best dancer in that line in the States, I determined to come over here and show it to you in the old country. I began in the usual way as a child and continued practice has led up to the result you have seen. I came over last June and I shall stay at least another year as I am booked up so far. I appeared first at the London Empire and after that was with B. G. Knowles in 'A Trip to Chinatown'. I like England [Wales] and the English [Welsh] so much I shall have lots of good things to say about them when I get home. I appreciated

my reception very much and I think Swansea people will like my dancing.

This solo performer, an African American woman given star status by the local paper and the opportunity to talk about her history and culture, was indeed an innovation and rightly of benefit to the local audiences.[59] Towards the end of the century, with competition on the boards rife, ever more surreal additions were tagged on to the now fading minstrelsy genre. The touring Kentucky Am-Euro Original Coloured Operatic Minstrels featured boxing kangaroos in Swansea for their American Plantation Walkaround scene. Other performers were the Midget Minstrels from London; the Crown Minstrels, featuring 'Laughing Gas' for the 'Funny Little Nigger' number; Wil Canlish the 'Negro Comedian', who played the bagpipes; Sergeant Simms' Black Boys from the Bahamas, who did a 'Military Extract from the Bivouac'; Clayton, Jenkins and Jasper, who included the Darktown Circus in their act; the McNulty Sisters, who performed the 'Novel Plantation Cane Dance'; and the Marvellous Salambos, who truly brought modern innovations into their show with the 'Powerful Electric Arc Light by Current Through the Human Body'.[60]

Minstrelsy was gasping its last breath, now driven out by a new fashion in south Wales entertainment – the 'animated and moving picture shows' screened in theatre buildings by companies such as the Original Lumière Cinematographer, the Cinematographe, Animatographe, American Biograph, Polveini's Cinematographe, Klondike Pictures, Bio-Tableaux, Poole's Myrioramas (see below), Bioscope, Hyper-Myrioramas, and so on, into the new century with St Louis Pictures and Kineopticons. Wales had its own pioneers of film-making, Arthur Cheetham and William Haggar, who created popular melodramas from 1896 to 1910.[61] In 1890 the local press advertised, at Swansea's Drill Hall, 'Chas. W. Poole's Greatest Myriorama on Earth', with magnificent 'Tableaux of Darkest Africa and Full Horrors of the Slave Trade'. The evening was supported by a local band described as 'powerful and highly efficient'. Two weeks later Poole's Myriorama presented the same event at the New Theatre and Star Opera House.[62] These Myrioramas were touring presentations, which were illustrated 'Vocally, Musically and Pictorially – a moving Panorama of scenic surprises, picturesque trips abroad, all over the world, in sunshine, storm, peace and war'. This particular presentation, on the slave trade, gave a graphic account of 'that horrible traffic in human flesh'.[63]

With animated and moving pictures capturing theatre and music hall audiences, the working lives of women were about to change, too, with the invention of the Caligraph Writing Machine, called the 'Perfect Typewriter'. Women's complexions would also be taken care of with 'New Sunlight Soap for Women's Liberation'. Advertisements for bicycles were aimed at women with disposable incomes. Households could also install, for easy terms of 3 guineas (£3 3s.) per annum, a telephone from the National Telephone Co. Ltd, and the 'Gram-o-Phone that Talks, Sings and Plays' was available for home entertainment from Brader's Music Emporium. Minstrelsy was beginning to fade away.[64]

At the beginning of this chapter there is a photograph (possibly c.1900–10) of the Harry Collins Minstrels. All are white men in 'blackface' except for the man standing back row, first left. He is genuine, name unknown. Did he leave a memoir behind? What were his private thoughts on his colleagues' 'blacking up' to represent a parody of his cultural heritage?

Whether we disprove now of the Welsh penchant for blacking-up, and feel that African Americans demeaned themselves by joining minstrelsy troupes, or alternatively if we consider that they used the conventions of the genre to portray a more positive image of black people, there is no denying that Negro minstrelsy was a particular product of its time, born out of bigotry and then disappearing at the cusp of the new jazz age, with its extraordinary proliferation of black musical talent. During its fifty-year heyday, minstrelsy left its mark on the people of south Wales and it is an open and interesting question as to whether this is an example of exploitation of African American culture by white performers, or whether, as I suspect, something quite different was going on, in that the fifty years of minstrelsy performances in south Wales represented an early form of Pickering's 'socio-cultural interchange' between African Americans and the Welsh; or, as Williams puts it, 'that involvement also brought African Americans to Wales during a crucial period in the nation's modern history, and laid the basis for future instances of transatlantic exchange'.[65]

It is at this juncture that the course of popular music in south Wales was tilted on its axis by the arrival in Wales of the Fisk Jubilee Singers, freed slaves on a fundraising tour for their new campus buildings at Fisk University in Nashville. They sang 'weird slave songs', what we would now call gospel songs, music the next chapter will explore.

Chapter Three

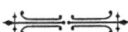

The Fisk Jubilee Singers in Wales, Freed Slaves and their Songs

FISK UNIVERSITY, NASHVILLE, Tennessee, set up in 1866, was one of the first educational establishments in the United States for the education of freed slaves and their children. The Fisk Jubilee Singers, on a fundraising tour around Britain for their university campus buildings, had a profound impact on the people of Wales. The Fisk Jubilee Singers were usually made up of five women to three men, or six women to four men, depending on the state of health of individuals and travel arrangements. The choir included Ella Shepherd, the harmonium and piano player and occasional guitarist. The account of their travels kept by J. B. T. Marsh and F. J. Loudin, of the 'little company of emancipated slaves', traces their journeys; a copy is held at Jazz Heritage Wales.[1]

The Fisk Jubilee Singers set out from the US in 1873 to raise money for the Jubilee Hall, their first campus building. With the intention of raising $20,000 for the Fisk University Building Fund, the Jubilee Singers raised $100,000 in three years of touring, and a further $50,000 with later tours. The College President stated in 1880 that students were dependent upon themselves financially and the university expenses had, thus far,

84 ❧ Freedom Music

Figure 6a: The Fisk Jubilee Singers, 1882 (Fisk University Special Collections Library, Nashville, TN)

Figure 6b: The Fisk Jubilee Singers, 1881–2 (Fisk University Special Collections Library, Nashville, TN)

been met by the American Missionary Association. Within a few years of its formation in 1871, twenty-four persons had been associated with the Fisk Jubilee Singers; twenty of the number had actually served as slaves, whilst three of the remaining four were of slave parentage. Ella Shepherd, described as 'a skilled young pianist' in Marsh's account, was also a singer. She had been separated from her mother as a baby, her mother having been 'sold down river'. Ella Shepherd was described as being 20 years old when they started touring, Maggie Tate as being 14, Jennie Jackson, 19, and Eliza Walker, also 14. The Fisk Jubilee Singers were led by F. J. Loudin, 'Basso, Manager and Director', described as having 'an exceptionally deep bass voice' and also as speaking out on civil rights.[2]

Just before leaving Nashville they sang at the National Teachers' Association of the USA Annual Convention, causing great disgust among some that 'the niggers could not be kept in their own places'. With 'barely enough money', the pioneering choir set out to cross the Ohio River (the river Jordan in their songs) to Cincinnati on the north, the freedom side. 'Full audiences met them in Cincinnati, with free concerts given.'[3] At the Rev. Moore's Congregational Church the Cincinnati press reported that it was

> probably the first concert ever given by a colored troupe in this temple, which has resounded with the notes of the best vocalists of the land. The sweetness of the voices, the accuracy of the executive, and the precision of the time, carried the mind back to the early concerts of the Hutchinsons, the Gibsons, and other famous families, who years ago delighted audiences and taught them with sentiment while they pleased them with melody. Jennie Jackson's rendering of the 'Old Folks at Home' as an encore, was received with rapturous applause. Over two seasons of fundraising, a tract of land of twenty-five acres, on a commanding site overlooking the city of Nashville, had been purchased for the permanent location of Fisk University . . . the students had worked with the laborers to level the earthworks, and the foundations had been laid for a noble building for university purposes, to be called

Jubilee Hall. A visit to England with a view to raising funds for its completion was under discussion.[4]

The Presbyterian minister of the Lafayette Avenue Church, Brooklyn, NY, and avid abolitionist, Dr Theo L. Cuyler, writing in the *New York Tribune* before they left for Britain, described the Fisk Jubilee Singers as

> these living representatives of the only true native school of American music. We have long enough had its coarse caricatures in corked faces; our people can now listen to the genuine soul-music of the slave cabins, before the Lord led his children 'out of the land of Egypt, out of the house of bondage!'[5]

The Singers had previously sung for Queen Victoria in April 1873 and had toured many worthy aristocratic and philanthropic venues. They were now about to step on to the stage of the Swansea Music Hall, Craddock Street, for the first time. We have a splendid, vituperative description of the Swansea of 1874 into which the Fisk Jubilee Singers arrived. The local paper had published with relish a letter in full from 'Anon.', who ranted about the town as follows:

> Besides no public monuments, the houses low, small irregularly built, and generally of a dirty and miserable aspect. No squares, no promenades no literary or scientific institutions, no social intercourse amongst its inhabitants but an infinite number of public taverns crammed with topers staggering under the influence of intoxications; brothels and dens of thieves; the streets dirty, narrow tortuous, unequal, here and there dangerously steep, generally unpaved and deprived of footpaths, continually obstructed, whether by carts, wheelbarrows, trucks, hackney-coaches, private carriages belonging to the nascent and proud nobility of this important borough, still in its infancy ... servants flirting about, wasting the time they owe to their mistresses; dogs, oxen, cows, sheep, pigs, horses and donkeys ... forming altogether a moving gigantic

confused mass of agglomerated beings and things of both sexes, of every species – or rapidly crossed by coal-merchants, society-makers, ship-owners, brokers, grocers, bakers, shop-keepers and valets, who, thinking only of themselves and their business, run like mad people, knocking down and trampling underfoot whoever offers any resistance to their unguarded long steps; the local authority not respected and powerless . . . here is Swansea: happy they who in its present state are not compelled to live in it!

The anonymous letter-writer does finally acknowledge the town's more positive points:

One must not believe that Swansea, with all these conflicting imperfections is beyond redemption, far from it. Situated on the border of a large bay, surrounded by the richest coal mines in the world; having very important manufactories of steel, copper, tin, iron, silver etc., many foundries, an extensive maritime commerce of importations and exportations, a vast commercial intercourse with all the nations in the world, endowed with great riches and much industry; Swansea possesses all the elements that can be desired to make it happy and one of the most important and civilised counties in Wales. All depends on those who are at the head of its government – they may make of it a Sodom in its full, or a Rome in the height of its splendour – there the Tarpeian Rock, – here the Capitol.[6]

The disgruntled letter-writer signed off the tirade to the good burghers of the town as 'A Pessimist whilst in a fit of dejection'. The current good burghers of the town (now a city) might heed the advice.

For all its faults, Swansea was not 'beyond redemption', as the Fisk Jubilee Singers were to discover. The local paper carried two pieces on their visit. The first, an advertisement for their performance at Swansea's Music Hall (opened in 1864 and renamed the Albert Hall in 1881), for March 1874, described their programme as:

88 ❦ Freedom Music

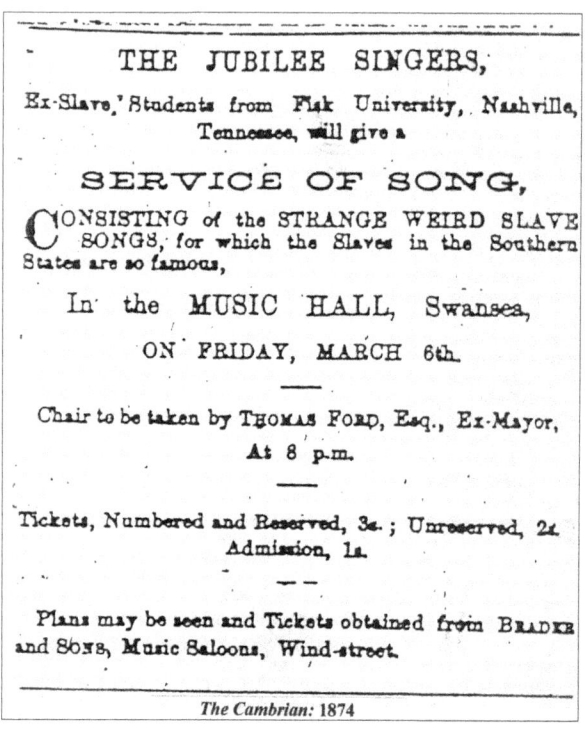

Figure 7: 'Weird Slave Songs', 1874 (SWW Media)

A Service of Song, Consisting of the Strange, Weird Slave Songs for which The Slaves in the Southern States are so famous. Chair to be taken by the ex-mayor of Swansea Thomas Ford Esq. Tickets from Brader's Music Saloons Wind St. tickets 1s. reserved 3s. unreserved 2s.

The second piece, a news item, gave more details about the students from Fisk University:

> It will be gratifying to most persons to find that Swansea is to be visited by the band of ex-slave students from Fisk University, Nashville, USA. After so successful a tour through the States and through the principal parts of England, they will be hailed with satisfaction in Wales as the exponents of true Nigger minstrelsy, and as the praiseworthy labourers

in the good work of raising the money necessary to perpetuate the Fisk University. The merits of the students are so well known by the almost invariably favourable critiques that have appeared in the English Press, that it needs but a reminder of the advent of the company to draw large and appreciative audiences.[7]

The Cambrian, although aware of the innovative style of the Fisk Jubilee Singers, was confused as to what the choir represented, assuming they would be similar to the popular 'Nigger minstrelsy' troupes. Pickering discusses 'tastes and conventions' and perceptions of the Fisk Jubilee Singers; he cites the Birmingham press displaying 'racial arrogance' in their coverage of the tour.[8]

The Jubilee Singers caused a sensation, in that cultural expectations in Wales were overturned by the sight of something quite different: a choir and musician performing with concert-hall authority and great dignity, even though their Negro spirituals were perhaps a whitewashed, anglicised version of their African inheritance. Theo. F. Seward, writing a 'Preface to the Music', in their volumes of gospel songs for sale to their audiences, notes:

> Its unique origin, and that the melodies are never composed, but spring into life. Another noticeable feature of the songs is the rare occurrence of triple time, or three-part measure among them. The reason for this is doubtless to be found in the beating of the foot and the swaying of the body which are such frequent accompaniments of the singing . . . its irregularities invariably conform to the higher law of the perfect rhythmic flow.[9]

The recognition above that melodies were 'never composed', or were improvisational, is now recognised as primitivism in black folk culture: 'The term primitive was often used to describe the people, cultures, and objets d'art of African origin or descent . . . but it is also intended to acknowledge the fact that marginalized and despised black cultures were pivotal in the creation of transatlantic modernism.'[10]

Or, in other words, an awareness of their new black cultural heritage and identity as a force for change. It was not such a revelation to the Welsh that slave songs could be rendered in such a manner that invoked spontaneous body movement and foot-tapping from the music washing over audiences from the stage. The Welsh were familiar with the *hwyl*[11] of the Welsh Baptist tradition, the half-singing, half-shouting in Welsh from the minister up in the pulpit while he worked himself into a sweat, thumping his Bible and encouraging his congregation to respond to the sermon with 'Amens' and 'Praise the Lords'. Wales, too, had its Amen Corner just like the Southern Baptist churches. The nearest the Welsh had previously got to swaying and foot-tapping was when interpreting the *Sankey Hymn Book*, hymns which did at least contain good solid tunes, some of which were quite rumbustious and popular on Victorian parlour pianos. Sankey was known as the Sweet Singer of Methodism, an American singer, organist and composer, associated with the evangelist Dwight L. Moody since 1870. Sankey and Moody events are still regularly held in Wales, such as the annual 'All Day Sacred Singing and Sankey Evening' at Gwehelog Chapel, Monmouthshire. Another example, featuring the Llandrindod Wells Silver Band, for 11 March 2006 is listed in the *Magazine for the Irfon and Wye Valley Churches*, issue 81 (March 2006). A copy of *Sacred Songs and Solos and New Hymns* resides in the Jazz Heritage Wales library.[12]

The Fisk Jubilee Singers had met Messrs Moody and Sankey on various occasions, the first time being at Newcastle on Tyne:

> lending daily assistance . . . and there went up in sweet, low notes a chorus as of angels. None could tell us where the Singers were – on the floor, in the gallery, or in the air. The crowd was close, and the Singers – wherever they were – were sitting. Everyone was thrilled, for this was the song they sang:
>
> > There are angels hovering around
> > To carry the tidings home.

... On one Sunday evening Mr. Moody preached, and they sang to an audience of between six and seven thousand working people[.][13]

The ability of the Fisk Jubilee Singers' music to appeal to both working and upper classes can be established from Loudin's evaluation of their work in his *Supplement* to the *Story of the Jubilee Singers*. Loudin explains that although doors were opened for the Fisk Jubilee Singers into royal homes and concert halls, thousands of 'excursionists from all parts of the kingdom' thronged to Crystal Palace to witness a choir of 5,000 children from churches and chapels, with a finale by the Jubilee Singers. Jenkins points out that Welsh chapels in particular had a healthy tradition of weekly collections for events such as these to enable excursions to be undertaken, as well as collections aimed at sustaining large overseas ventures.[14]

Their music, according to Marsh, remained a puzzle to the public, who could not understand 'the reason for enjoying so thoroughly these simple, unpretending songs'. It would not have been such a big puzzle to the Welsh. Marsh quotes from a critique by Colin Brown, Ewing Lecturer on Music in the Andersonian University, Glasgow, in a series of articles, in which he said:

> The highest triumph of art is to be natural. The singing of these strangers is so natural that it does not at once strike us how much of true art is in it, and how careful and discriminating has been the training bestowed upon them by their accomplished instructor and leader . . . the exquisite refinement of the piano as contrasted with the power of the forte, fill us with delight, and at the same time make us feel how strange it is that these unpretending singers should come over here to teach us what is the true refinement of music, make us feel its moral and religious power.[15]

Certainly, when playing the music from the *Fisk Jubilee Songbook*, one cannot but be moved by no. 23, 'Many Thousand Gone' with the line 'No more auction block for me', which can be contrasted with the rousing tub-thumper no. 73, 'I've Been Redeemed'. The Fisk Jubilee Singers were skilful in being able to convey a state of mind with an espousal of musical tradition. The Welsh, in particular, would have been equally skilful in identifying this state of mind as *hwyl*. The women of the Fisk Jubilee Singers, particularly Ella Shepherd, portrayed powerful and complex images.

By transcending cultural and economic boundaries, the Fisk Jubilee Singers brought their musical inheritance to a populace ready to embrace the Jubilee Singers' sincerity. The proud portrayal of their historical culture, via their slave songs and spirituals, was met not just with passive consumption, but by working-class men and women being exposed to cultural influences from which they, in turn, began to practise the songs within their own homes, churches, chapels and communities. Audiences bought the *Fisk Jubilee Songbook* in their thousands; evidence is Marsh's instances of large sales of the *Songbook* to the working classes. He gives as an example the receipts for tickets to a concert at Glasgow's Crystal Palace and profits on the sale of songbooks amounting to nearly £325. In addition, there are many instances in Marsh's diary accounts of 'hundreds' and 'thousands' of people attending free concerts in public arenas. Church helpers or volunteers collected donations in buckets. Marsh cites a Sunday summer evening in Hull when the Fisk Jubilee Singers spontaneously took to the King William monument as a platform and sang to a crowd that filled the street. In Scarborough a free concert yielded a collection of £90. At Manchester, they enlisted the services of Richard Johnson, the apostle of Ragged Schools. With good advertising, the proceeds of four concerts in the Free Trade Hall amounted to over £1,200, further swollen by the sales of the *Fisk Jubilee Songbook*, which also contained the history of their first American campaign. Marsh continues that the Fisk Jubilee Singers targeted areas of special need, for example a garden party was held 'for the poor and the lame' from crowded London tenements. Women with babes in arms were particularly welcomed to their free concerts, and no one was compelled to donate. Total receipts for the month of January 1874 amounted to £3,800, or about $19,000. Marsh cites a tour of Scotland where a crowd of 2,000 people flocked over two nights to Greenock Town Hall.[16] Certainly, it might be construed that Welsh literacy levels may have been sufficiently adequate circa 1873–7 for congregations to read and sing from the *Fisk Jubilee Songbook*, as Philip Phillips's *The American Sacred Songster* (1868) was already widely used in south Wales chapel services and Sunday schools, copies still being available.[17] The Welsh public were also able to purchase copies of the *Fisk Jubilee Songbook* which the Singers had brought with them from the USA as early as 1873, with an average day's sales amounting to £40. These contained notations, enabling people to take the music back to their own church choirs and communities.[18]

The significance of the tours of the Fisk Jubilee Singers, and their effect on Welsh working-class women as positive role models, also had a profound effect on the preconceptions on white audiences of black women's cultural identity. Wales was now experiencing the phenomenon of black American ex-slave university students performing exuberant music. Higginbotham discusses a 'positive racial accord', which can contrast with stereotypical perceptions of black women.[19] She argues that the position of black women embodied the added perception of 'sexual deviance'. That positive racial accord is endemic in the Fisk Jubilee Singers, who helped overturn these misconceptions and inherent inferiority brought about through conditions of slavery in America.

The Fisk Jubilee Singers, therefore, were in the forefront of changing the cultural stereotyping previously witnessed by Welsh audiences. They provided positive role models not only through being accepted at Court, but also for their eagerness to perform, and later fundraise, for the poor of Wales and England. The Fisk Jubilee Singers provided an opportunity to emphasise achievement for African American and African Caribbean women. Women were not discouraged from singing along at the Jubilee concerts, where songbooks could be purchased for use at home. Loudin continued his evaluation by pointing out that four of the Fisk Jubilee Singers, including himself and two of the women, eventually settled in Britain to study, to teach other black men and women, and to begin their own process of bridging cultural and racial divides. Oliver argues that the working classes were learning to live together in racial harmony, not only through work, but also through cultural exchange of music and related performance.[20]

Pickering confirms that the new music of the twentieth century attracted a great number of black male and female performers from the American stage shows, some settling in London and major cities in Britain at this time. He gives as examples Callender's All-Coloured Minstrels, including the Bohee Brothers, who stayed on in Britain, running banjo studios, touring regularly and providing free street entertainment, as did the Black Swan Trio featuring Carlene Cushman (mentioned in chapter 2). The musicians and singers enjoyed the freedom from racial harassment, and plentiful job opportunities, in the rapidly developing club culture of the towns and cities of Britain. Pickering also states that their teaching skills were an added form of employment.[21]

Green confirms that women such as Lilian Jemmott, the piano player from Cardiff, Ida Shepley, singer, and Amy Barbour-James all passed on their skills to young black British women eager to learn to play the piano. Amy Barbour-James, who died in 1988, left a legacy of published music of black composers. Amanda Ira Aldridge taught classical piano as well as giving concerts at Steinway Hall; the children of London's black community attended her home for piano lessons. Green cites Marie Lawrence, the soprano, who moved to Britain with the Native Choir of Jamaica in 1906, and went on to sing in London restaurants in the 1920s, making films in the 1930s.[22]

Abbott states that the Fisk Jubilee Singers' performances were an early expression of Black Pride:

> In the heightened religious atmosphere of the missionary freemen's schools, the idea was nurtured that the spiritual songs of slavery were 'genuine jewels that we brought from our bondage'. Jewels which harboured the potential to undo white prejudice and generate black pride.

Abbott states that their songs were 'an antidote to "negro minstrelsy" and an affirmation of racial merit. Each concert was, in effect, a civil rights demonstration.'[23]

With the Fisk Jubilee Singers performing their first concert in Swansea on Friday 6 March 1874, what was happening at the Music Hall just prior to their visit? A package from Scotland: Birrell's *New Diorama of Scotland* and the Royal Caledonian Minstrels. The Minstrels were performing 'selections of songs, droll stories, duologues, pibrochs [Highland pipes], dancers, broadsword combats, with descriptive lecture by Louis Richard Esq. the popular elocutionist'.[24] The Fisk Jubilee Singers also must have seen, or been aware of, troupes performing in blackface, such as Tute's Minstrels, a company of ten persons, who were appearing at the Music Hall, run by Mr James Tute, RAM, also in blackface. Swansea audiences were now in a position to compare and contrast the two genres. Sadly, there was no review of that first Jubilee Singers' concert.[25]

The following year, 1875, the Fisk Jubilee Singers returned to the Craddock Street Music Hall for another performance of their slave songs. The review read: 'The Fisk Jubilee Singers gave their services of songs to a large and attentive audience . . . the independence of the music of poverty . . . their programme is highly instructive and entertaining'.[26] Adjacent to the review was an article by Dr Rimbault discussing the harmonies of Welsh music, arguing that its

> particular character was derived from its geography (soft from Welsh valleys, wildness from the mountains), ancient melodies connected to religious purposes, elegies, and celebrations: the most agreeable coming nearest to nature and possessing a pleasing melancholy and soothing tranquillity, suitable to genial love. There are also dancing tunes and jigs which are extremely gay and inspiring. The national music of Wales differs from that of the Scotch and Irish in its being constructed upon the diatonic scale. Welsh tones, on this account, sound very modern to our ears . . . accompanied by its original harmony.[27]

The Craddock Street Music Hall catered for a variety of tastes; at the end of 1874 it was advertising the return visit of the Livermore Brothers' Court Minstrels, and, for those with more refined tastes, the annual Grand Concert of Edith Wynne and Mme Patti.[28]

While the Fisk Jubilee Singers were booked for that one night on Monday 2 August 1875 at the Music Hall, the rest of the bookings for the week were taken up by the Queen's Minstrels Troupe, formerly known as the Original Christys, white performers in blackface. *The Cambrian* described their programme as 'A Musical Melange, Grotesque and Eccentric Dances, The Coons of Minstrelsy by the Greatest Combination of Minstrel Talent in The UK, also touring Aberdare and Briton Ferry'.[29] The Fisk Jubilee Singers' personal thoughts on minstrelsy were not recorded.

It would appear, therefore, that south Wales audiences in the 1870s were being offered conflicting values of sociocultural African American identity, together with the confused notion of gender identity prevailing at the time. Confronted by the African American men and women in the Fisk Jubilee Singers, the audiences were offered a positive political voice, a perspective of which 'blackface nigger minstrel' groups were themselves not aware. Welsh women, perhaps, looked at the African American women in the choir with a larger perspective than they had ever done before, becoming aware through the songs and the introductions spoken by the performers, usually Frederick Loudin, of a little of their history and reasons for their rendering of slave songs. Music is politics. Early white radical feminists in their arguments and debates ignored class and racial difference and how black women perceived themselves; black women were usually perceived by whites as helpless victims. Black feminists, such as Ladner, argue that they resent the black/racial issue being seen by white middle-class radical feminists as an 'added-on' assemblage, because black feminists do not perceive themselves as marginalised or in a minority. Also, the term 'marginalised' is not a black feminist term, but one that is presented by white feminists within academic and theoretical debate. For example, Ladner views the black feminist perspective as positivism, and black women as being victims of the product of white American social policy, and not racial subordination.[30] Davis considers that black women had experienced oppression as social equals by whites, but that their punishment exceeded that meted out to black men, in that women were not only whipped and mutilated, but also raped. Davis calls rape a 'weapon of domination', but a weapon also used by their slave owners to 'demoralize their men'. Black feminists argue that this hidden racial subordination suffered by black women cannot be referred to as a 'commonality' experienced by all women.[31]

Higginbotham points out that some well-respected historians portrayed slave women not as victims, but as 'lazy, promiscuous and brutish figures'.[32] Nannie Helen Burroughs cites the racism of white women as a cause for the limited participation of black women in the organised suffragist movements.[33] Black feminists tell us to 'read our history'; in other words, if we do not know, go and find out. Oral history collections within libraries and archives are one way to find out. The Fisk Jubilee Singers would have been familiar with the following experiences. Sutcliffe writes:

> The stories in this volume are first-person accounts of slavery as recalled by former slaves living in Tennessee in the late 1920s and 1930s . . . the result of a project of the Social Sciences Department of Fisk University in 1929 and 1930 . . . the Fisk interviews were conducted by Ophelia Settle Egypt, a Howard University graduate who was working for Dr. Charles Johnson, a professor in Fisk's Social Science Department. Both were black, and it is possible that the former slaves felt comfortable relating their experiences to a black professional woman who encouraged them to speak about their experiences, good and bad.[34]

Name unknown:

> I am eighty-eight years old, born March 15 1843. I was sold four times in my life . . . and when I come to the age of twelve my own half-brother sold me. His father and my father and Abe Lincoln was first cousins.

My father was a Mudd, Abe Lincoln and him was brother and sister's children. It is very seldom you can get a colored person to tell you anything about slavery. The white folks ain't gonna tell you. Women wasn't anything but cattle . . . Dr. White organised the Fisk Jubilee Singers (during the) time I was at McKeeve's School . . . and I was in the first crowd. Dr. White took a good deal of pains with me 'cause I had such a good voice. The first five hundred dollars that was paid in the building of Jubilee Hall (on Fisk University Campus), we made it singing round town and places, and we paid it in that.[35]

Emma Grisham:

I was born in Nashville. I's up to ninety years, but I tell them I's still young. I lived on Gallatin Pike long 'fore the war and used to see the soldiers ride by . . . I educated my daughter at Fisk, and she's been teaching school since 1893.[36]

Cecilia Chappel:

I was born in Marshall County, Tennessee. I'm the oldest of two chillum, and I'm 102 years old . . . My mammy was brought to Nashville and sold to some people that took her to Mississippi to live . . . I don't know how to read or write.[37]

Hurmence researched some harrowing personal stories that would also have been familiar to the Fisk Jubilee Singers. Adeline Johnson, aged 93 in c.1930, told of her duties at the Jesse Gladden place: 'I wait on the missus and the chillun. I was whipped one time for marking the mantelpiece with a dead coal of fire. They make the Mammy do the lashing.' Rebecca Jane Grant, aged 92 when interviewed in c.1930, tells her story:

It was a raw cowhide strap about two feet long, and she (Missus) started to pouring it on me all the way upstairs. I didn't know what she was whipping me about. But I had not called the baby 'Marster Henry', Marster Henry was just a little boy . . . come halfway up to me. (Missus) wanted me to say 'Marster' to him – a baby!

Ben Horry was 87 in 1937; his worst memory was his mother being whipped by

> the colored overseer. He was the one straight from Africa. He the boss . . . and if womans don't do all he say, he lay task on 'em they ain't able to do. My mother won't do all he say. He have it in for my mother, my mother is take to the barn and strapped down on thing called The Pony. Hands spread like this and strapped to the floor and all two both she feet been tied like this. And she been give twenty-five to fifty lashes till the blood flow. And my father and me stand right there and look and ain't able to lift a hand! Blood on floor in that rice barn.[38]

Might it have been for his own survival in a white supremacist culture that the overseer from Africa could inflict such punishment? Owners also took slave women as second 'wives'; some did provide for their mixed-race children, although it was more usual that slave women were raped by their owners and left with the consequences.[39]

It could be argued that the Welsh were another society denied freedom of expression, regarded as second-class citizens by the English. This was brought home to the Welsh by the effects of the Reports into the State of Education in Wales in 1847, the notorious Blue Books, now residing at the National Library of Wales in Aberystwyth, commissioned by the Committee of Council on Education, Whitehall, 1 October 1846, 'to direct an inquiry to be made into "the means afforded to the labouring classes of acquiring a knowledge of the English language"'. Welsh women were singled out: the Report condemned their 'morals', accusing them of being corrupt and sinful, and their children were dismissed as having no virtue. Many Welsh women vanished from mining and agriculture, some having to leave Wales to work as servants in London. On the Welsh language, the Report stated:

> IX The Welsh Language is a vast drawback to Wales, and a manifold barrier to the moral progress and commercial prosperity of the people. It is not easy to overestimate its evil effects . . . As a proof of this, there is no Welsh literature worthy of the name[.][40]

Williams comments on the authors of the Report:

> The three Anglican, English monolingual young barristers who prepared the bulky Blue Books reinforced these views in their reports, and drew on appropriate evidence to buttress their prejudices. They quoted the barrister E. C. Hall, for instance, who argued not only that ignorance of English was 'a decided drawback in a Court of Justice', but also that there were fundamental defects in the Welsh language itself:
>
>> 'Their (the Welsh people's) mode of numeration produces great errors; they have almost to do an Addition sum in their heads before they can express some numbers. The Welsh language is peculiarly evasive, which originates from its having been the language of slavery.'[41]

Ieuan Gwynedd in 1850 added to the 'morals' furore in the periodical *Y Gymraes* (the Welshwoman), the first Welsh-language periodical for women. Ieuan Gwynedd stated that Welsh women should improve their standing by becoming 'faithful girls, virtuous women, thrifty wives and intelligent mothers, who would instil Christian morality and virtue into the men and boys of Wales'.[42] *Y Gymraes* used its pages as propaganda for instilling appropriate female behaviour, encouraging mothers to rear their children in the English language. Sian Rhiannon Williams comments in *Our Mothers' Land*:

> The magazine's attitude towards women's work was unsympathetic . . . Those women who worked in heavy industry were completely ignored by *Y Gymraes*, while the main occupation of Welsh women, domestic service, was romanticized and seen as the ideal opportunity for women to exhibit their natural feminine instincts of service and deference.[43]

To those Welsh women, then, in the Music Hall audiences listening to the music emanating from the Fisk Jubilee Singers, what they saw on stage was indeed Higginbotham's 'positive racial accord'. Audiences bought the *Fisk Jubilee Songbook* and took it home. They learnt, sang and played the songs, some of which had seemingly familiar themes, although they were in fact messages and signs from another emerging culture, asking to be set free:

No. 33 'Come Let Us All Go Down'
As I went down in the valley to pray,
Studying about that good old way;
You shall wear the starry crown,
Good Lord, show me the way.
By and by we'll all go down, all go down, all go down
By and by we'll all go down,
Down in the valley to pray.

No. 41 'He's the Lily of the Valley'
He's the lily of the valley, Oh! my Lord;
He's the lily of the valley, Oh! my Lord.
What kind of shoes are those you wear
That you can ride upon the air.
These shoes I wear are gospel shoes,
And you can wear them if you choose.
He's the lily of the valley, Oh! my Lord. (*etc.*)

Although the words were pleas from the slaves to be set free, they had connotations for three distinct groups of Welsh people: the valley Welsh could also sing about their communities being trapped in the business of hewing coal; the urban south Wales Welsh about the labour of shipping coal out of the docks; and Welsh women of the domestic drudgery entailed in both.

No. 65 'There's a Meeting Here Tonight'
Get you ready, there's a meeting here tonight
Come along, there's a meeting here tonight;
I know you by your daily walk, there's a meeting here tonight.
Camp-meeting down in the wilderness
There's a meeting here tonight
I know it's among the Methodists,
There's a meeting here tonight.

And what members of the audience could not but identify with the words and be roused to join in and sing on the way home? I am sure the women of Wales did sing on the way home, toiling back up to their valleys or climbing up to their Swansea terraces, to their chapels and churches, community halls, front parlours and back sculleries. They must have enjoyed the more liberated voicings, timings and chord structures of the music. They were also able to clap in time on the way home and not worry about causing offence to the deacons. This must have been the case as, a year later, in 1876, Swansea formed its own Jubilee Singers under the direction of Stephen Williams. They performed, for example, at Swansea's Agricultural Hall, possibly during the interval, when Mr Walter Rendell gave a 'Literary Evening' entitled 'Two Hours with the Best Authors'.[44] Music is indeed politics. It enables people to foster a dialogue, even if the politics behind it were too complicated for some to contemplate and the dialogue was in its infancy.

The Fisk Jubilee Singers continued on their way, visiting Newport, Cardiff and Merthyr Tydfil, with funds gathering apace. The Jubilee Hall, back on the Fisk University campus, became fully occupied and funds were now required for a companion building, the Livingstone Missionary Hall. As Marsh points out: 'Behind them were all the disabilities and cruelties of that bondage in which their lives began. Before them were all the possibilities of culture, distinction, and usefulness that are open to the citizens of one of the foremost nations of the earth.'[45]

The Fisk Jubilee Singers were not to return to Wales until fourteen years later, on 13 and 15 February 1889, at Swansea's Albert Hall (the

Figure 8: 'Troubled In Mind', *Negro Spirituals, or The Songs of the Jubilee Singers* (undated, out of copyright)

old Music Hall), over which presided Mayor R. Martin and ex-Mayor Howell Watkins. The programme for this visit was retained by Syd Jones, aged over 90, who resided in a Swansea care home, saving it with his grandmother's belongings. Mr Jones believed his grandmother, Mary Llewellyn Jones, had been born about 1860. He remembered she liked music and was the last surviving member of the Caradog Choir. He thought it possible that she attended the concert with her friends in the Choir. She was sufficiently impressed by the Fisk Jubilee Singers to have kept their programme safe, passing it on to her grandson, enabling it to have survived for over a hundred years.[46]

In 1889, at the same time as the Fisk Jubilee Singers were performing in Britain, Oliver points out in his introduction to *Black Music in*

Britain that a troupe from South Africa, referred to as 'authentic' in their publicity, performed a show called *Savage South Africa*.

> Two hundred Matabeles, Hottentots and Swazis were displayed in their Kraals and re-enacted the war in Frank Fillis's extravaganza at the Empress Theatre, Earl's Court in 1900. They performed as 'savages', which pandered to racist stereotypes. This troupe was shipped to Britain with a cargo of South African animals.[47]

There is no record of whether the Fisk Jubilee Singers were aware of the show or of any comments the Fisk Jubilee Singers might have made. However, such a large company would have been reviewed extensively in the press. Those performing in *Savage South Africa* were earning a living on stage and probably kept their opinions to themselves.

At this time, a proposal was put forward to erect a Temperance Hall as 'after all, money could be found for the Devil's Music'.[48] In 1899 the press reported a 'Unique Entertainment at Swansea':

> It is fourteen years since the Fisk University Singers visited Swansea, and but three of the original troupe now remain. Their entertainment is a unique one in many respects, consisting as it does of those peculiar negro melodies composed by an illiterate people, and sung with great fervour at camp and revival meetings. Mr F. J. Loudin, who possesses a powerful bass voice of splendid compass, delighted the audience by his rendition of 'Deep in the Mine', and in response to numerous demands for an encore sang 'Poor Old Joe'.[49]

F. J. Loudin (1836–1904) was an astute and clever man and knew how to work a local audience by choosing to sing W. H. Jude's 'Deep in the Mine' on his last appearance in Swansea. The song would have appealed considerably to a south Wales coalfield audience familiar with mining accidents and disasters. The song was written by Jude in 1882; there is an account of how the song came to be written in the *Advertiser, Adelaide*, as follows:

There was another large attendance at the Town Hall on Monday evening, when Mr W. H. Jude gave his third descriptive musical evening. The programme opened with the descriptive song 'Deep in the Mine,' a quaintly melodious song, dramatic in treatment and as sung by Mr Jude angularly impressive.[50]

There had been an accident in a north Wales mine, and rescuers had heard the 300 trapped men singing. The lyrics read:

> Though soldiers may to battle go
> By hopes of glory led,
> The miner fights no earthly foe
> To win his children bread.
> Firedamp is the cry that brings
> Terror to the miner brave,
> As through the dark it rings,
> And turns it to a grave.[51]

Jude might have written the song in memory of the pit disaster at Bersham Colliery, Wrexham, Denbighshire, which occurred on 3 August 1880, where nine men died, or of the Henwaen, Blaina, disaster on 3 March 1882, in which five men lost their lives. Loudin's interpretation of 'Deep in the Mine' must have left a deep impression on his audience.[52] The Fisk Jubilee Singers continued on their 1899 tour.

Seven years on, in April 1906, the Jamaican Native Choir, members of the Kingston Choral Union, arrived in Swansea to perform four concerts at the Grand Theatre and the Albert Hall.[53] There are similarities in the mode of dress of both the Jamaican Native Choir and Fisk Jubilee Singers, namely Victorian ankle-length dresses and black-tie evening wear. A sponsor was encouraged to invite them to perform in England and Wales, Sir Alfred Lewis Jones RA, PRBS, KCMG (1845–1909). He was born in Carmarthen, but brought up, educated and worked in Liverpool. A Victorian entrepreneur, businessman and ship owner, he opened up new trade with the West Indies. He was 'affectionately known to the residents of Llanddulas as "Banana Jones".'[54] Green sets out the story. Sir Alfred was well placed to help support a tour for the Jamaican Native Choir with Liverpool as his centre of operations, coinciding with his Colonial Products Exhibition 1906, at which they performed. Postcards were printed with a photograph of the Choir. The local press reported: 'Then the choir sang in a manner which brought tears to some eyes and a catch in the throat. To look at those dusky faces and to hear those melodious voices singing our "Rule Britannia" and our National Anthem was an experience apart.'[55] The Jamaican Native Choir visited Swansea again in 1908, performing on the Mumbles Pier with Wingate's Temperance Prize Band.[56]

There was one last visit to south Wales by the Fisk Jubilee Singers in 1907, this time as a Trio. Into these changing and innovative times, just at that very moment when music was evolving into the early sounds of 'hot' and 'syncopated' rhythms, history again gave a nudge to the shoulder. This time the Fisk Jubilee Trio were on a goodwill mission. Their impending arrival was announced with a large advertisement which detailed that two Good Friday services would be held in Swansea's Grand Theatre by the 'World-renowned Original Fisk Jubilee Singers Trio', at 3 p.m. and 7.30 p.m., to be followed by another concert the following day at the imposing St Andrew's Presbyterian Church, St Helen's Road. It had been eight years since their last visit and the choir was now reduced in numbers; Swansea's memories were long, and word of mouth passing to the next generation ensured their popularity and longevity in people's minds. Confirmation of this hypothesis is the fact that the Grand Theatre had no qualms about booking two concerts in their large venue for the same day, even though another major concert was scheduled for the following day in the next street in St Andrew's Church. It is also interesting to note that the word 'slave' had disappeared from the newspaper advertisement, to be replaced with 'Coloured American Artistes', showing a sign of the times and the vogue for current vernacular.[57]

The earlier 3 p.m. Grand Theatre concert on 29 March was awarded sufficient status to be presided over by the formidable Miss Amy Dillwyn

(1845–1935), industrialist, feminist, educationalist, activist and writer. Amy Dillwyn had rescued her father's failing spelter works, eventually becoming the hands-on owner of Dillwyn and Co.[58] Supporting this afternoon concert were the Swansea Trombone Quartet, quite innovative for its day, and 1,500 people attended, with Miss Dillwyn in her tweed suit, pince-nez on her nose and smoking a cigar, sitting at the side of the stage behind her table holding court and encouraging donations into the buckets being passed along the seats. One would never dare *not* to drop in a little something. The evening concert was presided over by F. Rocke, JP, with the additional entertainment provided by the Swansea Temperance Silver Band. As there was no longer any need for the Fisk Jubilee Trio to raise money for the campus buildings back home in Nashville, these being well established by 1907, the two Grand Theatre concerts were 'thank you' fundraisers and a tribute for 'the poor of Swansea', coordinated by the YMCA, in recognition of the financial support Swansea had given Fisk University in the past. A Silver Collection took place during both concerts in the dress circle and stalls, where the people of means usually sat.

The success of the Grand Theatre and the St Andrew's concerts provoked a flurry of activity in the *South Wales Daily Post* (previously *The Cambrian*), the following week. A photograph appeared of the Fisk Jubilee Trio, emphasising its importance. The credit states it was a 'hitherto unpublished photo of the famous negro entertainers Miss Emma Mocara, Mr McAdoo, Miss Laura A. Carr'. The *South Wales Daily Post* remembered the popularity of the full choir's earlier visits, acted accordingly, and sent a reporter for an in-depth interview. Eugene McAdoo willingly sat for an hour in the library at Swansea's YMCA building and recounted 'an interesting history' comparing Welsh and English audiences. The unnamed reporter felt it necessary to describe Mr McAdoo's colour and features in the first paragraph for journalistic accuracy, assuring us that Mr McAdoo was a 'fine representative of the coloured race, a well-shaped athletic figure; features bright and of intellectual cast – lacking the flatnesses usual with the dark races, and shiny dark yellow, rather than dusky'. This statement has more to say about the reporter than the public's perceived sensibilities. Mr McAdoo's voice was described as a 'real floor scraper of a bass'. But we must forgive the shortcomings of the reporter in their enthusiasm for accuracy, and praise the quality of the shorthand and obvious interest in the visit. What follows is a fascinating account of the history of the Fisk Jubilee Singers 1874 to the current Trio of 1907, from one still proud to carry the name into the next century. The *South Wales Daily Post* tells Mr McAdoo's story:

> Mr McAdoo's brother, Orpheus, was manager of the Southern Hemisphere party. When Mr Orpheus McAdoo died a few years ago, the contracts with the singers of course became null and void, and most of the eleven singers desired to return home. There were left only Miss Mocara, Miss Carr and Mr McAdoo . . . The trio have no fewer than 480 of the curious and famous negro choruses in their repertoire . . . And here Mr McAdoo pointed out a difference between the old Jubilee Singers and the present Trio. The former would hear these melodies in their rough state, but would never present them as heard. They would add something of the magician's magic touch. The trio, on the contrary, sing the melodies exactly as the slaves used to sing them. 'The Jubilee Singers', added Mr McAdoo, 'were known for their harmony, whereas we have sacrificed harmony to give the real living effect of the quaintness and eccentricity of the songs. For instance, our 'Peter on the Sea' is surely the most peculiar thing you ever heard. There is no attention to rhythm or tune, and very little to time; it is sung just as I heard a congregation of 800 sing it. It is a screech and a yell; yet it is musical.' Those who heard 'Peter on the Sea' on Saturday will be agreed as to its peculiarity! 'I have been most favourably deceived in regard to the Welsh,' Mr McAdoo said. 'We were told we would not raise any enthusiasm here at all; that the Welsh do so much singing that they will not acknowledge anyone else can sing; They are not perhaps so supercilious as the English – there is not so much surface feeling. For instance, an English audience claps you when you appear, before they know what you are going to do. Yesterday I noticed the people sat with arms folded until we had sung, and they found they liked us.'[59]

After the Fisk Jubilee Trio interview appeared in the press, they were inundated with requests for further concerts. Two more were hastily organised at St Andrew's Church for 3 April 1907. Another added attraction was advertised for Sunday 7 April at the YMCA 'Monthly Tea and Conference' at 4.30 p.m., when Mr E. McAdoo gave a talk on the 'Life Experience of the Famous Fisk Jubilee Singers Trio', and 'Ladies are Heartily Invited'. A large notice appeared in the *South Wales Daily Post* warning of the Fisk Jubilee Trio's farewell and praising the success of the extra concerts by the Trio, which 1,500 people attended. The review added:

> The Trio were in their top form, and their harmonious, cultured singing, combined with the strangeness of their melodies, made their concert one to be remembered. 'Peter on the Sea' surely about the most peculiar hymn ever written; 'Mother is Massa Gwine Ter Sell Me Tomorrow?' a Negro lament; 'Hear Them Bells', and several other favourites were given, and many were the calls for encores.[60]

This success prompted yet further hurriedly arranged extra concerts, in fact a five-day tour of the south Wales valleys from 8–13 April 1907. The Trio performed at Calvaria Chapel, Clydach; The Tabernacle, Pontardawe; Public Hall, Aberavon; Wern Chapel, Ystalyfera; Hermon Chapel, Pontardulais; and on 13 April the Forward Movement Hall, Morriston. The Fisk Jubilee Trio ensured their music was heard in isolated areas away from the big towns. More than 12,000 people attended this five-day tour.

The Fisk Jubilee Singers and later the Trio were the first to come and perform in Wales with a particular political and sociocultural message. With the continuing runaway success of Harriet Beecher Stowe's *Uncle Tom's Cabin* and its spin-off stage productions still very popular with working-class Welsh audiences, the Fisk Jubilee Singers and subsequent Trio were the pioneers in bridging the music of plantation slavery, gospel, secular melodies and popular music with concert hall authority. Some choir members decided to settle in Britain.[61]

Frederick Loudin, who temporarily settled in Britain, eventually returned home to Ohio, dying in 1904. Tom Rutling, after completing a tour of Europe, refused to return to racist America. He lived the rest of his life in Great Britain as a performer and teacher, suffering a fatal stroke on the beach at Morecambe in 1915. He wrote his autobiography, *Tom*. 'The very earliest thing I remember was this selling of my mother', he recalled when he was a Jubilee Singer.[62] Isaac Dickerson 'settled in Plumstead, southeast London about 1890, where he found audiences at the working-class St. Paul's Mission'.[63]

The original Fisk Jubilee Singers, singing stories of bondage and freedom, are surrounded by contemporary myths and legends. They had all the attributes and qualities that Wales admired and revered. But the Fisk Jubilee Singers were also human. Not all was plain sailing. For an account of what life was really like on the road for the Fisk Jubilee Singers in their early days, see Graham (2010).[64] In 1925, veterans of the Fisk Jubilee Singers Trio who appeared to be in their eighties were photographed on a railway platform on their way to perform before the Royal Family at Windsor Castle. It was Britain's last glimpse of them.[65]

That last performance of the Fisk Jubilee Trio in 1907 came at a time when ragtime music, together with its cake walk dance, was thundering on to Welsh stages, blowing away those lovely old traditional 'weird slave songs' . . . not forever, but just for a while.

Chapter Four

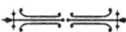

Ragtime and the Cake Walk: On Stage and in the Workhouse

RAGTIME MUSIC, AND ITS associated dance, the cake walk, had to find spaces on the boards amongst a cornucopia of bizarre and certainly sometimes eccentric performers, all competing for the attention of a predominantly working-class clientele. In the two decades leading up to 1900, the variety artistes touring the south Wales boards were a kaleidoscope of the bizarre, unlikely, homespun, eccentric, outlandish, folksy and surreal, all out to make an honest buck in the entertainment business. Disability was an advantage for some groups, such as the acrobats the Monopieds (all missing limbs) who returned regularly to packed houses. Most variety artistes were assisted by a weird and wonderful assortment of props, such as skipping ropes, horses (educated), fire engines, Fred Karno's Army, live animals, insect impersonators (Sylvester the Manfly), fighting kangaroos, knife-throwers and sharpshooters (the Kentucky Rifle Team), the first motor car on stage, ectoplasm (muslin, various), spectre and ghost shows, male impersonators with 'accoutrements', water tanks (real mermaids), water tanks (performing fish) and corpses. Nevertheless, however odd the turns, the variety stage also offered space for musicians, not only in pit bands and orchestras, but also as instrumentalists, performing in their own right as legitimate stage acts, for example the Ten Lady Drummers, who wowed audiences on their regular visits.[1]

By 1900 the musical tastes of the Welsh working class were adapting to changing cultural influences. Beddoe points out that Welsh women were beginning to demand more control of their lives, property and economic independence, and to campaign for the vote; and the nineteenth century saw an expansion in the number of women 'whose pattern of life was unlike that of women in the past'. Working women began to redefine their social position, developing middle class aspirations and burgeoning leisure opportunities:

> This group provided the overwhelming majority of feminists or 'New Women'. It was these bourgeois women whom John Stuart Mill had in mind when he pleaded for equality of the sexes in *The Subjection of Women* in 1869 and it was they who took up the challenge.[2]

Summerfield states that there was growing dissent from patriotic fervour for celebrating such battles as the Boer War and the Relief of Mafeking. Audiences were demanding more glamour, colour and music instead of, for example, a diet of Negro minstrelsy (see chapter 2) undertaken against a backdrop of British imperialism and the building of the Empire. Proprietors of theatre and music halls began adapting to change, away from productions offering 'founts of patriotism', which made audiences restless, and on to theatres of variety. Summerfield points out that theatre chains, such as Moss, Stoll and Thornton, encouraged a socially heterogeneous audience. These new audiences demanded more sophisticated fare, such as revues, which enabled the solo performer to 'star' within a company of singers and dancers. These short, fast acts became the staple of the national variety circuit, attracting local, working-class, family audiences, and thereby encouraging girls and women to attend, some of whom brought their babies.[3]

Oliver notes that sheet music up to the 1890s was selling in its millions, with some examples of the genre being: 'Spirituals, Parlour

Songs, Heart Songs and Familiar Plantation Ditties, Banjo pieces, jigs, cakewalks and coon songs'.[4] Theatres of variety drew an audience attracted by cheap ticket prices of 6d to 1s., but did not neglect their middle classes in the better seats, which sold at anything up to 2 guineas (£2 2s.). Traies describes the cultural and musical innovation as 'vehicles of change... embodying messages about class and gender roles... and the response of a working-class member of a music-hall audience might, for instance, combine class contempt with family affection'. She argues that by the beginning of the twentieth century, Victorian middle-class family values with emphasis on cultural elitism, had given way to the popular demands of the Edwardian new working class with its loosening of Victorian conventions of social behaviour. The new working class were artisans, tradesmen and women, shopkeepers, assistants, clerks, typists, holding a 'common cultural context', as audience and players of music.[5] In 1899 those with sufficient disposable income were able to purchase the new 'Gram-O-Phone' – 'it talks, sings and plays' – available at Brader's Musical Emporium in Swansea.[6]

'Nigger minstrelsy' was still popular but had to compete with the new glamorous and sophisticated shows in the big, plush theatres. The American Troubadours toured their 'Plantation Glees' and the cake walk, making several return visits to the Empire in Swansea. The American Troubadours were possibly the Black Patti's Troubadours, featuring Madame Sissieretta Joyner, dubbed the Black Patti (after Madame Adelina Patti, 1843–1919), the highest paid black performer of her day.[7]

One of these new musical crazes was ragtime. Ragtime, the shortened form of 'raggedy time' – a straight four-four left hand with a syncopated right hand – personified this new excitement in music and its dance spin-offs, like the cake walk, with its parody of class distinctions. The cake walk, as originally performed by black working-class men and women in the USA, parodied white upper-class mannerisms with a high-stepping, mincing walk and an arm-in-arm glide. The etymology can be derived from competitions held in American dance halls, with the best dancers competing for the prize of a large chocolate confection, thereby initiating the phrase 'to take the cake'.[8] It was another example of African Americans subverting white cultural mores.

One of the first ragtime hits, 'Eli Green's Cakewalk', was written by a woman, Sadie Koninski, a music teacher, in 1896, and became part of the repertoire of the Queen City Concert Band in Sedalia, Missouri, for whom composer and pianist Scott Joplin was an early cornetist.[9] Another early successful ragtime composer was Adaline Shepherd. Her composition 'Pickles and Peppers', published in 1906, became so popular it sold over two million copies and was used in the (unsuccessful) presidential candidacy campaign of William Bryant in 1908. Another early nationwide hit in America was 'Dusty Rag' by May Frances Aufderheide.[10] These early composers were white and middle class. The African American Scott Joplin, composer of over forty rags, a ballet and two operas, attained fame with his 'Maple Leaf Rag', published in 1899, erasing the earlier women from memory.

Rags were very popular played on pianos in 'sporting houses', which were usually run by 'Madames'. O'Connell writes that women bawdy-house managers were the 'true patrons' of piano jazz.[11] Colin points out that many new dances associated with ragtime were becoming popular in Britain, including the Tango, Cake Walk, the Boston (a walking dance), the Ramble, the Three-Step, the Shimmy, the Grizzly Bear and the Charleston. These new dances and the musicians who serviced them became so popular they startled the Imperial Society of Dance Teachers, formed in 1904, to the extent that 'they decreed that henceforth ballroom dancing should confine itself to four basic steps: the waltz, the foxtrot, the quick-step and the tango'. Victor Sylvester, doyenne of 'metronomic exactitude' strict tempo ballroom dancing, formed his own band to support this cause.[12]

The theatres made sure their interiors were fashionable and their decor was regularly refurbished in order to keep the patrons happy. Swansea's Grand Theatre featured the Globe Choir and Scenorama, a 'marvellous combination of Panoramic, Dioramic, Limelight and Electrical effects with twenty Lady Artistes'. This show included 'vocals, duets, part-songs, quartets, pretty actions, instrumental selections and bands

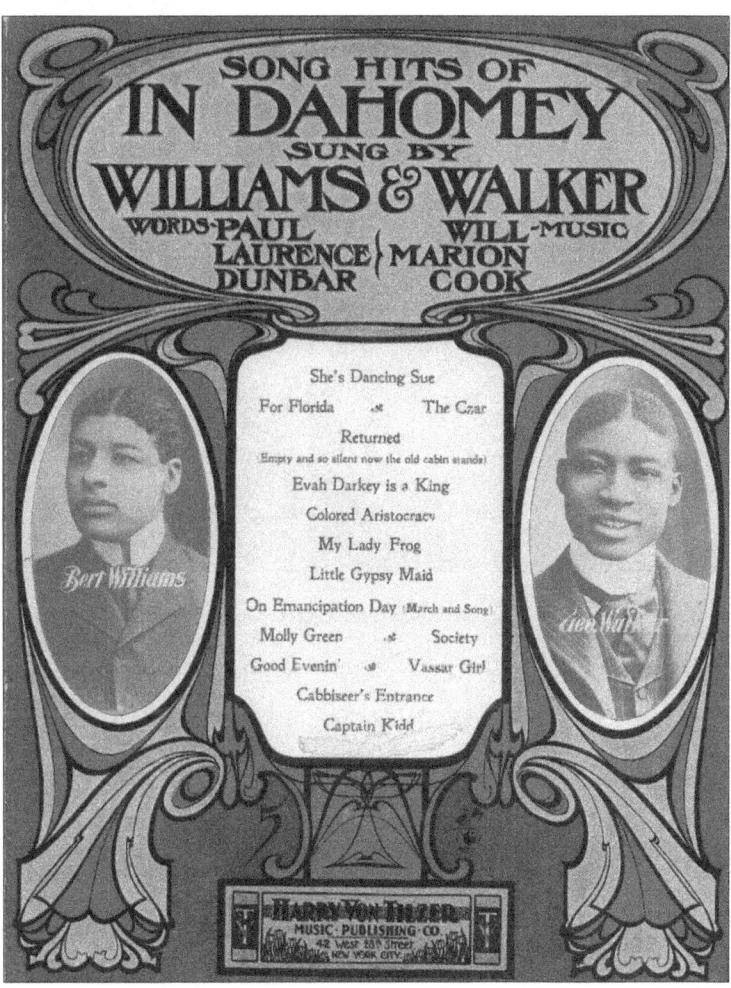

Figure 9: *In Dahomey*, 1903 (Brown University Library African American Sheet Music Collection, Providence, RI)

Figure 10: *In Dahomey*, trio of dancers (Williams, Walker, Walker) 1903 (out of copyright)

of guitars, mandolins and banjos'. The Palace Theatre a few streets away offered 'A Troupe of Six Lady Wrestlers and a Radiograph'. Every taste catered for.[13]

The new music of rags, rhythms and dances, was personified in the first big all African American production, *In Dahomey*, composed and conducted by Wil Marion Cook. This show opened at London's Shaftesbury Theatre in May 1903, arriving at Swansea's Grand Theatre in January 1905. The production touring Wales was advertised as 'The Negro Musical Comedy'; some audiences might have been expecting a 'Negro minstrelsy' show, which it was not. It featured over fifty members in the cast, with Stella Hart as the female lead. *In Dahomey* caused a sensation. Oliver points out that the production's success was primarily due to a performance given at Buckingham Palace before King Edward VII, ensuring a successful national tour. Oliver argued that there were 'clear advantages in conforming to the expectations of white society, while being sufficiently skilled or innovative for colour to be a sign of quality'.[14]

Africa had been exploited for its lands, labour and assets, its people 'Christianised'. Now Welsh audiences appeared to relish the sight of black people satirising imperial values. The production, said the *South Wales Daily Post*:

> presents a phase of entertainment that is entirely novel locally. The musical ragtime is conspicuous throughout, and though the plot is thin, it serves as a useful peg on which the eccentricities of those clever comedians Dan Avery and Charles Hart depend. This pair are responsible for the humour, and the whole time they are on the stage the audience is kept a titter. The tout ensemble is a special feature, the negro combination seemingly to be continuously on the move across the stage, and they ever readily join in song and dance . . . Avery and Hart are well supported by Messrs. Pete Hampton, F. Douglas, W. Dixon, Leon Williams, and W. Garland, and Laura Bowan, Mamie Anderson, and Pauline Freeman. The company is coloured throughout.[15]

The best production numbers were listed as 'Molly Green', 'Bearskin Baby', 'Good Night Lucinda', and 'I'm Unlucky'. *In Dahomey* also included a Cake Walk Competition for the local audiences. Four couples would be chosen each night, with the winning couple to be given a prize at the end of the week. The show was 'well supported by Wil Garland'. Women performers singled out for praise in the Swansea production were Laura Bowan, Mamie Anderson and Pauline Freeman. The original London 1903 production starred Bert Williams and George Walker, with featured women Aida Overton Walker, Rhoda King, Birdie Williams and Ida Gigas. Innovative as *In Dahomey* clearly was, Welsh audiences eagerly supported the production during its week's stay in Swansea and countless couples learned how to do the cake walk. However, there were dissenters at the time, Rudyard Kipling commenting: 'The cakewalk tells us why the negro and the white can never lie down together.

It is a grotesque, savage and lustful heathen dance, quite proper in Ashanti but shocking on the boards of a London hall.'[16]

Parsonage discusses the significance of *In Dahomey* in depth, pointing out that Dahomey (now Benin) 'had been conquered by the French in 1851, and so this setting provided an opportunity for the civilizing influence of white Europeans to be shown against the stereotype of "savage Africa"'. Dahomey was 'the last major port-of-call for slave ships making the infamous "middle passage" in the early nineteenth century'. There was plenty of humour and slapstick in the show, and Parsonage cites Riis upon the 'dual identity' of the stars, Williams and Walker, who described themselves as portraying 'native African characters as far as we could, and still remain American, and make our acting interesting and entertaining to American audiences'. The *In Dahomey* company made adjustments and alterations in order to please their British audiences, as there had been some criticism that the original production had been intended as a Negro opera.

The music of *In Dahomey* had several features that may have prompted comparisons with earlier British experiences of black and blackface entertainment. The choral style of some of the numbers recalls spirituals, which had been presented in Britain by the Fisk Jubilee Singers in the late nineteenth century and had become part of the later minstrel shows, as the standard and size of choruses had improved and enlarged.

Some critics had also regarded *In Dahomey* as a skit on the Back to Africa campaign, or Colonisation Movement. Parsonage continues:

> The show also references the conflicts between natives and African-American settlers that could result from the repatriation policies of the American Colonization Association. However, *In Dahomey* concludes with the failure of the settlement and return of the colonizers to America, illuminating the need for African-Americans to be accepted in America rather than being segregated.

Parsonage also quotes an interview given by the director of *In Dahomey*, Wil Marion Cook, to the *Daily News*,[17] pointing out that they had been treated better in London by the British than by fellow Americans. Cook says, 'There is no feeling against us here . . . We wanted to put up at the Cecil, and the management were willing enough to take us, but the (white) Americans stopping there objected to our presence, so we had to go to another hotel.' This contrasted with the company's invitation to perform at Buckingham Palace where: 'We were received royally. That is the only word for it. We had champagne from the Royal cellar and strawberries and cream from the Royal garden.' Parsonage comments: 'This apparent lack of racism that performers experienced in Britain compared with America may explain why the show remained in Britain for such a long period of time.'[18]

By the time *In Dahomey* arrived in Swansea in 1905 the show, with an eye to pleasing its ever-increasing audiences and responding to critical comments, had been tightened up with additions or deletions of songs and acts. Cook's plan of serving up an authentic Negro opera with *In Dahomey* 'was not particularly successful in Britain, although the show itself was undoubtedly popular'. Parsonage suggests that audiences were still expecting blackface minstrelsy, owing to the extent 'to which the image of the blackface minstrel had permeated British society, due to its prominence on the British stage during the preceding century'.[19]

Nevertheless, regarded as light opera or not, *In Dahomey* made a significant impact on south Wales. Wil Marion Cook with *In Dahomey* paved the way for other all-black productions to follow, such as Will Garland's *A Trip To Coontown* which toured in 1906, *Coloured Society* in 1917 and *Coloured Lights* in 1927, a successful formula for Wil Garland.[20]

Shortly after the departure of *In Dahomey*, the summer of 1905 saw the arrival of ragtime connoisseurs and 'American Coloured Fashion Plates' Johnson and Dean to sell-out audiences at the Swansea Empire. They were a truly innovative pair, in that they took great care of their marketing and pre-performance press releases and were the first African Americans to have their photograph in full evening dress included in their advertising press release. Charles E. Johnson was elegant in top hat, kid gloves, black tie and tails, Dora Dean sophisticated in a lacy ballgown, a far cry from the minstrelsy plantation genre. Johnson had introduced

Figure 11: Johnson and Dean, 'In Society', 1905 (Harvard Theatre Collection, Houghton Library, Harvard University)

steel plates into his shoes for tap dancing, and both danced in front of a black background under flicker spotlights to suggest silent movies, their own invention. According to an *Ebony* article of February 1953, Dora Dean was the sister of Clarence Babbige, the first black judge in Kentucky, and her mother was a former slave. Dean featured on cigarette cards, taking advantage of her good looks. Charles E. Johnson was the son of Eliza Diggs Johnson, a former slave in Missouri who 'had told him about cakewalks on the plantation'. Both showed off their skills with a soft-shoe shuffle, 'putting themselves over with personality and elegance'. Johnson was described as a 'strutter and eccentric dancer who employed legomania [*sic*], a rhythmic twisting and turning of the legs'.[21]

In Swansea, Johnson and Dean organised cake walk competitions during the week for the locals, culminating in the dance-off competition on the Saturday night, a huge hit with the Welsh. Johnson and Dean were probably unaware of the intricacies and complications of the Welsh/English cultural divide but it did offer an unexpected opportunity for working-class Welsh to poke fun at upper-class values. It was, therefore, a genuine African American/Welsh collusion. Johnson and Dean continued touring throughout Europe, and in May 1907 opened in St Petersburg, Russia. At practically the same time in Swansea, Harry Bartlett inaugurated the first ladies' mandolin and banjo band in Wales, probably including some ragtime in their repertoire, at St Gabriel's Hall, 'already in great demand at local bazaars, concerts and charitable events'.[22] Bert Williams, star of the original production of *In Dahomey*, wrote a song about Dora Dean:

> Oh, have you ever seen Miss Dora Dean,
> She is the sweetest gal you ever seen.
> Someday I'm going to make this Gal my Queen.
> On next Sunday morning, I'm going to marry
> Miss Dora Dean.[23]

It was probable that the polished performance of Johnson and Dean influenced Swansea's own 'Real Coon' Lonzo Brown, as he too was photographed in the press in full evening dress. Brown, a young 'coloured' man, made a 'decided hit at the Palace and the Shaftesbury' as a 'real singing coon and expert sand dancer'. Lonzo Brown then began his south Wales tour the following week at the Morriston Bioscope Theatre, sadly to disappear from the pages of the newspapers.[24]

Ragtime continued to wow the crowds. In 1913 Swansea's Empire Theatre trumpeted *Hullo Ragtime!*, the most 'elaborate and sumptuous production ever staged at an English [sic] Theatre', boasting a 'Beauty Chorus of 40 Girls'. This production was described as a revue, not a musical, and featured Irving Berlin performing his own music. He would sometimes respond to requests from audiences to perform his previous hits, such as 'Alexander's Ragtime Band' and 'Everybody's Doing It Now'.[25] Despite the unusually hot weather the local press reported there were crowded houses:

> The ragtime invasion from America has the British public within its grip and the haunting melodies had the audiences swaying in time on Monday evening. The Revue is a brand new thing to Swansea and it scored an instantaneous success. The final scene of the Ragtime Wedding is a beautiful one and is alone worth seeing. The Revue is packed with humour, melody and beauty, beautiful girls and gorgeous scenery. Tom E. Finglass, the Cowboy Coon, made a bit hit with his popular song 'My Baby', whilst his Indian scene song brought the house down . . . Lulu Williams was a charming little comedienne and dancer and Fred Keeton scored a great success with his song 'Early Closing Day'.[26]

Women performers were regularly demeaned as 'little', losing credence compared with male performers despite the professionalism in women's performance, as women performers were usually regarded as second class to the males. It must have been galling for women performers reading their reviews. Another 'little' example is Daisy Dormer, one of the stars of another large song-and-dance production called *OH-I-O Girls*. Having been described as 'an artiste to her finger tips', she was then referred to in the press as 'A little lady who quite captured those in front . . . in dance and ditty proved herself just as she was billed.' None of the gentlemen had to 'prove' themselves, as the assumption was that they were going to be good anyway. The show *OH-I-O Girls* was described as:

> 30 trained voices In the Conception of Old-Time Minstrel Songs and Ragtime Successes, and pretty costumes. One of the best turns of its kind yet staged at Swansea Empire aroused decided enthusiasm on Monday evening in the shape of a bevy of 30 comely maidens who, as the Oh-I-O girls go through a delightful programme of song and dance,

embodying the old and the new negro ditties together with some very well sung solo ballads.[27]

The winter programme for the Mumbles Pier Pavilion featured the society dancers Herbert and Lily St Johns with an article and photograph in the press headlined 'DO YOU TANGO?' The St Johns had been engaged 'by the management' to deliver five exhibitions of tango dancing, together with their pianist, Miss Martin. The Pavilion was especially decorated for the occasion. The first exhibition dance was the Tango Parisian, the 'real tango as danced in the ballrooms of Paris'. The Tango Mattchiche was described as being 'a dainty form of the old cake walk'. The Valse Pop-Pourri was a

> mixture of the Tango, Boston and Ragtime dances intermixed with the ordinary valse step. This item, which has more abandon than the others, proved to be the most popular. In a chat with the *Post* Representative, the artistes informed him the dances were easily learned. There were really only 8 or 9 steps to be mastered, the rest being variations given in a different manner, but it was essential for a couple to learn from the same teacher as each teacher had his or her own interpretation of the steps, which is apt to lead to confusion with a strange partner. The dance music was very striking and admirably played by Miss Martin.[28]

In the innocent pre-war days of spring and summer 1914, south Wales's appetite for 'coloured' song and dance acts was insatiable. Starring at the Empire were Pauline and her Madcap Dancers, 'America's greatest coloured singing and dancing act'. The review reads: 'Despite ever-increasing counter attractions in the town, the public of South Wales continues to accord the Empire that patronage it deserves.'[29]

The theatres, cafés and Mumbles pier continued to do good business. The press declared a 'Red Letter Week at the Carlton' with good houses and excellent orchestra. The Empire hosted shows such as Kate Carney's Cockney Revue *I Should Say So*, G. H. Elliott the 'Chocolate Coloured Coon', the 'Six Brown Brothers New American Act', Percy

Henri's *Big Tango Revue* with 200 'Parisienne model Gowns', and Bella Davis and her Cracker Jacks, 'young coloured artistes in Southern Pastures'.[30]

With war raging the Empire had no trouble filling its vast interior with ever more flamboyant productions, all helping to divert worries about the plight of loved ones. *The Million Dollar Girl*, 'with its complement chorus of forty Blonde Beauties', was such a one, only this time 'for recruiting reasons the male parts in the chorus will be played by ladies'. The Grand Theatre offered the big production, *Sealed Orders*, with a cast of sixty on the deck of a battleship. A 'magnificent review' was given to Beattie and Babs, the youthful stars leading a 'capital cast' in the *All Woman Revue*, 'intended to keep the home fires burning'. Another all-woman production was described as a 'daring innovation', as there was not a 'mere man in the cast . . . and the girls were exceptionally clever'. Reviews made it clear that it was a surprise that women could be so clever.[31] Trams brought the crowds into the town's variety halls and theatres. Emmy Harries, born in 1892, worked as a conductress on the trams (Badge 209) in 1914 aged 22. 'The Swansea Empire car was always busy with people standing on the bumpers outside, jam-packed it was', Emmy said.[32]

Ragtime music, cake walk dancing and revues were not just confined to the plush, art nouveau theatres of south Wales. The Swansea Board of Guardians ran a tight ship at the Swansea Union Workhouse on Mount Pleasant's Gibbet Hill (1861–1929) and made sure the inmates were up to date in their access to culture and leisure pursuits. Of the elected twenty-nine Guardians, only one was a woman, described as 'a spinster'.[33] From as early as 1874, concerts had been regularly given at the Workhouse. A good review was published of the programme given at the Annual Workhouse Concert that included 'excellent selections of glees, songs, duets and readings by various gentlemen and ladies of the town'. Gifts from the Christmas tree were distributed to the pauper children, and prizes were given to the children who 'best sung the little pastoral song "While I'm at School" and best recited the poem "Conscience"'.[34]

At their annual Christmas dinner in 1919 five hundred inmates had a 'splendid dinner followed by the playing of gramophone records by the new Mayor Dewitt followed by musical events'.[35] Killjoy Bert Cronin rose at a Board of Guardians meeting to protest at money being spent on 'entertainment of the inmates, it was not fitting that such things are held in the Institution'. Happily, he was overruled.[36] Headlines in the press screamed: 'Hellish! Dances at the Workhouse!' Spirited discussions took place at the monthly Board of Guardians meetings, where Mr C. Jeffreys moved that dancing not be allowed as he had never been to one in his life and it was 'hellish'. 'Shame!' cried Mr Harry Williams. Mr Phillips said if the nurses wanted to dance they could go to the Patti Pavilion. Two women on the Board started arguing and were called to order by the Chair, who added that 'the cause of young girls' misfortunes was that there was not sufficient respectable indoor attractions to keep them from the streets'. Motion carried.[37]

Nevertheless inmates, presumably a captive audience, were regularly entertained by concert parties, glees, instrumental music and variety acts, with the Billy Ace Concert Party advertised to perform in October 1921.[38] At one musical event the Mayor and Mayoress provided two kinds of cake, fruit and sweets, plus tobacco. After tea, the inmates enjoyed a concert, with Dilys Davies on piano, and *penillion* (vocal improvisation over a harp melody) with Mr Jenkins.[39] Rumbles of discontent began to rise from some Board members, Mr Hanlin protesting that it was a 'most dangerous thing to advocate dancing at any workhouse'. Mrs Williams in reply asked the Board not to be 'bigoted'. The local paper pointed out that the Board themselves used the Workhouse as a 'supper resort and that Labour members invited other members of the Board to tea ... why condemn soirees and dances?' Killjoys defeated.[40]

Swansea's David Evans department store took their Christmas 1921 production of *Castle Follies* into the Workhouse; the show had previously been staged at their showroom in aid of Swansea's Aged Poor Fund, with employees rehearsing out of hours. The staging was in black and white check and featured a chorus line with 'a youthful Miss Seavell' singing 'Movieland' followed by 'Going Back to Dixie', accompanied by

Miss Graham on ragtime piano. (Dixie was the old nickname for the southern United States.) This toe-tapping sentimental song conjured up life on the old plantation for those unfortunates confined in the Workhouse:

> I'm going back to Dixie, I'm going back to Dixie
> I'm goin' where the orange blossoms grow
> 'Cause I miss my old plantation, my home and my relations
> My heart turns back to Dixie, and I must go
>
> I miss my beans and hominy, my pumpkin and red gravy
> My appitite is fadin', so says my uncle Davey
> And if my friends forsake me, I pray the Lord to take me
> My heart turned back to Dixie, and I must go.[41]

The inmates' Christmas dinner for 1921 was 'Roast Beef and Pork followed by Plum Pud'. By January 1922 another row erupted amongst the Board. Alf George wanted to give the inmates a concert with an extension until midnight, strongly objected to by Mr Phillips, who insisted that undesirables would 'turn up to dance when the Mayor brought respectable people with him'. Alf George accused the Chair of being the 'Kaiser'. Permission for the concert was granted.[42] The convivial atmosphere at the Workhouse encouraged an unnamed nurse and porter to get married by special license, departing for London by train. They left a note behind with a month's wages that said 'Thanks to all for your kindness to us',[43] a case of working-class philanthropy subsidising the town council's required duty. However, their donation had probably given them great pleasure.

The Workhouse entertainments continued, with Jennie Lewis on ragtime piano for the Georgians Concert Party.[44] For the big Christmas 1922 production the dining hall was fitted up as an Old Kentucky Plantation, and the Empire Theatre minstrel troupe, the White Eyed Coons, gave a 'capital entertainment to the inmates, jazz bands and fun galore'. Guardian Mrs Lennard moved 'a hearty vote of thanks'. The downside was that the inmates had over-indulged their beer ration, so 'No Beer for Christmas Day' was reported, but 580 inmates were entertained by the Salvation Army on Boxing Day, followed by a staff dance.[45]

The New Year of 1923 saw Miss Loxton's Jazz Wallahs playing for the inmates' dance, which had been sponsored by the Fruiterer's Association. Fred Ley said any inmates calling at his store could have free fruit.[46] On the whole, the Board of Guardians were quite modern in their approach to cultural activities, though kept in line by the more Victorian members of the Board. Mr Jeffreys objected to staff having leaves of absence. When it was explained that some staff wanted to attend a dance at Thomas's Café in aid of the Poor Law Benevolent Fund, Mr Jeffreys said 'who knows, these young probationers may carry on and who knows what the downward step means'. Despite the arguments, the motion was carried, with an extension granted until midnight. A Board member, Dr Marks, questioned whether extensions at the Workhouse (now called the less threatening Tawe Lodge) should be at the expense of the ratepayers, and voiced his disapproval. Alf George replied it was to 'help the lives of those less fortunate'.[47]

Jazz bands at the Workhouse/Tawe Lodge continued, despite the grumbles. Under the auspices of the Commercial Travellers Fraternity, the Manhattan Syncopated Orchestra were the next visitors.[48] The Board then appointed a woman locum, Dr Morris Williams, one of four daughters of the Assistant Medical Officer, to the Board of Guardians.[49] Once again there was no beer for the inmates at Christmas 1923. Mrs Essie Harris complained inmates had been without beer for many years and it ought to be reinstated, but Harry Williams replied it was his duty to protect and safeguard the inmates. A row ensued, with seventeen against having beer and ten for. Unfortunately, the motion was carried. To compensate, the inmates did get the Salvation Army Band, a roast beef dinner, a late dance and a Boxing Night concert and dance.[50]

Probationer nurses at the Workhouse/Tawe Lodge struggled to enjoy a private life, with one nurse complaining of the restrictions on extension passes. She was summoned to appear before the Board.

Outcome unknown. Swansea Fruiterers were regular sponsors of entertainments at Tawe Lodge, hosting the Black Cat Concert Party with Amy Loxton on ragtime piano, followed by a dance. Another dance, with Morry's Nine Stars, was billed as 'A Treat For Inmates'.[51] These enterprising local businesspeople were prepared to repay their economic good fortune by ensuring the less fortunate were able to at least partake in some small way of the delights of good entertainment, as enjoyed by working-class audiences down in the town.

Ragtime music was fading away, and Tawe Lodge became Mount Pleasant Hospital within the new National Health Service in 1947, with a large geriatric section and a maternity unit. The old building continued to offer live music and dances to the 'geriatric' patients on the wards into the 1980s, organised on a weekly basis by the nurses. The hospital was shut down in 1995 and the site buildings were refurbished for residential use.[52]

Chapter Five

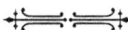

The First World War: Ragtime Trenches and Suffragettes

As blues singer Ottilie Patterson astutely remarked, 'Jazz didn't come out of a vacuum.'[1] Jazz was busy defining itself in its birth throes in America and preparing for an imminent arrival in Wales. It wasn't quite jazz yet; it was spelt 'jass' back then, and formed from an amalgam of ancient African rhythms, African American slave songs and work songs, European jigs and reels, and a variety of improvised music and dance. Welsh miners emigrated to the Appalachian coalfields during the 1800s to work on the bituminous drift mines in what is now West Virginia, and Welsh jigs and reels must have been added to the mix of music emerging at the time. Jamison traces the hybrids of music from their European, African American and Native American roots, including the dances that accompanied the music:

> Finally as opposed to the phrased, melodic music of the European dance tradition, African dances are performed with rhythmic accompaniment. Black dancers in North America commonly danced to tambourines, bones, jawbones, handclapping, and foot stomping, as well as body percussion known as 'patting Juba . . .' A dance instruction

manual from 1873 recommends this 'old fashioned patting on the thighs' as the appropriate accompaniment for 'plantation breakdowns'.[2]

Flatfootin' was a popular early form of dancing to improvised music, a tradition that is enthusiastically carried on today in a wealth of West Virginian music and dance festivals.[3]

Sheet music had 'jas' or 'jass' in the titles, such as 'That Funny Jas Band from Dixieland' (1916), or 'Everybody Loves a "Jass" Band' (1917), with lyrics that read:

> I heard a band the other day
> And let me tell you, they can play
> In such a funny manner
> That your feet 'er going to
> Make your body sway
> I heard 'em down in New Orleans
> They play a rag called 'Pork and Beans'
> Say, you can't get enough,
> Of that raggy stuff,
> Although I don't know what it means.
>
> *Chorus*
> Everybody Loves a 'Jass' Band, *etc.*[4]

Reading the lyrics, even before the music is heard, will convey the syncopated, or off-beat, patterns of the rag, or raggedy-time music. This was the music that reverberated around the music halls, theatres and cafés in Wales during the First World War, which ignited as the first jazz age into the 1920s.

Music responded to a fast-changing world by redefining the boundaries of two distinct forms: what was deemed high culture for the concert hall, and appropriate music for the masses, or popular culture. This redefinition also applied to the people who produced the music, which Pickering describes as a 'cross-cultural fertilisation'.[5] Forty years earlier

Figure 12: 'Everybody Loves A "Jass" Band', 1917 (Brown University Library, African American Sheet Music Collection)

Wales had witnessed freed slaves perform with concert hall authority on the international stage. Working-class Welsh attended the concerts and purchased their songbooks, learning the slave songs to sing in their churches and chapels. Now, the music was once more adapting to change, a faster pace of life, and the Welsh kicked their heels up in delight to ragtime music and outrageous dances, handed on by a new generation of African Americans.

Britain danced its way towards the First World War, just at a point when the social and working conditions of its population were beginning to be investigated and questioned, and women's voices for equality were becoming louder. The massive slaughter of ordinary people would cause wider questioning of traditional values of King and Country. Beddoe confirms that the Great War did challenge the entrenched gendered roles prevalent in Wales, and that contemporary images of women were a revelation to some women and disturbing to others, depending on how one regarded depictions of one's own gender. For women the usual conventions applied: to service the home; to suffer unemployment, as the middle classes dismissed their servants; to perform voluntary work for the community; or to don a nurse's uniform, which was regarded as a respectable occupation or vocation. It was an irony, as Beddoe points out, that the Great War enabled many women to 'stand tall for the first time in their lives'.[6]

Just prior to the First World War, women had started to find their feet politically. One of the largest promotions to be undertaken by women was the 1910 *Pageant of Famous Women* booked into Swansea's Albert Hall in aid of Votes for Women. This production was accompanied by a full Women's Orchestra. Press interviews were given by the *Pageant* producer Edith Craig, daughter of Ellen Terry, with Mrs Cleeves, the Hon. Sec. of the Women's Freedom League, in charge of ticket sales. The script was by Cicely Hamilton. Edith Craig said the *Pageant* had only previously been produced twice in London. One hundred women took part in the *Pageant*, representing 'the work that woman has done for the world, the part she has played and to bring that home effectively'. The three speaking parts would be Justice from her throne, holding the scales, between Woman and Man, with Woman calling for the great names of history in support of her cause. As the historical characters appeared they filled the stage, and then descended and marched around the hall to the uplifting strains of the orchestra. Hypatia, Jane Austen, Grace Darling, Sappho, Mrs Siddons, Boadicea, Black Agnes and Joan of

Figure 13: 'Gramophone' advertisement, Oxford Music Stores, Swansea, 1919 (SWW Media)

Arc were some of the characters, with Mrs Charlotte Despard, the suffragist and anti-war campaigner, playing Florence Nightingale. Photographic reproductions (stills) were for sale in the foyer. The *South Wales Daily Post* reported that:

> Mrs. Despard, the President of the Women's Freedom League, spoke with accustomed force and ability and told how, when a young woman,

she rebelled against the appealing helplessness of the women of mid-Victorian time, and how women nowadays were realising the strength of their true womanhood. She did not, however, desire that women should enter into politics an unorganised mob as some of the men did (to laughs). She concluded that the present period of political quiet afforded the Government 'a splendid chance of conferring this tardy act of justice upon women'.

Edith Craig maintained that the movement's greatest foes were 'prejudice and ignorance'. Although the news review a few days later conceded that the crowded audience were highly delighted with the event, a slightly sniffy put-down ended with 'Mere man can and does admire the important part that woman has played in the world's history. The wisdom of giving votes to women is perhaps another matter.'[7] Masson identifies similar comments as 'these local newspapers often exuded a sticky feeling of small-pond middle-class clubbiness'.[8]

Just to remind women of their place, Swansea's Star Theatre, feeling threatened by this rising tide of women's voices, continued to present their weekly melodramas aimed at the domestic market, such woman-as-enticer-and-temptress fodder as *The Woman Pays*, *Can a Woman be Good?*, *Bad Girl of the Family*, *From Convent to Throne* and *The White Slave*. However, new music and smart revues would soon arrive, kicking these demeaning and condescending plot-lines out of the window.[9]

The suffragettes, with the Swansea branch being particularly active, took their campaign all over Wales. Things got lively in Llanelli in 1912, with the press reporting that suffragettes were 'Undaunted', after Miss Barratt of the Women's Social and Political Union had to 'seek aid of the police'.[10] Sylvia Pankhurst spoke from the stage of Swansea's Star Theatre in January 1913 on 'Political Equality for Women'. The Star was an unusual choice of venue, considering its track record in anti-women melodramas. Pankhurst, a member of the Independent Labour Party, was to break away from her mother Emmeline, when Pankhurst senior urged women to support the war effort, and Sylvia urged peace and human rights. Sylvia Pankhurst spoke on the low wages of women, in which she was 'in favour of labour representation, time would come when every woman's trade would have its representation, and Maternity Benefit should be paid direct to every woman; fifty years of peaceful agitation had brought nothing'.

Pankhurst also reported on bad housing and urged the vote for women. The suffragettes became more militant, breaking away from the suffragists, and Mrs Pankhurst senior was sentenced to three years' penal servitude for 'bomb outrages' against Lloyd George's new house.[11] Masson writes that there had been vicious attacks on the suffragettes in Lloyd George's home village of Llanystumdwy, 'rowdyism which had a strong flavour of Welsh chauvinism'. Masson dissects the complex local conditions under which the Welsh suffragettes campaigned, with women 'pulled one way by feminism and another by class, party and family loyalty'. The National Union of Women's Suffrage Societies (NUWSS), adopted a policy of electoral support for the Labour Party, known as the Election Fighting Fund (EFF). In Wales, however, Masson examines the opposition to the EEF by the South Wales Federation of Women's Suffrage Societies, finding 'south Wales women feeling alienated from the national leadership, their own understanding of the politics of their region set aside'. Masson concludes that the complex and diverse politics of women in Wales 'needs to be integrated into our understanding of the richness, as well as the difficulty, of feminist politics in Britain, and also into the political history of Wales'. It was not just an English middle-class movement but, as Masson points out, part of the 'political history of working-class women' which is not yet fully explored.[12] For example, during National Baby Week, a special film, *Motherhood*, was showing at the Carlton Cinema. Lady Mond was in attendance, 'To Help the Mothers Save the Babies'. Lady Mond was the wife of the industrialist and Liberal MP Sir Alfred Mond, who was serving in the Lloyd George wartime government. Lady Mond undertook extensive philanthropic work relating to women and children, and in 1914 had converted her country residence into a hospital, philanthropy and culture working successfully alongside each other.[13] In contrast, Lady Rhondda (Margaret Haig Thomas), was a political activist and suffragette, placing her home-made bomb in a pillarbox in Risca Road, Newport, in June 1913, with smoke soon seen rising from the aperture. Lady Rhondda wrote: 'my heart was beating like a steam engine, my throat was dry'.[14]

Political unrest encouraged some women to replace their constricting clothing and to experiment with new modes of dress, with women's skirts and hair becoming shorter. Consternation grew in local worthies' minds concerning the moral lapses among women. Girls, after all, were educated accordingly for their role as domestic servants, wives and mothers. A typical example of the ideal mould was a large photograph published in the local press showing a classroom of Dyfatty schoolgirls 'being instructed by Mr Wakefield on how to feed babies'.[15] Dr Rawlings, who listed his interests in *Who's Who in Wales 1920* as 'YMCA, Temperance, Social Purity and Municipal Work', penned an article under the headline 'Fallen Sisters', blaming the 'Domestic Servant Problem' on dancing. He warned that dancing was an 'immoral training' and dancers showed 'no fear of God before their eyes'. It is apparent that domestic servants had not taken heed of Dr Rawlings's advice, considering the increasing number of dances being held in local halls and the number of musicians competing ever more resolutely for the business of supplying the music.[16]

Dances were so popular that they were held in any venue that had a roof and a floor, a good example being in November 1911 when the Royal Institution Dance for 200 people took place from 9 p.m. to 1 a.m. in the Royal Institution Library, now Swansea Museum, which would be unheard of today.[17] Another, the RSPCA Ball, went on until 2 a.m. and a *South Wales Daily Post* journalist, bylined 'Joan', was assigned to cover these events. Her duty was to describe the new fashions ('Gowns by Joan'), but Joan also took it upon herself to occasionally name the bands and the dances, leaving us a patchy but welcome record of what went on, written by a presumably young journalist who saw opportunities beyond describing a nice frock.[18]

Dance troupes were popular on the theatre stage, bringing their latest sheet music for the local pit orchestras to play. The 'domestic servants' and 'fallen sisters' described by Dr Rawlings crowded the theatres to see troupes such as the Six Lancashire Lasses, the Dainty Damsels, the Nine College Girls, the Stella Girls, the Eight Empire Girls, the Girton Girls, the Rousby Girls, the Cora Sisters, the Three Belles Hurricane Dancers, Olive Lenton and her Girls, the Caselli High Kickers, and many others. With the opportunity for theatre audiences to see how it was done close up, together with the profusion of local halls available and bands to fuel the urge to dance, it is no wonder that Wales's dancers were propelled on to the floors to have a go themselves. Anna Chandler from America was headlined at the Empire in 1911 performing the 'Turkey Trot', with Lily Flexmore, the circus, vaudeville and cabaret artiste, arriving shortly afterwards with her 'Remarkable Bite My Toe Dance'.[19]

Women musicians were now highly prominent on stage, in theatre pit orchestras, as solo pianists or small groups accompanying silent films, or within orchestras or small combos in dance halls and municipal functions. They were also active within the Musicians' Union. Kate Leigh, from a famous theatrical family, became the Amalgamated Musicians' Union's first Assistant Secretary, when it was founded in April 1893. Swansea formed its AMU branch in November 1896. Kate Leigh became known as the Mother of the Union. 'The Union that we require is a protecting Union . . . from Amateurs, and protect us from unscrupulous employers.' One of the first awards was to guarantee musicians in London 30s. per week as minimum pay, although drummers received only 28s.[20]

With noisy suffragettes urging the vote, there is little doubt that women musicians were keen to sign up to the Amalgamated Musicians' Union, sensing the need to be represented. The Three Dixons (banjoists), Ten Dixie Girls, Win Etherington (piano), Maude Kramer (banjo), the Sisters Caselli, the Sisters Julian, and many others were popular on the bandstands, in the theatre pits and on the Mumbles Pier.[21] By the spring of 1913 crowds gathered at the new Pierrot Pavilion on Swansea's sands, which offered two performances daily, children welcome for a halfpenny.[22]

Beddoe points out that women were beginning to demand more control of their lives, property and economic independence, as well as campaigning for the vote, and that the nineteenth century saw an expansion in the number of women whose lives diverged from those of women in the past. Women were able to spend a little more on clothes and entertainment for themselves.[23] Boulton states that women in Britain at this time, such as Miss Egerton Welch, opened up venues for dancing to teach the new fads, as well as inventing new job opportunities for themselves.[24] This is confirmed by Colin, featuring an advertisement for 'Dancing Taught by Experts' at the Empress Rooms, Royal Palace Hotel, London, run by Gipsey Strudwick with a stable of women dance teachers.[25] Wales was no different. Welsh women entrepreneurs with an eye on the main chance opened dance emporiums, most of which were held in their own front parlours. Swansea had its own speciality dance, called the Marina Saunter. The craze for the new dances fuelled dance competitions intended to show off dancers' skills and were opportunities to showcase the skills of the American stars on stage.

The Grand Theatre hosted a Grand Tango Competition with prizes of £2, £1 and 10 shillings. The press encouraged anyone to compete including two ladies dancing together or two gentlemen; 'anyone wishing to conceal their identity could adopt a nom-de-plume and wear a mask. No professionals allowed'. The second house on a Friday night was the place for couples to strut their stuff and may have encouraged gay and lesbian couples to take part without worrying how their public persona was viewed.[26]

Descriptive vernacular was changing as fast as the music. 'Exhilarating Swing' was used for the first time in 1914 to describe the Blow and Collins Company's *Red Heads* show at the Empire, which contained 'vividly coloured burlesque and gorgeous Parisien [sic] creations'.[27] That lovely summer of June 1914, just two months before the outbreak of war, saw headlines screaming 'Swansea Sold Out', as 100,000 people headed for the south Wales beaches and patronised local shows. Then within weeks the headlines were demanding 'King and Country Need You – Join the Army Today'. French reservists marched to High

Street station with the tricolor and Union Jack entwined.[28] Eighty-five German prisoners of war (probably innocent residents and bystanders) were rounded up in Swansea and sent to a Cheshire concentration camp. During August 1914 the government appealed for 100,000 more men, and those that hadn't already joined up were accused of being 'Petticoats'. Soldiers' wives queued for the new Separation Allowance.[29]

As part of the war effort Gladys Dawson donned her nursing uniform and sang recruiting songs at the Elysium. She became increasingly popular, singing 'Tipperary' from the stage of the newly reopened Star Theatre, now referred to as 'Swansea's Historic Playhouse'. Dance teacher Miss Langdon swiftly advertised that her classes had not been cancelled. Nervous music-store managers immediately slashed the price of pianos (useful for keeping up morale in the front parlour) by half to 15 guineas (£15 15s.).[30]

The locals turned out to support the war effort. Eight Welsh miners from Ogmore Vale appeared at the Empire performing comedy and part-singing. Swansea Art College students donned authentic uniforms to sing 'Britain and Her Allies', putting on a 'magnificent show' for the War Relief Fund, with student Mr Collins from Neath impersonating G. H. Elliott, the 'Chocolate Coloured Coon'. There was a dance afterward with refreshments. St Gabriel's, in the Uplands, opened its doors for the Women's Freedom League, who performed sketches with Miss Clark at the piano, including a sketch, 'Bakehouse on the Twmp, Aberpandy', delivered all in Welsh, with benefits going to the Serbian Hospital Relief Fund.[31]

Theatres were cutting back their stage programmes in order to show more news footage and recruiting drives on their new cinema screens. Miss Maisie Lynne appeared at the Grand Theatre in the wild extravaganza *Little Miss Ragtime*, with an appeal issued from the stage for recruits, urgently needed for the 6th Battalion Welsh Regiment.[32] Exuberant and uplifting music was a successful recruitment tool. Two brothers from St Asaph, north Wales, were responsible for one of the most successful. 'Smile, Smile, Smile! (Pack Up Your Troubles in Your Old Kit Bag)' was written by Felix Lloyd (music) and George Powell (lyrics). They had entered the piece in a contest for a marching song for troops, and to their astonishment it won. It was published in 1915 and translated into several languages, including German, becoming a huge hit. Felix Powell became a Staff Sergeant and toured with his song, but gradually realised his uplifting music was encouraging thousands of young lads to their deaths. He suffered a breakdown in the trenches, eventually taking his own life in 1942, during another world war he had thought would never occur.[33]

Also doing its bit for the war effort was the Albert Hall, which hosted a Grand Evening Concert given by blind musicians accompanying the Swansea and District Male Voice Choir, a programme in aid of blinded soldiers and sailors.[34] Nearby, at the Grand Theatre, a cast of sixty took to the stage for the production of *Sealed Orders* with the main scene being a ball danced on the deck of a battleship.[35] Show-stopping productions increased, in line with the carnage.

A letter appeared in the press posted from 'Somewhere in France from One of the Men'. The writer reported that his battalion had been making the most of a short respite before returning to the trenches and had formed the Swansea Battalion Minstrels, to 'get a little enjoyment after our perilous stay in the lines'. On the evening of 28 February they were bombarded by 'whiz bangs, rifles, grenades and trench mortar bombs, which did a lot of damage to the dugouts, but no lives lost'. He said the Minstrels were a 'recognised combination' and their divisional recreation room was packed for the show. Major Dyson Williams was at the piano to accompany the variety show. Amongst the turns was a 'large troupe and chorus, and Lance-Corporal Thomas and Sgt Stephens did a Ragtime Duet "The Barber's Ball", followed by Corporal Gwynne who sang "A Nigger's Love"'. General Philipps addressed the gathering, saying 'how pleased and proud he was with the work of the Welsh Division both in and out of combat'. The packed show concluded with the national anthem. The letter's by-line was 'By One Of The Men'.[36]

While ragtime was being performed on the battlefield, in the trenches and the billets, Professor Payne and his Leading American Ragtime Orchestra enjoyed a week's residency at Swansea's Mackworth

Hotel. A specially constructed stage had to be erected in the well of the grand staircase to accommodate the orchestra. The week was described as 'the last word in syncopation'.[37]

A week later, as if to fuel the need for consolation during increasingly bad news from the front, another huge production was set for the Empire, this time *Watch Your Step*, with a cast of eighty-five and a twenty-five-piece augmented orchestra directed by Jackson (later Jack) Hylton, who would go on to become a popular mainstay on the wireless. *Watch Your Step* was the first musical by 26-year-old Irving Berlin, the composer of 'Alexander's Ragtime Band' and 'Everybody's Doin' It'. The *Watch Your Step* score was 'all ragtime' and the original American cast featured dancers Vernon and Irene Castle, the latest dance duo phenomenon and inspiration for Ginger Rogers and Fred Astaire. This Wales tour featured the 'Champion American Trap Drummer' Hughes Pollard from Chicago, also known as 'Black Lightning'. In this production, 'new songs and tricky dances were showcased by Kitty Curtis, Dorothy Levy and the Lottie Stone Troupe of sixteen'. *Watch Your Step* was revived in 2000 under the American Classics banner at the Longy School of Music in Cambridge, Massachusetts. There is no doubt that Wales was served the very best in music and dance during those early years of the First World War.[38]

An *All Women Revue* toured the south Wales stages during the summer of 1916. It is apparent that, owing to increasing numbers of men required for military duties, women were quick to spot job opportunities as entrepreneurs, producers, directors, musicians, stage hands and designers. The original ad for the *All Woman Revue* featured a photograph of the stars Beattie and Babs, described as a talented pair whether singing, dancing or engaging in 'tomboy frolics'. The revue, which featured 'artistic stage pictures', was intended to show how women can 'keep the home fires burning'. The press reported that there had been

> much speculation in Swansea as to whether an *All Woman Revue* would prove successful, but all doubt was dispelled on Monday evening

when the production was an instant and pronounced success, winning the hearty approbation of the crowded audiences at both performances. Not a dull moment, thanks largely to Beattie and Babs, the youthful stars whose mimicry, singing and dancing were simply 'great'.

The cast of the *All Woman Revue* also included a platoon of the Women's War Work Emergency Corps, which undertook the work of men in various capacities – munitions workers, policemen, dustmen, painters, carpenters and gardeners. The show also featured Grace Vicat, Audrey Stafford, Lucy Clements, Frankie Carlos, Mona Magnet and Violet Essex, the 'charming soprano' from the Royal Opera House. Again, a war didn't dilute the level of high talent delivered in these popular productions.[39] Another successful touring production at the Empire was *The High Explosives Revue*, which included 'much capital dancing including the Mexican dance and the Japanese Foxtrot. This Show Goes With A Bang', reported the press.[40]

Women were taking the bull by the horns. *The Kodak Girl* was another all-woman touring production at the Empire with a company of forty, while over at the Grand Theatre a comedy drama called *Woman Power* was advertised as the first comedy drama ever written 'without a man character in it'. The review pronounced it 'a daring innovation for this all lady production company . . . girls exceptionally clever and capital staging'. *Woman Power* was again supported by the Women's War Work Emergency Corps.[41] Audiences flocked to these productions not only to forget their troubles, but also to feel they were supporting the war effort.

During Easter weekend 1917, Swansea's Victoria Park hosted a Monster War Fund Carnival, with the Bonymaen Minstrel Troupe, wire-walkers, roundabouts and a boxing tournament. A young lad billed as 'Master Willie' appeared, depicting the new young star of silent film, Charlie Chaplin. Lil Griffiths, May Price and Amy Loxton provided the music, together with the Swansea Banjo and Mandolin Band. This was the first mention in the press of May Price and Amy Loxton, both later becoming pioneers of early jazz music in Wales, Price in particular being

Ragtime Trenches and Suffragettes ❋ 143

Figure 14: 'Munition Girls Concert Party' advertisement, 1917
(SWW Media)

involved in productions for Swansea café society (see chapter 6).[42] In May 1917 Swansea was given special praise by the government for its wartime enterprises, in which the Women's Auxiliary Army had taken a leading part. The summer had seen a profusion of carnivals and fetes, all to raise funds for the Welsh prisoners of war in Germany, or the Swansea munition girls' hostel.

Discharged war-wounded took to the stage of the Empire for a *Lads of the Village Revue*. The show included a full company of fifty, including showgirls as Maids of the Village in ten novel battle scenes, described as a 'comedy with tremendous swing and racy plot from Salisbury Plain to the Submarine Attack'. Evelyn Parker was on piano with instrumentalists the Rowe Sisters. There were three holders of the DCM (Distinguished

Figure 15: 'Thanks', Royal Theatre advertisement, 1918 (SWW Media)

Conduct Medal) in the cast. A wounded Sergeant Carlsbrook paid tribute to Swansea's artistes, writing that 'this show was the finest he has ever heard', seconded by Corporal Bowen, who added that 'he was proud to be in the Brynmill Red Cross Hospital in his town after being out in France'.[43]

Women did not only risk their lives working in munitions. Pioneers and stalwart Welsh women such as Miss Lena Ashwell risked theirs taking Welsh concert parties' touring shows out to the front line. Lena Ashwell described her enterprise as 'a gift from Wales'. She took with her Megan Foster, Winifred Clark, Thelma Bentwich, Olive Davies, Auriol Jones, Patric Playfair, David Brazille and Emily Pickford. That Ashwell's troupe survived to tour for four years was remarkable, with a tragedy occurring only after the war was over, in 1919. Emily Pickford, a 'well respected teacher of music and tireless worker for charitable causes', was with the troupe of seven who had put on a concert at Guoy, France. In February 1919, the car Pickford was travelling in with baritone Frederick Taylor slid on the icy towpath of the river Somme and entered the water. They both drowned and are buried alongside each other in Abbeville communal extension cemetery.[44]

That summer of 1917, over 100,000 people were carried on the trams during August bank holiday, with 15,000 attending the Swansea Fete and Gala. Huge audiences enjoyed the *All Khaki Concert* with 'first class musical attainment' at the Albert Hall by the 4th King's Shropshire Light Infantry, with Ben Evans Stores supplying the bunting and Brader's Musical Emporium the piano.[45] The London Hippodrome's 'Beauty Chorus' of sixty, featuring Edna Morgan, Marjorie Ford and Betty Green, kicked their way to glory on the Empire stage for the revue *Razzle Dazzle*, with the 'added attraction of a tank on stage recently returned from the front'. There was consternation amongst variety acts that the revue format would kick them out of business, but not yet . . . variety still had a way to go.[46]

Swansea was indeed keeping its end up. 'All Khaki' concerts were popular with the visiting military, and the cinemas reflected popular public taste with films such as *Munition Girl's Romance* and other melodramas. It is also a fact that despite the real-life carnage suffered abroad and the impact it was having on Welsh families, huge audiences were still attracted to the cinemas to see such bloodthirsty fare as a 'Two Hour Programme of Disaster Movies' featuring 'Foxhunting, Blood Tingling Auto Disasters, Auto and Train Races and Terrible Rail Wrecks!'[47]

News on the war front was slightly better by the end of November 1917, when the Hindenburg Line was smashed and a 'Glorious British Victory by the Third Army' was reported, with thousands taken prisoner. To cheer everyone up at Christmas the Empire showcased *Joyland*, featuring the talents of Isobel Scott and Eric Marshall plus a full chorus of sixty Joybelles; gowns were described as 'chic confections'.[48] These big productions provided increasing dancer opportunities, with recruitment focused on the working classes to supply the demand; the pay equalled that of textile workers.[49]

In January 1918 some women had won the vote, with the press stating that about six million women would be placed on the Parliamentary Register, and that five million 'who have not hitherto exercised the municipal vote will enjoy that privilege and responsibility'.[50] The Empire did record business for its next big touring production *Flying Colours*, as it featured the popular troupe of lady drummers from the London Hippodrome Revue, plus the now obligatory chorus of sixty high-kickers, starring Cress and Leonard, Cora Engleton, and Ethel Martel.[51]

During the summer of 1918, women's dominance on the stage and bandstand was unassailable, developing, rehearsing and delivering their own productions as well as supplying the music. Trippers flocked on to the Mumbles Pier to hear the ragtime performers in small concert party revues. Florence Davey, on piano, ran the 'Gypsies' Concert Party' in the Pier Pavilion; then Betty Laurie the ragtime pianist performed on the Pier, followed by another pianist Alice Branson in the 'Controllers' Concert Party', then Cissie Jackson playing for the 'Utopians Concert Party'. The availability of cheap pianos to the Welsh working class, coupled with the profusion of cheap sheet music, was another significant

Figure 16: Record sleeve for Snell and Sons, established 1900
(Jazz Heritage Wales Record Collection)

factor, offering new career opportunities for women and possible introductions into the new genre of black popular music. Loesser states that piano production in Britain escalated from 25,000 in 1851 to 75,000 in 1910, an increase of 200 per cent. As this was a product well adapted to the new factory production methods, the cost to the purchaser was reduced. Loesser also points out that during the early 1800s, Longman and Broderip, piano dealers, were already in the second-hand piano business, enabling the piano to eventually 'lose its badge of gentility . . . becoming pianos for the people'. Piano playing for women escalated from being a domestic accomplishment, blossoming into a means of employment.[52]

The Welsh certainly took advantage of the new hire purchase credit agreements, which led to a profusion of pianos in the parlour. New 'Art Model' pianos and organs could be purchased for 10s. 6d per month from establishments such as the Western Piano Co. catalogue, or from the South Wales Musical Repository. Harding confirms that the piano was a 'respectable accomplishment' for women, which led, in turn, to a respectable career.[53] Bourke points out that the First World War pushed working-class households into a higher income bracket, with many women choosing to remain in employment after the war. Bourke cites the average working-class weekly income as £1 1s. to £1 10s. 'Goods representing status could also be the focus of intense competition . . . The piano and (by the 1920s) the radio, were other objects around which competition flourished.'[54] Women from south Wales were taking advantage of these new opportunities not only to earn a wage packet, but for cultural fulfilment.

Nearing the end of 1918, the hint of peace was in the air mixing with the tang of salt water and seaweed on the Mumbles Pier boardwalk.[55] Articles in the press were daring to suggest that perhaps the war would be over soon. By 22 October 1918 the press reported a conditional surrender, and on 11 November 1918 the Armistice between the Allies and Germany was signed. Press reports headlined 'HEROES ALL' and 'LOCAL LADS WHO HELPED MAKE HISTORY' covered the pages, although local lasses were not mentioned at all. The 'World's Greatest War' was at an end.[56]

Wales erupted. There were 'Parades of Joy and Striking Processions'. In Swansea the police band marched down through the beflagged streets from the Central Police Station playing American airs, followed by the Salvation Army Band, the St Joseph's Band, and the Post Office Band, all converging on St Mary's Church, which was filled to overflowing. Children discharged crackers and fireworks in public thoroughfares without hindrance. The night streets were crowded, and 'bands of revellers made merry with squibs, rockets and the singing of popular airs'. They were described as exuberant but restrained, as decreed by the mayor's request earlier in the day. Briton Ferry's town band marched with hundreds of children carrying flags. In Carmarthen, church bells rang, and the blasting of works' hooters had to be suspended owing to the racket. Wounded soldiers carrying flags, headed by the Salvation

Army Band, also paraded. Neath, gaily decorated with bunting, sirens sounding and bells ringing, gave schoolchildren the day off. Women and children marched with banners, singing patriotic songs. In Port Talbot and Aberavon the press reported everyone 'agog with excitement. Hooters and guns were let off with deafening result.' The Theatre Royal in Swansea placed a large ad in the press thanking its patrons for their support during the war years.[57]

Throughout 1918 those women not involved with war work continued to keep the south Wales bandstands filled, the dance floors crowded and morale running high. Let us not forget Lena Ashwell who had taken bands to France to entertain the troops, who survived and returned to encourage dancing classes in convalescent camps to help repair the shell-shocked. We should also remember Doris Page, May Price, Gretta John and Laurie Melville, who became producers and directors of café floor shows during the war (see chapter 6), 'the best for popular taste, fashion and music'. Miss Gweneth Williams and her Jazz Orchestra performed for the dependants of fallen soldiers and sailors. Madame Allport (an eyebrow- raiser of a name), with Mabel Thomas on ragtime piano, got the naval base men step-dancing to ragtime and nautical numbers at the Exchange Restaurant, supported by a large cast of women. Homecoming Tommies (soldiers) and Jacks (sailors) made a beeline to the Mackworth Café for the twice-daily vaudeville show *The Rip Van Winkle Burlesque Revue*.[58]

Into this razzle-dazzle of noise, flags, bunting and music sailed the US fleet of over fifty submarine chasers towing a captured U-boat, U-91, for a ten-day visit. U-91 was credited with having sunk the USS *President Lincoln* on 31 May 1918 (although official sites credit U-boat U-90), and other Allied first-class shipping, and now carried the captured six German officers and twenty-seven men. On-board tours of the submarine cost the local sightseers 6d. The US fleet personnel decamped to Swansea town for the delights of its noisy cafés and nightlife of jazz, burlesque and revue. Theatre shows featured nautical revues, 'bathing beauties', 'flighty flappers' and showgirls referred to as 'smart things'. There was even a *Christmas Burlesque Panto*, which sadly was not reviewed; it would have been enlightening to discover what the Americans thought of cross-dressing and slapstick.[59]

Also returning safely home to New York were the Harlem Hellfighters. Lieutenant Jim Europe was the leader of the 369th Infantry Hellfighters Band, introducing the sounds of American ragtime to Europeans during the First World War:

> Jim Europe had established the New York's Clef Club in 1910, the club also acting as a booking agency and a trade union for black performers . . . Noble Sissle (songwriting partner of Eubie Blake) and Jim Europe had enlisted in the army together and organised a regimental band, accompanying the acclaimed 369 Infantry Regiment, the first American unit to arrive in France . . . The brave black unit, including the band, earned the nickname 'Hellfighters' for its participation in several vital military campaigns. Returning home after the war, Europe led his Hellfighters in the first parade of returning war heroes with a million fans cheering them up New York's Fifth Avenue to Harlem. Europe and Sissle had written *On Patrol in No Man's Land* which became a favourite among US veterans.[60]

For those Americans sailing into port that December day in 1918, Swansea town, with its sophisticated shows and latest music and dances, must have compared well with New York's Broadway and London's Soho. Music that was being heard in smart London supper clubs and cafés arrived in Wales within weeks. But most surprising of all was the new south Wales café culture that had emerged during the war, a café society fuelled by the rivalry between Swansea and Cardiff to provide the best floor shows, the best bands, the best dancing and fashions, the best interior designs and awnings, all run by women, who produced, directed and performed (see chapter 6). The cafés, sometimes offering free buns with a cup of tea, became a support network for bereaved women, encouraging them to come in with babes in arms and children to relax, take a couple of hours off from worrying and fretting about their husbands and sons in the trenches, and listen to the music. That some of

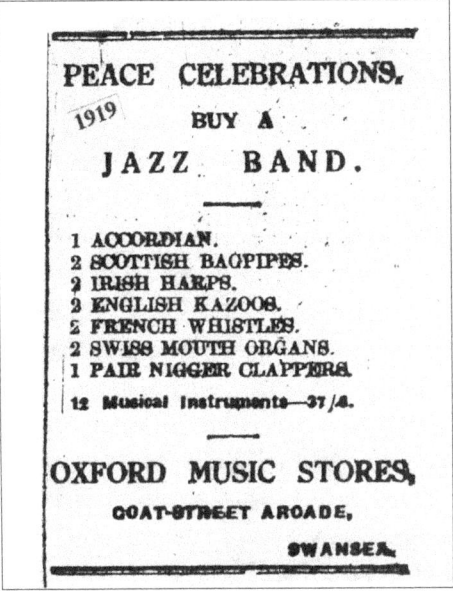

Figure 17: 'Buy A Jazz Band' advertisement, 1919
(SWW Media)

the music was produced and performed by African Americans was not a surprise, but a given.

The word 'jazz' made its first appearance in print in the south Wales press on 15 February 1919.[61] It was perceived as being part syncopation and part dance music, 'thus the word "jazz" was initially a vague, all-embracing term for current syncopated dance music in Britain, as were "cakewalk", "foxtrot" and "ragtime" before it'.[62] Brass and wind instruments, such as trumpets, trombones and saxophones became embedded within the jazz combo or band, with violins and cellos gradually losing appeal. Percussionists and drummers extended their repertoire with the new additions of tom-toms, wood blocks, cymbals and a large bass drum, usually decorated or painted.

Peace celebrations continued well into 1919. There were Victory balls, The Zig Zag Revue with a chorus of fifty, 'JAZZ – JAZZ – JAZZ' dancing lessons, and a VAD (Voluntary Aid Detachment) nurses' dance at the Albert Hall. A masked ball for 400 on the Mumbles Pier included wounded men, with music supplied by Mrs Williams and her Orchestra, which included three discharged soldiers; Mrs Williams would go on to lead jazz and augmented orchestras throughout the 1920s. The Grand Theatre put on the revue Luck of the Navy, with the Theatre Royal competing with another similar show, Over The Top. A Swansea Peace Day was advertised to take place in all the parks, with marching bands. Victoria Park held its own Monster Peace Fete, and sixteen bands took part in a competition. The Mayor's Procession held in November 1919 required an extended route, owing to the number of bands that wanted to play: the Discharged and Demobbed Soldiers and Sailors Band, the Tramways Band, Salvation Army Band, Telegraph Messengers Band, St Joseph's Brass Band and the Police Band. The two big Christmas shows for 1919 didn't have to worry about competition for audience attendances; both shows were packed out for weeks. Swansea, which also drew its audiences from the Swansea, Neath, Dulais and Garw valleys, had never seen anything like it. The Grand Theatre featured the astonishing production The Female Hun Revue, with scenes that included 'High Speed Aeroplanes, Submarines, and an Escape from a German POW Camp'. Over at the Empire, the Oh Joy! Revue excelled in musical numbers and was 'full of vigour on the feminine side' with several numbers having to be repeated to feed the insatiable appetites of the audiences.[63]

The last word on the First World War goes to Betsy Arnold, aged 104. Betsy 'danced gaily' around the Verdun oak tree, which had been planted by the Mayor of Abergavenny at Bryngwyn. Betsy said she had given up smoking when she was 100, and didn't know quite how old she was, as she was born at a time when the registering of births was not the rule. Betsy has now been retrieved from obscurity. Dance on, Betsy![64]

Chapter Six

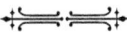

Café Society: The Jazz Age

A CAFÉ SOCIETY, MUSIC-LED, flourished in south Wales during the First World War, a creative surge fuelled by a reinterpretation of the African American music that had left a legacy in Wales. Café society eventually faded away when the era of the big bands took over the stages and ballrooms during the 1930s.

The café society movement emerged during an uneasy period of rumours of war and a preparation for the implementation of the machinery of war that scooped up young men from towns and valleys and deposited them in trenches across an unfamiliar Europe. Williams examines the fascinating transatlantic discussions that took place between the African American Langston Hughes writing for 'the low down folk', and Welshman Idris Davies writing for 'the folk in South Wales . . . who have never heard of NEW VERSE and literary cliques'. Williams identifies a two-way process of discovery between the Welsh and African Americans. Citing Paul Robeson writing of his experiences in south Wales, and Ralph Ellison tracing his wartime experiences as a GI in Swansea, Williams discusses 'mutual constructions of African American and Welsh identities'.[1] Williams points out the transformation of Wales by

1911 owing to mass population movement into the south Wales coalfields, and compares this movement with African Americans moving from a rural workplace to city employment. Williams discusses the 'notion that racial uplift could be achieved through cultural accomplishment'.[2]

The African American writer W. E. B. Du Bois had set out new ideas on music as early as 1903, in *The Souls of Black Folk*, influencing debate by the next generation of cultural and political activists. Stuart Hall, writing in the *Guardian*, said 'Du Bois is remembered for his single-minded commitment to racial justice and his capacity to shape black consciousness'. Hall quotes Du Bois's biographer, David Levering Lewis, describing *The Souls of Black Folk* as 'like a firework going off in a cemetery'.[3] Du Bois had written:

> I turn from these well-tended acres with a comfortable feeling that the Negro is rising . . . They that walked in darkness sang songs in the olden days – Sorrow Songs – for they were weary at heart. Ever since I was a child these songs have stirred me strangely . . . yet at once I knew them as of me and of mine.[4]

Contributors to what would later become known as the Harlem Renaissance movement picked apart the class system within which the black people's movement operated. Vincent argues that jazz and its related musics were an early form of American patriotism fighting for a voice against European fascism; African Americans were promoting early forms of jazz as a dignified music. An example is Black Swan Records, founded in Harlem in 1921, long before white historians and collectors arrived on the scene in the early 1930s to document the music and claim it for posterity.[5] John Lomax, fieldworker, folklorist and ethnomusicologist, archivist, writer and son of folklorist and collector John A. Lomax, documented songs and interviews for the Archive of American Folk Song at the Library of Congress, Washington DC (see chapter 8).

Swansea's café society appeared to be an amalgam of the Welsh working class embracing aspects of an African American cultural force, from which the Welsh communities adapted music and dance for their

Figure 18: 'Jazz it' advertisement, 1922 (SWW Media)

own enlightenment, presenting it remade for their eager audiences. The instability of wartime created seeds of opportunity for young entrepreneurs to grab a chance and make a statement. In order to have organised floor shows twice a day for years, Swansea's cultural aesthetes would have employed writers, directors, producers, musicians, dancers, administrators, promoters and volunteers, who were predominantly women during the war years. There was a burgeoning of a new cultural awareness, a café identity that surprised even the Welsh press when it realised how popular the cafés were and the enthusiasm with which they were embraced by the general public in such troubled times. Wales was and is a cultural nation, or, as Dylan Thomas satirically wrote in *Under Milk Wood*, 'Praise the Lord, we are a musical nation.'[6]

The cafés of south Wales contributed greatly to an awakening of youthful vitality, verve, entrepreneurship and what we would refer to these days as the 'cultural industries'. Thomas was very familiar with Swansea cafés and the Kardomah in particular. The Kardomah Exhibition Salon opened its doors in Castle Street, Swansea, in August 1914. Dylan Thomas was born a few weeks later, and as a teenager in the 1930s was a frequent user of the Kardomah, together with his pals, the 'Kardomah Boys': poets Vernon Watkins, Charlie Fisher and John Pritchard, painters Mervyn Levy, Alfred Janes, Tom Warner and Mabley Owen, and occasional frequenter the composer Dan Jones, who was at university.[7] They discussed philosophers, composers, writers, poets, film stars, death, religion and girls. However, Swansea cafés had an earlier claim to fame, which has been undocumented, the café society that heralded the birth of the first jazz age.

The Kardomah Exhibition Salon opened with great fanfare, encouraging 'ladies' into its new tea rooms on the first floor with 'luxurious comfort and pleasing decorations for their daily meetings and opportunities to enjoy the delicious tea and coffee'.[8] Beddoe points out that Welsh women were beginning to demand more control of their lives, property and economic independence, as well as campaigning for the vote. The Kardomah recognised this, paying special attention to encouraging women to come inside and use the premises for their meetings. Political groups such as the Women's Freedom League, Votes for Women and suffragettes would have been attracted to this convivial new meeting space.[9]

Café society was to expand quickly, and rather surprisingly, during the early war years. Not only did cafés present a convivial meeting place for women, but they also offered new work opportunities for local musicians, dancers and entrepreneurs. Another innovation was the occasional hiring of small combos of African Americans from the larger theatre touring productions and revues, who were eager to take an extra afternoon gig before their main evening performances on the national theatre circuit tour. In Swansea alone, twelve cafés opened, with some offering shows and revues twice daily; the smallest café catered for 400 people, the largest for over 1,000; for example, the Carlton Café with its American Bar 'n Grill and Floorshow was a big attraction. Cafés such as the Chantant, the Continental, the Baltic Lounge, the Metropole Winter Gardens, the Exchange and the Mumbles Pier Pavilion were employers of musicians and performers on a grand scale. The other most important aspect for women of this burgeoning café culture was that it was free and accessible during the daytime. Cafés were initially alcohol free and welcomed mothers with children and babes in arms.

In September 1915 the local paper carried a news item 'Café Life', stating, with some surprise:

> Who would have predicted that Swansea would ever be a café town? It is extremely doubtful whether there is a provincial town so bountifully equipped and so well patronised as ours. The new Café Chantant of the Mackworth Hotel in High Street seats 1000 people. There will be a regular orchestra and musical programme, fully licensed and all round catering.[10]

It should not have been a surprise. Why not? Swansea had something with which London could not compete: five miles of golden sands and the sea. South Wales was a magnet for the workers from heavy industry and their families to come and enjoy themselves, that is those workers who had not been scooped up as cannon fodder. The local press said 'Swansea needed to laugh and there was a War Workers' need for leisure, with some foreign restaurants accused of not uplifting the morale of the people.'[11] This unfair insult regarding 'foreign restaurants' was not elaborated on, but Italian cafés and ice-cream parlours may have been in the press's firing line. For example, the Cascarini family were one of many Italian families running cafés and ice-cream parlours in Wales from the early 1900s. Joe, the Cascarinis' eldest son, is immortalised today in Joe's Ice Cream Parlour in Swansea, with its famed Knickerbocker Glory a required part of the tourist experience.[12]

The local entrepreneurs R. E. Jones Ltd (the Tea Shop Kings) certainly did their bit for uplifting the morale of the people. They were owners of several local cafés and businesses, and offered 'Musical Teas' from 5 p.m. to 6 p.m. as the latest innovation, sometimes with free cake or buns. R. E. Jones Ltd later went on to open catering establishments and hotels in London.[13]

Cafés competed for the best in art deco scenic designs and effects, with some cafés sporting striped awnings stretching over the pavements, emulating the finest establishments in New York or London. Competition was rife between Cardiff and Swansea for the very best in the latest innovations. Cardiff had been made a city in 1905, while Swansea's city status was not awarded until 1969; Swansea always felt the need to show its mettle as the underdog.

The Carlton Café with its American Bar 'n Grill was particularly good at advertising its shows with regular cartoons published in the local press as well as the usual written ads.[14] However, good as the cartoons were for bringing in the crowds, we would now find the depiction of the African Americans on the bill to be derogatory caricatures with exaggerated features and minstrelsy make-up. In October 1915 the Continental Café, not to be outdone by the Carlton Café, offered a £10 prize (a considerable amount of money at the time) for the best impersonation of 'Mabel Normand and Charlie Chaplain' (*sic*). The Continental also advertised its floor show with the cartoon 'Ye Old Blackamoors Minstrels and Augmented Orchestra', white performers in blackface.[15]

Figure 19: Advertisement cartoon, 'At Carlton Café', 1915
(SWW Media)

Shortly afterwards, in February 1916, Professor Payne and the American Leading Ragtime Orchestra, the 'last word in syncopation', had a week's residency at the Continental, headlined 'Ragtime Week'. The Carlton, with a sideways glance at this innovative competition, erected a specially constructed stage in the well of its grand staircase, giving its shows some extra pomp;[16] the beneficiaries of this rivalry were, of course, the patrons, mostly women during those war years.

The Café Chantant hosted Sybil Jones and the Pocket Pierrots, featuring her 'Teddy Bear Song'.[17] Also appearing with the Pocket Pierrots was Freddie Warner, performing the 'Michigan – a delightful dance'. Freddie Warner, aged 11, was the son of Larry Warner, a song-and-dance man, charity worker, entrepreneur, 'coon impersonator', manager of Clydach's Globe Theatre and stage manager at Swansea's Palace Theatre.[18] The Warner family's enterprising charitable endeavours meant they were able to send regular parcels to wounded military personnel overseas. Freddie was known as the 'Animated Spark', one of his featured numbers being 'Night Time Down in Dixie', probably Irving Berlin's 1914 hit 'When It's Night Time in Dixieland'. Songs about Dixie were popular, especially so with the visiting American military coming off Swansea docks and heading for the town's entertainment hotspots. 'Singing Dixie' is described by Mullen as the 'Old South being depicted in nostalgic voice, conjuring up a warm rural paradise of Kentucky, Tennessee and other places'. The Old South was as distant to audiences as the war going on in the trenches. Mullen makes the point that 'the singer . . . invites the audience to imagine themselves as White people from the South, not as Black people', as presumably did Freddie Warner when he sang the following:

> *Chorus*
> Night time down in Dixieland
> Darkies strolling hand in hand
> Southern melodies
> Floating on the breeze
> Let me tell you it's grand
> For when you
> Hear those darkies harmonize
> Tears of gladness fill your eyes
> Baritones and Basses
> Lounging round the places
> Dixieland embraces the happiest of races
> All you see is smiling faces
> When it's night time in Dixieland.[19]

These types of lyrics generally reflected the attitudes of the composers of the time. The family of composer Irving Berlin (1888–1989), one of eight children, had fled the Russian anti-Jewish pogroms and settled in

New York in 1893. Berlin's music has become part of the Great American Songbook, but he was probably writing lyrics such as these as survival tactics in his early days on the streets of New York 'working as a busker singing for pennies',[20] possibly failing to recognise, or deciding to ignore, the current derogatory and racist language to earn a quick buck, when no doubt he was experiencing a Jewish backlash of his own. The gradations of the social and political realities of the circumstances of the African Americans portrayed in songs such as these would probably have been lost on Welsh audiences enjoying the local youngster, Freddie Warner, singing in blackface and dancing ragtime steps. It is easy to make assumptions about audiences' interpretations of the genre as, generally speaking, the working classes rarely left their impressions in print, neither were they sought. We therefore have to rely on the press for audience response, and Freddie Warner was very popular. He grew up to find fame as a drummer in the Bernard Ash Capital Dance Band, touring the UK, and performed the Charleston at the Patti Pavilion in 1926.[21]

All this activity, together with the latest in ragtime music and increasingly sophisticated floor shows, boosted competition between the cafés, thereby increasing work opportunities for musicians. R. E. Jones's musical teas were hugely popular: 'We have had matinées galore but to have tea while a performer is in full swing is a pleasant novelty . . . adults flock in ever increasing numbers to their burlesque revues . . . the musical tea fits the bill.'[22]

Burlesque, the latest innovation from America, had originated in the late 1890s, a combination of ragtime music, minstrelsy, dance, leg show and comedic numbers. Cullen writes that burlesque derived from the vaudevillian tradition of 'people's culture . . . variety arts have been expressions of religion, community ritual, politics and casual entertainment'. Burlesque was where women wielded the power, with innovative pioneers such as May Howard, who was touring her own production company from as early as 1888. By 1914 there were nearly eighty burlesque touring productions in the USA. Some burlesque shows also offered areas of exposed female flesh, for which higher ticket prices were charged.[23] That south Wales café society should offer a rather risqué melange of music, dance, leg shows, sketches and news items, usually satirising political or contemporary figures, was indeed unexpected and surprising. Not only that, it was south Wales's own distinct version of a burlesque show and would have included local and topical items. Sadly, detailed descriptions of performance are scant in the press. However, there cannot have been much bared female flesh on show in the afternoons, presumably just the odd ankle or calf, as it would have caused a huge scandal making headline news, and there were no instances of outrage reported in the press. The other reason that the cafés were pulling in the crowds was, of course, free entry.

Outside the cafés, the war raged on. The extent of the carnage was kept to a minimum in the local press, but occasionally reports would surface, such as: 'two hundred and fifty wounded soldiers were entertained at the Metropole Winter Gardens by the RAOB (Buffs), the Royal Antediluvian Order of Buffaloes, a charitable and philanthropic organisation'. The huge numbers of café patrons, predominantly women and children, were continually added to by wounded military and those lucky enough to be on leave unscathed.[24]

The cafés had to look to their laurels with their decor and presentations, regularly bringing their establishments up to date, owing to the competition of big theatre productions coming through on the touring circuit. In one week in Swansea, the Empire Theatre featured *The Kodak Girl* with a company of forty, while at the same time the Grand Theatre staged *Woman Power*, a 'Daring Innovation with not a man in sight'. These shows were followed shortly afterwards by another theatre production, Fred Karno's 'All Women' *Five Temperaments* show, supported by the Women's Emergency Corps, founded in 1914 to contribute to the war effort and later evolving into the Women's Volunteer Reserve. All these shows were packed out. By May 1917, the local press were gloating that Swansea had been 'praised in Government circles for its wartime enterprise'.[25] But whatever the competition, the cafés survived and prospered, making enough profit on teas and cakes to maintain free admission to showtime.

In the summer of 1917, at the height of the war, the cafés were a noisy, intercultural blast of talent and innovation. They had to be, owing to ferocious competition. The crowds, still mostly women, sought solace and companionship amongst others with similar heartaches suffering the anguish of dead or missing menfolk. No doubt conversations were questioning how they would be able to bring up their families on their own. As well as providing top-class entertainment, the cafés provided a safe environment and an arm around the shoulder, a place to seek help and support when needed.[26] Providing positive distraction, café floor shows vied to be the best. A headline declared: 'What talent at the Continental – a futurist Music Hall show. Beats all London shows to a Frazzle, vim and éclat of the entertainment, full to overflowing.'[27]

On the same day at the Empire Theatre, the London Hippodrome's 'Beauty Chorus' of sixty staged a show called *Razzle Dazzle*, the 'finest revue starring Edna Morgan, Marjorie Ford, and Betty Green'. That the cafés were able to fill all their hundreds of tables, when big touring productions like this example were on at the same time at the major theatres, confirms the café talent on offer, albeit there still being no cover charge.

The cafés had been flourishing for almost two years. Women were now beginning to make their mark as producers, directors and performers at the floor shows. Swansea locals Gretta John, May Price and Doris Page were frequently mentioned, sometimes in rival shows, or sometimes working together. Doris Page and Laura Emm's 'unique talent' got special mention at the Continental as Jack and Jill from the Munition Works, singing 'sixty songs from *Girl of the Golden West*, a record number of songs for a revue'. *Girl of the Golden West* was a 1915 American silent film, a Western, directed by Cecil B. DeMille, based on a 1905 play about the American Gold Rush. Doris Page and Laura Emm's production with sixty songs must have been home-grown, as the film was 'silent' and the original play did not have music; further, munition workers would not have appeared in the original 1905 play. So for Page and Emm to have produced sixty songs on a contemporary theme, together with rehearsing the musicians, was professionalism of the highest order.[28]

A few weeks later the Continental was hosting talent contests with prizes, accompanied by the usual 'Swinging Choruses and Merry Abandon'.[29] The talent contests were shortly followed by a theatrical and cultural coup. The hot floor show that week at the Continental was Harrie Coonie – 'The Coloured Kid from the show *Way Down South*' – again showcasing those Southern images of a stylised plantation life, as previously sung by the eleven-year-old Swansea boy Freddie Warner in blackface. Now here was the genuine article. Coonie was described as the 'Sensational Coon Dancer and Singer', a 'clever exponent of Plantation Style dancing'. At the time, 'coon' was the usual vernacular for describing a Negro or African American, which we would find an insulting or derogatory word today. However, performers would include 'coon' in their advertising literature as a popular and familiar enticement for the audience's benefit, the performers knowing this ploy would increase audience numbers. Coonie danced with 'lightning-like rapidity, his arms and legs spiralling like a windmill'. Original plantation- style dancing would have been just voice and percussion, provided by hands and feet, with maybe a washboard, sandbox, bones (usually turkey), tambourine or a home-made instrument. Harrie Coonie would probably have been accompanied by a small ragtime combo, although the band was not mentioned. Crowds duly flocked in. Harrie Coonie was subsequently called up to the US army for the duration of the war.[30]

There were full houses again a month later at the Continental for their *Potted Revues*, featuring Doris Page with Griff and Maurice.[31] Then the Continental came up with something new, a seance, with 'Wonder Woman' Mlle Aazelia. It was reported that crowds flocked to the seance, a confirmation of the anguish suffered by those with missing or dead loved ones. To conclude the Continental's very successful year, they put on *Aladdin* and allowed patrons in to witness rehearsals; 'a daring in-novation' said the press. The American Jackies (Jack Tars, sailors) declared the Continental had a 'bully cabaret', although there was no mention of what the Americans thought of a panto with cross-dressing and innuendo. However, it broke records for business.[32]

The new year of 1918 had the Continental Café showcasing their new revue, this time something really daring, the 'Continental Burlesque Revue with Saucy Flappers' in *The Girl from Ciro's*.[33] Brooks has examined the life and times of Ciro's, the smart London supper club that opened in 1915 in Orange Street near Leicester Square, whose clientele included socialites and the military flocking to see 'coloured' musicians and dancers. Ciro's is described as being decorated in:

> Louis XVI style with a sliding roof and a dance floor on springs that could be tightened or loosened as needed. The premises also included a gallery and a grill room. It was operated basically as a private club for the upper crust, who were not about to let wartime stringencies get in the way of having a night on the town.[34]

With that level of investment spent on it, together with licensed bars, Ciro's was a far cry from the south Wales cafés that catered for the working classes with tea and buns. Nevertheless, the south Wales cafés did a sterling job by keeping up with the latest in art deco design and hiring the best of professional entertainers.

The resident band at the London Ciro's with a year's contract was pianist Dan Kildare and his Clef Club Orchestra from New York, a seven-piece which included his brother Walter on cello, Seth Jones, Joseph Meyers and George Watters, all on banjos, Louis Mitchell on drums and vocal, and John Ricks on double bass. Kildare had been one of the first African American bandleaders to secure a residency in the UK, which obviously was a spur for others to follow. Ciro's was renowned for its African American ragtime musicians, who offered a dash of decadence for its racy clientele.[35] This band also made some early recordings: 'Oh! How She Could Yacki, Wicki, Wacki, Woo', 'Where Did Robinson Crusoe Go with Friday on Saturday Night?' and W. C. Handy's 'St Louis Blues'. Did the Seven Spades Syncopated Band appear at the Continental Café to accompany *The Girl from Ciro's* floor show? Unfortunately, there was no mention of the band in the press, but we can assume they did accompany the show, as *The Girl from Ciro's* was on a national tour.[36]

In March 1918, the Continental erected a new awning over its pavement with '*SMILES*' emblazoned on it, advertising its forthcoming show, another innovation. 'Smiles' was the hit number from the original Broadway musical *The Passing Show of 1918*, described as a 'spoof' on the past year's theatrical productions, or what is recognised now as satire. The young Fred and Adele Astaire danced in the original show. The Continental was quick to pick up on current trends. The lyrics of 'Smiles' were:

> There are smiles that make us happy
> There are smiles that make us blue
> There are smiles that steal away the teardrops
> As the sunbeams steal away the dew
> There are smiles that have a tender meaning
> That the eyes of love alone may see
> And the smiles that fill my life with sunshine
> Are the smiles that you give to me.[37]

The promise of this exciting new show, the jolly hit number 'Smiles', together with more positive news from the front, must have cheered up the Continental's war-ravaged clientele. Other numbers featured in the original show were 'I Really Can't Make My Feet Behave', 'Trombone Jazz', 'The Shimmy Sisters' and 'I'm Forever Blowing Bubbles'. Starring in the Continental's version of the show were Gretta John and Laurie Melville, telling 'a tale of impudent waiters'. Again, Gretta John was in charge of production and rehearsals as well as performing.[38]

The next show at the Continental was *Out Of It*, which was described as an antidote to the war's alarms. This may have been a locally conceived production.[39] If the Continental's latest production did not attract that weekend, then maybe a game of women's soccer might do instead. Swansea Ladies soccer team drew with Newport XI.

Eight thousand turned up at St Helen's ground, with the match described as 'thrilling'.[40]

The summer of 1918 had plenty on offer for the locals as well as the tourists. The Carlton Café had *The Waverley Girls* show, which went down 'great guns', but with no further information in the press. The Mumbles Pier Pavilion had a busy summer, hosting a Confetti Battle and Dance with full orchestra. Two thousand people attended the Mumbles Carnival, with an afternoon dance and concert on the pier with an all-woman orchestra. Also on the pier were the Gypsies Concert Party (CP), led by Florence Davey on piano. Another concert party was led by Dorothy Evelyn on piano. The All Woman Cornubion CP, featuring Pat Forde at the piano, was also on the pier. Betty Laurie on ragtime piano shortly followed. The next Pier Pavilion show was the Controllers CP, with Alice Branson on piano, followed by the Utopians CP, with Cissie Jackson on piano, plus many others. These are the forgotten women of early jazz. Welcome back, ladies.[41]

The press declared:

> They'll want entertainment of the right kind and the Café Chantant supplies it – good singing, clean business, striking songs. Anyone can come and sing themselves if they pass muster in the rehearsal room, and many have done so. Shows at the Continental are 4.30 p.m. and 7 p.m., so get busy.[42]

Miss Delor was already busy supplying ragtime piano at the Café Chantant. The Chantant later declared that it was 'hard put on to entertain all would-be patrons who flock for its vocal and edible wares'.[43]

At the end of the First World War there was great rejoicing in town.[44] The British and Allied navies sailed in. Demobbed and wounded soldiers packed the streets, and there was no shortage of venues to quench the thirst of those needing to be entertained. They flocked to the cafés, and the local paper announced 'CAFÉ SOCIETY: Great Crowds clamouring for admission!' Over at the Café Chantant, Gretta John and Maye Price performed 'Are You From Dixie? (Cause I'm From Dixie

Too)'. This was written in 1915, as part of the *Rip Van Winkle Burlesque Revue*, vaudeville era songs celebrating the American South.[45]

The regular 'Café Society' column roared: 'The Best for popular taste, fashion and music. The cafés are a high watermark of the flowing tide of popularity. Doris Page and Maye Price are now seriously challenged by Gretta John and Laurie Melville.' At the time, classical concerts were having difficulty filling their venues, with the press stating that Swansea's Albert Hall with the well-known mezzo-contralto Carrie Tubb had only 'moderate attendances, but all the cafés were packed'. Certainly, free admission to the cafés was having a detrimental effect on other venues and music genres.[46]

Café business continued to boom. Cut-throat competition was the norm. The Café Chantant offered a 'Special Tea and Doughnuts Cabaret', and six thousand doughnuts were baked for the occasion. The Metropole Winter Gardens Café hosted a 9 p.m. to 2 a.m. dance featuring 'all new music'. Fashions were described as 'fashionable black or white satin, with the young in strikingly artistic shades'.[47] The Café Chantant next featured the new entrepreneurs Doris Page and Gretta John, described by the press as 'right on'. This expression was possibly derived from 'right on target', a wartime colloquialism which survived as a trendy and hippy term until the 1960s.

On 4 February 1919, the word 'jazz' first appeared in print in the Welsh press, in an advertisement offering a free copy of the sheet music for the song 'Jazz', available in the *Ideas* periodical and sung by Ethel Levey and Nat. D. Ayer.[48] Sheet music proliferated and became an integral part of popularising jazz music. Parsonage quotes the *Dancing Times* report in 1919:

> Jazz was always primarily a word. It was a word which to some suggested the acme of poetical motion, while to others it conveyed conceptions of the lowest depths of immorality and degradation . . . Dancing, or 'jazzing' is used as a more direct sexual metaphor in jazz songs . . . linked with flirting. Jazz was beginning to develop its own identity.[49]

There is scant historical evidence of what 'jazz' music in Wales at this time actually sounded like, owing to multiple adaptions for Welsh taste, novelty turns mixed with nostalgia, and rhythmic versatility in abundance to propel dancers on to the dance floors. Louis Mitchell, drummer with Dan Kildare and his Clef Club Orchestra from New York, mentioned above, maintained he was actually the first person to bring jazz to Britain, as leaving clubland behind he had embarked on a music-hall career, thereby spreading the 'new rhythms' across the country. Rye states that Mitchell made a lot of noise, not to everyone's taste, 'varying his work on the drum with the use of all sorts and conditions of contrivances arranged upon a huge horseshoe . . . Black Lightning [Louis Mitchell] is destined to become a favourite with orchestras.'[50]

Fish and chip shops, eager to cash in on the café youth scene, applied for music and dancing licenses but were rejected, on the grounds that they were fish and chip shops. Local authorities, too, were anxious to get in on the licensing act, to officially promote and host their own dances and make some money. The Local Government Board (Ministry of Health) stated that this application was the first of its kind, the issue being whether dancing came under the scope of the Baths and Wash-houses Act as a healthful form of recreation. Local authorities were generally allowed to utilise swimming baths, while whist drives would probably not be considered healthful. Any losses incurred on the dances would not be made good out of the rates and would have to be met by private guarantee. It was decided that dances were a legitimate means of healthful recreation. R. E. Jones Ltd, the 'Tea Shop Kings', also applied for the new music and dancing license, but surprisingly their application was turned down. They did not seem too bothered as they were highly successful locally, had already bought another hotel in London and were busy expanding their empire.[51]

It was the fashionable young fuelling the new trends, and women's bands provided the jazz. The war had been won, the young wanted to dance and celebrate. That first year of peace in Wales in 1919 was an astonishing declaration that youth and feminism had come into its own. Joy, coupled with a need for flamboyant youthful exuberance, released any lingering inhibitions. Dancing was now fuelled by the new jazz music, and peace and freedom were shouted from the rooftops; literally, in fact, as large department stores such as Ben Evans regularly employed bands and orchestras in their emporiums to entertain the crowds in their rooftop cafés or for fashion shows and in-store dances.[52]

Newly unemployed First World War pilots, led by Captain Dalton of Blackpill, a young lad looking for new business opportunities after the war, opened AVRO Aerodrome, flying daily excursions to Mumbles, Gower and Ilfracombe from Swansea sands, tickets one guinea (£1 1s.). By the summer of 1919 AVRO had undertaken 15,000 leisure and business flights from the sands; there were no health and safety regulations then to hinder the new business entrepreneurs.[53]

Young women took full advantage of the new freedom of expression in fashion, quickly throwing off Victorian corsets. Wales had only just got used to seeing the suffragettes, in their tight, stiff jackets, high-necked blouses, long, heavy skirts, and large hats decorated with birds and fruit. Now, young women were taking to the dance floors in racy attire. Complaints started to appear in the press of 'Parisien vaguaries [sic] and bare women's backs'. There were also protests from haberdashers that women were buying less dress material and that backless dresses should be altered accordingly with inserts. This incurred the wrath of dressmakers, who retorted that their artistic designs would be ruined by alteration.[54] The press anxiously reported that women were 'suffering from trouseritis', shocked at the number of young women appearing in trousers at the Victory Ball. The clergy were upset, shouting from the pulpit that no woman should be allowed to attend services in a low-cut dress or a skirt that did not reach the ankle. One priest refused to marry a bride because she showed too much silk stocking. Pyjama parties were all the rage, with much hand-wringing from vicars.[55]

The cafés continued to upset the establishment and clergy, with the latest show at the Café Chantant described by one alarmed reviewer as 'Obstreperous ignorance screaming through a megaphone to a million scullery maids'. It was obvious that scullery maids were finding their feet and paid no heed to these warnings. Café Chantant productions sometimes lasted into long residencies, one example being the *Aboard the Lugger* revue, which played for seven weeks. Old-school class distinctions and 'respectable' music were fighting a losing battle against jazz, the music of protest and rebellion, as jazz was helping to break those boundaries down. Some men felt threatened by women's newfound voice, and organised male-only Grand Smoking Concerts at the Salisbury Club. One concert had Alderman Molyneux in the Chair. Definitely no jazz music, and certainly no scullery maids in attendance there.[56]

One enterprising Swansea woman, Madame Jessie Davies, advertised jazz dancing classes 'Direct from London' in her front parlour, a small terraced house in George Street. Another, Miss Treharne, gave jazz dancing lessons in her house in Buckingham Terrace. Educational establishments, threatened by these modern infiltrators, felt a professional requirement to offer new courses reflecting new trends in order to attract the youth of Wales away from purely hedonistic activities. Swansea Technical College's Mount Pleasant campus (now UWTSD), offered five lectures on 'Modern and Practical Music' at 2s. 6d. Another series of lectures, this time illustrated at the piano, was taught by D. Vaughan Thomas (Oxon), to make sure respectable music was on the curriculum.[57]

A School of Dramatic Art, the first in Wales, was established in Swansea by educational pioneers Evelyn Gleaves and Muriel Hutten, both women being experienced in drama productions in Swansea, London and Manchester. The new School's first home was the Unitarian Schoolroom, where evening and Saturday morning classes were held in 'deportment, gesture, elocution, operatic dancing, and all branches of dramatic work . . . including Shakespeare's Tempest'.[58]

Glamorgan Education Committee members were realising that women were demanding a voice, and a meeting was held to discuss married teachers. The Director of Education Mr T. J. Rees pointed out 'there was an objection to married women teachers as they became Head Mistresses and stopped the promotion of men'. The Swansea branch of the National Association of Schoolmasters declared in the press that 'women teachers were unsuitable for the teaching of boys'.[59] An article appeared in the local press appealing for women to join the Organised Demo of Women to protest at the price of milk. Did the teachers, with concerns about their careers being blocked, show their solidarity and join the marchers on the women's demo?[60] Jones writes of community actions in the south Wales coalfields, with women working collectively to achieve the main goal.

Office 'girls', who had taken over from men reluctant to use the newfangled typewriters, were discovering that their wages were too low to live on and were, by necessity, being thrown back on to domestic service. Business women were finding that men returning from the battlefields were first in line for business employment. Newspaper headlines, such as 'Flapper's Fire Up', reported that there was jealousy amongst the men owing to women's increasing job opportunities. This caused outrage amongst women trying to earn 'an honest wage' and taking up training opportunities. The Grosvenor Place Secretarial Training Bureau reported that fifty female students were 'typing away in perfect time to dance tunes on the radiogram', with the supervisor stating that it was the 'rhythmic system and some of our advanced pupils can even transcribe shorthand notes to a quick foxtrot'.[61] Beddoe has investigated this period of women's increasing political and feminist actions and their anxiety to get their voices heard and respected in this new world of work in the jazz age.[62]

As 1919 drew to a momentous close, the newspapers recorded the 'race riots' in Cardiff. Evans gives a full account of the tensions between returning demobbed men causing a surplus of labour and increasing competition for jobs on the docks.[63] Bourne points out that although 1919 was the first year of peace, it was also the year in which

> racial tensions exploded throughout Britain . . . fuelled by white ex-servicemen who felt that they had returned home from the battlefields to a country that was not fit for heroes. A scapegoat was needed . . . and in 1919 it was Britain's African and Caribbean community that was targeted [including in Cardiff].

However, the south Wales local press were very supportive of striking 'coloured' men, as a photograph showed large numbers of 'coloured' men at Swansea Docks waiting for employment on ships and reported, 'with few exceptions [they] are very particular about their attire as can be seen by our picture'. All the 'coloured' men were wearing suits, ties and trilby hats, and one was holding a smart walking cane.[64]

Before 1919 ended, patrons of the Café Chantant were treated to two new shows. Doris Page wrote the music for the 'daringly unconventional pirate ship scenes in *Aboard the Lugger*', which went into a seventh week. The next production was the *Mutt and Jeff Show*, Swansea's take on the popular American cartoon strip of two dimwits and their increasingly outlandish get-rich-quick schemes.[65]

Café society and women's direct action both continued to flourish during 1920. Swansea telephonists Miss Gwynne and Miss Martin organised a Leap Year Dance where ladies could choose their partners, and hired Mr Turner's Jazz Band, which featured a 'drummer to accompany the new dances' – new dances also fuelled record sales. Snell's in Swansea's High Street became the official agent for Columbia Records, selling all the latest ten-inch, shellac-based, 78rpm jazz recordings at 3s. 6d or 5s. 6d for a twelve-inch record. If dancers got sore feet they could purchase a 'TIZ' bath, recommended for 'before and after jazzing'.[66]

The ever-innovative Café Chantant underwent a complete refurbishment for its 1920 New Year floor show, with orange and black scenic decor effects, the emporium reaching a 'dizzy pinnacle of popularity'. Gretta John and Doris Page were in charge. Their big new show was *Way Down South*, featuring sand dancing, buck dancing (from 'buck and wing', flatfootin' and pigeon wing) and tango jazzing. *Way Down South* featured an all-black orchestra of 'Cullud Gemmen', the vernacular as printed in the local press. Sheet music titles from the show were 'Mammy's Sleepy Time Songs', 'Mistah Turkey' and 'Hick'ry Tea'. This production featured a return visit from the very popular Harrie Coonie (see chapter 6), who had happily survived serving in the military during the First World War, this show being a repeat of the successful

1917 production. Coonie's 'plantation singing' received a good review, with 'laughter echoing through the huge hall'. Coonie was described as a 'typical US Southerner who, being a real live coon, and a clever artiste, interprets the amusing ways of plantation cullud folk'. The local press reported that the enterprising Café Chantant regime had introduced Harrie Coonie to Wales back in 1917. It described him as 'the real article brought from the cottonfields', urging patrons to 'Go Waydown to Dixie' at the Chantant to see 'how the cullud folk dance and sing on the plantation' and promising that Mr Coonie would perform new steps at the end of the show. A week later, the Café Chantant, always looking for a new angle, introduced their in-house performing waiters and waitresses, who sang and danced on top of the bars and counters. Perhaps they performed some of the new steps shown the previous week by Harrie Coonie. If that was the case, it was truly a genuine cultural exchange.[67]

The pace of innovation at the Café Chantant was blistering. During April 1920, the Café Chantant roared that its new Gretta John production was to be *Everything is Peaches Down in Georgia*, offering daily matinées of 'popular song and cream puffs'. John knew her audience's tastes, and built her production around the popular 1918 sheet music by Milton Ager and Geo. W. Meyer:

> Down in Georgia there are peaches
> Waiting for you, yes, and each is sweet
> As any peach that you could reach for on a tree.
> Southern beauties they are famous
> Georgia's where they grow
> My folks write me, they invite me,
> Don't you want to go?
>
> *Chorus*
> Everything is peaches down in Georgia,
> What a peach of a clime,
> For a peach of a time
> Believe me Paradise is waiting down there for you.[68]

That particular month, Swansea's café society truly embraced women entrepreneurs at the top of their game, an innovative delivery of popular culture and catering, a historic sociocultural exchange of working-class ideas, performance and artistic variables from one (black American) working-class culture to another (white Welsh). Gretta John would have observed Harrie Coonie with his interpretations of song and dance 'from the plantations' in the previous weeks. John, with her co-producers, usually Doris Page and Maye Price, adapted and reworked these popular styles and images to suit the Café Chantant clientele.[69] Not only did Gretta John provide new opportunities for women to learn their craft in café society, the women were quick to grab any opportunities. One instance of a young woman who was prepared to take off for pastures new was Sybil May Jones from the Café Chantant regime. Sybil was one of Gretta John's vaudeville revue team, and the press reported that Sybil was now leading lady in the *Set Fair* revue and touring the Midlands. The experience Sybil Jones had gained working at the Café Chantant provided her with the confidence to enhance her career on the national stage.[70]

That august institution, the Swansea Chamber of Commerce, instigated front-page news by hiring a jazz band for its annual dance. Held at the Metropole Winter Gardens Café, the venue was specially decorated in pink with fresh flowers and trailing smilax, with dancing from 7.30 p.m. until the 'small hours' to Murray's River Club Band. The fashions were described as 'blended together like a rainbow'.[71]

It was at this point, with Swansea becoming what we would refer to today as a recognised destination for the arts and cultural industries, the county borough thought it prudent to advertise for an entertainments manager, to be responsible for the management and conduct of entertainments, concert parties and bands, with a commencing salary of £4 10s. per week. Swansea was on the up. However, the new entertainments manager would soon be made aware of impending unrest over working conditions for café women. Hotel and café workers received no extra pay for working until midnight or 1 a.m., whereas musicians were governed by the Musicians' Union. Grumbles over several months erupted into a full-blown strike by twenty-five waitresses at Swansea's Baltic Lounge Café. The Baltic Lounge had undergone a refurbishment and opened a new ballroom, inaugurated with a grand ball led by the New Missouri Band, together with a dancing exhibition by Millie and Max. Large crowds gathered in Castle Street as Baltic Lounge waitresses voiced their grievances on the street.[72]

Beddoe confirms that 358,000 British women belonged to unions by 1914. During the first jazz age women in Wales aged 21 to 30 enjoyed more disposable income than ever before. 'Yet, although they took over men's jobs, they rarely were paid men's rates – though many, even so, had never been better off.'[73] The Baltic Lounge was deserted inside, but for Mrs Aird, the manageress, and the Café Buffet Band. Mrs Aird had given the 'girls' a week's notice as they had 'not given satisfaction'; a woman employer not supporting her workforce of women, as not all twenty-five waitresses could have been unsatisfactory. The United Catering Trades Union were taking up their case, and a public appeal went out to refrain from patronising the Baltic Lounge. The waitresses were photographed with placards, with their complaints highlighted against 'foreign non-union labour'. The electricity supply to the café was suspended and the gas-workers all 'downed tools in sympathy'. Sympathetic colliers and coal trimmers organised a takeover of the Baltic Lounge to support the waitresses, all seated with blackened faces and dirty clothing at the 'nicely laid tables watched by the crowds outside'. However, Mrs Aird's four-week campaign against the waitresses and employees' union ended successfully for her. The aftermath was twenty-five waitresses losing their jobs, and Swansea Corporation was urged to provide official attractions, with properly paid staff. Unfortunately, it was also apparent that the Amalgamated Musicians' Union did not come out in support of the waitresses' action, as the Baltic Lounge Buffet Band had remained on the premises and had not supported the strike; perhaps the Buffet Band were not members of the AMU.[74]

The high-life experienced by café society clientele was also causing concern with the medical profession, who raised issues about young women preferring the pursuit of pleasure to that of being wives and mothers. The local press headlined a news article 'Everybody's Doing It – Dance Halls Multiplying and Birth Rate Dropping!' taking their lead from another Irving Berlin hit song 'Everybody's Doing It' (Irving Berlin denied any double entendre):

> See that ragtime couple over there
> Watch them throw their shoulders in the air . . .
> Everybody's doin' it, doin' it, doin' it[75]

Dr Lewis, the Medical Officer of Health in Pontardawe, had responded to a question asked at a meeting as to 'whether it was the working classes or the well-to-do that were always dancing?' Dr Lewis replied that it was all classes, and pointed out that there was also a wider knowledge of 'preventatives and a tendency to follow physical culture pursuits'. He added that 'women today would rather attend tennis courts and dance halls than rear children'. Popular Swansea exhibition dancers Millie and Max advertised their new classes with a photograph in the press, with the puff 'the models of rhythm and style with their exclusive dance creations', propelling yet more youngsters on to the dance floors of Wales.[76]

The Neath Medical Officer of Health was worried about the behaviour and morals of modern youth and issued his annual report, entitled 'Moral Slackness and Peril on the Streets'. His report stated that 'Much of our moral slackness was as a result of imperfect training in games'.[77] Owing to the popularity of café society, further unrest had spread to waitresses in Neath. The local press reported that several had been sacked for having their hair bobbed and were described as 'flappers'. The outcome of these sackings went unreported. Women having their hair bobbed also upset the Amman Valley School literary society. Their boys had voted en bloc against bobbing for girls, saying it was 'unnatural and added to a lack of charm and graces, and an absence of dignity', males once again dictating boundaries of women's behaviour. Women wishing to make hair statements could take advantage of the new

'Speciality of Bingling, Shingling and Bobbin" at the Exchange Toilet Saloon, with its Ladies' Private Room, based at Sir James German and Son (Swansea) Ltd, shipping and freight brokers in Adelaide Street, the industrial heartland of Swansea shipping and coal exporters. The Exchange Toilet Saloon continued to service clientele into the 1960s, but by then for men only, from the local shipping and coal offices.[78]

Apart from musicians and dancers, women were endeavouring to better their working lives. There had been complaints in the press that women no longer wanted to do domestic work, not helped by the government's new policy of suspension of benefit for refusal to take domestic work. Social clubs were to be established, girl apprentice schemes to be instigated, and girls given better status by being named house assistants. Mrs Williams, a government spokesperson, endeavoured to bring about agreement between mistresses and maids. She thought 'all girls should receive domestic training in their last year of school life, that social clubs be established, girls apprenticed, less bullying by mistresses, and girls be given better status as House Assistants'. Mrs Williams added that 'girls had taken to domestic service when their unemployment pay had stopped'. This was a form of government-sanctioned employment blackmail. The fight for equality continued. At the subsequent Domestic Service Enquiry (*sic*), exception was taken to opinions voiced by Dorothy Hedges, who said 'dole should not be given to girls declining domestic service, they should experience starvation'. The chairman dryly remarked 'some were very near it already'. Dorothy Hedges continued: 'I cannot say I'm particularly sorry, it is the only thing that will bring this class of girl to her senses.' Working-class girls did not want to be brought to their senses; they wanted good jobs and better pay and career prospects, like the men.[79] Some women wanted to improve their lot by applying for jobs in heavy industry. An unnamed woman had applied for a mining job at Amman Valley Colliery, but was rejected. She angrily retorted to the press:

> I don't see why I could not do the work. I have lived amongst miners. There is nothing impossible for women to do nowadays and I do not see

why the Miners' Federation should raise any objection to the employment of women as colliers. Women are employed at Tinworks and other industries.[80]

With these domestic, political and class issues bubbling constantly under the surface, café society continued to flourish and became ever more sophisticated over the next five years. Established cafés underwent regular refurbishment to keep up with the competition, and new ones opened to fanfares. First of the new crop of cafés was the Patti Pavilion, opened at the end of May 1920 with the intention of building an attached shelter in which to house a band to entertain visitors during wet weather.[81] The venue is still in use today as Patti Raj, an Asian restaurant and function suite. Mme Patti was the world-renowned opera star who resided at Craig-y-Nos Castle in the Swansea valley, the Patti Pavilion being a replica of her theatre at her castle. Amy Framer was one of the first women pianists to be employed at the new Patti Pavilion, accompanying Jessie Templeton's 'Chinks the Vaudeville Entertainers'. The flagship David Evans department store opened their café and luncheon lounge with thirty tables. It had a smoking room panelled with hunting scenes, and draughts and dominos were provided for patrons, who were serenaded daily by the high-class Saunterers Jazz Orchestra. David Evans held an annual café open day and later added an American soda fountain to their amenities with 'American Ices and Sundaes'. The Baltic Lounge Café, having recovered from its coal trimmers sit-in, offered a 'thé dansant' (tea-dance) with full orchestra every Saturday afternoon. Other new cafés to open up were the Regent, Lovells, and the Cutglass Temperance Bar, although it is not clear what artistic provision was offered at the Cutglass.

The people of Swansea also wanted to dance on the sands, but the council thundered, 'No Dancing on the Foreshore', and the newly installed entertainments manager had to comply with booking dances in established venues to appease the masses. The Welsh Aviation Company (previously AVRO) was now offering flights from the beach for two passengers at 7s. 6d, a greatly reduced price from the original 1 guinea (£1 1s.). Take off and landings were a hazardous occupation, as hundreds of unemployed and homeless people, including the demobbed unable to find accommodation on returning from the First World War, had taken to sleeping on the beach during the hot weather. Temperatures soared to 82°F (28°C). Dancers shook the Mumbles pier foundations when a thousand took to the boardwalk for jazz dancing, assured by the *Daily Post* that it was indeed safe to do so and the boardwalk would not collapse into the sea.[82]

R. E. Jones Ltd, Swansea 'Tea Shop Kings' and owners of the Café Chantant, had come out of the war well, purchasing the London Piccadilly Hotel for £2 million. In 1923 the death of R. E. Jones was reported. R. E. Jones was survived by his four sons, one of whom, Leigh Jones, went into the film business, shooting the silent film *The Piccadilly Playtime Girls in Gower*. This film was premiered at the Trade Exhibition at the Café de Paris, Leicester Square, London. A Swansea premiere was held at the Castle Cinema. Newspaper reports stated Gower was to be the new Hollywood of Britain, with the 'film industry searching for a suitable centre and producers deciding on a Co-operative Film Policy'. Swansea parliamentary committee had put in £100 towards the £1,000 cost of *The Piccadilly Playtime Girls in Gower*, with a further £150 from the finance committee. An anxious Swansea Borough Council was reluctant to finance any more films, and opportunities for an innovative and pioneering film industry running alongside the highly successful jazz scene were lost. *The Piccadilly Playtime Girls in Gower* has completely disappeared.[83]

Jazz music during the 1920s slowly began evolving again. The smart, fast revues continued in the cafés, and larger jazz bands and orchestras serviced the new big ballrooms with their sprung dance floors. Some orchestras still managed to squeeze themselves on to the café bandstands. Women's contributions to jazz music in south Wales during that first jazz age should not be forgotten; here are some of the women's bands that contributed to Wales's cultural emergence: Mrs Rhys Burman's Sylvian Jazz Band was very popular, as were Mrs Gilbert Williams's Jazz and Syncopated Orchestra (Mrs Williams also led the Langland Bay Dance Orchestra), Mrs Gwynne and her Premier Orchestra, Miss Aplin's Orchestra, the Miss E. Jones Orchestra, Lena Shearson's

Society Six, Miss Oxton's Orchestra, Winnie Talbot's Music with Two Masters of Ceremonies, the Live Wires with Daisy, Mavis and Dolly, the Five Drummer Girls, and Miss Winnie Scannel's Orchestra. Women jazz musicians did exist, and they worked just as hard alongside men's orchestras, working long hours into the night after rehearsing during the day. The women jazz entrepreneurs, such as Gretta John, Maye Price and Doris Page, also enabled the music to flourish, absorbing influences from African American bands passing through town, adapting and subverting where necessary to fulfil a need for the dancing throngs.[84]

The Kardomah Exhibition Salon, opened in 1914, was quiet on the jazz front, with hardly any mention of flappers or dance floors; it kept its aspiring middle-class distance from the noisier elements. By the mid-1930s changes were again in the air. The *Melody Maker* reported in January 1935 that it was a 'sad day for Swansea', as the sole surviving café orchestra, the Ladies Trio at the Castle Restaurant, had received notice to quit, the last of the 'flesh and blood music'. The Castle was to install wireless and speakers, like most of the other venues. The *Melody Maker* complained that:

> Swansea patrons were now to receive educational teas and eat to the accompaniment of lectures on Foundations of Music. Oh for the palmy days when all the cafés had their orchestras: Mackworth, Lovells, Baltic Lounge, Carlton, Castle etc. . . . all in all, café work for musicians in Swansea seems doomed.[85]

The Kardomah survived, without music, and continues to be a popular café in Swansea's town centre. Its name is haunted by Dylan Thomas and his friends, mentioned at the beginning of this chapter: bohemian cultural aesthetes, poets, writers, artists and musicians, who influenced international debate. They knew as youngsters that what they were producing was as good, as innovative and exciting as anything anybody else was producing in Britain. So too thought the innovative women bandleaders and entrepreneurs of the south Wales 1920s café society, a decade before Dylan Thomas took to discussing poems and girls. Dylan Thomas and the Kardomah live on in history and continue to be celebrated. The café society musicians and entrepreneurs, with their embracing and celebration of African American music in the 1920s jazz age, were forgotten.[86]

Chapter Seven

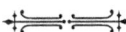

Cutting a Rug to the Second World War: Jews and 'Negro Morals'

MUSICIANS, DANCERS, AND ENTREPRENEURS in the arts looked to the future, eager to participate in a new way of expressing themselves; they were modern women and these were modern times when the old way of doing things were done by retrogressive men. Modernism was a disregard for the establishment; for old men who had sent young men to slaughter. Modernism was the avant-garde flinging off convention and embracing risqué decadence. Jazz music fitted the bill with its aspects of 'primitivism' and 'authenticity' emanating from African Americans' freedom of expression in their music. Women grabbed at the opportunities the new music offered, with its elements of high art aesthetics coupled with syncopated and rhythmic abandon, and the risks inherent in both. Jazz was modern and, with its African American heritage, it was also 'exotic'. Parsonage discusses jazz and its 'modernism' and 'primitivism' aesthetics further. To perform it or to dance to it meant that one had the opportunity to indulge in self-expression and become part of the new wave.[1] It also meant that working-class Welsh women could participate in a movement which transcended artistic and sexual boundaries and allowed them access to a cultural movement previously indulged in by the English upper classes, or wealthy socialites of the London supper clubs. The First World War had fractured establishment order and hierarchy. Jazz allowed optimism and was a stimulant to free expression.

Londoners may be forgiven for thinking that their city was the only place to be for the current trends in culture and entertainment during the 1920s, but Wales was only weeks behind the latest London innovations. Wales's dance entrepreneur Miss Millie Durk took her opportunity and offered 'Blues Dance' classes at Swansea's Uplands School of Dance on 7 September 1923, commenting:

> Dancing has become an integral part of our social life. The dance spirit dwells in everyone that is sound in limb and general constitution. She is the spirit that moves us since the dawn of civilisation, to explore our personality, our thoughts and emotions by means of rhythmic movements of the body.[2]

African American composer W. C. Handy (1873–1958) is acknowledged as the 'Father of the Blues', as he recognised the early folk character within traditional work songs. Arna Bontemps, who taught at Fisk University for many years, edited Handy's autobiography. Handy writes of the first time his 'St Louis Blues' was played in 1914:

> When *St. Louis Blues* was written the tango was in vogue. I tricked the dancers by arranging a tango introduction, breaking abruptly into a low-down blues. My eyes swept the floor anxiously, then suddenly I saw lightning strike. The dancers seemed electrified. Something within them came suddenly to life. An instinct that wanted so much to live, to fling its arms and to spread joy, took them by the heels.[3]

Millie Durk felt this 'joy' instantly and was the first to offer blues dancing in Wales; musicians recognise blues as the flattened third, fifth and seventh tones of the scale. African American Charlotte Forten (1837–1914), abolitionist, teacher and nurse wrote down her feelings when listening to slaves working on the plantation at which she worked and called them 'the blues'.[4] Paul Oliver writes: 'Charlotte Forten's entry is one of the first recorded references to "the blues" as a state of mind.'[5]

In Swansea rival classes in blues and jazz dancing sprung up in quick profusion, run by women in their front parlours, to service those eager to hit the dance floor. A profusion of dance bands and orchestras were started by women, such as Mrs Rhys Burman's Sylvian Jazz Band, Miss Winnie Scannel's Orchestra and Mrs Gill Williams Syncopated Orchestra. That these and many other women entrepreneurs played early jazz music is testament to the legacy that had been left behind by the touring African American revues, stage shows and floorshows (see chapter 6). South Wales musicians grabbed all these opportunities and showered the passing trade with a non-stop diet of jazz, with its particular blend of cultural interchange, which, surprisingly, extended beyond the traditional stage, bandstands and floor shows, into unexpected venues, such as the Workhouse and the Sailors' Home (see chapter 4).[6]

In the early 1920s, 'flappers' was the new expression to describe young women who dressed in an unconventional manner and took to the new fashion scene, encouraged by jazz music and enticed by modern marketing techniques: for example, Jazz Fashions, Jazz Jumpers, Jazz Effects and Jazz Colours were the latest summer fashions in vogue in 1921 at Ben Evans's store. Jazz Dye Soap was a new invention for women who wanted 'jazz-coloured' dresses. Dance frocks at David Evans store cost 2 guineas (£2 2s.). Joan and Viola were sent out from the local press to describe the dance-floor fashions, though some descriptions we would now find offensive, such as 'nigger charmeuse trimmed with silk lace and flame roses'. The dance floors dazzled: a 'jazz pantaloon suit of gold and blue brocade tissue with gold cap and large black tulle bow', Miss Thomas in a 'Jazz Folly of mauve and green diamond silk with overtulle skirt', Mr A. Janes 'cutting a rug in a Jazz Pierrot suit of chintz', Miss Mitchell in a 'Jazz Turk mauve gown with brown floral crepe', Miss McMillan in 'Jazz Pierette'. Light and airy frocks for the heatwave were advertised, in jazz cretonne, striped zephyrs and floral foulards of mustard and black, and any colour of striped crêpe-de-Chine. Paris gowns and French modes were now available at Ben Evans's store ('Ben's'). Steel bead trimmings were popular, but must have caused some bruising when doing the shimmy. Miss Treharne wore 'olive green crêpe-de-Chine with black and gold lace'. 'Flannel balls' were held, at which the men could wear flannel trousers instead of a lounge suit. Anthonie Ltd of Castle Street advertised 'Smart Dancing Frocks and Art Models of our own design in night shades at 5 guineas' (expensive).[7]

By 1924 skirts were short with no waistline. Ostrich feathers were a must. Plus fours (breeches below the knee) were de rigueur for men, until Oxford bags came in, with twenty-four-inch turn-ups which flapped fashionably when doing the Charleston. The Patti Fashion Show strutted knee-length skirts, and at the Baltic Lounge Miss Ceinwen Roberts wore a fetching white tissue tube dress with flame ostrich feathers. Over at Baldwin's Dance at the Patti, Mrs Trevor Griffiths wowed them with her cyclamen silk chiffon taffeta trimmed with ostrich feathers on the hem. Women competed with ever more eye-watering fashion statements. Mrs Leonard Davies wore black silk georgette over gold with rows of fringes. Swansea banks held their annual knees-up at the Metropole, featuring Miss Parkes doing the Polo Trot, and Ivy Price and Eileen Davies executing the Apache Dance. The Kit Kat Club opened their season at the Patti with the Capitol Jazz Band and Miss Ethel Parsley performing Charleston exhibition dances. The Frisco Seven Syncopations held court at the Assembly Rooms, and one could dance every Tuesday and Saturday at the Conservative Club for one shilling. At the Armistice Supper Dance Mrs Woolston was 'attired in black silk with scarlet beads, and Mrs Fletcher in silver lamé trimmed with white fur'. At the Drill Hall Priory Ball, Miss P. Jacob danced to Jack Hylton's London Band wearing 'a jazz outfit of green, gold and red with feather trimming on her hat'. The Christmas 1925 newspaper advertisements urged boyfriends to buy for their flapper girlfriends and bright young things the latest trends in fashion and accessories, such as frocks in crêpe-de-Chine or georgette plus the new on-trend wristlets, Apache neckties, suede volumes of poetry, perfumed sachets and gold tiepins for sports girls. Hilda Ward, 'The Greatest Lady Saxophonist', led her 'magnificent lady band' at the Empire to crowded houses. South Wales could hardly be described as a backwater for fashion and musical trends. Feminism was looking up, but with it came increased competition from male bands busy reforming after the First World War and trying to edge out women musicians. Dr Rawlings, now a JP, addressed the Sketty Brotherhood thus: 'The Town was like a lunatic asylum. Dance bands and dancing were a product of barbarism and childishness... and needed to be Christianised'. Hot music was to blame.[8]

Both the new 'hot' or 'syncopated' music, and the opportunities for performance it generated, offered career avenues for women. The main function in syncopated music is to encourage improvisation. Parsonage states:

> Cross-referencing recordings with contemporary comment shows that the word 'hot' was generally used from around the mid-1920s to identify musical qualities that are considered inherent in a modern understanding of jazz. The first issue of *Melody Maker* identified the latest releases by Hylton's Kit-Cat Club band under the leadership of American saxophonist Al Starita as 'red-hot syncopated rhythm with a good deal of "dirt" thrown in' to 'appease the appetites of "jazz" lovers'.[9]

Women with a history of using music as a career path adapted to the exciting challenge. The ability to improvise meant that women musicians, through imaginative or impressionistic improvisational skills, had now become lady syncopators, such as Jennie Millar's Lady Syncopators.[10] Within south Wales, for example, women were employed as jazz musicians at cafés, department store roof-gardens, the Sailors' Home, school halls, hotels, lounges, restaurants, on the beach, on the pier and at Snell's recording studio in Swansea's arcade. Women were also employed in shop windows to demonstrate the pianos and the sheet music on sale. Women grabbed these opportunities for new jobs.

For example Peggy Dell, whom the *Melody Maker* described as 'Pianist with Plaits', was later employed as a piano player at Woolworths, aged 14, eventually becoming vocalist with the Roy Fox Band.[11] The local press followed jazz's progress as a new music genre with gasps of incredulity and fascination, using bold headlines and exclamation marks for emphasis. The press were also eager to present articles discussing the minutiae of the music, such as that by Arthur Mason, writing:

> The jazz band and the jazz music of our day are doing more than was ever done to make music an excitement. What is the value of music that merely excites? What is its value by comparison with that of music which soothes, which exalts, which inspires?[12]

The local press were careful to point out if performers were 'coloured' and usually wrote their pieces with respect, sometimes describing the correct degree of skin tone. They also wrote of 'Negro' artists performing in London, such as the Harmony Kings Quartet performing at the Wesleyan Hall, Tooting:

> Mr. Ivan Browning (the Quartet's Manager), addressing the congregation after the first song, said that in many instances negro spirituals were known as sorrow songs. They were the only music that America could claim, and they had been the cause of a better understanding of the negro race.[13]

Although the first gospel recording by American acapella group Dinwiddie Colored Quartet on the Monarch label was made as early as 1902, 'race recording did not properly begin until about 1921, the year in which record sales in America first hit the one hundred million mark'.[14] In Britain women jazz musicians became role models in the recording studio. Women were recording as early as 1912. Schleman documents many of them, such as vocalist Louisa Zeitlin, who recorded on Columbia with Jacob's Trocaderians, as well as appearing at London's

Regent Palace Hotel; the Trocaderians were associated with the well-known British caterers, Lyons. The explosion of recording artists began in the late 1920s on the Zonophone, Decca, Parlophone and Brunswick labels. Edison Bell Phonograph promoted their new 'Winner' label, specialising in cheap records catering to home dancing. Elsie Carlisle, vocalist with Ambrose, became a collectable photograph on Wills cigarette cards; there was no shortage of role models for young women.[15]

Women musicians also joined the Musicians' Union. The MU centenary *Illustrated History* states that women musicians were in abundance when the Amalgamated Musicians' Union was founded in 1893, largely because music was seen as a suitable skill for young middle-class women to acquire, and more working-class women had access to musical instruments than ever before. New opportunities opened up for many women musicians, who had previously found it difficult to develop a full-time professional career; also by 1926 Swansea had over four hundred women motorists, making it easier for them to travel to work. According to the MU publication, some women were skilled at a variety of musical genres; these would include working in theatre pit orchestras, who were expert at reading musical scores. Women piano players and small combos were very popular accompanying silent movies, which required improvisational skill and incidental music. The programmes were usually changed twice weekly, with working hours from 1 p.m. until midnight; some of these women would have easily adapted to the new 'hot and syncopated' style of music burgeoning in the 1920s.[16] Swansea's Carlton Cinema de Luxe opened in January 1914. The Elysium Cinema opened in 1914, the Albert Hall was converted from a music hall to a cinema in 1922, and the Shaftesbury in St Helen's Road was operating in 1913. In 1921 cinema musicians demanded better wages, which was rejected, and patrons were faced with 'music-less films'. A good wage for cinema musicians was an average of £6 per week, but not many musicians received it. The Musicians' Union voiced grievances and a strike threatened. Some cinema managers protested the extra £2 per week demanded meant there would be piano-only cinemas. Several cinemas were non-unionised, employing cheaper musicians.

Meetings were held and deputations received. It was agreed pay had to be improved as 'Swansea was £1 below other districts'.[17]

Women working in the music business led a financially precarious but culturally rewarding life. Standards at theatrical digs or lodgings for performers on tour were usually basic and quite costly; complaints about facilities were common.[18] Theatrical companies seemed to get stranded more often in south Wales than in London, with some companies reduced to singing in the streets in order to pay for their digs.[19] Although jazz had its attractions as a career move, it could also be a risky occupation.

Women were quick to grab any opportunity to become entrepreneurs by organising events, booking bands and designing artistic decorations for venues. Swansea's Madame Jessie Davies organised many a 'Long Night' dance with jazz bands. The College of Nursing held a Grand Fete featuring a jazz band, at Parcwern hospital grounds. For the Chamber of Commerce Ball, mauve and gold decorations decked the Hotel Metropole ballroom, with Murray's River Club Band supplying the music. Christmas at the Sailors' Home saw 'high jinks with brown, black and white men taking part in the festivities'. But not everything ran smoothly, as many an official committee meeting would be engulfed in argument. For example, the Swansea school building sub-committee, with an eye on additional income, met to discuss the use of schools for dances, being a 'considerable source of revenue from these functions and any amount of pleasure to young people . . . the sub-Committee will clear at least £1000'. Dr Stephens, debating the implications of dances in schools, said he would pay 2s. 6d to see Alderman Griffiths dancing. Motion carried.[20]

During the New Year of 1921 department stores held dances for their staff, such as the Woolworth Hop in their own ballroom in Swansea's High Street with dancing until 1 a.m. to the T. Williams Orchestra; maypoles decorated in red, white and blue festooned the dance floor. Ben Evans department store held a fundraiser for Swansea hospital in their costume showroom; five hundred people attended. Mrs Eddy's Orchestra, featuring Limelight Dances, played at the National Union of

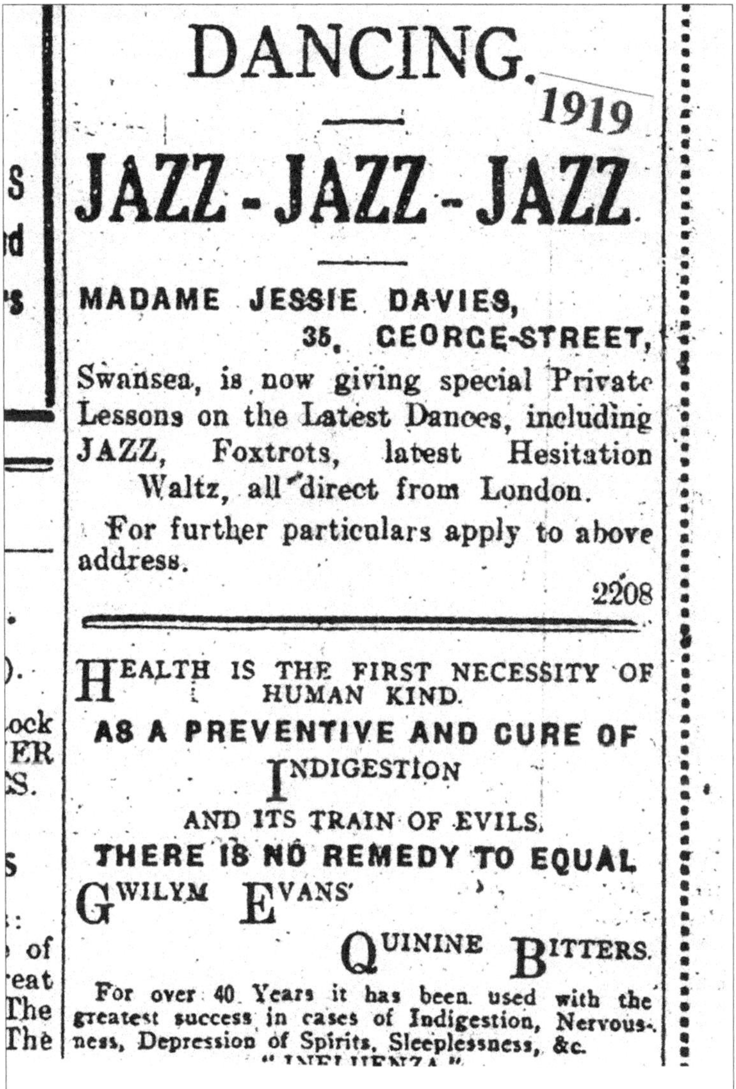

DANCING.

1919

JAZZ - JAZZ - JAZZ.

MADAME JESSIE DAVIES,
35, GEORGE-STREET,
Swansea, is now giving special Private Lessons on the Latest Dances, including JAZZ, Foxtrots, latest Hesitation Waltz, all direct from London.

For further particulars apply to above address.

2208

HEALTH IS THE FIRST NECESSITY OF HUMAN KIND.

AS A PREVENTIVE AND CURE OF
INDIGESTION
AND ITS TRAIN OF EVILS.
THERE IS NO REMEDY TO EQUAL
GWILYM EVANS'
QUININE BITTERS.

For over 40 Years it has been used with the greatest success in cases of Indigestion, Nervousness, Depression of Spirits, Sleeplessness, &c.

Figure 20: Jazz dance lessons advertisement , 1919
(SWW Media)

Ex-Servicemen at the Patti Pavilion; Mrs Eddy's Orchestra was also busy that week at Manselton school. The new dances the Chicago Maze, the Dazzle Foxtrot and Swansea's own Marina Saunter were featured at the Bohemians Dance at Hafod boys' school. With new dances appearing in quick succession on the scene, bandleaders had to adapt quickly, making sure to have new arrangements for band charts ready in time for their musicians to keep up with the dance trends. The Swansea school building committee agreed to overhaul the gas jets for better lighting for the dances in school halls. Some organisations felt dancing was a therapeutic and health-giving experience, as did the Swansea Dockers Educational and Social Council, which held its Hop to 'provide mutual and social culture for the workers'. February 1921 headliners at the Empire were 'Martini the Jazz Pianist and his Rollicking Rags', followed by *The Spangles Revue* with the Syncopated Jazz Five. *The Spangles Revue* staged fifteen scenes, featuring Isabelle Dillon, Ivy Dewey, Audree Claire and Hilda Newsome, with the press reporting 'a jazz quintette makes joyous noises and worth a trip'. Local bands and musicians had to be on top of their game to satisfy the youngsters on the dance floors.[21]

In February 1921 a 'Long Night' dance was organised by Mrs Parsley at Brynmill girls' school. With increasing numbers of dances, hops and cake-walking competitions taking place, Swansea parks committee came up with a proposal to organise open-air dances in the parks, citing successful outdoor dances run by Manchester, Liverpool, Brighton and Glasgow councils. It was suggested that hard flooring could be laid around Victoria Park bandstand with the cheapest estimated cost of £1,100. Mr Ball said it would be an ideal attraction for young people, and the elderly could sit and watch. The chairman of the parks committee declared that 'decent people would not go to the park to see dancing'. Mr Ball pointed out that some churches and chapels ran dances, to be interrupted by an angry chairman, who shouted, 'and if I had my way I would not allow them in churches and chapels'. The matter of dancing in the parks was deferred for a year.[22]

Before Swansea parks committee could reconvene, a headline screamed 'SKETTY JAZZ ORGIES', Sketty being a very well-to-do area of town and therefore implying a great public scandal. This was caused by two presumably middle-class women. A case had come to the county court concerning complaints of 'War Dances' being held at De La Beche Road. The next-door neighbour had complained about terrible noise and vibrations until 2 a.m., and that these 'orgies' were happening on a regular basis. Mr Wrightman, the aggrieved neighbour, said he had been in the shipping business for forty-five years and had 'knocked about' the Strand (near the docks), but had never heard such goings-on. The defence argued that thin walls were the cause of the problem, as the two women had only been playing their music until midnight on a gramophone they had borrowed from next door, while accompanying themselves with a mandolin. His Honour observed: 'You two women have parties and make a noise when your husbands are away, is that it?' 'No sir, that's an untruth,' replied Mrs Barratt, 'my husband can come in any time of the night', since he was a night watchman. Mrs Lewis's husband was in the army. His Honour required the police to do a full investigation and adjourned the case for a week. The Sketty church and social groups had to fan themselves, while police time and finances were wasted in investigating non-existent orgies. Outcome not reported. Those pillars of the community, the Freemasons, hired the Davies's Jazz Orchestra for their Masonic Ball at the Patti, while over at the Sailors' Rest a concert took place with eight women musicians supplying the music. The Neath Medical Officer in his annual report wrote he was worried about youth's 'moral slackness and evils on the streets'. This was grossly unfair, as there was no trouble at all when 18,000 people thronged the crowded streets after watching the ladies' football teams at the Vetch parade through the town in charabancs. Ladies Internationals 6, Swansea 1.[23]

The wringing of hands over women's 'moral slackness' (and it was usually women who were fretted over) was of concern to the leaders of Welsh Nonconformity. Aaron states that the behaviour of Welsh women was to be 'heavily policed ... well into the twentieth century'. However, Welsh women were trying to assert their identity, to find their own voice, to not conform, to find self-expression, while not incurring the wrath of public scorn or accepting the 'English definition of [the Welshwoman] as the libidinous hoyden of primitive Wild Wales'. To be Welsh and 'respectable', as Aaron points out, 'entailed severe curbs on her freedom'.[24] Women were therefore finding a new confidence to exert freedom of expression, whether as musicians or on the dance floor, defying old-fashioned notions of duty to self, men and the church hierarchy while risking personal and public ridicule.

The jazz age had barely got started when in 1921 church politics raised its head over the pulpit. The Swansea Free Church Council held a meeting at Calvary Baptist Church, Danygraig, to discuss 'Immoral Sex Dancing', to ascertain to which class it belonged and what attitude the church should take. Was dancing healthy or degenerate? These issues were heatedly discussed. Mr Davies suggested that the Church had failed to keep up with the times, but it was not impossible to concentrate the mind of youth into the service of religion. The meeting remembered previous negative attitudes to musical instruments in churches and chapels, and caution needed to be undertaken with the present climate in case the young were turned off attending church services. The Pastor of Mount Calvary expressed his view that it was the 'Sex Dancing' that was immoral and that if dancing was indeed proper, why could not men dance together? Silence. A letter was read out from Dr D. A. Rawlings, an adviser to the Workhouse Board of Guardians, expressing sympathy with the Church's cautionary attitude. The Pastor of Calvary Baptist commented that if all the others were only of the same frame of mind (as Dr Rawlings), Great Britain would be a better country.[25] Meanwhile south Wales danced on into the 1920s. The Gwyn Hall, Neath, hosted the Oilville Dance for the National oil refineries, music supplied by the Neath Borough Orchestra. At the Patti, the Electrical Trades Union held theirs from 6.30 p.m. until 1 a.m. with Brayley's Orchestra and limelight effects in the ballroom. Swansea health department held their dance at the National School with Basil Radford's Orchestra. Therefore, there were plenty of job opportunities for musicians during 1921.[26]

However, the debates concerning 'Sex Dancing' deteriorated into racist attacks against 'Negroes and their Morals', blaming them for

Welsh youth's degenerate behaviour. Dr Hurn addressed the Workers' Education Committee, stating 'modern dances were taken from the immodest and immoral dances of the Negroes'. A letter from 'Freethinker' appeared in the *Daily Post* objecting vehemently to this comparison, arguing that 'Negroes' Morals' were in fact better than those of some civilised countries. 'Freethinker' argued that it was only after the visits from missionaries that Negroes were deemed to be immoral. 'Freethinker' concluded that s/he was all for uplifting the culture of Swansea, but instead of the Church's teaching, s/he would have 'Free thought', and instead of faith s/he would advocate 'Reason'. We can only guess whether Dr Hurn tested his theories on degenerate Negroes' morals by going to see Abbie Mitchell and her Harmonic Quartette at the Empire. Their programme of vernacular songs was described as 'plaintive melodies of the Southern States – The Real Thing in the way of Darkie Folk Songs'. The review described Abbie Mitchell's singing as a 'sweet and full soprano blending very pleasingly with the deeper notes of the males; an enjoyable and artistic performance'. There was no mention of depravity and immoral behaviour among young people on the streets after exiting the Swansea Empire.[27]

A highlight of 1921 on the Swansea Empire stage was the 'outstanding success' of the Southern Syncopated Orchestra on tour from London, featuring the Royal Southern Singers Quartette. They were described as being given a 'rousing reception and popular items were old negro camp meeting glees'.[28] The original Southern Syncopated Orchestra, formed in America in 1918, arrived in Britain in 1919 with twenty-seven musicians and nineteen vocalists, from Africa, the West Indies, the Americas and the United States. Rye writes 'they would have performed spirituals, ragtime, plantation or 'coon' songs, and formal compositions such as those of Samuel Coleridge-Taylor'. The local press gave no detail and it cannot be confirmed whether this 1921 orchestra was as large as the original. In October, the Swansea Empire advertised: 'Plaintive melodies of the Southern States exercised a peculiar fascination world over, with no finer exponent than Abbie Mitchell the silver-voiced singer from the Syncopated Orchestra and a full harmonic quartette . . .

An enjoyable and artistic performance.'[29] Rye described them: 'the orchestra's ranks included at least two apostles of the new jazz in trumpeter Arthur Briggs, and, importantly, the New Orleans clarinettist Sidney Bechet, widely acknowledged as one of the music's greatest figures'; new jazz was improvisational, having evolved from earlier genres. Tragically, a few months later the local press reported that two men walking along the shore at Wigtownshire (now part of the council area of Dumfries and Galloway) saw the body of a man in the sea, a Negro, believed to be Walter B. Williams, a member of the Southern Syncopated Orchestra who were on board the ill-fated steamer SS *Rowan*. Rye continues:

> By the time that nine of the then thirty-two members were lost in the sinking of the SS *Rowan*, on which they were travelling between engagements in Glasgow and Dublin on the night of 8–9 October 1921, it included Trinidadian brothers Cyril and George Blake, Jamaican trumpeter Joe Smith, Sierra Leonian pianist Frank Lacton, and Nigerian banjoist Gay Bafunke Martins.[30]

The loss of nine musicians from the Southern Syncopated Orchestra was surely a tremendous loss for jazz music. The Orchestra performed a mixture of styles. Jazz pianist, composer and BBC presenter Julian Joseph describes them as 'energetic and life affirming, all the more poignant after the Great War'. In 2014 Julian Joseph brought together descendants of those lost in 1921, sharing his 'impression of the music of the Southern Syncopated Orchestra that they would have played to the King and Queen: "Tin Pan Alley Blues" and "St Louis Blues" just two examples of the music that form the basis of modern popular music'.[31]

The Rev. Morgan Jones, preaching at Brynhyfryd, strongly criticised the present generation of Wales for its 'degrading condition', referring to sex dancing and 'Negro morals'. He predicted that 'fifty years hence it would be written in history that the present generation were found to be the weakest people that Wales had ever had'. Jazz was targeted again in 1921 by Dr Walford Davies, Director of Music at the University of Wales. He advised the Swansea education committee that 'jazz music was positively iniquitous, positively immoral and positively pernicious'. Again, there was that nod to 'Negroes' Morals' in this remark.[32] The Rev. Phillips, addressing the Sketty Brotherhood and Sisterhood, said that '75% of loose women in New York had got there through dancing saloons . . . and was it not possible for the church to (be able to) divert the passion?' He obviously had the recent Sketty 'orgies' on his mind. Dr Rawlings, now a JP, replied that Wales would 'go down in darkness. I've never known such debauchery and self indulgence.'

Another Swansea magistrate, Mr J. W. Jones, reported to the Swansea parks committee alleged improper behaviour on the Patti dance floor, with couples having 'their heads glued together', also suggesting that 'immoral women' attended these dances. Mr Lindsey, also a member of the deputation, said he had seen 'Jews dancing rather improperly together'. It was pointed out that there was no 'Shimmy or Stunt Dancing allowed at the Patti', but Alderman Owen JP said that he had heard there was 'scanty clothing' worn and some people had been asked to leave. He added that 'it was impossible for a man to kiss a girl while he is dancing with her'. Mr Darwin, manager of the Patti, trying desperately to defend its reputation, said he 'had no particular feelings against Jews but they were the only people he took exception to as they were always improvising on the dance floor to the annoyance of other people'. Mr Darwin never offered an explanation of how he distinguished Jews from other dancers. Eventually, a resolution was passed that 'no evidence of anything improper had taken place at the Patti'. The mention of Jews and 'dirty' dancing set off weeks of heated anti-Semitic debate within the local press which did, however, allow some temporary respite from racist comments about Negroes and their morals. Jews and Negros were now linked together as the perpetrators of Wales' loose morals.[33]

The year 1923 saw an increase in news items on racial slurs upon the Jewish community, which blew up into a storm in February. Swansea parks committee received a deputation from the Swansea social and whist drive committee complaining about anti-Semitic remarks made by magistrate J. W. Jones. Another of the deputation, Mr Gardiner, also defended the Patti and its dancers. The chairman asked if there were 'any ill-famed women there?' 'Certainly not,' replied an angry Mr Gardiner, 'I would take my wife there.' Alderman John Lewis said that he and the vice-chairman had interrogated the Chief Constable on this question of 'glued heads' and there had been nothing untoward; in fact the police had 'spoken highly' of the way the Patti had been run. There was mention that the press were 'prodded' to write offensive articles concerning Jews' stunt dancing and the wearing of 'scanti [*sic*] clothing'. Mr Darwin, the Patti manager, was asked about 'cheap dances'. He replied that there was a cheap dance on a Saturday night, admission being 1s. and 1s. 6d, but he had less trouble with cheap dances than with those costing a little more with refreshments, and he had to provide a service for everybody. A resolution was passed: 'That the reflections passed by the *Leader* newspaper are most detrimental to a useful Corporation property, which is much appreciated, and are entirely unfounded. No evidence whatever has been adduced of anything improper taking place at the Patti.' That official resolution should have ended any controversy, but disquiet continued.[34]

The first hints of trouble had been discernible earlier, in December 1922. The press had reported that the Polish Blackshirt Fascist movement was causing 'alarming situations', and stated that the government needed to take strong action to 'dampen the sparks before they became flames'. Sparks flew again when public discussion of dances and morals erupted in the press. The Rev. Watkin Davies of St Jude's observed that 'dancing was a splendid thing when under proper provision for young people as we have them for the Girls' Friendly Society and the Girl Guides'. Asked if they did stunt or shimmy dances, the Rev. Davies replied 'Oh no, they are so suggestive'. Bandleaders became targeted by anti-Semitic racist slurs, and were outraged at 'immorality' jibes thrown at them. A reporter had gone to interview an indignant Mr Snipper of the Jazz Wallahs Jazz Band who had been held personally responsible for immorality at the Patti. Mr Snipper pointed out that of five members of his band, two were Gentiles and his band was not responsible for any wrongdoing taking place. Mr Snipper also pointed out that stunt dancing was very common on the dance floors, but denied there was any immorality involved in its execution. Dr Rawlings, JP, said he 'had no objection to dancing per se in selected company and at reasonable hours, but I strongly object to promiscuous dancing at midnight or the early hours'. Asked what he meant, Dr Rawlings replied 'jazz dances were open to great abuse and of moral and physical evil'. Letters flooded into the newspaper under the headline 'JEWS AND DANCING', objecting to the slurs heaped upon dancers and Jews. The letter-writer, 'Terpsichorean Judaean', said the Jazz Wallahs conducted their dances 'in a most decorous manner'. The writer went on:

> I take exception to Mr Darwin saying in one breath that he had no feeling against the Jews, and then in the next saying that he objected to the way they improvised on the dance floor. Has he not seen non-Jewish couples doing this? . . . As a whole, Jewish young dancers, by reason of their aptitude and grace, always attract the attention of others who look to them for the introduction of the latest steps.[35]

Another letter-writer, 'Fairplay', wrote in support of 'Terpsichorean Judaean', confirming that the remarks were 'a slur upon the Jazz Wallahs' morality . . . and the people . . . and were objectionable, distasteful and insulting'. 'Fairplay' reminded readers that the Jazz Wallahs had spent two days performing on street corners raising money for the Swansea Hospital Carnival'. An apology was called for. Further letters flowed in. A 'Young Person' wrote to defend the youth and dancing:

> I am young, active, and feel that I am entitled to spend what little money I have left over from my weekly earnings as I see fit, and without being dictated to by a group of narrow minded killjoys many of whom have served their usefulness and their opinions like other pieces of worn-out and broken-down machinery, should be scrapped without further ceremony. I should say that the class of people who frequent

dance halls are too busy with their work and play to pry into the affairs of other people . . . it's an old saying that it takes an evil mind to detect anything that suggests evil. The gentlemen who are responsible for bringing up this insulting campaign can do no better than apologise.

The same day, the press reported that 'UNREST' had spread to the valleys with a headline 'Valley Morals – Disturbing State of Affairs'. Then coal-stealing was added to the anti-Semitic mix. A letter-writer had suggested that there were 'hotbeds of corruption and immorality at Rhydyfro, Pontardawe, Alltwen and Ynysmeudw'. A vigilance committee was called for. Ammanford was declared a 'wicked town and the hardest town we have touched' by evangelists at the Ammanford Revival, parading through the streets with banners reading 'Spirit of Evil at Ammanford'.[36] The jazz age in Wales was hotting up.

The Ammanford Silver Band were caught up in the rows and got tarred with the same brush as jazz musicians. They had applied for permission to hold open-air concerts on the Gorsedd site, which led to 'scenes' at the council meeting. The National Eisteddfod rehearsals on Sundays had not been objected to, as 'they were regarded as something sacred in Welsh life, and there was nothing anti-Christian in the great works of Handel, Beethoven or Mendelsohn'. A 'hubbub' followed between Mr Williams and Mr Evans, who shouted at each other. Mr Evans said of Mr Williams 'most people require rest on Sunday and do not go about getting bets on a Sunday morning'. 'You Shut Up', said Mr Williams, 'you've been on the council for eighteen years but you have not yet learnt how to conduct yourself.' Permission was granted for the open-air concerts.[37]

Fuelling the flames, a notice appeared in the press declaring a 'hoard of ruffians dressed as the Ku Klux Klan' had paraded through Swansea on a float, playing jazz. They turned out to be Swansea University students collecting for Rag Week. With these local confrontations being reported on at some length, Dr Walford Williams chose to deliver a lecture on 'Colour in Music' at the Swansea University musical society, his theme being 'public taste has been warped by ragtime music but we must live it out', implying that questionable 'Negro morals' had infiltrated respectable music circles. Another lecturer, Dr Vaughan Thomas, spoke on 'Municipal Apathy', declaring there was musical neglect in the town as Swansea did not have an opera house. That could be explained, he said, by 'the love of dividend and money' taking precedence over music.[38]

The arguments over dancing, Jews and Negro morals spread to Cwmamman Council, where fisticuffs nearly ensued at the council chambers. The Rev. John Thomas called for the authorities to ban dancing after 11 p.m. at Garnant Palace de Dance (sic) and Drill Hall, owing to 'Morals'. Willie Owen pointed out that there was a lot of indecency with people attending eisteddfodau and churches allowing their vestries to be kept open until midnight. Mr Owen added that functions 'where young people congregated should terminate at 10 p.m.'. Councillor Edwards contended the motion 'out of order as the council were not administrators of morals and it was an insult the Rev. gentleman had brought such a motion forward'. The Reverend Thomas retorted, 'you are splashing mud all right – I'll throw some at you also.' There was 'a scene', with Councillor Edwards challenging the Reverend to repeat the remark outside. Edwards got to his feet saying, 'I regret that you, a Reverend have gone into personalities, you who are supposed to uphold humanity.' There were cries of 'Chair! Chair!' from the floor. Motion carried.[39]

Surprisingly, there were a few brave dissenting men of the cloth who were prepared to accept jazz music into their services. A fine example was the Wesleyan Chapel on Swansea's Alexandra Road, which offered banjos at the Mission and the 'Pillars of Fire Missionaries' at services. Solos were given on bongos and accordion to 'warm up lukewarm Christians', with no reports of youth displaying 'Negro morals' in the congregation. Not to be outdone, Pastor Jeffreys of Mount Zion Chapel initiated ragtime hymns, accompanied by handclapping and leaps into the air, to enliven his congregation, all at a time when the rest of the country regarded Wales as a God-fearing cultural backwater. Pastor Jeffreys, who had spent 'seven wonderful years in Llanelli' before moving to Swansea, remarked 'Our singing has been called ragtime, but if it keeps the people together what does it matter? Let us thank God for it.' Wales, therefore, celebrated the Almighty not only in God-fearing solemnity, but with an outpouring of liberated behaviour similar to that on the dance floors.[40]

At the end of 1923 the local press advertised the new HMV gramophone records available for purchase. The list included 'Running Wild', an 'Ebony Jazz Tune' available at 3s., performed by English duo Norah Blaney, piano, and Gwen Farrar, cello; both sang, bridging the gap between variety and revue. Their stage show, which featured their recordings, was described as 'belonging to the sophistication of the nineteen twenties rather than to the old world of the music-halls which it invaded'. Blaney and Farrar were household names who also enjoyed an off-stage relationship, 'living together openly and enjoying the starry life' of Bright Young Things. Farrar would sometimes exit the stage after a number 'slinging her cello across her shoulder'.[41] Blaney and Farrar had been part of the Lena Ashwell Concert Party tours of the First World War (see chapter 5). South Wales could now purchase their latest record from the hit show *Running Wild*, the show in which the Charleston dance first appeared. Blaney and Farrar's life and times were featured at the 2015 Brighton Fringe in a touring stage show called *All The Nice Girls*, a Behind The Lines production, starring Ali Child and Rosie Wakley as Blaney and Farrar.

The Charleston became the latest dance floor spectacle, the steps a throwback to the fast tap footwork of African Americans, with add-ons of kicking up the heels, crossing the hands over the knees, and incorporating the 'glide' of sliding one leg behind the other in a circular motion. It was an exhilarating and exciting time to be on the dance floor – a time when women could indulge in exhibitionism without, they hoped, being called to account. Young women and girls, wearing short flapper dresses above the knee, were able to show off their steps uninhibited by constricting fashion. Most dresses sported layers of fringes, which swayed and shook, and some women also wore long strings of beads, which added to the visual motion of the dress. A headband with an ostrich feather usually completed the outfit. In 1925 Charleston exhibition dances were given by Miss Ethel Parsley and her partner, advertised from 7.30 p.m. to 1.30 a.m. for the new season at the Kit Kat Club, opening at the Patti with music provided by the Capitol Jazz Band and Kenways Dance Band, tickets priced at 3s. 6d. This ticket price was well within the means of most youngsters and was good value for a long night, a dance exhibition and two bands.[42]

African American composer James P. Johnson was responsible for the Charleston phenomenon. Johnson had pioneered the 'stride' piano style of ragtime and syncopated rhythms, and remembered:

> first seeing the Charleston danced at a dive called the Jungles Casino in New York in 1913. The Jungles was just a cellar without fixings. The people who came ... were mostly from Charleston, South Carolina. Most of them worked ... as longshoremen or on the ships. They danced hollering and screaming until they were cooked. They kept up all night or until their shoes wore off, most of them after a heavy day's work on the docks. The Charleston was a regulation cotillion step without a name. While I was playing for these Southern dancers I composed a number of 'Charlestons' – eight in all, all with that damn rhythm. One of these later became my famous 'Charleston' on Broadway.[43]

Trouble was brewing again in south Wales. A disconcerting article appeared in October 1924 informing the public that the British Fascists had opened a branch in Swansea.[44] Morals and Fascists notwithstanding, dances continued into 1925. Eight hundred attended the St Patrick's Day Ball at St Joseph's Hall, with music provided by the Crowley Bros Augmented Orchestra. In contrast, over 1,000 hymn-singing Revivalists formed a procession outside Calfaria Baptist Church in Llanelli, led by the renowned Revivalist David Matthews. They marched through the streets, stopping outside Llanelli Workingmen's Club, until club members came out to complain about the noise. The size of the crowd in the road prevented traffic from passing, and the police were called. There was a stand-off. The Revivalists eventually moved off singing, and the drinkers returned to the peace of their bar.[45]

During 1925 and into 1926 relations between political factions in Swansea town deteriorated when members of the local branch of the British Fascists were charged with assaulting Harry Pollitt, secretary of the National Minority Movement, and imprisoning him against his will. Pollitt had been attacked on a train to Liverpool. Pollitt's appreciation for the south Wales coalfield's 'sacrifices of the workers and their international solidarity' is documented by Hywel Francis.[46]

Swansea Fascists, anxious to make amends for bullying tactics, placed a wreath on the Cenotaph at the Armistice parade. The wreath-laying was to no avail, as complaints had been received regarding their undisciplined behaviour. Swansea Fascists then numbered between 500 and 600, and their chair, Mr Leeder, demanded that members must remain disciplined. He suggested a fundraising dance, as such good membership figures ensured a financial success. Two jazz bands, the Orpheans and the Blue Havanas, were hired for the British Fascists Dance held at the Patti on 2 February 1926, with 250 attending. This event was so successful that a British Fascists Carnival Ball was hastily organised for the following month, again at the Patti, with the same bands. Jazz musicians, Jewish or otherwise, were not going to turn down well-paid gigs even if they were for the British Fascists. The Jewish Association Football Club, who had previously held their Select Dance with Morry's Nine Stars Jazz Band at Swansea's 'newest ballroom', at Thomas's Café – advertised as the finest dance floor in Wales – were probably feeling threatened. With sabre-rattling continuing between the Jewish communities and Fascists, jazz bands such as the Blue Havanas and the Orpheans took the bookings regardless of the hirer's politics. Membership of the Swansea Fascists was increasing and causing some disquiet in the town. A counter-demonstration and rally was duly organised by a Miss James, initially against strikes and lockouts, but her efforts inspired 300 Swansea women to travel to London to demonstrate for peace and prosperity at the Royal Albert Hall. Fenner Brockway, J. H. Hudson, George Lansbury and Arthur Ponsonby were the speakers, and a pamphlet, *Why We Will Not Fight!*, was produced.[47] It would appear that growing Fascist unrest and bullyboy tactics, combined with the government strategy of ignoring the worker's political activities for their basic right to better pay and conditions, inspired Miss James and the 300 to take action and travel to London to voice their concerns. While the women from Swansea saw the need for a firmer political approach to austerity strikes and lockouts which were affecting local communities, the Evangelical Council were more worried about Welsh youth and morals. They appealed to Carmarthen Town Council to close dance halls at 10 p.m., as they had the 'moral and spiritual welfare of the young at heart'. Dances were described by the Evangelical Council as being:

> rugby scrums, seesawing from right to left like ships in a swell, flies trying to wriggle out of condensed milk, quivering like unset jelly, with girls tugging hopeless partners around the floor . . . with cat-like creeping and flying bracelets travelling at 200 mph., all brazen huzzies.[48]

Females always got the blame and had to take full responsibility for any seeming failings in public behaviour. 'Rugby scrum' was a popular description for dances. The following description was of the usually respectable annual Swansea Hospital Dance, now high on the disapproval list:

> MCs could do a lot more. The modern MC [Master of Ceremonies] gathers loungers around him and grabbing a partner for himself and legging her into the melee. So many people admitted it was like Swansea market on a Saturday night. Plus Fours (the latest in trouser fashion), boys and men standing in the middle of the dance floor, others walking in and out amongst dancers. Youths kissing girls . . . cigarette packets and fag ends, and no attempt at the MC to encourage wallflowers to dance. Couples foxtrotting or doing a waltz were allowed to slink with long panther-like creeps across the rhythm of the music and there were many collisions. There was a complaint that

organisers were too prone to sell 500 tickets at 4s. each, with the result – scrummage.[49]

The jazz police would soon be out in force again, as an advertisement for the following week at Swansea's Empire heralded the arrival of Hilda Ward, 'The Greatest Lady Saxophonist and her Lady Syncopators':

> Just from a session at Covent Garden. The magnificent lady band of syncopators were hit of the evening. Numbers given in masterly style and audience showed approval in remarkable manner. Programme all too short. Pop girls added to the gaiety with their choruses and clever dancing.[50]

This is one of the earliest references to 'pop' music. There was criticism that Swansea Corporation parks committee should tighten up procedures, as 'the prestige of the town should not be sacrificed for a few irresponsible young people'.[51] Neath Town Council fixed their curfew for dances at midnight. It was true that dances were a riot of fun and noise, fuelled by 'hot music' on the bandstands. However, youth could not be blamed for kicking up their heels; life was generally tough for most young working-class people in Wales and it was to get a lot tougher. It was 1926, and the General Strike. Music changed, and Wales's youth sang 'The Red Flag' in demonstrations outside the Elysium Hall.[52]

In 1926 the *Melody Maker* began publishing, priced 3d, a monthly jazz magazine later to become a weekly newspaper. It was the first publication to review American jazz records and articles as well as British ones. It was a very popular and important publication, giving jazz music performed by both men and women credence and relevance. It was an early supporter of women's jazz, but unfortunately lapsed occasionally into discriminatory practices (see chapter 8).

As can be seen from the African American contribution to café society in chapter 6, African American performers were held in high regard in south Wales, despite many insults hurled from the pulpits.

Black men and women performers were to suffer further discrimination from articles published in the *Melody Maker* in September 1927. Dr Farnell, the Rector of Exeter College, Oxford University, had written: 'Nigger Music Comes from the Devil'. He continued:

> There was nothing more degrading than vulgar music, which was worse than poisonous drink. Our civilisation was threatened by our Americanisms and jazz music. Do not take your music from America or from the niggers, take it from God, the source of all good music.[53]

Dr Farnell was writing from a doctrine enmeshed in self-righteous bigotry, racism and misogyny. To him, jazz was sinful and the black men who played it were sinful. Black women were branded 'sexual savages' and the embodiment of 'female evil' – for leading black men astray to play the music, and white men astray, from 'spiritual purity into sin', to listen to it.[54]

Debates on race issues were rife within the *Melody Maker*. An article by Maurice Burman, headed 'Hot Music Is It Negroid or Hebrew?', was published in 1931, in which the author compared and contrasted the music of the 'coloured races' with 'Hebrew sacred music'. Burman gave examples, arguing that this was not an attempt to prove anything, merely to draw attention to a fact which he had not seen before in print. Similarly, *Melody Maker* critic Leonard Feather, on the 'colour question' in 1933, offered the opinion that 'white musicians have contributed more to the advancement of hot music than coloured musicians'. This line was thoroughly opposed with reasoned argument by a champion of women jazz musicians, Bettie Edwards, who accused Feather of not knowing his history. Feather had opined that cornet player Bix Beiderbecke and saxophonist Frankie Trumbauer (both white) had inspired critics to make a study of the music, stating they were 'years ahead of their time'. Edwards counter-attacked, saying both musicians had got their inspiration from early ragtime:

which history will tell you it's a Negro expression of musical thought. The blues idiom of the Mississippi is the only evolution of modern music that will hold a permanent place. Stomps and gut-bucket music can have no survival beyond the dance fashions of the day.

Feather retaliated by saying that white musicians copied their ideas and 'refined them and that refinement has made hot music what it is today'. He went on,

America would still exist . . . but it would be an enormous forest of primeval savages, instead of a civilised country . . . white men have a greater practical knowledge of music . . . which enables them to make use of theory.

Edwards bounced back: 'Really? Then how would you account for the fact that the four most accomplished musicians in the whole of jazz were Hawkins (Coleman, tenor sax), Armstrong (Louis, trumpet/cornet), Hines (Earl, pianist) and Venuti, (Joe, Italian/American violin/vocalist) – three out of four!' Feather conceded that 'coloured' (black) players' music 'comes from the soul . . . but coloured players are so temperamental . . . the great men of white jazz don't have to be forgiven, because they don't make any slips!' Feather remarked that Armstrong played compositions by white musicians, giving pianist Hoagy Carmichael as an example. Edwards retorted that 'it goes to show that you cannot successfully dissociate white from black at the present stage of development in hot music' and urged Feather to see Armstrong's show the following week.[55] Bettie Edwards won that argument on points, realising the significance of the music that spoke a universal language.

Louis Armstrong continued on his 1933–4 tour of the UK with his Harlem Hot Rhythm Band, arriving in Swansea for a week's residency from 21 May 1934 at the Swansea Empire.[56] Armstrong's visits to Swansea left lingering memories. Mrs Whipp, interviewed by the *South Wales Evening Post* in 2013, aged 100, was born in Sketty, Swansea, in

1913. She grew up at a bed and breakfast in Oystermouth Road, run by her parents, and she recalled that the B & B guests included musicians and comics, including Armstrong's band on this tour. They 'took her out to the Bath Hotel on her 18th birthday and she was treated to a surprise performance from the crooner'.[57] Armstrong would later be accused of 'commercialism' in the 1940s by the jazz purists, but as Humphrey Lyttelton (trumpet) pointed out, 'Louis's professional career involved every facet of showmanship from featured solo spots to accompanying floor shows and, for a while, silent movies.' Lyttelton continued that the musicians who recorded with Armstrong in these early days were blissfully ignorant of the significance of what they were producing, which, in turn, enhanced the innovative vitality of the music. Armstrong in an interview said:

> Those people who make the restrictions, they don't know nothing about the music, it's no crime for cats of any colour to get together and blow ... You'll always get critics of showmanship. Critics in England say I was a clown, but a clown, that's hard. If you can make people chuckle a little, it's happiness to me to see people happy, and most of the people who criticise don't know one note from another.[58]

Jazz in Wales continued in popularity to such an extent that the threat to public morals and decorum continued to be raised by religious bodies. The Free Churches of Aberystwyth, for example, sent a deputation to the town council protesting against council permission for the public to apply for dance licences; it added a pledge to ratepayers that there was to be 'no more drinking'. Ignoring the fact that jazz bands had donated proceeds from benefits and fundraisers to the Wrexham coal mining disaster in 1934, Welsh churches and chapels continued to protest against the music with the ultimate goal of banning jazz altogether, as, in their opinion, it continued to induce 'Negro morals' in Welsh youth. Welsh youth ignored the churches' campaign.[59]

Wales rarely got mentioned in the *Melody Maker*, other than occasional notifications for musicians of forthcoming dance-band

> # The Links Between the Hwyl and the Negro Spiritual
>
> ### VARIOUS FORMS OF EXTEMPORISED RHYTHMIC CHANTING
>
> by
> The Reverend
> E. EBRARD REES
>
> WHEN the average person hears a Negro spiritual for the first time it either appears to be ludicrous or it rouses a deep emotional experience.
>
> Any new Negro spiritual does the same; it makes us laugh in ridicule at the simplicity of the sentiment, or weep at its emotional appeal to us.
>
> What is generally forgotten is that the Negro spiritual is a religious *vehicle*. It belongs to man on his lower planes of religious experience; man not quite grown up, but man everywhere for all that.
>
> **Origin**
>
> The spiritual came to this country from the Negroes of South America, where the preachers are natural singers.
>
> These preachers get their sermon going, and soon they have worked themselves and their congregations into an ecstasy of emotion. When that point is reached, they *sing* their text, or a sentence, or a paragraph, and their " song " bears away the congregation on an emotional wave.
>
> Thus the Negro spiritual is a very important part of the Negro preacher's equipment.
>
> their hearers by chanting or singing a rhythmic tune. Not only the preacher, but the congregation as well, are completely carried away. The hypnotic spiritual has won them, and the " truth " the preacher is desirous of getting over is got over.
>
> But the spiritual goes much further back into history In Persia, India and other Eastern places we find movements that have come into some form or other. The Celts were used to it, for the Druid priests incantated their messages.
>
> **Similarity**
>
> That is why an immemorial trait is found among Welsh preachers known as the Hwyl. If a stranger to the Welsh hwyl were to go to a rural Welsh church and hear the preacher half-way through his sermon he would be surprised to hear a spiritual which is as like a Negro spiritual as two peas.
>
> a rhythmic flow of niagaras of nouns and avalanches of adjectives.
>
> A strange fact about this Welsh hwyl is that it cannot function except as the vehicle of religion. The preacher cannot do it apart from a congregation.
>
> It is a pity that some of the best Welsh hwylers have not been recorded for gramophone purposes, and their " spirituals " recorded in musical scores for other purposes.
>
> **A New Field**
>
> The Welsh hwyl presents a new field to the Negro spiritual lover. And as it is fast dying out, the sooner it is recorded in some way the better, or it will be too late.
>
> It is said that Handel got the idea of his fugues for oratorio purposes from the Welsh hwyl. He heard a Welsh preacher under the sway of this emotion on a " fugue," and he captured it for *The Messiah*. The fugue is dominant in the spiritual and in the hwyl.
>
> It is a strange fact that these religious chantings, both Negro and Welsh, seem to have some definite connecting link with modern dance music. It is not so much the mere extemporisation which is of course

Figure 21: 'The Links between the Hwyl and the Negro Spiritual', 1934, *Melody Maker* (©Time Inc. (UK) Ltd)

contests, such as that for 1934.[60] However, under the headline 'Where There's a Hwyl' the *Melody Maker* reported that a second programme of Negro spirituals in Welsh would be given on BBC Radio, the first broadcast having been an experiment. Listeners had remarked after the first broadcast that they felt the spirituals resembled Welsh hymns, and a further programme was aired. The *Melody Maker* reminded readers of a recent article by the Rev. Ebrard Rees, who likened the Negro spiritual to Welsh *hwyl*. *Hwyl* translates as 'a state of fervent arousal within the Welsh-language Baptist service of call and response'. A similar 'soul' exists within African American Baptist services. This was the first time the comparison had been made in print. The Rev. Ebrard Rees's positive response to the history of jazz music was one of the few beacons of light amongst the mostly negative and racist attitudes of the rest of the ecclesiastics.[61]

In 1935 the *Melody Maker* reported that 'annoyed Swansea Clerics' had drawn up a resolution in Welsh, which was circulated to all churches and chapels and passed unanimously. It asked young people to stay away from 'hot' music for the sake of their health and well-being, claiming that the current position was becoming 'ugly'. The Pontardawe Women's Institute was not amused. They had earlier applied to the Pontardawe Magistrates Court for an extension for their St Valentine's Day Dance at Gwaun-Cae-Gurwen, and could see one of their fundraising efforts being scuppered. The nervous Chairman of the Magistrates warned the Pontardawe Women's Institute about the whole issue of dancing, licensing and 'Negro morals', reminding them of the Church's recent resolution. The Women's Institute, champions of many good causes, sailed like galleons on the tide of public opinion, and their licence was eventually granted. The Women's Institute and Wales danced on, and women's jazz in Wales continued to thrive, despite the odds.[62]

By the mid-1930s in Britain, debates on the 'race issue' continued to be discussed within the *Melody Maker*'s pages. A report appeared regarding Germany banning the playing of 'interpolated entertainments', i.e. jazz music. Pamphlets urging bands to 'expel all Jewish musicians' were distributed in London's Archer Street, the main hiring venue for musicians in the city. Under the headline 'Hitlerism in Leeds', the *Melody Maker* reported that Jewish dancers were to be barred from venues on 'certain nights'. Advertisements had been placed by 101 dance clubs in Leeds extolling 'strictly English clientele only'. The anti-Jewish ads initiative was, in fact, congratulated by the Sheffield music tour operator Sir Henry Coward, who stated at a Leeds women's luncheon club that: 'Hitler did a great thing . . . for the sake of art, morality and the Anglo Saxon Race. Jazz debases the morals and has destroyed the former prestige of the white races.'[63]

Hitler was having no impact in Wales. In May 1935 the *Melody Maker* reported that Wales was to have its own BBC programmes, broadcast from Cardiff, and wondered whether Welsh bands would get a chance to be heard.[64] Tony Small was pictured recording from the Coney Beach Restaurant, Porthcawl, and advertising the 'Streamline Trumpet' at 4 guineas (£4 4s.) or 2s. per week. In the same issue, the close-harmony group the Boswell Sisters broadcast several songs, including 'St Louis Blues', and a number entitled 'Rock and Roll' – they were singing about the sea. This issue also included a rather racist comment on Wales. Edgar Daniels of Blaenau Festiniog had sent in his amateur song manuscript for review. The *Melody Maker* reported: 'A Flat is not a commercial key . . . Don't they sell pens and inks in the unpronounceable place where you live? Your tune "That's why it's 'Home Sweet Home to Me'" is too long and hackneyed.'[65]

The *Melody Maker* advised its musicians that BBC Radio's Third Programme (the forerunner of Radio 3) had now mastered their microphone technique and advised a deep voice was preferable for 'lady vocalists' to sing pop dance-band numbers.[66] It also reported that fifteen-year-old Swansea crooner Joan (no surname) had been broadcast whistling, although she had sung with bands such as Roy Allen and the Manhattans, and the Sylvians Dance Orchestra. Also advertised in the *Melody Maker* was Mumbles pier, which had now opened its new ballroom for dances every Saturday night, the contract having gone to Roy Clifford and his Band.[67] In 1936, the death of King George V was announced in the press, with the comment 'our world of jazz collapses'. The country was of 'heavy heart with grief'. Bands that were due to be broadcast were now cancelled; they were probably grieving too at the loss of income.[68]

The *Melody Maker* flagged up the BBC in 1936 for giving airtime to the Zulu musician Thola'Kele Caluza, who had given a talk on the origins of jazz, 'one of the few African native music professors and full blooded member of the Zulu nation'. Caluza talked on the history of the African drums and about how he had made gramophone records with his Zulu Native Choir and had also studied piano and organ.[69] This appraisal is in contrast to the 'Negro morals' rows debated earlier in the local press.

Swansea was briefly mentioned in the *Melody Maker* regarding a broadcast from the Swansea studio by Arthur Wyn on vibes and xylophone, with Leonard Morris on piano. An item also appeared by reporter G. E. Pfrötzschner about Germany's new dance band 'Dictator' for the 1936 Olympic Games broadcasts, Hans Bund, 'the German Henry Hall'.[70] The *Melody Maker* then grouped its small items under 'South Wales Notes', enabling a clearer picture of what was happening on the jazz scene in Wales:

> Evered Davies broadcasting from Aberystwyth; Lou Preager and His Band booked for the Ritz Ballroom, Llanelli; the Club Four band resident at the Pier, Mumbles; the Lyricals had left the Pavilion, Pontardawe; Len Calvin and the Denza Players of Llanelli had secured a broadcasting contract; the Keskersays and the Manhattans were still working; and Frank Hughes was now back in the Sylvians featuring Hawaiian guitar, after his season at Tenby.[71]

By the mid-1930s the Bangor-born clarinettist Harry Parry (1912–56) was making a name performing in Eddie Shaw's band at Payne's Café in Llandudno. Parry went on to form his own sextet and various other bands, with an emphasis on swing music. His later quintet featured George Shearing on piano. Parry became a fixture on the BBC with his Radio Rhythm Club Sextet and later recorded for the Parlophone label. He was a public figure as host and compère of BBC Radio's Jazz Club and worked extensively in London, later recording with Dill (Dillwyn) Jones on piano. When bebop became the latest jazz innovation in the late 1940s Parry faded out of the limelight, unable to adapt.[72] Dill Jones (1923–84), however, did adapt. Jones was born in Newcastle Emlyn, Carmarthen, and became ship's pianist on the *Queen Mary* sailing to New York, thereby taking the opportunity to see and hear the finest modern jazz musicians perform live. Jones featured on piano in London bands led by Tony Kinsey, Joe Harriott and Ronnie Scott, before forming his own trio and eventually emigrating to New York. Jones died of cancer and his obituary in the *New York Times* read: 'A versatile, accomplished pianist, he was a master of the Harlem stride style ... and was the host of "The BBC Jazz Club", the program that introduced jazz to British television.'[73]

In October 1936 the *Melody Maker* reported a threatening scandal regarding dance bands and the BBC. Serious allegations had been made of a new 'racket' by the BBC, in which unpaid bands were encouraged to play one-night hotel gigs under the pretence of a 'resident' broadcast, thereby exploiting the musicians. Although the accolade of broadcasting was highly sought after, it was at the expense of the purse for those who acquiesced to get airtime. In the same issue, it was reported that the BBC had taken over the old Public Assistance offices in Swansea's Alexandra Road to be refurbished as their new studio for south Wales.[74] The International Peace Campaign was also reported on, with musicians encouraged to get organised and 'Declare for World Peace'.[75]

During 1937 the mentions of Wales in the *Melody Mak*er began to increase; male bands predominated, with an occasional reference to women. Mae Jones was the popular Welsh piano player and director of the Rhythmic Ten, and had written the whole of the music for the *Brown Bird* show, recently broadcast from the Bristol studio.[76] In contrast, ten male bands were featured, with a photograph of one, the Ambassadors from Treherbert, who would be competing in the Big Welsh Contest at the Brangwyn Hall, judged by Henry Hall, the regular BBC broadcaster. The other bands competing were Roy Allen and his Band from Gorseinon, Eric Wall and his Players from Port Talbot, Vic Haynes and his Lyrics from Swansea, Teddy Holmes and his Band from Ammanford, the Blue Four from Swansea, the Blue Rhythm Boys from Treherbert, the Manhattans from Swansea, Frank Wride and his Band from Pontypridd, Glyn Samuel and his Rhythm Boys from Treorchy, and Eric Dare and his Band from Gorseinon. No women. Was this because they were overlooked in preference to male bands, or had the women not applied?[77] First prize of £35 went to Glyn Samuel and his Rhythm Boys, with Swansea hospitals 'benefitting handsomely and many discoveries made by the BBC'.[78] There were increasing opportunities for Welsh bands to be on air, as Hopkin Morris had taken over as BBC Welsh 'chief' and was committed to 'better and brighter programmes'.[79]

Women continued to plough their own furrow. Cardiff piano player Clare Deniz had a gig in May 1937 at the Old Florida Swing Spot, South

Bruton, with Ken 'Snake Hips' Johnson (named for his dancing style) and his Rhythm Swingers, an eleven-piece band.[80] Deniz was the daughter of a Barbadian seaman and a Somerset mother, and she continued to perform into her 80s. Wilmer, writing in the *Guardian*, says of Deniz, who died aged 91, 'she was one of a handful of black Cardiff musicians to establish themselves in London two decades before Shirley Bassey'. Deniz travelled to London, pretending to be an American and dressing stylishly in order to attract the work. She also featured with a Benny Goodman-styled sextet called Frank's Spirits of Rhythm, and later experimented with bebop with Jamaican arrivals trumpeter Dizzy Reece and saxophonist 'Pet' Campbell.[81]

Musicians and singers in Wales with the talent to try were eager to make a career for themselves in London or other major cities. For example, in 1937 the *Melody Maker* reported that 17-year-old vocalist Sylvia Stuart had left Swansea 'for the wicked metropolis' for her first big break, with Al Tabar and his Band at the smart Prince's Restaurant, Piccadilly, London. Stuart had also signed a six-month contract to sing rhythm numbers in Budapest at the Parisien Grill, with the management having an option for a further six months at the exclusive Hotel Esplanade in Prague.[82] Three male performers who left Swansea in 1937 were 'brilliant pianist' Leonard Morris, editor of a book of Welsh folk songs, to join the Forum Theatre in London, and two members of the Esplanade Hotel Dance Band, who joined Doug Swallow's Band at the Ritz, Manchester, namely Leo Morris, tenor sax, and Harry Smith, violin and sax; Wales was losing some of its best musicians.[83] In 1938 Mrs Wilf Hamer and her Band broadcast twice with the BBC from Rhyl, and the Glyn Samuel Band from Treorchy did likewise from the Swansea studios, the *Melody Maker* pronouncing in 1938 that 'South Wales can Swing' when it reported on the dance band contests. The winners that year were Roy Allen and the Modernists.[84]

The *Melody Maker* noted the rise of hostilities in 1938 and reported on missing musicians, such as band leader Teddy White, who got stranded in Vienna during Hitler's invasion, with some of his band missing and Germany having confiscated their money.[85] Also mentioned approvingly was the BBC policy of favouring dance bands.[86] The good relations didn't last long, as the *Melody Maker* reported that the BBC

> were driving a new nail into jazz's coffin as they had abandoned the midnight gramophone recitals which was a threat to the future of pop, jazz and dance bands . . . contemptuous treatment, and jazz is being slowly interned in a slough of bureaucratic intolerance.[87]

The BBC should have taken note of the popularity of jazz, as 4,000 fans from all over Britain had attended the first Jazz Jamboree, in 1939 at the Trocadero Cinema, London. Proceeds were to go to the Musician's Union Benevolent Fund, as the MUBF needed the money, and tickets were for sale at 5s. The Jamboree was described in the *Melody Maker* as a 'Mighty Spectacle' but no other details were given.[88]

As 1939 progressed, there was increased reportage in the *Melody Maker* of hostilities across Europe. In Cardiff there was unrest between neighbours when Geraint Jones, a boogie-woogie pianist with a 'long training' in classical music, upset his neighbour Mrs Thomas, who complained about the noise. In response he composed 'Mrs. Thomas Blues' and played it for her. Mrs Thomas's comments were not recorded.[89] The *Melody Maker* also reported that the Nazis were 'still listening to good jazz', as five bands had been touring in 'high-class' bars in Berlin.[90]

War was declared in Britain on 3 September 1939. The following week's publication of *Melody Maker* declared 'Jazz Swings Into Khaki', the paper's job being to 'keep music alive' and the musicians' job to 'keep up morale in civilian defence'.[91] Wartime dance music 'was booming as musicians had recovered from the shock'. The *Melody Maker* featured south Wales's jazz efforts to keep up morale:

> Teddy Joyce was using a fifteen-piece band for his Joyce Jamboree which included Tony Lombardo and Gloria Brent; Ron Davies on drums was at the Marina Ballroom, Penarth and also doing ARP (Air Raid Precaution) duties; Ron Smith, altoist, had joined the RAF; Len Stevens and his Band was at Cold Knap Bay, Barry Island; Murray

and his Band played for RAF St Athan's Aerodrome; Frank Davies at the Capitol Theatre, Cardiff, had been compelled to disband his twelve-piece and install a 'snappy' four-piece instead, and Peter Colman was still resident at Cardiff's Carlton Rest.[92]

By December 1939, a 17-year-old Welsh 'girl', Terry Wilson, had been snapped up by Harry Leader and his Band, 'The Masters of Melody'. Leader had discovered Wilson singing with a trio in cabaret in the West End and signed her for twelve months; she became a 'smash hit' at his Sunday concerts. The Keskersays were now playing regularly at Swansea's Langland Bay Hotel, with the leader Georgie Charles also working as a special constable for the war effort.[93] The *Melody Maker* became the official organ of ENSA (Entertainments National Service Association) Musical and Band section. ENSA had paid £1,966 towards dance musicians' wages for troop concerts. An appeal was sent out for 'croonettes' to audition for 'wax recordings', and 150 applied.[94]

Margaret Carlson from Swansea recalled her war work as a 17-year-old in Bridgend munitions factory filling bombs and shells. With such dangerous work occasionally resulting in horrendous injuries and sometimes death, the filling line were only too eager to be entertained in the factory canteen. Visiting stars did turns, girls from the factory floor would go up to sing or dance, and once film star Clark Gable arrived to sell War Bonds for a kiss. A factory group was formed, called the Pellettes, to which the girls jitterbugged – an exuberant, freewheeling dance spread initially by the American armed forces, featuring swings, lifts and throws between the legs and incorporating nifty footwork. After their shift Margaret and her friends on the line hot-footed it to Swansea dance halls to jitterbug to national touring bands such as Joe Loss and Ambrose, as well as to the local bands. The best local band in town, according to Margaret, were the Excelsiors, who were resident at the Patti Pavilion. It cost 6d to go in, a halfpenny for a cup of tea, and 3d for a glass of beer. Margaret's starting pay in 1939 was £4 10s. per week, a large increase from the 10s. per week at her previous job, rolling sheets through the press in Swansea Baths and Laundry. By

218 ❦ Freedom Music

Figure 22: Margaret Morris in a shop window, 1947
(Jazz Heritage Wales Collection)

the time she left Bridgend Munitions in 1946 it had risen to £11 19s. 6d, including bonds and bonuses, enabling her to keep her mother and sisters. Margaret recalled the polite African American GIs billeted in Swansea passing her in the street on her way to catch the train to Bridgend munitions factory. They always said 'Good morning' to her. Margaret commented that the GIs were only 'courted long enough for them to part with their silk stockings, sweets and make-up'.[95]

Wartime sheet music was hugely popular. Music publishers cashed in, especially when America entered the war and GI Joes were 'over here'. The lyrics to this derogatory and racist 1944 sheet music, 'Choc'late

Soldier from the USA', the cover depicting a smiling African American soldier at the wheel of a jeep, read:

> Choc'late drop, always fast asleep,
> Dozin' in his cosy bed,
> Choc'late drop has got no time for sleep,
> He's riding in a jeep instead;
> They used to call him Lazy Bones in Harlem
> Lazy good for nothin' all the day;
> But now they're mighty proud of him in Harlem
> Choc'late Soldier from the USA.[96]

Cinemas and ballrooms did not escape the bombing during the 1941 Swansea Blitz. The Tower Cinema in Townhill, however, did, and became a sanctuary when Emlyn Road in Townhill had a direct hit. Maureen Andrews, then 8 years old, recalled being in the Tower watching a film with her father when the alarm went over the tannoy. Her father placed her with a family and ran to Emlyn Road to see if their home had been hit. He later returned for Maureen and took her home, their house having escaped damage. The Blitz continued for a further two nights. Joan and Val Phillips watched the bombs raining down on Townhill and Mayhill; they described the scene as 'looking like fairyland', but it was the incendiaries giving this impression.[97]

The most famous of the all-woman orchestras that blazed a pioneering trail during the Second World War was the Ivy Benson All Girl Orchestra. Ivy ran a tight ship and expected the best from her 'girls' on and off the bandstand; she auditioned young women from all over the country. Her swing arrangements, as well as her stage presentation, were immaculate. The hugely popular orchestra toured non-stop, with air-force bases high on the agenda.[98] Joan and Val Phillips recalled the queues outside the Tower Ballroom for the Ivy Benson Band being 'a mile long stretching along the street. We went to dances with our girlfriends as it was more fun and we always liked to see what the new ballrooms were like.'[99]

Figure 23: Ivy Benson, Vienna, 1947 (Jazz Heritage Wales Collection, donated by Diana Lusher and Richard Arnatt from Sheila Tracy Collection)

Ballrooms during and after the Second World War kept jazz music alive: during the war to keep up morale, and after the war to celebrate being alive, offering new opportunities to dance the jitterbug and later the jive. The Tower Ballroom officially opened as a ballroom in August 1958 with a sprung dance floor, a Bamboo Buffet and Bar, fish net decor and storm lanterns. It included a Rank Organisation sound system and spotlights. The resident Tower Orchestra was led by Ray Jones. Joyce Cannock saw Johnny Dankworth and Cleo Laine at the Tower: 'fabulous nights! I used to walk home to Penlan as there was no transport in them days'.[100]

Huge ballrooms, expensive in upkeep with the payment of fees for twenty-two musicians in big bands and more in orchestras, had to diversify in order to survive. Rock and roll arrived in 1958, and small rock bands and jazz combos were employed to fulfil the new dance craze, the jive. Derek Morgan, bandleader and drummer with the Rockets, recalled, 'My band entered the 1958 Tower Rock n' roll contest and won! We were all jazz musicians. We used to play a lot at the Tower.'

Another drummer, John Evans, leader of Swansea's ten-piece Jazz Senators, who also played at the Tower, diversified into rock music when jazz gigs dried up. He joined the Fireflies rock group which played at the Tower Ballroom and supported rock stars on tour, such as Jimmy Justice and the Exchequers, Johnny Kidd and the Pirates, Emil Ford, Adam Faith, and Freddy and the Dreamers. Roy Denver, the Fireflies' singer, recalls: 'We entered a competition at Sophia Gardens in Cardiff beating Tom Jones before he had made his first record! We usually played for four hours and got 10s. each . . . the halls closed once pubs started putting in live bands.'[101]

Jazz was sidelined, surviving the onslaught of rock music in small jazz rooms and clubs through the enthusiasm of its fans. Derek Gabriel, the renowned Swansea jazz photographer, has documented the post-1950 jazz venues in Swansea: the Patti, the Glanmor Jazz Club, Swansea Townhill College, Swansea University, the Columba Club, the Liberal Club, and the St James's Club, which now hosts Swansea's Jazzland, run by pianist Dave Cottle. Jazzland began life in 1959 as Swansea Modern Music Society, with their first newsletter dated 13 April 1959 and signed 'Shirley Bateman – your Club Editor'.[102]

Jazz, as does most popular music, reinvents itself for contemporary audiences. New jazz festivals sprang up, such as Brecon Jazz Festival, with its artistic director Jed Williams, which trumpeted its arrival in 1984 on a huge scale and seemed invincible, attracting international stars. It survives on a smaller scale as the Brecon Jazz Weekend and Spirit of the Festival. The Swansea International Jazz Festival celebrated its fifth summer of events in 2018, its artistic director being Dave Cottle.

It is remarkable that a minority music which welcomed the first African Americans to south Wales in the mid-1800s, and supported them and an evolving music through the 1920s into the first jazz age, should survive through segregation, discrimination, the First and Second World Wars, and the onslaught of rock music. Jazz music, through generations of protests and rebellions, continues to flout boundaries. Theoretical discussions on race (did European music influence African American music?) and gender (are women encouraged enough to apply for university jazz courses?) are on-going. The music remains a source of economic disadvantage for most jazz musicians, who have to augment their incomes by teaching, running workshops and diversifying. Jazz music, however, continues to innovate, and Wales played a significant part in its heritage.

Chapter Eight

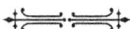

Fair Treatment for the 'Fair Sex'?

CHITI ARGUES THAT WOMEN jazz musicians were often overlooked and rarely recognised, despite the historical evidence, with jazz historians and critics systematically silencing or denigrating the voice of women.[1] Jazz music celebrates its hundredth anniversary in 2019, so it is timely to ask who wrote the history and critical analysis of early jazz music; were women represented in that critique, and, if so, was it gender neutral? Were women performers regarded as novelty acts, and therefore not awarded due attention to their capabilities? Bailey suggests there was a mythology that women were 'unskilled . . . [that] was so embedded in contemporary sources that these myths have now spread to the secondary literature'. For women, playing jazz was not a straightforward pursuit but a negotiation around obstacles within a patriarchal system.[2]

Male authors and critics wrote about what they knew and understood – male bands. When women jazz musicians took to the stage, this was perceived as a threat to jazz's sociocultural hegemony, with critics writing with derisive tones at women's expense. The male jazz performer was the status quo; women did not require equal status as they hardly existed in critiques. It was easy, therefore, for women to be dismissed and written out of jazz history. This chapter will discuss whether jazz women received fair treatment from the music press in the early days, and why Welsh women in particular were badly hit by the *Melody Maker*, the main national British music newspaper published from 1926, with hardly any mention in its pages at all, even though we have established in this book that Welsh women were abundant on stage, in café floor shows and in the halls. However, the Welsh local press did give due regard to women's endeavours.

Parsonage and Dyson confirm that British women jazz musicians contributed to the evolution of jazz from the beginning of the twentieth century. They refer to jazz guitarist Deirdre Cartwright, famous for the 1983 BBC television's *Rock School* programmes, as identifying a 'lack of role models for women when she started out in her career'. It was thought that women played an irrelevant and undistinguished part in the formation of the music, and the literary canon mostly reflected this theory. Women engaging in political activism during the 1960s and 1970s, and discovering feminist history, began to influence the way women perceived themselves, which, in turn, helped to overcome some of the barriers placed in their way. Parsonage and Dyson write that 'the changing nature of music education and increasing opportunities for this to be accessed by women on an equal basis to men has been influential on the development of female jazz musicians in Britain'.[3]

Additionally, music schools and university courses must take a look at their curriculum and offer compositions by women composers, either as an alternative to the male genre or at least on an equal basis. Jazz courses should offer modules on women in jazz history, not just as an add-on, but to showcase positive role models for youngsters and to illustrate the perilous nature of the journey the early jazz pioneers took. Some jazz courses are now led by women, such as the inspirational double bassist, composer and arranger Paula Gardiner, Course Director at the Royal Welsh College of Music and Drama (RWCMD) in Cardiff. Paula runs a Junior Jazz summer course for 8–18-year-olds, aimed at first-timers and also those who wish to go on to higher education. She has been a beacon and role model for women musicians in Wales for many years. Gardiner recalls:

> The College [RWCMD] was looking for someone to create and co-ordinate a jazz programme back in 2001. They asked me in the interview what I thought was important for jazz training, and I had a lot of ideas about that, because I'd previously set up my own workshops. The two roles of academic and jazz musician complement each other well indeed: I have an allowance of time to pursue my own personal development. Obviously I can't be out playing bass until the small hours every night when I have a full-time job, and I'm a parent too, so it's a question of balance. But when I play, it's so enjoyable; it still feels fresh and exciting.[4]

Paula Gardiner began her career by combining structured workshops at the Wavendon Centre in the 1980s, a registered charity founded by Sir John Dankworth and Dame Cleo Laine, with writing and composing her own music; both Paula Gardiner and Dame Cleo Laine are Patrons of Jazz Heritage Wales. At the age of 27, after being admitted to the Association of Professional Composers, Paula undertook a Master's degree in Jazz Composition at the Guildhall School of Music. She felt then it was crucial that she passed on her skills to others.[5]

Rieger argues that concepts of music stem from masculine cultural characteristics. Jazz women might, therefore, have appeared to be a threat to the jazz fraternity by overturning those cultural constructs and competing for work in what was perceived to be a male field.[6] At the beginning of the twentieth century women jazz musicians were fully participating in this explosion of cultural dynamism and vitality, making a significant contribution to the twenty-first century. These women perceived themselves as being in the forefront of changing patterns of social behaviour in both public and private life. However, such positive female role models are rarely included in written accounts of the period or thought worthy of conservation or discussion. This is in contrast with the folk tradition of Wales which has cherished its history and conserved its resources, and which continues to be celebrated by contemporary musicians, such as Catrin Finch and Cerys Matthews, for the enlightenment of worldwide audiences.

The Welsh folk music tradition has an illustrious history of collecting and conservation, saving it for the nation and future generations. A pioneer of rescuing folk songs from obscurity was Maria Jane Williams, born 1794/5 in Aberpergwm House, Glynneath, south Wales. An accomplished performer on guitar and harp, she was associated with the Welsh cultural society known as *Cwmreigyddion y Fenni* (Composers of Abergavenny). In 1844 her collection of Welsh folk songs was published as *The Ancient National Airs of Gwent and Morgannwg*. There, Maria Jane Williams claimed that: 'The songs were given as obtained . . . in their wild and original state; no embellishments of the melody have been attempted, and the accompanying words are those sung to the airs.'[7]

A later pioneer in the Welsh folk music tradition, especially in the collecting, conserving and recording of traditional airs and songs, was Morfydd Owen (1891–1918), born in Trefforest. Pike writes: 'Owen was one of the most promising singer-composers Wales has ever produced . . .probably the best mezzo-soprano of her day, a brilliant pianist, and an original and eclectic composer.'[8] Owen composed a nocturne for full orchestra, performed in Queen's Hall, London, in 1914, and went on to compose forty songs. She had a particular interest in folk song and was a pioneer collector in her field, a member of the Welsh Folk Song Society, and notated old songs from phonographs on which she had recorded elderly people singing. Many of these old Welsh folk songs were arranged for voice and piano by Morfydd Owen. Welsh was her first language and she also spoke English, French, German and Russian. Owen studied at University College, Cardiff, with David Evans, gaining a BA in Music in 1912, and was admitted to the Gorsedd of Bards the same year. She set poems by Blake, de Musset, Keats, Alfred Noyes and Robert Bryan to music. Owen later met Lady Ruth Lewis, 'an avid collector of Welsh folk songs', wife of the Liberal MP for Flintshire, Herbert Lewis. Inspired, Owen identified, notated and recorded the old

Figure 24: Maria Jane Williams (1795–1873)
(St Fagans National Museum of History, Wales)

songs on cylinders on the then state-of-the-art Edison phonograph. In 1914 Owen published thirteen folk-song arrangements in Ruth Lewis's

Folk Songs Collected in Flintshire and the Vale of Clwyd. Appointed a sub-professor of Composition at the Royal Academy in 1914, Owen's desire to study folk music in Russia was thwarted by the outbreak of war. She died suddenly, aged 26, and is buried in Oystermouth Cemetery. Pike quotes Professor David Evans, Owen's Cardiff teacher: 'I regard her early death as an incalculable loss to Welsh music, indeed I know of no young British composer who showed such promise.'[9] In the summer of 2015 the life and times of Morfydd Owen were resurrected by the dance-theatre group Sweetshop Revolution for their production *I Loved You and I Loved You*, described as:

> part concert, part dance piece with three incredible dancers . . . as well as a singer and pianist playing live. Much of the music has not been heard for 100 years. The aim of Sweetshop Revolution is to make dance theatre that both questions and entertains, where movement, music and text sit seamlessly as one.[10]

The renowned Swansea-born soprano Elin Manahan Thomas with Brian Ellsbury (piano) celebrate and perform the music of Morfydd Owen on their 2016 recording *Portrait of a Lost Icon*.[11] Morfydd Owen's early conservation work and her 180 compositions produced over ten years are testament to the regard her name holds in Wales; she realised that old songs would be lost to Wales if she did not undertake the collecting work herself. Wales has produced inspiring women composers who would have remained obscure but for organisations such as Tŷ Cerdd and the Welsh Folk Song Society, which cherish and nurture the music and heritage of women such as Grace Williams (1906–77). Williams, recorded for the *Composer's Workshop* series for the BBC Welsh Home Service, said:

> To compose music is to do something off the beaten track, even if you're a man. But if you're a woman composer it is considered very odd indeed. But at the age of four I began to have tantrums because I couldn't play the piano. I preferred to be let loose on anything

that came my way; and a vast amount of music did come my way. Most of it was by the great composers, with Beethoven and Chopin as first favourites, but . . . when jazz first came to Wales I played Alexander's Ragtime Band with great gusto. In those pre-radio days it was tremendously exciting for me to hear an orchestra.[12]

The conservation and interpretation of Welsh folk song has importance for Wales's cultural heritage. Morfydd Owen was collecting and recording Wales's folk heritage in the early twentieth century, but it would be another twenty years or so before John and Alan Lomax would set out in the early 1930s and record for posterity the blues men and women of the southern states of America. The conservation of cultural heritage accomplished by Wales and by the southern states could not be more diverse, but the end result was similar: to preserve the music for future generations before it was lost. Lomax writes:

My father, John A. Lomax, and I began recording Southern black folk songs in the field in the 1930s. The portable recording machine, which my father and I were the first to use, provided the first breakthrough. Thus the portable recorder put neglected cultures and silenced people into the communication chain.[13]

Morfydd Owen realised this too. By giving voice to the voiceless, there is a record of how things were and how things sounded, a counterpoint to those who prefer the safe and familiar status quo. The institutions that preserve the history of women in music are also responsible for the way in which women who produced the music are represented. Women in jazz, and that includes jazz women in Wales, did not get an easy ride in the music media; they were denigrated and misrepresented. Uncovering the neglected or hidden history of women is part of the jazz story. There cannot be a history of jazz music without women, so it is crucial that there is an examination of how women were perceived in the early music press in order to show women of the future how far they have come.

Figure 25: Song collecting, Llandysul, 1911
(St Fagans National Museum of History, Wales)

The *Melody Maker*, the first and important voice for jazz, published from 1926, offered work for women in their advertisements, provided they sent in photographs with the job application, a requirement not necessary for men. In 1928 Welsh male jazz musicians got a brief, derogatory mention with the headline 'An All-Welsh Dance Band!' The piece featured the Memorial Hall Dance Band, with the suggestion that it was unusual that Welsh people could play jazz. Its opening sentence reads:

> Can it be possible, you ask, that Wales, the recognised home of 'highbrow' music and musicians, has produced a dance band composed entirely of its own countrymen? Ah indeed to goodness, but this is the case . . . The band performs four nights per week at the Memorial Hall Pontypridd. Taffy – we beg his pardon – W. Davies (leader) on piano and organ etc.[14]

Women in Wales were barely mentioned during these early years, so assumptions have to be made that Welsh women were included in general comments about women performers. Women in the UK able to perform jazz music were reviewed as not being feminine. If they were 'feminine', wearing stage gowns and lipstick on the bandstand, then it was held that they could not play jazz, as they had to dress up to hide deficiencies. A typical example:

> Sensational . . . only way of describing the reception given to the twenty-two Ingénues on the occasion of their recent performances at the London Palladium. Although the girls played well, outstandingly well considering their sex, the real honours go to their showmanship, slickness, well-conceived lighting arrangements. Musical virtuosity was certainly not the reason . . . nor their musicianship.[15]

Such preoccupation with visual aspects was part of condescending attitudes about women's level of ability, implying that their degree of ability was not equal to men's, but that they had gained public popularity through their feminine appeal or, alternatively, that they were regarded as a novelty item. Women were devalued as musicians and they certainly would not have been booked into the prestigious London Palladium unless they were exceptionally good. The media and promoters of the time enforced gender stereotypes and women became trapped in compulsory glamour, reinforcing assumptions that their music did not really count. Women's jazz had to fight from a position of disadvantage.

Jazz women, however, did not feel that their lives had to be dictated by their sexuality, reproductive systems or degree of femininity, but instead by their musical ability in order to perform a complex music which could provide a living wage and a satisfying career. If women did, in fact, display an intellectual understanding of the music and conveyed it through a high level of performance, they were regarded as having masculine characteristics, or portraying deviancy. Jazz music since its inception had been defined through male terms as a male art form. This is no longer the case, although old preconceived notions can occasionally be sniffed wafting on hot air.

In the 1920s women jazz musicians in Wales were in a more difficult position than those, for example, living in London, as Welsh women had to find their niche performing a new music within the traditional culture of Wales as the land of song, male voice choirs, *eisteddfodau* and *penillion* (a vocal improvisation over a harp counter-melody). It might, therefore, be seen from the pages of the London-centric *Melody Maker* that Wales was a cultural backwater for jazz music, preconceptions limiting its investigation. Wales, too, was busy trying to recover from the damning of the 1847 Blue Books[16] and perhaps needed to show a respectable face to the world. Chapels and churches tried their best to throw jazz out, but youth and the music won out.

Women, whichever part of the UK they came from, were rarely mentioned in the *Melody Maker*. In the late 1920s, women began to attract increasing attention in its pages, but then from 1931, when Spike Hughes, a Cambridge graduate, bass player, composer and arranger, was offered a weekly column as well as his regular record reviews, they suffered marginalising and alienation. His columns and opinions became a 'must read' for fans and musicians, bookers and promoters. His autobiography, *Second Movement*, traces his influential career as both performer and writer and critic for jazz newspapers and journals, dictating opinion which became received wisdom. He wrote in the *Melody Maker* under the pseudonym of 'Mike' or 'Anonymous', eventually confessing his 'veil of secrecy' in the edition of 15 November 1952. He referred to himself as 'the voice of experience', and wished to see his name in bold type in the *Melody Maker* as a 'theorist promoting propaganda defining public taste'. Unfortunately, his preference was for propaganda and public taste of his own definition, which was to promote male jazz musicians and eliminate women, any women, from the bandstand. On his band tours, he confessed to 'looking for pretty Eurasians or delicious full-bosomed and exotic girls from the East Indies'.[17]

The following judgement on women musicians, from Hughes's autobiography, written in 1951, is quoted because of the implications his opinions had at the time for all women, be they Welsh or not (and

Figure 26: Spike Hughes (*Second Movement – Continuing the Autobiography* (London: Museum Press, 1951))

Hughes referred to all British women as English), and from which they struggled to recover:

> I have always viewed with alarm the growing tendency of women to compose music; not merely because they do not compose very well, but because their presence in the company of a group of male musicians is embarrassing and unnatural. As men we have our own language and our own codes of behaviour among ourselves . . . a woman who

demands artistic, professional and social equality among us . . . is acutely unwelcome and disturbing. There can never be such a thing as true equality of the sexes. Economic equality, perhaps – I am married to a woman who, thank heavens, not only earns her own living, but often mine as well. Women lack originality and creative ability . . . The Englishwoman is at her best only when she is dressed for the company of those horses and dogs which she so much resembles.[18]

Spike Hughes became one of the pool of judges for the *Melody Maker* National Dance Band competitions, but his decidedly sexist views of women musicians cast doubt on his abilities for impartiality as a judge. Hughes wrote:

These contests were organised up and down the country by the *Melody Maker* for the benefit of semi-professional bands . . . It was all thoroughly good publicity for the paper which, in return for supplying a few judges, giving the successful band a nice write-up in its columns and presenting the leader with a banner and a certificate . . . I managed to remain sober on most occasions . . . My fellow-judges all seemed to relish a temporary escape from their wives . . . More than once I found myself having to brush quite pretty chamber-maids off my Hotel bed . . . In spite of a pretty liberal education in Berlin and elsewhere, I had to admit myself a beginner in licentiousness when faced with the frontal attack put on by the young women of Bolton and Nottingham . . . I was given handsome expenses (as a judge) and a fee for my trouble[.][19]

As a middle-class Cambridge man, Hughes implies his superiority to and sexual authority over women. He took every opportunity to undermine women's performance. He asserted in his *Melody Maker* column of April 1928 that it is only because women are 'cheap and look nice' that they are given the work.[20] Hughes socialised and drank with record producers at HMV and Decca and regularly broadcast for the BBC, claiming that his musicians were a cut above the rank and file. The conservatism of the BBC, together with the broadcasting monopolies of Spike Hughes and Victor Silvester, the strict-tempo bandleader, became entrenched, keeping women off the airwaves. Harker reports that:

> In Britain in 1925, there were two million radio sets in use, almost all of them tuned in to the BBC . . . Given this general situation, it is no surprise that the most successful British recording artists in 1955 were Victor Silvester and his band. He and they had by then sold 27,000,000 records . . . Silvester also managed to gain regular access to the BBC. How did this happen? Part of the answer lies in the fact that American bands were not allowed to tour Britain, and vice versa, until the mid 1950s, so competition from the real thing could come only in the record market, which was in any case relatively unimportant. Silvester was a product of monopoly: when that monopoly was broken so was he.[21]

Hughes also maintained that 'in recording and broadcasting, women's bands are unheard of, and this fact alone surely speaks volumes for their tardy progress'. What Hughes failed to mention was that women were denied the opportunity to record and broadcast, as Hughes himself was a controlling influence within the recording studios and the BBC, through Oxbridge connections and by promoting his own work over others. Hughes operated on a double front: professional sexism and class discrimination.

Women were 'allowed space', as the *Melody Maker* put it, to oppose Hughes's opinions within its columns, and a healthy debate ensued, which raged throughout 1928. Hughes, writing as 'Anonymous', delivered a one-page tirade against women, headlined 'Where the Fair Sex Fails'. He commented:

> she has not yet established her claim, even as a bad second, when it comes to the art of playing syncopated music, and the sooner she realises it, the better for us all. Everyone concerned in exploiting syncopated bands and consequently in a position to know the good

> from the bad, agrees with me for never will they dream of paying a female band anything like the money they offer the men. In fact, it's usually only because they are cheap and look nice that the ladies are even given a showing... Women syncopators also appear to lack originality and creative ability . . . But, let us also ask them to uphold their reputation of being 'the fair sex' by admitting, in their turn, that they have had their chance in syncopation and have failed.[22]

It might be questioned why Hughes's opinions of women musicians should be given any credence today, the answer being that these statements, in the only newspaper covering jazz at the time, have never been questioned until now. Surely any contemporary writings on jazz music must examine the legitimacy of his views regarding those early pioneer women, especially as his opinions continue to be quoted in contemporary volumes.[23]

Hughes's discriminatory argument was deftly dismissed by Miss Molly Pearl, who countered with an article entitled 'The Case for the Fair Sex'. Miss Pearl not only articulated the aesthetic value of jazz as a creative art form to which women were capable of contributing, but also dared to suggest that some jazz women were superior musicians to men. Miss Pearl recognised that women were becoming a threat and were being denied access to control their own careers in recording and broadcasting, writing:

> It only goes to show that magnificent Man is afraid of the progress which woman is making . . . in the art of syncopation . . . and are making musical headway at a speed which is evidently causing the opposite sex the gravest concern. Syncopation seems to bring a woman a sense of ecstasy when she is playing . . . and work together in perfect accord. Musical achievement is the great thing which counts in establishing our claims to equality or even superiority . . . the pioneers have fully established their claim to recognition. Recording and broadcasting may be open to our sex when man ceases to be the sole governing power in these directions.[24]

Hughes ('Anonymous') replied in the *Melody Maker* the following month:

> To my mind her case is as hopelessly illogical as you expect from a woman. It can be torn to threads and I stand by all the nasty things I said in my first ultimatum! My main concern is to show up the weak spots in the defence . . . however, let's get on with the washing. My point is that although the ladies are in the majority . . . for every mediocre syncopating female musician, there are anything up to a hundred good male performers, and for every might-pass-with-a-push ladies' dance band, there are at least twenty good ones composed of men . . . What I want to know is what are the disadvantages of her sex? I would have thought women had every advantage. First of all, nature made them – at least most of them – decidedly more pleasing to look upon . . . Secondly, they can afford to start off at less money. Compared with the number of men, few women have to keep themselves[.][25]

Hughes, with a wife who earned her own salary, had little or no understanding of the lengths working-class women, especially those in Wales, had to go to in order to survive as musicians, or of the amount of rubbish they had to read in the music press about themselves and their music, and the effect his opinions had on their professionalism. Hughes stated that in the 'Victorian and Edwardian eras music was considered an essential part of women's education and men would be looked on as effeminate if they devoted too much time to it'. He also opined that when modern dance music came into vogue the best male professional musicians considered it 'beneath their dignity to go in for it as they had a prestige they did not want to lose'. Women, he went on, never had that prestige as professional musicians to start with, and men's bands were 'proof of his superior musical standing . . . and women have not advanced anything to show that man will ever have to relinquish his governing powers in the BBC or HMV in favour of Venus'.[26]

Edna Rogers, bandleader, with three sisters who were also musicians, Gwen, Agnes and Stella, of Welsh parents, delivered the 'last word' championing women jazz musicians with an acerbic piece called 'A Vindication of the Fair Sex', describing Hughes as 'dangerously clever . . . patronising and sarcastic'. Rogers asserted that he got his points across with 'cheap humour . . . but omits factors of importance', arguing that Hughes manipulated evidence to suit his own arguments. Rogers stated that men's bands had undercut the going rate, making the business a 'precarious and almost derogative occupation', thereby spoiling the profession for all. She also argued that many men's musical ability was so negligible that women's could hardly be defined as inferior to it. Rogers wondered how some men were able to keep in employment, declaring that firstly the public were not sufficiently educated to 'differentiate between good and bad and accept showmanship', and secondly, that male bands worked in 'cliques', helping pals to keep a job. She maintained that this loyalty between men to keep their colleagues in work, even if their ability was questionable, undermined women who might have spent years studying to become proficient, only to then discover jobs were distributed through favouritism. Rogers stated that even though women's emancipation was far advanced, workwise they were still at a disadvantage; it was expected that women work for less pay, as there was an assumption there was a man earning her keep, but women's stage gowns were an extra expense, when men were only required to wear a lounge suit. Rogers summed up by saying that it was no surprise that some women musicians had witnessed the drawbacks and declined to enter the fray, preferring a profession where they 'have a better chance to succeed'. Her 'last word' was that women could be equally successful in syncopation if it was worth their while to try.[27]

Edna Rogers, a multi-instrumentalist, was well qualified to rebuff Spike Hughes ('Anonymous') in 'A Vindication of the Fair Sex'. She had led Gwen Rogers and her Musical Dolls, 'a snappy little band of ten', resident at Covent Garden Opera House, also supplying music for the Olympia Dance Hall, and previously at the Alhambra.[28] A review (not by Hughes) in the *Melody Maker* of the Musical Dolls at the Opera House reads:

The Musical Dolls gave pleasure to the thousands who attended the recent dances . . . Also on 25 March to those still incapacitated soldiers of the Great War who attended the concert given in their service at the Wigmore Hall by the Adair Wounded Fund. Whoever is responsible for the programmes certainly knows how to select the best. A month ago it was Jack Hylton and his Band; and now that the Musical Dolls have performed, it can be fairly said that the best of both sexes have been chosen . . . and inspiring ability.[29]

Rogers continued her career despite Hughes's vindictiveness. Her points can now be verified by evidence in Hughes's own autobiography. Hughes writes that for greater efficiency he installed one of his male friends as band secretary to represent the Hughes name, and to contract the work for the Hughes band, and to distribute the work amongst other male bands if Hughes's band was already engaged. Hughes then took a percentage for lending his name to the enterprise, as well as being paid for the work, arguing that music was a business for 'people with brains'. Hughes also refused to accept the Musicians' Union rate for work at the BBC, as he considered his musicians were 'a cut above the rank and file' and were worth more', thereby initiating credibility problems for women attempting to acquire any broadcasting opportunities at the BBC, even at the MU rate for the work.[30]

From Hughes's own evidence, women were denied work and broadcast opportunities, and he continued to foster the concept that women were a threat to male promoters and booking agents. His autobiography reveals that he further went on to discriminate against women by his friendship with Hyam Greenbaum, musical director of Decca Record Company. Greenbaum filtered recording work Hughes's way. When Greenbaum left the company in 1932, Hughes took over Greenbaum's conducting role in addition to his own band work. Decca's chief recording engineer, Norman Angier, was also a friend of Hughes and helped put recording work his way. A successful old boys' network was operating. Hughes also received a full-page spread in the *Melody Maker* promoting his own records.[31] It must be remembered that at this time Hughes was chief journalist and reviewer for the *Melody Maker*, the only national paper covering jazz and dance band music.

More usually, the sexism suffered by women musicians was less overt than that delivered by Hughes, but equally insidious. For example, the *Melody Maker* critic ends his review of the four-piece Bob'd Uns performance with the remark, 'Attired in most effective novel costumes . . . the girls should have no difficulty in attracting the squires of the Midlands'.[32] Appearance was all. Women were generally referred to as 'little', or 'pretty little' in both performance and record reviews, thereby again valuing appearance and devaluing performance.[33] In contrast, looks are deemed irrelevant for men. Men's appearances were never commented upon, although there were many men's bands during the 1920s and 1930s performing in frilly lace and satin rumba shirts, loosely gathered gypsy shirts, headscarves and earrings, or, in the case of Don Rico, an embroidered and appliquéd frilly shirt, fur-trimmed knee-length cape and black leather boots with tassels, which dominated a page of the *Melody Maker*, a mode of attire not editorially commented on.[34]

Although it is not known whether there were any Welsh women included in the band, in 1927 Ynet Miles and her All Ladies Band won the Greater London Open Dance Band Contest at the Hammersmith Palais de Danse. While giving the band credit for its achievement, the *Melody Maker* critic reported that: 'this winning combination could only be explained by the fact that the ladies were obviously aware of their charm and . . . their silver frocks made a charming picture which possibly was the cause of the downfall of many of the male competitors'.[35]

There is an implicit assumption in the above report that Ynet Miles and her All Ladies Band won the competition by their looks and not their professional ability, that male jazz musicians were therefore at a disadvantage, and women jazz musicians could prove a future threat to jobs and status. Reg Mote's Syncopated Orchestra came second, but was described as having 'better instrumentalists', and although Ynet Miles's band was described as 'brilliant', the instrumental and winning performance was denigrated. Indeed, denigration of women's instrumental technique was far from uncommon. The view that women generally had little ability was sometimes expressed as the criticism that they lacked rhythm, as with Miss Jerry Stevens, trumpet player with the ten-piece Alex Hyde's Modern Maids, performing at the Palladium in 1931, whose technique on *St Louis Blues* was described as giving 'ample indications of a power of rhythmic interpretation that would be extremely creditable in a man, and which in a lady is highly unexpected, and most refreshing'.[36] It is the reviewer who has decided that Stevens's power of rhythmic interpretation is 'highly unexpected', certainly not the performer.

Women were hardly ever allowed a positive review. When Ivy Read and her Ladies' Band are congratulated for the 'excellent standard of playing', the musicians are immediately put down for not showing 'a little more restraint in their playing', a contradiction in terms.[37] Again, although drummer Chrissie Beard, performing at Edmonton with her Society Ladies, is described as 'a drummer of considerable experience and her quartet's outstanding merit of the performance is the extraordinary vigour which they put into everything they do', the review goes on:

> In these enlightened days of sex equality and feminist emancipation, and so on, it is with great trepidation that I venture to suggest that this may be because of the mental and physical limitations of feminine sustaining power. It cannot, however, be a coincidence that in all ladies' bands this lack of any sustained tone is so curiously noticeable. Vitality there is in a marked degree and, of course, charm.[38]

Contradictions continued between a genuine critical review of a band's performance and denigration of that performance by comments on the women's appearance. Hughes was not alone in discriminatory reviews; this time it is 'VNL' (identity unknown). This *Melody Maker* correspondent gives all due approval to Hilda Ward's Band of Ten Lady Syncopators (we cannot assume they are all English), 'pioneers of ladies' bands in this country', thus:

> The combination . . . tackles its ambitious programme with courage and energy . . . stage effects are well conceived . . . effective arrangements (The Birth of the Blues and Lost Chord) . . . Miss Ward leads the sax section with her customary showmanship and power.

But the reader is left with a nasty taste in the mouth by the critic ('VNL') then commenting that the women's dresses have 'not healed the wound to my aesthetic sense. I fear it is mortal.'[39]

Again, here is Hughes ('Anonymous'): 'Playing dance music is one of the few things which I suppose that even the members of the fair sex themselves will admit they cannot do as well as us poor wretches doomed to trousers.'[40] In December 1928 the *Melody Maker* produced a Christmas photographic souvenir supplement of Britain's Famous Dance Bands and personalities. No women's bands featured.[41] Undeterred, women battled on to get their voices heard, with Wales continuing to be ignored within the paper's pages.

Ray Starita, saxophonist and clarinettist and member of London's Savoy Orpheans, wrote a piece for the *Melody Maker* in 1931, aimed at all male musicians, called 'Single Men Preferred', for the series 'News and Views of Those Who Matter'. He stresses from the beginning that the 'right fellows' are chosen in order for the band to work together, that younger men were more adaptable than older ones, and that dance and jazz music was a 'single man's game'. He concludes that 'if you've got boys with the right temperament you can't go wrong'.[42] Women reading articles such as these would have felt excluded and demeaned.

Refreshingly, for a change, quite a balanced article appeared in 1929 in the *Melody Maker*, entitled 'The Challenge of Eve, Male or Mixed Kinema Orchestras', in which Arthur W. Owen discussed women working in cinemas. 'Talkies' started to make their mark in the cinemas in the early 1930s. Prior to then, cinema pianists and trios were booked to play improvised music, taking their cue from action on the screen, with women piano players to the fore; larger orchestras would have used written band charts especially composed for some silent films. Owen decried the 'bitter attacks' that women had received, and declared they were unmerited, as music was an art equally suited to both sexes. Women, too, had graduated from music colleges, and were 'thus equipped to compete on equal terms as bona-fide professionals' and were paying Musicians' Union membership on an equal basis. Owen pointed out that many 'kinema' musical directors favoured hiring males, but others appreciated that 'women responded to discipline just as readily as men . . . and that in a well conducted orchestra the presence of the female element is a refining influence'. He added that a woman was 'the equal of, if not superior to, the men . . . giving more attention to her duties, playing with far more energy and taxing her artistic ability to a greater extent'. Owen wrote that because men in general were more ambitious they left orchestras regularly for better positions and were therefore less reliable than women, who tended to hang on to subordinate positions and were more consistent; a woman knew that a leader's job or a sub-conductor's post was 'in most cases beyond her reach'. However, he ends the article by saying in the 'very isolated places' where a woman is in charge of a mixed orchestra, the result 'sooner or later is bound to be unsatisfactory, and few men will accept engagements under such conditions'. Owen concludes by stating that a woman musician is content to stay in her position for years 'which is often unworthy of her ability'.[13]

From Owen's fair and interesting discussion on the role of women in cinema orchestras, discrimination was again heaped upon women in the *Melody Maker* by writer and critic Leonard Feather, who asked in his *Melody Maker* column of August 1933, 'Why such a small proportion of the fair sex professes any interest in or appreciation of hot music?' A whole page in October 1933 was given over to letters from women ('Pat' London, Bettie Edwards, Marion Downey and André Ache, Secretary of the Hot Club de Belgique) in defence of women jazz musicians. They offered the following reasons for the continued demeaning of their chosen careers:

i. lack of opportunities offered to girls at school, university and in the community

ii. lack of opportunity leading to narrower vision of technical ability
iii. lack of knowledge leading to lack of understanding of jazz's merits
iv. the natural conceit of the male tribe encouraging the work of men only
v. the male language of jazz
vi. misogyny[44]

Feather wrote to the *Melody Maker* in November 1933, under the headline 'Asking For It', saying that he congratulated the noble 'Fem-Fans' who did their best to explode his theory. He was 'not struck by misogyny' he wrote but 'merely logic', as there were large numbers of the 'gentler sex who refuse to be educated in hot music' and they should join 'rhythm circles' or 'rhythm clubs', where they were 'conspicuous by their absence and use their feminine organising ability'. He concluded his letter by asking the women to write to him personally. He did not state why he wanted women to write to him personally.[45] Women were absent from rhythm clubs because most barred women altogether and nurtured an elitist and patriarchal hierarchy.[46] Although Wales was not specifically mentioned in these arguments, we can infer that all women in the UK were targeted. For example, some rhythm clubs withheld membership from women, although allowing them into meetings. The Forest Gate and District Rhythm Club only reluctantly offered membership and voting access to women after a change of secretary, the previous secretary having resigned.[47] From the above, with a knowledge of the patriarchal jazz hierarchy operating at the time, it is not surprising that some women were reluctant to become involved in the rhythm clubs and circles. Kathleen M. Stevens, of London, SW1, replied by letter to the *Melody Maker* regarding Feather's criticism of women being absent from rhythm clubs. She said: 'I am a member of the No.1 Rhythm Club. Constructive criticism would, I feel sure, be welcomed by all those who have our cause at heart, but his letter certainly indicates a somewhat biased non-comprehension of the facts.'[48] Rhythm clubs opened in Wales, with those in Newport and Cardiff established in December 1933, and Swansea's in 1934.[49]

It is evident that during the 1930s British jazz women were not only professionally competent to play jazz, but were deeply offended at how their work was denigrated and perceived in public. Feather, writing elsewhere, quoted the *New Yorker* critic Whitney Balliet's comments on women:

> Most women lacked the physical equipment – to say nothing of the poise – for blowing trumpets and trombones, slapping bass fiddles, or beating drums. Female instrumentalists . . . in the past thirty or forty years . . . in the main . . . have dropped quickly out of sight.[50]

It was not that women had 'dropped quickly out of sight', it was more that they were never given the attention on the scale that men were. Feather and Balliet both discriminated against women on grounds of gender and ability, and regarded music created and/or performed by women as disrupting the assumed masculinity of the music. Jazz in particular transcends definability as masculine, as improvisation offers a new interpretation at each performance by whatever sex – part of the idiom's attraction. Another point against the Feather/Balliet argument is that the playing of, for example, wind instruments, is not about power, but technique, and therefore has nothing to do with body size and strength. Leonard Feather was caught out when he took the *Melody Maker* record review 'Blindfold Test' in November 1937; he thought he was listening to Fats Waller on piano when in fact it was Una Mae Carlisle, composer, arranger and broadcaster.[51]

In 1934 the *Melody Maker* finally woke up to the fact that jazz was being played in Wales and felt obliged to provide a very occasional special column called 'South Wales Look You'; the first one featured Swansea. Headlines included such items as 'The Taffies are Dancing . . . More Orchestras find themselves Active'. It was also reported that Edwards department store had orchestras on their roof garden every Friday and Saturday, and bands such as the Manhattans and Vic Haynes and his Lyricals were given a mention. However, a female trio were not mentioned by name, merely referred to as '3 girls play in a café',[52] thereby neglecting the previous ten years of women's innovative contribution to café society and stage performance.

In October 1934 the *Melody Maker* had a large spread on the South Wales Dance Band Contest held at Swansea's Patti Pavilion, declaring 'Terrific Enthusiasm but Low Standard'. Winners were Roy Allan and his Band, second were the Ramblers' Dance Band and third Eric Dare and his Band. Twelve bands competed, none were women. The comment was that most of the bands 'seemed to play "all-out" with amazing zeal to produce the maximum amount of noise'.[53] Did women's bands fail to apply because they felt they were not good enough? The *Melody Maker* review particularly mentioned that the men's bands were of a low standard; perhaps this comment would inspire good female bands to apply next time around.

There must have been sufficient competition from female bands to threaten the male preserve, as Leon Goodman wrote in the June 1935 *Melody Maker* asking for 'men with their sex well-defined' to join him in his new 'No More Women Movement', to eliminate women from the profession. The new movement's slogan was to be 'Keep the Business Clean'. Geoffrey Clayton responded with a piece titled 'The DANGER of WOMEN in JAZZ'. Clayton's first paragraph advises men how best to view women through binoculars, then quotes an unnamed 'famous poet-fellow':

> Oh, woman, in thine hour of ease,
> Uncertain, coy and hard to please.
> But when rehearsals sear our brow
> She will butt in: and what a cow![54]

Clayton then confirms he is going to join the 'anti-feminine league' and encourages 'you chaps . . . to go and do likewise'. He continues by asking who is ruining the music profession: 'The price-cutters? Certainly not! The agent's commissions? Nothing of the kind! The BBC? Don't be a BBF! The *women* that's what it is – the women!' He then advises male readers to 'take a strong line with these women and don't let them bully us', and finishes by detailing the duties his wife requires of him at home. This comment on women added to the destabilisation of any positive perceptions of women's music, rendering them only as a useful part of the male debate and their preference for how women should be perceived. Williams argues that women musicians were 'seen as interlopers. Female musicians were often positioned and seen as Other to the masculine norm'.[55] Alternatively, women musicians saw themselves as experiencing a collective way of working and offering a culturally rewarding performance for themselves and audiences, requiring male bands and critics to form a new perspective on gender norms. Unfortunately this repositioning would take a further fifty years to formulate any positive analyses on women's jazz by men. Williams confirms that the jazz press have been 'historically negative' but concludes that for women who put in the time and effort to play well, 'there is no implicit barrier to women being successful in jazz'.[56]

Occasionally the *Melody Maker* did make some positive comments. In May 1939 it produced a full-page spread, written by Ken Evans, headlined 'Feminine Jazz'. He commented that there was not much of it, but what there was 'is good'. He wrote mostly about American women, but did mention British women Peggy Dell, Diana Miller, Mary Lee, Marjorie Stedeford, the Rhythm Sisters, Ivy Benson and Ella Logan.[57] The next month, June 1939, the *Melody Maker* made a surprising stand for women's rights against Blackpool Holiday Camp. An advertisement placed in the Birmingham Mail by the holiday camp required 'two attractive girls to play sax and drums in the camp band, but they also had to assist at table and work as hostesses' in exchange for full board and 15s. per week. No male musician would have been required to undertake two jobs. An incensed *Melody Maker* thought this was 'disgraceful, presumptuous and an insult to musical professionalism'.[58] The *Melody Maker* was at last recognising that to denigrate female musicians was not in the music profession's best interests, especially as women read the *Melody Maker* and would expect the newspaper to champion their music.

The now up-and-coming Ivy Benson and her All Girl Band opened at Norwich Hippodrome for their 'Meet the Girls' season, 'attracting the biggest audience to date', reported the *Melody Maker*. Benson auditioned 'girls' from all over the country and paid tribute to the way in which 'the girls have worked at rehearsals'. The reviewer commented the band was not yet a world-beater but improvement was seen during the opening week, with Ann Joyce, piano, and Pat Sheridan, vocals. A new speciality number of the band was called 'Hitler, Goebbels and Goering'. The reviewer added, 'Perhaps a mere male should not criticise such a thing but it does seem that the band might have been dressed more attractively, the dresses seem rather severe.' Even with the Ivy Benson Band adhering to wartime austerity and ditching the froth and petticoats, the new attire still did not satisfy the male gaze.[59]

Regarding pay, the *Melody Maker* said it had 'opened its doors to Girls Dance Bands', who would receive men's rates. The report went on that there were over sixty women members of the Musicians Union, but 'Miss Benson and her Band are the first out and out dance band to enrol within our ranks'. It continued that the 'fashion in industry' was to pay women less, but in 'musical circles we are out to stop that and we are negotiating with other ladies' orchestras'.[60] However, the Ivy Benson name would not appear in any of the future acknowledged authoritative books on big bands.[61] Benson felt women's music was not taken seriously by the BBC, and in fact during the whole of 1950 her band was awarded only thirty minutes' airtime, compared with over forty-three hours that year for Victor Silvester's strict-tempo dance band.[62]

In February 1940 the *Melody Maker* reviewer 'Mike' (Spike Hughes), perhaps realising his entrenched attitudes towards women musicians were becoming passé with the increasing popularity of women's orchestras, signed off his column with the words: 'Jazz is like a woman. So long as you don't expect your love affair to last forever, you will be able to look back afterwards and say that was fun. I've had my fun.'[63]

The *Melody Maker* eventually lifted the 'veil of secrecy that hid the identity of one of its most (in)famous contributors Spike Hughes', when it published an article by him on 15 November 1952 in Chris Hayes's memoir, *Melody Maker Memories*. Hughes (1908–87) recalled his thirteen years writing as 'Mike' or 'Anonymous'. He never acknowledged his appalling sexism, or questioned whether his views had damaged women's career prospects. He never acknowledged that perhaps his opinions had become received wisdom, influencing future critics. Women got on with their careers, leaving a legacy to inspire us today in which women can play jazz on their own terms.

In the 1946 *Melody Maker*, Eric Winstone targeted female vocalists, writing on 'The Female of the Musical Species – Another Psychological Thesis on the Musical Profession'. He felt that women were more 'savage . . . and that the feminine mind was like a bottomless well'. He continues, an 'average range for a girl singer is seldom more than six notes' and provided she keeps her head 'she cannot help but achieve fame and fortune with possibly a couple of BBC producers and a fur coat on the side'. He opines that 'girls without a voice at all apart from the face of Lauren Bacall, the legs of Betty Grable and the comfortable contours of Rita Hayworth, . . . have nothing to offer'. He concludes that there are some musicians 'who actually like doing one night stands', a double entendre assuming women will always give sexual favours for the chance of a gig.[64] Although women's bands had done well during the Second World War, music critics continued to treat women as invisible, and not worthy of contributing to the music profession, or they were objectified and discussed in terms of sexual availability.

Did women receive fair treatment? On the whole the *South Wales Daily Post* did a far better job of recognising women jazz musicians' capabilities and entrepreneurship, during the early café society days and beyond, than the *Melody Maker* newspaper, tasked with the specific job of promoting jazz music and those who played it, regardless of gender. The *South Wales Daily Post* penned their articles seemingly rather surprised that Swansea was a town renowned for its jazz, the café culture it embraced and the men and women who played it. The paper gave this new music its due regard, anxious that not only the musicians but the whole town would benefit from its positive promotion as a new tourist attraction, which it did. The *Melody Maker*, in contrast, although quite positive to women in the very beginning, allowed its main reviewers to victimise and degrade women, a position from which women had to fight for their right to play the music in the way they saw fit, and to fly free.

It is to be hoped that music students, young girls and women can now take advantage of the opportunities available to them on jazz courses and be inspired. Paula Gardiner, Head of Jazz Studies at the Royal Welsh College of Music and Drama in Cardiff, interviewed in 2015 by *BASCA* (British Academy of Songwriters, Composers and Authors), comments:

> In 2001, I went back to the Royal Welsh College of Music and Drama. They asked me to set up a jazz syllabus. By 2004, when my daughter was two, I went full-time. We created undergraduate and postgraduate courses and the popularity grew. Composition is a very important element – everyone is encouraged to create their own material.
>
> As part of the Cultural Olympiad in 2012, I was involved in Mzansi Cymru – a joint project between South Wales and Cape Town. The idea was to show a fusion of Welsh music and South African music. We had a community choir with singers aged from 8 to 87, an orchestra of 50 people, an indigenous percussion band from South Africa. It was amazing – and I had to conduct it all.
>
> There are always new challenges. My next one is a Welsh language jazz project. I've been learning Welsh on and off for years, but this time I need to do it properly.[65]

It is to be hoped that music students, young girls and women will take advantage of the many opportunities available to them on the jazz courses offered throughout the country, as well as at RWCND. Students can campaign for more women tutors and lecturers and query whether there are opportunities to study women composers and manuscripts on their courses. Harpist and composer, Welsh-speaking Catrin Finch straddles both classical and jazz genres. She has several academic honours, toured Patagonia with the National Orchestra of Wales, and performed on the recording of *Cantata Memoria* by Karl Jenkins – a choral with orchestra dedicated to the children who perished in the 1966 Aberfan disaster. In 2018, Catrin Finch released her second album with the Senegalese kora player Seckou Keita. Wales can be proud of its cultural heritage.

Conclusion

Freedom Music: Wales, Emancipation and Jazz 1850–1950 is an attempt to portray the story of how jazz music came to Wales from a sociocultural and feminist point of view. There are many books on jazz and the people who played it. Jazz was predominantly theorised and discussed as a London centric genre, with the first theoretical discussions taking place within the pages of the national newspaper *Melody Maker*, published from 1926, which concentrated on hot music and dance bands in its early days. However, W. B. E. Du Bois, the African American social historian, was already challenging how black music – 'sorrow songs' – and its people were perceived, in his groundbreaking book *The Souls of Black Folk*.[1] He wrote of African Americans living within 'the Veil', which he raises in order for us to understand 'the meaning of its religion, the passion of its human sorrow, and the struggle of its greater souls', giving African Americans a voice. This voice Du Bois described as 'the rhythmic cry of the slave . . . neglected . . . half despised, and above all it has been persistently mistaken and misunderstood . . . but . . . it still remains as the singular spiritual heritage of the nation and the greatest gift of the Negro people'.[2]

To trace this 'gift of the Negro people' I took as my starting point 1950, as it was within my own living memory and family stories, and followed a trail back into history. It was never a straight path, and some of the tracks veered off into unexpected places, but it was truly a fascinating journey with a cast of characters I never expected to meet. Jazz has always been linked to the human struggle for freedom: freedom from slavery, freedom from restrictions placed on gender, freedom for self-expression and self-actualisation. Although white races have inevitably exploited black resources in music as in other fields of human endeavour, the mixed input from European musical heritage, as well as across genders, has contributed to an enrichment of the music. Attempts at controlling this outburst of creativity (detailed in these pages) were in vain, for the excitement and enthusiasm transmitted with this ever-evolving music enthralled the people of Wales. The links between working people of Wales and the oppressed African American diaspora, the solidarity expressed in mutual aid as well as cultural exchange, brings a richness to this part of our shared history of struggle against oppression, and our shared joy in the music.

This book reached back into history and found the abolitionists and their campaign songs, together with the slave songs or 'sorrow songs' of freed slaves who toured Wales from the 1870s. In piecing together the story of the Fisk Jubilee Singers from Nashville, their 'weird slave songs', tours around Wales and return visits, I realised that it was interlinked with that of the Welsh abolitionists who set out from south and mid Wales from the 1820s and 1850s, and who went on to engage with international politics on a grand scale and run safe houses for runaway slaves. One story could not be told without the other. I had found my starting point. By the time the Fisk Jubilee Singers had made their last visit to Swansea in 1907, ragtime was all the rage.

This book could have started in the jazz age of the 1920s but the music was already evolving from ragtime, that raggedy-time syncopation embedded within the minstrelsy tradition of the late 1800s. People in Wales took it to their hearts, imitating not just the music but the appearance of the performers by painting their faces with burnt charcoal, while African Americans themselves were adapting their take on the music to accommodate local audiences. The bands and minstrel shows showcased for the 'inmates' of the Swansea Workhouse, together with decisions made by the Board of Guardians as to whether a cultural education in the latest in popular music should be allowed in a place upholding the Poor Law, were discussed. To discover that ragtime and minstrelsy were taken into the Workhouse does show that whatever we now think of workhouses, Swansea's was run by a mainly pioneering Board of Guardians who fought for a cultural education of equal importance to that of basic care in food and clothing.

The First World War threw up a wealth of fascinating detail of the music weaving its way through noisy suffragettes fighting for the vote, and military men writing home from their ragtime trenches. All-woman dance troupes and orchestras filled the stages, and women were demanding more control of their lives. Swansea's own popular dance, the Marina Saunter, took hold, and the victorious US naval fleet sailed into port in 1918 to partake of the noisy nightlife. The end-of-war celebrations continued into November 1919, with bands marching through town. By this time, café culture was in full swing.

The unexpected discovery that a café culture existed in town a decade before Dylan Thomas frequented the Kardomah in the 1930s, to discuss poems and girls, was a revelation. The women who ran the floor shows were not only businesswomen, but cultural innovators in their own right. African American revues were passing through town and would fit in a quick café spot in the afternoon before their big stage appearance in the main theatres at night. The local Welsh women watched and listened, took hold of the music and ran with it, displaying flair and imagination, with little by way of capital but plenty in the way of enthusiasm for the music. This period of excitement and diversion, an antidote to wartime horrors and bereavement, propelled the jazz age into Wales, which continued until the Second World War ushered in a new type of jazz.

Jazz between the wars saw 'flappers' dancing in backless frocks in 'jazz colours' with men in flapping Oxford bags. Many orchestras and jazz combos were led by women, usually with the honorific 'Mrs' before their name to denote respectability. But it was also the time when racist and misogynistic bile flowed from the pulpits, led by academics and men of the cloth. The music was denigrated and despised by them, with Jews and 'Negro morals' in the firing line, together with women who danced to the music, branded as 'brazen huzzies'. Louis Armstrong, trumpeter, singer, composer and early ambassador for jazz, did a week's residency in Swansea, leaving behind a legacy that lasted into living memory.

The last chapter discusses how women were represented in the popular music media of the time, the *Melody Maker*, and compares and contrasts this with how the local south Wales press viewed the music, and its effects on the people and the town. Women musicians had to endure a steady stream of misogynistic attitudes from in the music press, from which they took decades to recover. The *Melody Maker* was the only music newspaper at that time reporting on jazz and the people who played it, ergo the reporting was London and England-centric, with Wales making a definite appearance only under the column 'South Wales Look You' in the 1930s. This book, therefore, can glean opinions about Wales only from meagre offerings. Nevertheless, the local press was much more positive and congratulatory, and gave a welcome to jazz music, together with the people who played it and the dancers who took to the dance halls, which enabled Swansea to become a vibrant and innovative town and helped to put south Wales on the international music map.

This cannot be the definitive story, as more work needs to be undertaken, particularly in the rural parts of west and north Wales. However, Wales, usually regarded as God-fearing, with a distinct cultural identity of traditional Eisteddfodau (festivals of literature, music and poetry) and male voice choirs, had an unexpected story of its own to tell, hitherto hidden from history. It is not only a feminist story, but also places women performers and entrepreneurs within a working-class context. There is a considerable volume of material housed in the Jazz Heritage Wales archives, including a specialist library with journals and periodicals, continuing the story from the ending of this book to the present day, as well as more information on current subject areas and collections. This book needed to be written, because not to write it would allow the conventional stories of the history of jazz music to prevail, with a continuation of historical amnesia. My research uncovered a wealth of cultural history and heritage pertinent to Wales, previously unacknowledged, a starting point for further academic research on what continues to be a fascinating and relevant part of Wales's popular culture.

Notes

Introduction

1. Gwyn Alf Williams, *When Was Wales? A History of the Welsh* (London: Black Raven Press, 1985; illus. repr. Harmondsworth: Penguin Books, 1991).
2. Giraldus Cambrensis/Gerald of Wales, *The Journey Through Wales/The Description of Wales, 1188–1214*, trans. Lewis Thorpe (Harmondsworth and New York: Penguin Books, 1978), pp. 236, 239, 242.
3. Osian Ellis, *The Story of the Harp in Wales* (Cardiff: University of Wales Press, 1991), pp. 27, 32.
4. Cris Haines, 'Early harp music of Wales and jazz musical patterns', personal email correspondence, 25 July 2016.
5. Paul Oliver, *The Story of the Blues* (London: Penguin Books, 1978), p. 13.
6. Linda Dahl, *Stormy Weather: The Music and Lives of a Century of Jazzwomen* (London: Quartet Books, 1984), p. 11.
7. Eric Hobsbawm, *The Jazz Scene* (London: Faber & Faber, 1959; repr. 2015), pp. 254–5.
8. W. E. B. Du Bois, *The Souls of Black Folk: Essays and Sketches* (Chicago: A. C. McClurg and Co., 1903; repr. New York: Fawcett Publications, Inc., Fawcett World Library, 1961), pp. 181–2.
9. Stuart Hall, 'Lives and Letters', *The Guardian*, 22 February 2003.

10. Evelyn Brooks Higginbotham, *Righteous Discontent: The Women's Movement in the Black Baptist Church 1880–1920* (Cambridge, MA: Harvard University Press, 1993), p. 14.
11. *The Cambrian*, 5 July 1861.
12. Daniel G. Williams, *Black Skin, Blue Books: African Americans and Wales 1845–1945* (Cardiff: University of Wales Press, 2012), p. 13.
13. Catherine Parsonage, *The Evolution of Jazz in Britain, 1880–1935* (Aldershot: Ashgate Publishing, 2005), p. 3.
14. W. J. Gibbs, *Negro Spirituals, or The Songs of the Jubilee Singers* (Bromley, Kent, and Ambleside, Clacton-on-Sea: W. J. Gibbs, c.1900).
15. Rudyard Kipling, quoted in Peter Bailey (ed.), *Music Hall. The Business of Pleasure* (Milton Keynes: Open University Press, 1986), p. xiv.
16. Parsonage, *The Evolution of Jazz in Britain, 1880–1935*, p. 96.

Chapter One

1. *The Cambrian*, obituary, 'Death of Mrs Donaldson – Record of a remarkable life', 13 September 1889.
2. Jen Wilson, 'Jessie Donaldson, 1799–1889, Swansea Abolitionist', in *Minerva, The Journal of Swansea History*, Transactions of the Royal Institution of South Wales, 12 (2004), 41–50.
3. Brian Perrins, Pete Thomas, Aaron Fortt and Mark Joseph, 'Swansea's Dark Past: A Link to the Slave Trade', *Community View*, 33 (May 2004). The Swansea Community Boat Trust runs heritage tours and floating classrooms up the River Tawe to Landore Copper Works in their barge *Copper Jack*.
4. Stanley Elkins and Eric McKitrick, *The Early American Republic, 1788–1800* (New York: Oxford University Press, 1992), p. 151.
5. 'Swansea's High Street Church, built 1698, in use until 1846', historical leaflet (n.d.).
6. *The Cambrian*, 7 July 1829.
7. *The Cambrian*, 14 May 1825.
8. I am indebted to Hilary Edmiston of Caswell, Swansea, a great-great-great-great-granddaughter of Mary Ann Perkins, who discovered a photograph of Jessie Donaldson and helped piece together her story.
9. *The Cambrian*, 19 January 1822.
10. D. Williams, 'The Return of the Welshman from Mexico', in *The Cambrian*, 6 March 1829.
11. *The Cambrian*, 10 April 1824. It reads: 'At Frandon, Cincinnati, in the state of Ohio, North America, on the 7th Jan. last, Francis Donaldson, Esq. formerly of Serjeant's Inn, a member of the Honourable Society of the Middle Temple,

and many years a resident of Perfunnor, near Rhayader, in Radnorshire; a gentleman, who most eminently and deservedly possessed the particular esteem of every person who had the pleasure of his acquaintance, and who, in June 1822, with an amiable wife and a large family, left England [sic] and made an extensive purchase of lands in the state where he died.'

12 Mrs Richard Alexander Donaldson, IV (researched and compiled), *Donaldson: A history of the William Donaldson family of St. Andrews, Fife, Scotland, the province of New Jersey, North America, and London, England, with a record of his descendants in the United States of America*, with Preface and Addenda compiled by Pat Donaldson (Georgetown, OH: Donaldson, 1978). On Frandon: 'The structure was built by the Donaldsons, ardent abolitionists, who came to New Richmond at a very early date and owned the largest store in town, as well as a farm on the outskirts. In 1935, when this sketch was made, the old building, that had had its heyday so long ago, bore a condemned sign on the entrance. It is interesting to note that when the waters receded after the history-making flood of 1937, in which much of the village was literally washed off its foundation, the Donaldson building was still sitting firmly on the corner, waiting for its thick walls to be torn down brick by brick, and not washed away by the waters of the Ohio it had watched for so many many years' (p. 97). I met the delightful genealogist Pat Donaldson in July 2001. I visited the splendid Cincinnati Library, Genealogy and Local History Department, held up the Mrs Donaldson obituary and asked the librarian how could I find out who this lady was. Confusion reigned, as my Welsh accent had defeated the woman behind the counter. Another came to help out, then smiled and said, 'Ah, we have a lady called Pat Donaldson who regularly calls in to work here, I wonder if she would know, as she has been researching the Donaldson family?' Phone calls were made, and Pat and I eventually met and settled into the library sofas, grinning and rather surprised that history had rapidly caught up with us. Pat did indeed know of a Mrs J. Donaldson, had not been able to trace her first name, and knew that she had left America for Wales. Pat presented me with a copy of her book, I told her all about Swansea, and we exchanged information and addresses. History can suddenly become the present, bringing alive long-dead folk who contributed so much to making this world a better place but who have nearly been forgotten. It is a historian's duty to write them back into history.

13 Lajuana Miller is a guide for the Secret Passages Tour, Cincinnati, presented by JLG (Journey Legacy Gratitude) and African American Heritage tours, which includes slave narratives, a re-enactment, a soul-food lunch, and a moving tribute at the river 'Jordan' (Ohio). When I took the tour we ended at the Ohio/Covington riverbank on Riverside Drive, Covington, and sat on the bench next to James Bradley looking over to Cincinnati and freedom.

Ms Miller writes: 'A statue of James Bradley sits on a bench, reading a book. He was a slave who bought his freedom. The way that worked was a slave worked all day for his owner, then be hired out at night to another owner. The slave's owner got half and the slave got half. When they saved enough, they bought freedom. Bradley played a role in the Lane Debates – to have a former slave lent credibility. This is where he crossed the river. We have a closing ceremony on the river where we hand out small flashlights. We stand with our lights on and pay tribute to ancestors – to our black ancestors who struggled to freedom and to our white ancestors who helped them.' *The Cincinnati Enquirer*, 1 July 2001.

14 Booker T. Washington, *Up From Slavery* (New York: Doubleday, Page and Co., 1901; London: Penguin Books, 1986), pp. 9–11.

15 *The Cambrian*, 3, 10, 17 May, 7, 14 June 1823.

16 Thomas Clarkson, 'Tour on Behalf of the Anti-Slavery Society', NLW MS14984A.

17 For further reading see Chris Evans, *Slave Wales: The Welsh and Atlantic Slavery, 1660–1850* (Cardiff: University of Wales Press, 2010).

18 For an explanation of the lyrics, see www.contemplator.com/america/gourd.html, www.followthedrinkinggourd.org/, accessed 15 July 2015.

19 No. 7, 'Roll, Jordan, Roll', from W. J. Gibbs, *Negro Spirituals, or The Songs of the Jubilee Singers* (n.d., c.1900). A copy is in the Jazz Heritage Wales library. The freed slaves, the Fisk Jubilee Singers, performed music from their songbook in Swansea in 1874, 1875, 1882, 1907 (see ch. 3). In 1991, playwright Alan Plater based his BBC Radio 4 three-part drama *The Devil's Music* on the story of the Fisk Jubilee Singers in Wales, and 'Roll, Jordan, Roll' is featured throughout. *The Devil's Music* is available at www.bbc.co.uk/programmes/b00fl777.

20 See 'Freedom and Slavery and Riverboats' at www.curiosity.cs.xu.edu/blogs/antebellumcincinnati/ accessed 22 July 2015.

21 No. 32, 'Across the River', from Philip Phillips, *The American Sacred Songster* (London: Sunday School Union, 1868). A copy is in the Jazz Heritage Wales library. Philip Phillips, 'The Singing Pilgrim of America', performed from his songbook at Swansea's Mount Pleasant Chapel on 10 November 1876, accompanying himself on the American organ. The 'Evening of Song' was a fundraiser held under the auspices of the Sunday School Union; *The Cambrian*, 10 November 1876. In 1860 at the age of 26 Philip Phillips set up in business in Cincinnati selling pianos, organs and Sunday School songbooks. His modus operandi was to park his cart or vehicle on a prominent corner and play his melodeon and sing, drawing large crowds; see www.hymntime.com/tch/bio/p/h/i/phillips_p/htm, accessed 22 July 2015. See also Martin Clarke (ed.), *Music and Theology in Nineteenth-Century Britain* (Farnham: Ashgate

Publishing, 2012). In ch. 6, '"Sing a Sankey": The Rise of Gospel Hymnody in Great Britain', Mel R. Wilhoit quotes Ian Bradey: 'The Victorian era coincided with a massive upsurge of interest in teaching singing at both school and adult level. Choral societies and glee clubs were started all over the country. Hymn singing was perhaps the greatest beneficiary of this new movement. Whether for reasons of respectability and religious sentiment or simply because they were easier and more fun to sing, it was hymns rather than parlour ballads, folk songs or music hall numbers that most exercised the nation's vocal chords – not just in churches and chapels but in school rooms, at public meetings and social gatherings, in the streets and, most of all, at home in the nursery or parlour', p. 103.

22   Donaldson (researched and compiled), *Donaldson: a history* . . ., p. 79.
23   *www.hamiltonavenueroadtofreedom.org*, accessed 15 July 2015. See also Richard Cooper and Dr Eric R. Jackson, *Cincinnati's Underground Railroad* (Charleston, SC: Arcadia Publishing, 2014), p. 32.
24   Donaldson (researched and compiled), *Donaldson: a history* . . ., p. 79.
25   Walter P. Herz, 'Such a Glaring Inconsistency: The Unitarian Laity and Anti-Slavery in Antebellum Cincinnati, Let Freedom Ring!' (Ohio Humanities Council, no date), p. 6; available at *www.lists.firstuu.com/LetFreedomRing/essay2.pdf*, accessed 20 July 2015.
26   *The Cincinnati Gazette*, 26 July 1836.
27   *The Cincinnati Gazette*, 3 August 1836. See also the Ohio Anti-Slavery Society, *Narrative of the Late Riotous Proceedings Against the Liberty of the Press in Cincinnati* (1836). Available at *https://archive.org/details/narrativeoflater00lcohio*, accessed 16 May 2002.
28   *Narrative of the Late Riotous Proceedings*, p. 39.
29   *Narrative of the Late Riotous Proceedings*, p. 44.
30   Walter P. Herz, 'Such a Glaring Inconsistency: The Unitarian Laity and Anti-Slavery in Antebellum Cincinnati', *Let Freedom Ring! First Unitarian Church Journey of Reconciliation* (n.d.), p. 11.
31   *New Orphan Asylum for Colored Children Records* 1875–1967 (n.d.). Available at *http://library.cincymuseum.org/archives.mss1000-1099/Mss1059-register.pdf*, accessed 21 July 2015.
32   Donaldson (researched and compiled), *Donaldson: a history* . . ., p. 80.
33   Dr E. Wyn James, 'Welsh ballads and American slavery', *The Welsh Journal of Religious History*, 2 (2007), 59–86. 'Like the anti-slavery poems by Morgan John Rhys and S.R., this song again is written in the first person, with the Little Negro addressing the descendants of the Ancient British. In addition to the version in the periodical (13 stanzas), which emphasises the fact that the "Welshman" and the "Negro" are brothers and that Christ died for both, a longer broadside version (27 stanzas) – whose extra stanzas were added after

the emancipation of 1834 – includes narrative material which tells of the Little Negro's being taken from Africa by the English to the Caribbean and expresses his wish to return to Africa as a Christian missionary. This longer version was printed both as a four-sided leaflet and as a one-sided broadside "proper", complete with a number of illustrations (which make it by far the best illustrated of all the anti-slavery ballad sheets in Welsh)\\UWRS35\Users\jenwilson\Desktop\Welsh Ballads and American Slavery.html - _edn59 . . . In addition, a considerably shortened and edited variant of the poem, in six stanzas with a chorus, to be sung to the tune "Sweet Home", is also to be found on ballad sheets, coupled with a poem on the subject of the exodus of the Israelites of the Old Testament from slavery in Egypt . . . The original 13-stanza version of the poem was included in the collected works of Benjamin Price, published posthumously in 1855. There the date of composition is given as 25 September 1830. In an introductory note, the editor of the volume emphasises the popularity of the poem and its significant influence in the shaping of public opinion in Wales against slavery and in favour of freedom in general. He describes it as one of the most "*tyner, teimladol, a thoddedig*" ("tender, sensitive, and emotional") of compositions ever to have appeared in any language and says that, at the time of the great efforts to abolish slavery in the West Indies in the 1830s, it was in the mind and on the lips of everyone, from the grey-haired old man to the child who had just learned to read. Indeed, he says, this song was the first thing a mother would teach her child.'

34 *The Cambrian*, 12 July 1850, 23 May 1851, 14 July 1854.
35 *The Cambrian* 7 March 1856.
36 Ashley Ford, Living History interpreter, Cincinnati Museum Center, personal email correspondence 2 July 2016.
37 Joanne O'Connell, 'Understanding Stephen Collins Foster His World and Music' (unpublished DPhil thesis, University of Pittsburgh School of Arts and Sciences, 2007), p. iv.
38 O'Connell, 'Understanding Stephen Collins Foster His World and Music', pp. 157, iv, 207.
39 *www.tour.pitt.edu/tour/stephen-foster-memorial*, accessed 27 July 2015.
40 Stan Stennett, *Fully Booked* (Skipton: Vertical Editions, 2010). See also *http://news.bbc.co.uk/local/southeastwales/stanstennet*, accessed 21 February 2017. For Dai Francis see his obituary, *The Telegraph*, 11 December 2003.
41 *www.pitt.edu/~amerimus/foster.htm*. Paul Robeson can be heard singing 'Old Folks at Home' in the vernacular on YouTube, *https://www.youtube.com/watch?v=36hJeMk1PLg*, accessed 27 July 2015.
42 *www.cincymuseum.org/historymuseum* accessed 27 July 2015. See also Ashley Ford, musician at *www.fostersongs.com/artist*

43 Cooper and Jackson, *Cincinnati's Underground Railroad*, pp. 27, 37.
44 *The Liberator*, 1 January 1831.
45 *The Letters of William Lloyd Garrison: From Disunionism to the Brink of War* (Cambridge, MA: Harvard University Press, 1975), p. 231.
46 Cooper and Jackson, *Cincinnati's Underground Railroad*, p. 27.
47 *The Liberator*, 23/18 (6 May 1853). Available at *http://fair-use.org/the-liberator/1853*, accessed 20 July 2015.
48 Robert S. Levine, *Martin Delany, Frederick Douglass, and the Politics of Representative Identity* (Chapel Hill and London: University of North Carolina Press, 1997). Stowe to Garrison, 19 December 1853, in Annie Fields (ed.), *Life and Letters of Harriet Beecher Stowe* (Boston: Houghton, Mifflin and Co., 1897; repr. Los Angeles, CA: HardPress Publishing, 2013), p. 124; Frederick Douglass, 'The Industrial College', 20 January 1854, Frederick Douglass Papers, p. 3. (Stowe had written the December 1853 letter to defend Douglass against Garrison's charge that he was an 'apostate' from the cause. She demanded of Garrison: 'Is there but one true anti-slavery church and all others infidels? Who shall declare what it is?', *Life and Letters of Harriet Beecher Stowe*, pp. 214–15. See also Philip S. Foner, *The Life and Writings of Frederick Douglass, Volume II, Pre-Civil War Decade 1850–1860* (New York: International Publishers, 1950); *www.pbs.org/wgbh/aia/part4/4h2926.html*, accessed 27 July 2015.
49 Frederick Douglass, *Narrative of the Life of Frederick Douglass* (New York and Oxford: Oxford University Press, Oxford World's Classics, 1999), p. 100.
50 Douglass, *Narrative*, p. xvii.
51 Daniel G. Williams, *Black Skin, Blue Books: African Americans and Wales 1845–1945* (Cardiff: University of Wales Press, 2012), p. 35.
52 William Tweedie, *Running a Thousand Miles for Freedom; or, The Escape of William and Ellen Craft from Slavery* (London: William Tweedie, 337 Strand, 1860). See also *www.docsouth.unc.edu/neh/craft/menu.html*, accessed 24 July 2015.
53 Tweedie, *Running a Thousand Miles for Freedom*, p. 82.
54 Letter from Wm. W. Brown to Williams Lloyd Garrison, Pineville (PA), 4 January 1849, in *www.docsouth.unc.edu/neh/craft.menu.html*, accessed 24 July 2015.
55 *The Cambrian*, 29 October 1858.
56 Alan Llwyd, *Cymru Ddu Black Wales: A History* (Cardiff: Butetown History and Arts Centre, Alan Llwyd/Hughes and Son, 2005), p. 56.
57 Stowe, letter to Gamaliel Bailey, 1851 (transcribed Stephen Railton/University of Virginia, 2006). This text is transcribed from Joan D. Hedrick (ed.), *The Oxford Harriet Beecher Stowe Reader* (New York: Oxford University Press, 1999) p. 66; Stowe's original letter survives only as a typed copy in the Boston Public Library. See also *www.utc.iath.virginia.edu/uncletom/utithbsht.html*.

58 Old Washington is one of the old historic towns in America, and visitors can step into the pre-1790 log cabin visitor centre to hear the stories about Harriet Beecher Stowe. See *www.washingtonky.com*, accessed 22 July 2015.
59 *The Cambrian*, 6 October 1876, 2 February 1877. Josiah Henson later told a Sheffield audience 'how his Grace Archbishop of Canterbury slipped a £50 note into his hand when leaving' and concluded by singing a slave song and a farewell hymn.
60 Josiah Henson, *The Life of Josiah Henson, Formerly a Slave, Now an inhabitant of Canada, as Narrated by Himself* (Boston: Arthur D. Phelps, 1849). See also John Lobb (ed.), *An Autobiography of the Rev. Josiah Henson* [Mrs Harriet Beecher Stowe's 'Uncle Tom'] *from 1789 to 1876, With a Preface by Mrs Harriet Beecher Stowe, and an Introductory Note by George Sturge, and S. Morley, Esq. MP.* (London: Christian Age Office, 89 Farringdon Street, 1876).
61 Williams, *Black Skins, Blue Books*, pp. 53–6.
62 'Josiah Henson', leaflet dated 19 June 1997 at the Harriet Beecher Stowe House, 2950 Gilbert Avenue, Cincinnati OH 45206.
63 *The Cambrian* 29 November 1877.
64 *The Cambrian*, 22 February 1878.
65 *The Cambrian*, 29 November, 6 December 1878.
66 Williams, *Black Skins, Blue Books*, p. 25.
67 *South Wales Daily Post*, 9 May 1899.
68 *The Cambrian*, 3 April 1863. Letter written by Samuel Heineken Jnr.
69 Fern Riddell, 'The End of the American Civil War', *History Today* (8 April 2015), available at *www.historytoday.com/author/fern-riddell*, accessed 27 July 2015, on the 150th anniversary of the end of the American Civil War.
70 Jerry Silverman, *Ballads & Songs of the Civil War* (Pacific, MO: Mel Bay Publications, 1993), p. 14.
71 *The Cambrian*, 27 February 1874, 6 August 1875. See also ch. 3, 'The Fisk Jubilee Singers in Wales'.
72 Maria Weston Chapman, *Songs of the Free and Hymns of Christian Freedom* (Boston: Isaac Knapp, Washington Street, 1836), in John A. Collins, *The Anti-Slavery Picknick – A Collection of Speeches, Poems, Dialogues and Songs: Intended for use in Schools and Anti-Slavery Meetings* (Cornell University Library digital collections, copyrighted material 1 January 1842), p. 4.
73 Jen Wilson, 'Before Freedom: The Story of Willis the Runaway Slave', schools resource pack (Swansea: Jazz Heritage Wales, 2010). Willis's story is told through music and images in the 'Before Freedom' schools touring package, performed by musicians from Jazz Heritage Wales. Each school receives a schools resource pack. Willis is played by vocalist Christian Rae.
74 John Hope Franklin and Schweninger Loren, *Runaway Slaves, Rebels on the Plantation* (New York: Oxford University Press, 1999), p. 222.

75 *The Cambrian*, 2 February 1833. The *Cambrian* newspaper reported: 'EMANCIPATION OF A SLAVE AT SWANSEA – A short time since, the St. Peter (H. Mickle, master) a large American ship, arrived at this port from Cabija, in Chilli, with copper ore; and on Thursday the 24th ult., a very fine young negro, about 20 years of age, of the name of Willis, applied to T. Edw. Thomas, Esq., Portreeve, stating that he was a slave acting as cook on board the St. Peter; that he had accidentally heard, that if he could but put his foot upon British ground, he would then be free, and requested advice upon this point. Mr T. instantly sent to the ship to ascertain whether Willis really had been a slave on board such vessel, but as the Captain was not to be met with at the instant, the worthy Magistrate lost no time in assuring the poor fellow, that by the laws of this happy country, he was emancipated – that he was no longer a slave!!! This gratifying information naturally gave the most heartfelt delight to all present, but more especially to Willis, who for the first moment of his life, felt that he was a free man!!! The following morning, as he would not return on board, he had a written discharge from the ship, and as he was not entitled to any wages, the Captain generously gave him two sovereigns. Willis belonged to the ship owners, and it will be gratifying to the friends of humanity to learn, that during the nine years he had served in the bonds of slavery, he had no complaint to make against his former or his present master, but that, on the contrary, he had experienced every indulgence and kindness compatible with his situation. Notwithstanding (and his good condition and well-dressed appearance, bespoke the truth of his statement) he was anxious to be free.'

76 *The Cambrian* 20 March 1841.

77 http://www.llanellich.org.uk/files/248-thomas-the-black-barber, accessed 6th February 2017.

78 *The Cambrian*, 16, 23 March 1855, 20 November 1863. See also Charles Stearns, *The Narrative of Henry Box Brown who Escaped from Slavery, Enclosed in a Box Three Feet Long, Two Wide and Two and a Half High. Written from a Statement of Facts Made by Himself. With Remarks Upon the Remedy for Slavery* (Boston: Brown and Stearns, 1849). See also www.docsouth.unc.edu/neh/boxbrown/summary.html and www.aaregistry.org/henry-box-brown, accessed 28th July 2015.

79 *The Cambrian* 11 September 1863.

80 *The Cambrian*, 17 December 1869.

81 Letter from National Underground Railroad Freedom Center, 50 East Freedom Way, Cincinnati OH 45202, USA, 17 June 2004, Jazz Heritage Wales Collection.

Chapter Two

1. *The Cambrian*, 2 February 1830, 7 July 1832, 6 July 1833.
2. Mandolin Band photograph property of Jazz Heritage Wales.
3. *The Cambrian*, 7 July 1844.
4. *The Cambrian*, 12 July 1850. *The Birmingham Journal*, 12 June 1847. See also www.search.connectinghistories.org.uk, accessed 7 February 2017.
5. *The Cambrian*, 23 May 1851.
6. *The Cambrian*, 14 July 1854.
7. Frantz Fanon, *Black Skin, White Masks*, trans. Charles Lam Markmann (London: Pluto Press, 1986), pp. 18, 110, 228–9. Originally published in France as *Peau Noire, Masques Blanc* (Paris: Éditions du Seuil, 1952).
8. Audre Lorde, *The Master's Tools Will Never Dismantle The Master's House*. Comments at 'The Personal and the Political Panel' ('Second Sex' conference, 29 October 1979), also in Audre Lorde, *Sister Outsider, Essays and Speeches* (Berkeley: Crossing Press, 1984).
9. Michael Pickering, 'White Skin, Black Masks: "Nigger" Minstrelsy in Victorian England', in J. S. Bratton (ed.) *Music Hall: Performance and Style* (Milton Keynes: Open University Press, 1986), pp. 70–91.
10. Michael Pickering, '"A Jet Ornament to Society": Black Music in Nineteenth Century Britain', in Paul Oliver (ed.), *Black Music in Britain: Essays on the Afro-Asian Contribution to Popular Music* (Milton Keynes: Open University Press, 1990), p. 16.
11. *The Cambrian*, 20 October 1854.
12. *The Cambrian*, 23 November 1860.
13. *The Cambrian*, 5 July 1861.
14. Jane Aaron, 'Finding a Voice in Two Tongues: Gender and Colonization', in *Our Sisters' Land: The Changing Identity of Women in Wales*, ed. Jane Aaron, Teresa Rees, Sandra Betts and Moira Vincentelli (Cardiff: University of Wales Press, 1994), p. 185.
15. *The Cambrian*, 31 March 1865.
16. *The Cambrian*, 15 September 1865. For further reading on the Grenfell family, see *Dictionary of Welsh Biography* (National Library of Wales); Stephen Hughes, *Copperopolis: Landscapes of the Early Industrial Period in Swansea* (British Library Cataloguing in Publication Data, 2000).
17. *The Cambrian*, 13 October 1865.
18. *The Cambrian*, 29 June 1866.
19. *The Cambrian*, 25 October 1867.
20. *The Cambrian*, 1 November 1867.
21. *The Cambrian*, 12 June 1868.
22. The song 'Alabama Sam' was probably in circulation via a broadside or word of mouth predating publication. It was published by the Poet's Box, probably

in Glasgow in April 1870, two years after its Swansea performance. For more information see *www.digital.nls.uk/broadside.cfm./id/16046*.
[23] See *www.traditionalmusic.co.uk/songster/13-de-ham-fat-man.htm*, accessed 28 April 2015. There is a fascinating account of minstrelsy troupes and their music in William L. Slout, *Burnt Cork and Tambourines: A Source Book for Negro Minstrelsy* (Library of Congress of Cataloguing in Publication Data, 2007), p. 231. African Americans had escaped their masters and plantations by the end of the American Civil War 1861–5.
[24] *The Cambrian*, 18 December 1868.
[25] *The Cambrian*, 5 March 1869.
[26] *The Cambrian*, 12, 19, 26 March 1869. For further reading on perceptions of African American style and substance, see Pickering, '"A Jet Ornament to Society"', pp. 16–33.
[27] Kimberlé Crenshaw, quoting Sojourner Truth, 'Ain't I a Woman?' at Women's Convention, Akron, OH, 28–9 May 1851, in 'Demarginalizing the Intersection of Race and Sex: A Black Feminist Critique of Antidiscrimination Doctrine, Feminist Theory, and Antiracist Politics', *University of Chicago Legal Forum*, 1/8 (1989), 153.
[28] bell hooks, *Ain't I A Woman: Black Women and Feminism* (London: Pluto Press, 1981), p. 160.
[29] *The Cambrian*, 9 April 1869.
[30] *The Cambrian*, 5, 12 September, 28 November 1873.
[31] *The Cambrian*, 6 March 1874.
[32] *The Cambrian*, 22 May 1874. For the illustration, see the Evanion Catalogue, British Library, *http://www.bl.uk/catalogues/evanion/Record.aspx?EvanID=024-000000415&ImageIndex=0*, accessed 12 May 2015.
[33] *The Cambrian*, 11 September 1874, 19 October, 2 November 1877.
[34] *The Cambrian*, 29 May 1874. For further investigation of the Coushatta Massacre, and the role played by Marshall H. Twitchell, who 'worked to promote education and civil rights to former slaves known as freedmen, see Wikipedia, 'Coushatta Massacre', *en.wikipedia.org/wiki/Coushatta_massacre*, accessed 1 May 2015.
[35] *The Cambrian*, 2 October 1874.
[36] *The Cambrian*, 19 November 1875.
[37] *The Cambrian*, 7 April 1876.
[38] *The Cambrian*, 28 April 1876. For working conditions of Welsh girls employed as servants, see Rosemary Scadden, *No Job For A Little Girl: Voices from Domestic Service* (Llandysul: Gomer Press, 2013).
[39] *The Cambrian*, 2 March 1877.
[40] *The Cambrian*, 5 October 1877, 25 January 1878.
[41] *The Cambrian*, 8, 15 March, 26 July 1878. See also *http://stageagent.clom/shows/play/3555/the-octoroon*. For Edith Wynne see *http://yba.llgc.org.uk/en/s-WYNN-ED-1842.html*, accessed 7 February 2017.

42   *The Cambrian*, 11 October 1878.
43   *The Cambrian*, 20 July 1883.
44   Daniel G. Williams, 'Frederick Douglass, Abolitionism and Victorian Wales', in *Black Skin, Blue Books: African Americans and Wales 1845–1945* (Cardiff: University of Wales Press, 2012), pp. 23, 39.
45   Pickering, '"A Jet Ornament to Society"', p. 26.
46   H. Reynolds, *Minstrel Memories: The story of burnt cork minstrelsy in Great Britain from 1836 to 1927* (London: Alston Rivers, 1928), p. 78.
47   *The Cambrian*, 3 November 1883.
48   *The Cambrian*, 7 September 1883. See also Pickering, 'A Jet Ornament to Society', pp. 16–33.
49   *The Cambrian*, 21 December 1883.
50   *The Cambrian*, 30 November 1888.
51   *The Cambrian*, 7 December 1888.
52   *The Cambrian*, 29 November 1889.
53   *South Wales Daily Post*, 15 June 1897.
54   *South Wales Daily Post*, 24 August 1897. Information about the British Empire campaigns is available at *www.britishempire.co.uk*, accessed 8 May 2015.
55   *The Cambrian*, 27 December 1889.
56   *The Cambrian*, 4 April 1890, 23 June 1893.
57   *The Cambrian*, 24 October 1890, 3 April 1891.
58   *The Cambrian*, 4 October 1894.
59   *South Wales Daily Post*, 20 March 1895.
60   *The Cambrian*, 24 March, 29 September 1893; *South Wales Daily Post*, 12 January 1894, 10 June 1895, 2 February 1897, 31 May 1898, 24 January, 16 May 1899.
61   *South Wales Daily Post*, 16 February, 15 March, 27 July, 4, 31 August, 21 December 1899, 9 January, 25 May 1900, 2 January 1902, 27 December 1905.
62   *The Cambrian*, 26 December 1890, 9 January 1891.
63   *https://archive.org/stream/chaswpoole*. The presentation included Mr Stanley commenting 'By September the expedition struck the famine region, a region so devastated by the raids of the slave owners in a manner so complete that where once existed populous villages not a single hut remains. The method adopted by the Arab slave raiders is to surround the villages for a two mile radius, hiding themselves in the long dry grass, which eventually they set fire to, also the huts of the natives, and by yelling and firing of guns so terrify the poor negroes that many of them are easily made captive. Any who show fight are mercilessly shot down, the remainder placed in chains and forked sticks, previously cut for the purpose, ready for the long and weary march. Infants who may be an encumbrance to their mothers, and old folks who are no use to see as slaves, they dispose of by either battering or blowing out their brains. Dr. Livingstone stated "that for every slave taken alive five were left dead".'

64 *The Cambrian*, 6 May, 3 June 1892; *South Wales Daily Post*, 1 April 1898, 17 January, 26 December 1899.
65 Williams, 'Frederick Douglass, Abolitionism and Victorian Wales', p. 75.

Chapter Three

1 J. T. Marsh and F. J. Loudin, *The Story of the Jubilee Singers, with Supplement by F. J. Loudin* (London: Hodder and Stoughton, 1902), with notation.
2 Lynn Abbott and Doug Seroff, *Out of Sight: The Rise of African American Popular Music 1889–1895* (Jackson, MS: University Press of Mississippi, 2002), p. 3. 'Loudin quickly became the Singers' most important soloist and added his exceptionally deep bass voice to the concerted harmony of the jubilee choruses. Throughout his career Loudin used the Jubilee platform to make public statements on the issue of civil rights. He was, in retrospect, the most politically outspoken black entertainer of the nineteenth century'.
3 Marsh and Loudin, *The Story of the Jubilee Singers*, pp. 14–16.
4 Marsh and Loudin, *The Story of the Jubilee Singers*, pp. 18, 46.
5 Dr Theo L. Cuyler, reviewing a concert at his church, in Marsh and Loudin, *The Story of the Jubilee Singers*, p. 30.
6 [Anon.], Letter to *The Cambrian*, 16 January 1874. The 'Tarpeian Rock' was a steep cliff overlooking the Roman Forum and the scene of executions where miscreants would be thrown off the top (*Wikipedia.org/wiki/Tarpeian_Rock*).
7 *The Cambrian*, 27 February 1874.
8 Michael Pickering, '"A Jet Ornament to Society": Black Music in Nineteenth-Century Britain', in Paul Oliver (ed.), *Black Music in Britain: Essays on the Afro-Asian Contribution to Popular Music* (Milton Keynes: Open University Press, 1990), pp. 16–33, quotes *Birmingham Daily Mail*, 10 April 1874.
9 Theo. F. Seward, Preface (n.d.), in W. J. Gibbs, *Negro Spirituals or The Songs of the Jubilee Singers* (Bromley, Kent, and Ambleside, Clacton-on-Sea: W. J. Gibbs, *c.*1901). A copy resides in the Jazz Heritage Wales library.
10 Sieglinde Lemke, *Primitivist Modernism: Black Culture and the Origins of Transatlantic Modernism* (Oxford and New York: Oxford University Press, 1998), p. 9.
11 *Hwyl* translates as 'a state of being, or condition . . . a stirring feeling of emotional motivation and energy' within the Welsh-language Baptist service of call and response. A similar state of fervent arousal, or 'soul', exists within African American Baptist services.
12 Ira D. Sankey, *Sacred Songs and Solos and New Hymns and Solos 888 Pieces* (London: Morgan and Scott, *c.*1872).
13 Marsh and Loudin, *The Story of the Jubilee Singers*, pp. 67–8.

14. For further reading on Welsh working-class communities' ability to raise funds and sustain financial ventures, see Nigel Jenkins, *Gwalia in Khasia: The Biggest Overseas Venture Ever Sustained by the Welsh* (Llandysul: Gomer Press, 1995). Sunday School children would be awarded ornately inscribed certificates for their fundraising activities (Jen Wilson, personal archive).

15. Marsh writes that the 'Jubilee Music was more or less of a puzzle to the critics; and even among those who sympathised with their mission, there was no little difference of opinion as to the artistic merit of their entertainments.' *The Story of the Jubilee Singers*, p. 66.

16. Marsh and Loudin, *The Story of the Jubilee Singers*, pp. 48–119.

17. Philip Phillips, 'The Singing Pilgrim', performed 'an evening of Sacred Song' at Swansea's Mount Pleasant Baptist Chapel on 9 November 1876 under the auspices of the Sunday School Union; some of the net proceeds were to be applied to the Continental Sunday School Mission and the general purposes of the London Sunday School Union. Mr Phillips sang a collection of what he called 'song sermons', accompanying himself on the American Organ. The Chair was taken by Mr. Ebenezer Davies, President of the Sunday School Union.

18. By 1900 W. J. Gibbs, Ambleside, Clacton-on-Sea, was retailing *Negro Spirituals, Fisk Jubilee Songbook* for 34s. 6d per 100 copies. Chapelgoers in Wales were already familiar with the Sankey hymnbooks, still currently in use, and the Negro spirituals also became part of the church and chapel repertoire.

19. Evelyn Brooks Higginbotham, *Righteous Discontent: The Women's Movement in the Black Baptist Church 1880–1920* (Cambridge, MA: Harvard University Press, 1993), pp. 88–119.

20. Paul Oliver, *The Story of the Blues* (London: Penguin Books, 1978), p. 6. 'For some people it is infinitely glamorous, for others it is a symbol of the oppression of a racial minority.'

21. Pickering, '"A Jet Ornament to Society"', pp. 27–8.

22. J. Green, 'Afro-American Symphony: Popular Black Concert Hall Performers 1900–1940', in Oliver (ed.), *Black Music in Britain*, pp. 34–44. See also Jeffrey Green, *Black Edwardians: Black People in Britain 1901–1914* (London and Portland, OR: Frank Cass, 1998) pp. 62, 143.

23. Lynn Abbott, '"Do Thyself a' no Harm": The Jubilee Singing Phenomenon and the "Only Original New Orleans University Singers"', *American Music Research Center Journal* (2013). Available at www.colorado.edu/amrc/node/277/attachment, accessed 20 January 2016.

24. *The Cambrian*, 6 February 1874.

25. *The Cambrian*, 23 March 1874.

26. *The Cambrian*, 6 August 1875.

27. *The Cambrian*, 6 August 1875. Dr Rimbault was an English organist, musicologist, book collector and author. He went on to state, 'Welsh music

was originally composed for the harp, which often resembled scientific music of the 17th and 18th century'. Perhaps Dr Rimbault had gone to see the Fisk Jubilee Singers.

28 *The Cambrian*, 13 November 1874. The Livermore Brothers Court Minstrels were whites in blackface. Edith Wynne, born in 1842 and known as the Welsh nightingale, was one of the world's 'most celebrated singers' and, according to the *Cambrian*, 'The first Welsh singer to make a name for herself in the USA'. Mme Patti was the renowned opera star who later made a home for herself outside Swansea in Craig-y-Nos Castle. A replica of her Adelina Patti Theatre still resides in Victoria Park, and is now an Asian restaurant.

29 *The Cambrian*, 30 July, August 1875.

30 J. Ladner, 'Introduction to *Tomorrow's Tomorrow: The Black Woman*', in S. Harding (ed.), *Feminism and Methodology: Social Science Issues* (Bloomington, IN: Indiana University Press, 1987), p. 80. Ladner informs us she was 'influenced by her Blackness . . . There is no single set of criteria for becoming a woman in the Black community, each girl is conditioned by a diversity of factors depending primarily upon her opportunities, role models, psychological disposition, and the influence of the values, customs and traditions of the Black community.'

31 Angela Davis, *Women, Race and Class* (London: Women's Press, 1982), p. 7. 'Since slave women were classified as "breeders" as opposed to "mothers", their infant children could be sold away from them like calves from cows . . . As females, slave women were inherently vulnerable to all forms of sexual coercion . . . Rape, in fact, was an uncamouflaged expression of the slaveholder's economic mastery and the overseer's control over Black women as workers.'

32 Higginbotham, *Righteous Discontent: The Women's Movement in the Black Baptist Church 1880–1920*, p. 191.

33 Nannie Helen Burroughs, Speech given at the National Baptist Church Twentieth Annual Session of the Women's Convention (1920). 'In 1909 Burroughs founded the National Training School for Women and Girls in Washington D.C. which uniquely provided academic, religious and vocational classes for black girls and young women at a time when education was segregated in the South; she operated it until her death. It has since been renamed the Nannie Helen Burroughs School in her honor' (*Wikipedia.org/wiki/Nannie_Helen_Burroughs*).

34 Andrea Sutcliffe (ed.), *Mighty Rough Times, I Tell You: Personal Accounts of Slavery in Tennessee* (Winston-Salem, NC: John F. Blair, 2000), pp. vii–ix.

35 Sutcliffe (ed.), *Mighty Rough Times, I Tell You*, pp. 52–7.

36 Sutcliffe (ed.), *Mighty Rough Times, I Tell You*, pp. 80–2.

37 Sutcliffe (ed.), *Mighty Rough Times, I Tell You*, pp. 109–10.

38 B. Hurmence (ed.), *Before Freedom, When I Just Can Remember: Personal Accounts of Slavery in South Carolina* (Winston-Salem, NC: John F. Blair, 1989; from the Penn School Collection, Penn Center, Library of Congress, 1966), pp. 55–7, 21–7.
39 Solomon Northup, *12 Years a Slave* (London: Penguin Books, 2012), p. 48. The film of the same name, directed by Steve McQueen, won three Academy Awards (Academy of Motion Picture Arts and Sciences) in 2013.
40 *Reports of the Commissioners of Inquiry into the State of Education in Wales, Appointed by the Committee of Council on Education* (London: HMSO, 1848), p. 66.
41 Daniel G. Williams, *Black Skin, Blue Books: African Americans and Wales 1845–1945* (Cardiff: University of Wales Press, 2012), p. 46. G. Tyson Roberts, *The Language of the Blue Books* (Cardiff: University of Wales Press, 2011), p. 203.
42 Evan Jones ['Ieuan Gwynedd'], editor, *Y Gymraes*, established 1850–2. *Y Gymraes* was revived from 1896–1934, editor Alice Gray Jones being described by the National Library of Wales as a 'less conservative editor than her predecessors, who constantly upheld the rights and status of women'.
43 Sian Rhiannon Williams, 'The True "Cymraes": Images of Women in Women's Nineteenth-Century Welsh Periodicals', in Angela V. John (ed.), *Our Mothers' Land: Chapters in Welsh Women's History 1830–1939* (Cardiff: University of Wales Press, 1991), pp. 76–7.
44 *The Cambrian*, 8 September 1876.
45 Marsh and Loudin, *The Story of the Jubilee Singers*, p. 77.
46 Programme (copy) of Fisk Jubilee Singers 13–15 February 1889, Jazz Heritage Wales. For further reading on the Caradog Choir and Griffith Rhys Jones 'Caradog' 1834–97, Conductor, see www.cynonculture.co.uk/wordpress/trecynon/griffith-rhys-jones-caradoc-1834-1897/, accessed 22 October 2018. There is a statue to Jones in Aberdare erected in 1920. Its inscription reads 'Conductor of the renowned South Wales Choral Union "Y Cor Mawr" 1872–1873. This statue is erected by his friends and fellow countrymen in appreciation of his musical genius and as a tribute of admiration and affection 1920.'
47 Oliver (ed.), *Black Music in Britain*, p. 14.
48 *The Cambrian*, 18 January 1889.
49 *South Wales Daily Post*, 14 February 1899.
50 *The Advertiser, Adelaide*, 16 May 1893. 'Deep in the Mine' is also mentioned in Lynn Abbott and Doug Seroff, *To Do This, You Must Know How: Music Pedagogy in the Black Gospel Quartet Tradition* (Jackson, MS: University Press of Mississippi, 2013), p. 37.
51 L. Morrison (lyricist) and William Herbert Jude (composer), 'Deep in the Mine' (London: J. B. Cramer and Co., 1882).
52 See www.welshcoalmines.co.uk/disasterslist, accessed 21 January 2016.
53 *South Wales Daily Post*, 27 April 1906.
54 See www.llanddulashiddenhistory.co.uk/joneslewis, accessed 21 January 2016.

55 Jeffrey Green, 'The Jamaica Native Choir in Britain, 1906–1908', in *Black Music Research Journal*, 13/1 (Spring 1993), 15–29.
56 *South Wales Daily Post*, 6 August 1908.
57 *South Wales Daily Post*, 26 March 1907.
58 Amy Dillwyn: industrialist (Dillwyn Spelter Works, producing zinc); writer (*The Rebecca Rioter* (1880) and others); philanthropist (Swansea Union Board member of the Workhouse); sportswoman (Dillwyn Hockey Club); politician (standing in Castle Ward in November 1907 as the Independent Candidate); campaigner (women's suffrage NUWSS) and cigar-chomping suffragette who referred to her friend Olive Talbot as her wife. Honno Press reissued Dillwyn's *The Rebecca Rioter* in 2001. David Painting's *Amy Dillwyn* (Cardiff: University of Wales Press, 1987, new edn 2013).
59 *South Wales Daily Post*, 2 April 1907.
60 *South Wales Daily Post*, 5 April 1907.
61 See www.jeffreygreen.co.uk, accessed 20 January 2016. Dr. Paul T. Kwami, Fisk University Associate Professor, Musical Director, and Mike Curb, Jubilee Singers Endowed Chair.
62 See www.blackpast.org, accessed 20 January 2016.
63 See www.jeffreygreen.co.uk, accessed 20 January 2016.
64 Sandra Graham, 'On the Road to Freedom: The Contracts of the Fisk Jubilee Singers', *American Music*, 24/1 (University of Illinois Press, Spring 2006), 1–29.
65 Pickering, '"A Jet Ornament to Society"', p. 33.

Chapter Four

1 *The Cambrian*, 10 January 1890; *South Wales Daily Post*, 12 March 1918.
2 Deirdre Beddoe, *Discovering Women's History: A Practical Manual* (London: Pandora Press, 1983), pp. 28–9.
3 Penelope Summerfield, 'Patriotism and Empire: Music Hall Entertainment 1870–1914', in John Mackenzie (ed.), *Imperialism and Popular Culture* (Manchester: Manchester University Press, 1986), pp. 17–48.
4 Paul Oliver (ed.), *Black Music in Britain: Essays on the Afro Asian Contribution to Popular Music* (Milton Keynes: Open University Press, 1990), p. 12.
5 J. Traies, 'Jones and the Working Girl: Class Marginality in Music Hall Song 1860–1900', in J. S. Bratton (ed.), *Music Hall: Performance and Style* (Milton Keynes: Open University Press, 1986), p. 23–48.
6 *South Wales Daily Post*, 17 January 1899.
7 *South Wales Daily Post*, 17 April 1900. For further reading on 'the Black Patti' see Henry Louis Gates Jr and Evelyn Brooks Higginbotham (eds), *African American Lives* (Oxford and New York: Oxford University Press, 2004), p. 477.

8   For an analysis of the ragtime era, see P. Gammond, *Scott Joplin and the Ragtime Era* (London: Sphere Books Ltd, 1975). See also Paul Oliver, 'Under the Chicken Tree: Songs from the Ragtime Era', in *Songsters and Saints: Vocal Traditions on Race Records* (Cambridge: Cambridge University Press, 1984).

9   Gilbert Chase, *America's Music: From the Pilgrims to the Present* (Urbana and Chicago: University of Illinois Press, rev. 3rd edn, 1987), p. 423.

10 Sadie Koninski (composer), 'Eli Green's Cakewalk', written in 1896 and published by Joseph W. Stern in 1898; Adaline Shepherd (composer), 'Pickles and Peppers', published by Joseph Flanner in 1906; May Francis Aufderheide (composer), 'Dusty Rag', published by J. H. Aufderheide, 1908. Biography notes by Bill Edwards at *http://ragpiano.com*, accessed 29 March 2017.

11 Sid O'Connell, *Women in Music Newsletter*, July 1992. See also *https://jscholarship.library.jhu.edu/handle/1774.2/26285* for the musical score.

12 Sid Colin, 'Do You Come Here Often?', in *And The Bands Played On* (London: Elm Tree Books, 1977), pp. 69–81.

13 *South Wales Daily Post*, 11 November 1902, 17 February 1903.

14 Oliver (ed.), *Black Music in Britain*, pp. 3–15.

15 *South Wales Daily Post*, 1 February 1905.

16 Kipling, quoted in Peter Bailey (ed.), *Music Hall. The Business of Pleasure* (Milton Keynes: Open University Press, 1986), p. xiv.

17 *Daily News*, 16 May 1903, 6.

18 Catherine Parsonage, 'In Dahomey: A Negro Musical Comedy', in *The Evolution of Jazz in Britain, 1880–1935* (Aldershot: Ashgate Publishing, 2005), p. 100.

19 Parsonage, 'In Dahomey: A Negro Musical Comedy', pp. 81–104; T. Riis, 'The Music and Scripts of "In Dahomey"', *Recent Researches in American Music, Vol. 25* (Madison: AR Editions, 1996), quoted by Catherine Parsonage.

20 Oliver (ed.), *Black Music in Britain*, p. 12.

21 *South Wales Daily Post*, 20 June 1905. Jessie Carney Smith (ed.), 'Dora Dean (1872–1949), Dancer, Entertainer', in *Notable Black American Women Book II* (Detroit, MI: Gale Research Inc., 1996), pp. 161–4.

22 *South Wales Daily Post*, 23 April 1907.

23 Frank Cullen, with Florence Hackman, Donald McNeilly and Charles E. Johnson, in *Vaudeville Old and New, An Encyclopedia of Variety Performers in America Volume I* (New York and London: Routledge, Taylor and Francis Group, 2006), pp. 570–1.

24 *South Wales Daily Post*, 20 June 1905, 2 March 1910.

25 Charles Hamm, *Irving Berlin, Songs from the Melting Pot: The Formative Years, 1907–1914* (New York: Oxford University Press, 1997), p. 208.

26 *South Wales Daily Post*, 16, 17 June 1913.

27 *South Wales Daily Post*, 25 November 1913.

28 *South Wales Daily Post*, 2 December 1913.

29 *South Wales Daily Post*, 5 May 1914.

30   *South Wales Daily Post*, 15 May, 9 June, 21 July, 11 August, 7 September 1914, 12 January, 12 March 1915.
31   *South Wales Daily Post*, 7, 28 December 1915, 3, 20 June 1916, 13 February 1917, 12 March 1918.
32   Jen Wilson, interview with Emmy Harries, 'Swansea Women's History Group Oral History Collection' (Swansea Women's History Group, 1983).
33   Bernard Lewis, *Swansea and the Workhouse: The Poor Law in 19th Century Swansea* (Swansea: West Glamorgan Archive Service, 2003), p. 23.
34   *The Cambrian*, 9 January 1874.
35   *South Wales Daily Post*, 19 November 1919.
36   *South Wales Daily Post*, 4 February 1921.
37   *South Wales Daily Post*, 4 March 1921.
38   *South Wales Daily Post*, 29 September 1921.
39   *South Wales Daily Post*, 8 November 1921. Penillion is the art of vocal improvisation or counter melody over a harp melody.
40   *South Wales Daily Post*, 11 November 1921.
41   *South Wales Daily Post*, 19, 30 November 1921. 'I'm Going Back to Dixie', a walkaround dance song composed by Dan Emmett in 1861, with sheet music published the same year by Firth, Pond and Co. John Hartford (1937–2001) can be seen on YouTube performing this song with banjo and fiddle against a backdrop of paddle steamers on the river, available at *https://www.youtube.com/watch?v=ihhRCEykygU*. Accessed 8 February 2017.
42   *South Wales Daily Post*, 30 November, 27 December 1921, 5 January 1922.
43   *South Wales Daily Post*, 18 January 1922.
44   *South Wales Daily Post*, 30 September 1922.
45   *South Wales Daily Post*, 3 November, 6, 27 December 1922.
46   *South Wales Daily Post*, 17 January 1923.
47   *South Wales Daily Post*, 2, 22 February 1923.
48   *South Wales Daily Post*, 13 April 1923.
49   *South Wales Daily Post*, 7 September 1923.
50   *South Wales Daily Post*, 14, 27 December 1923.
51   *South Wales Daily Post*, 1, 30 May 1924, 21 February, 14 May 1925.
52   Swansea Women's History Group filmed interviews with staff on their last day at the Maternity Unit, Mount Pleasant Hospital, formerly the Workhouse and Tawe Lodge; Hi-8 video documentary, *The Last Day at Mt. Pleasant's Maternity Unit* (1995/6). Documentary and archival material held at West Glamorgan County Archives Services, Swansea Civic Centre.

Chapter Five

1   Ottilie Patterson (1932–2011), Jazz Heritage Wales Oral History Collection (1990).

2. Philip Jamison, *Hoedowns Reels and Frolics: Roots and Branches of Southern Appalachian Dance* (Urbana and Chicago: University of Illinois Press, 2015), p. 131.
3. Flatfootin' can be viewed at 'Old Time Dance Party at Augusta Heritage Center' on YouTube, and at *http://flatfootandfancyfree.com/tradition*, accessed 15 February 2017.
4. Coleman Goetz and Leon Flatow, 'Everybody Loves a "Jass" Band' (New York: Leo Feist, 1917), reproduced with kind permission by Sheet Music Collection, Brown University Library, Providence, RI (2015).
5. Michael Pickering, '"A Jet Ornament to Society": Black Music in Nineteenth-Century Britain', in Paul Oliver (ed.), *Black Music in Britain, Essays on the Afro-Asian Contribution to Popular Music* (Open University Press: Milton Keynes, 1990), pp. 16–33.
6. Deirdre Beddoe, 'Fur Coats and Widows' Weeds: The Great War, 1914–1918', in Deirdre Beddoe, *Out of the Shadows: A History of Women in Twentieth-Century Wales* (Cardiff: University of Wales Press, 2000), pp. 47–73. Cardiff-born Ivor Novello penned the wartime hit 'Keep The Home Fires Burning' in 1914, with words by Lena Gilbert Ford, published by Chappell and Co.
7. *South Wales Daily Post*, 26 April, 4, 5, 6 May 1910.
8. Ursula Masson, 'The Swansea Suffragettes', by Swansea Women's History Group, in Luana Dee and Keineg Katell (eds), *Women in Wales* (Cardiff: Womenwrite Press, 1987), pp. 67–76.
9. *South Wales Daily Post*, 17 January, 16 February, 22 August, 3 October 1910, 10 December 1912.
10. *South Wales Daily Post*, 18 January 1912.
11. *South Wales Daily Post*, 2 January 1913.
12. Ursula Masson, '"Political conditions in Wales are quite different . . .": party politics and votes for women in Wales 1912–1915', in *Women's History Review*, 9/2 (2000), 373, 384–5.
13. *South Wales Daily Post*, 3 July 1917.
14. Angela John, *Turning the Tide: The Life of Lady Rhondda* (Cardigan: Parthian Books, 2013), pp. 100–1.
15. *South Wales Daily Post*, 13 December 1911.
16. *South Wales Daily Post*, 13 December 1911.
17. *South Wales Daily Post*, 17 November 1911.
18. *South Wales Daily Post*, 3 December 1911.
19. *South Wales Daily Post*, 7 November 1911, 17 September 1912. There is a remarkable photograph of Lily Flexmore (1905) in full flow, dancing and biting her toe, along with an array of fellow thespians, contortionists and performers, at *https://uk.pinterest.com/rileymo/cirque/*, accessed 23 March 2015.

[20] Mike Jempson, *The Musicians' Union: A Centenary Celebration* (London: Musicians' Union, 1993), pp. 6, 28. The centenary publication states that women musicians were in abundance when the Amalgamated Musicians' Union was founded in 1893, largely because music was seen as a suitable skill for young 'middle class' women to acquire, although more working-class women had access to musical instruments than ever before. New opportunities opened up for many women musicians, who had previously found it difficult to develop a full-time professional career. The publication goes on to state that some women were skilled at a variety of musical genres, and that women working in pit orchestras required a high level of ability in reading musical scores. With the improvisational skills needed for accompanying silent movies, some of these women would have easily adapted to the new 'hot' and 'syncopated' style of music burgeoning in the 1920s. Male bandleaders were scathing about women's musical skills and their physical appearance. Women had originally been barred from the London Orchestral Association in 1893, 'rejecting amateur and part-time musicians'. Although they had been allowed to join the Amalgamated Musicians Union in 1893, this took place in the face of some of their male colleagues' prejudices. The AMU claimed it was committed to equal pay for equal work (and those women in the Queen's Hall Orchestra were accorded equal status and pay with men, and their own band room). But most women were still being paid less than men, and some venues even excluded women musicians. By 1921 there were 20,000 members. Marie Lloyd was also an early member and used the rallying cry 'our demands are just and we must stand together as a profession'. For further reading see John Williamson and Martin Cloonan, *Players' Work Time: A History of the British Musicians' Union 1893–2013* (Manchester: Manchester University Press, 2016).

[21] *South Wales Daily Post*, 14, 21 January 1913.

[22] *South Wales Daily Post*, 9 June 1913.

[23] Deirdre Beddoe, *Discovering Women's History: A Practical Manual* (London: Pandora Press, 1983), pp. 206–20.

[24] David Boulton, *Jazz in Britain* (London: W. H. Allen, 1959), p. 25.

[25] Sid Colin, *And The Bands Played On. An Informal History of British Dance Bands* (London: Elm Tree Books, 1977), p. 8.

[26] *South Wales Daily Post*, 17 March 1914. For the history of gay, lesbian and transgender in Wales, see Norena Shopland, *Forbidden Lives: Lesbian, Gay, Bisexual and Transgender Stories from Wales* (Bridgend: Seren Books, 2017).

[27] *South Wales Daily Post*, 9 February 1914.

[28] *South Wales Daily Post*, 2 June, 4, 5 August 1914.

[29] *South Wales Daily Post*, 11 August, 1 September 1914.

[30] *South Wales Daily Post*, 7 September, 17 October, 23 November 1914.

[31] *South Wales Daily Post*, 20 October, 23 December 1914, 19 January 1915.

32 *South Wales Daily Post*, 25 May 1915. A letter appeared in the press from Sapper W. J. Williams of the Welsh Field Company, Dardanelles, Turkey: 'I have eight men in my trench which they called The Ragtime Villa. We're practically in the firing line, not much more than half a mile from the sea, and our warships and the land batteries near us make a terrific noise as they bombard the Turkish positions. Makes one's head ache, but they do awful execution among the Turks. We only work during the dark hours, too dangerous in the day. Yesterday the Turks dropped shrapnel and one shell dropped into the parapet of our trench just outside our dugout. It is very hot here, flies are an awful pest, millions of them. Shells are beginning to whiz over again, they must be preparing for a big move.' *South Wales Daily Post*, 2 October 1915.

33 George and Felix Lloyd Powell (composers), 'Smile, Smile, Smile! (Pack Up Your Troubles)' (New York: Chappell and Co., 1915), retrieved from Neil Prior, 'The woe behind World War One song "Pack Up Your Troubles"' (31 January 2014). Available at *bbc.co.uk/news/uk-wales*, accessed 18 September 2015.

34 *South Wales Daily Post*, 28 November 1915.

35 *South Wales Daily Post*, 28 December 1915.

36 *South Wales Daily Post*, 14 March 1916.

37 *South Wales Daily Post*, 15, 19, 22, 26 February 1916.

38 *South Wales Daily Post*, 29 February 1916. For further reading on early jazz musicians in Britain see Jayson Toynbee, Catherine Tackley and Mark Doffman (eds), *Black British Jazz: Routes, Ownership and Performance* (Farnham: Ashgate Publishing, 2014), p. 27. For further reading on Irving Berlin's first musical, see *www.americanclassicsmusic.org/watch-your-step*, accessed 10 September 2015.

39 *South Wales Daily Post*, 2, 3, 6 June 1916.

40 *South Wales Daily Post*, 5 September 1916.

41 *South Wales Daily Post*, 13, 27 February 1917.

42 *South Wales Daily Post*, 10 April 1917.

43 *South Wales Daily Post*, 16, 29 October 1917.

44 *South Wales Daily Post*, October 1917. With thanks to Women's Archive of Wales for information on Emily Ada Pickford, available at *http://www.powell76.talktalk.net/mrsemilypickford.htm*, accessed 8 September 2015.

45 *South Wales Daily Post*, 30 October 1917.

46 *South Wales Daily Post*, 3 July 1917. See also Dr John Mullen, *The Show Must Go On! Popular Song in Britain During the First World War* (Farnham: Ashgate Publishing, 2015), p. 49.

47 *South Wales Daily Post*, 30 October, 13 November, 4 December 1917, 19 January 1918.

48 *South Wales Daily Post*, 19, 20, 21 November, 11 December 1917.

49 Mullen, *The Show Must Go On!*, p. 47.

50 *South Wales Daily Post*, 11 January 1918.
51 *South Wales Daily Post*, 12 March 1918.
52 A. Loesser, *Men, Women and Pianos: A Social History* (New York: Dover Publications, 1990), pp. 228, 235–6, 258, 267–79. For the growing availability of pianos during the nineteenth century, see Cyril Ehrlich, *The Piano: A History* (London: J. M. Dent, 1976), p. 144, estimating annual production figures for pianos in England as 50,000 for 1890. See also C. Dickens, 'The Age Before Music Halls', in *All The Year Round*, ns 11 (1874), both cited in J. S. Bratton (ed.), *Music Hall: Performance and Style* (Milton Keynes: Open University Press, 1986), pp. 6–7, 26–7.
53 Rosamond E. M. Harding, *The Piano Forte: Its History Traced to the Great Exhibition of 1851* (Cambridge: Cambridge University Press, 1933), pp. 221–59.
54 J. Bourke, *Gender, Class and Ethnicity: Working-Class Cultures in Britain 1890–1960* (London: Routledge, 1994), pp. 5, 102–6, 160–1.
55 *South Wales Daily Post*, 23 July, 6 August, 3, 10 September 1918.
56 *South Wales Daily Post*, 2 July, 22 October, 11 November 1918.
57 *South Wales Daily Post*, 12, 16 November 1918.
58 *South Wales Daily Post*, 30 November 1918
59 *South Wales Daily Post*, 5 February, 12 March, 14 May, 18, 19, 22, 27, 28 June, 9, 16, 23 July, 6 August, 3, 10 September, 16 October, 5, 11, 12, 26, 30 November, 17, 23, 24, 27, 28 December 1918.
60 Floyd Levin, *Classic Jazz: A Personal View of the Music and the Musicians* (Berkeley, Los Angeles and London: University of California Press, 2000), pp. 65–8. See also http//www.redhotjazz.com/hellfighters.html, accessed 14 August 2017. Their CD, 'Jim Europe's 369th "Hell Fighters" Band, The Complete Recordings', is available from Inside Sounds/Memphis Archives, memphisarc@aol.com. BBC Radio 4 broadcast 'The Jazz Kings Go To War', as part of their season 'World War One: The Cultural Front', on 12 August 2017. The BBC website *www.bbc.co.uk/programmes/b090v3bj* reports: 'It was a time of segregation in America; a time when Jim Crow laws still dominated society. The American military would not allow black soldiers to fight alongside white recruits so they gifted the 15th regiment to the French, following their terrible losses at the Somme and Verdun the year before. The regiment was viewed as war fodder, they would entertain French villages before being sent off to the Frontline to fight, and most likely die. But that did not happen. The Harlem Hellfighters would not only go on to be the most decorated regiment in the American Expedition Force, but are credited with bringing jazz to Europe; a musical form which would define a generation.'
61 *South Wales Daily Post*, 15 February 1919.
62 Catherine Parsonage, *The Evolution of Jazz in Britain* (Aldershot: Ashgate Publishing, 2005), p. 32.

63. *South Wales Daily Post*, 27 December 1918, 28 January, 22 February, 11, 18, 25 March, 15 July, 14, 15 August, 15 November, 6, 23 December 1919.
64. *South Wales Daily Post*, 25 July 1919.

Chapter Six

1. Daniel G. Williams, *Black Skin, Blue Books, African Americans and Wales 1845–1945* (Cardiff: University of Wales Press, 2012), p. 104. Williams talks of 'an extended analysis of such moments of contact and comparison' p. 18.
2. Williams, *Black Skin, Blue Books*, pp. 154–7.
3. Stuart Hall, 'Tearing Down the Veil', in the *Guardian*, 22 February 2003, 34; David Levering Lewis, twice winner of the Pulitzer Prize for parts one and two of his biography of W. E. B. Du Bois, *W. E. B. Du Bois: Biography of a Race, 1868–1919* (New York: Owl Books, 1994) and *W. E. B. Du Bois: The Fight for Equality and the American Century 1916–1923* (New York: Owl Books, 2001).
4. W. E. B. Du Bois, *The Souls of Black Folk* (Chicago: A. C. McClurg and Co., 1903; repr. New York: Fawcett Publications, Inc., Fawcett World Library, 1961), pp. 99, 181.
5. Ted Vincent, *Keep Cool: The Black Activists Who Built the Jazz Age* (London: Pluto Press, 1995), p. 175.
6. Dylan Thomas, *Under Milk Wood: A play for voices*, first staged 14 May 1953 at the Poetry Center, New York. See also Liz Reitell's recollections at *www.dylanthomas.com/dylan/dylans-work/milk-wood-chronology/*, accessed 14 September 2015.
7. Dan Jones studied composition at the Royal Academy of Music in London, later working as a translator at Bletchley Park, where Vernon Watkins was also working. In 1977 Dan Jones wrote an account of his Swansea friends and his days with Dylan Thomas in *My Friend Dylan Thomas* (Worthing, W. Sussex: Littlehampton Book Services, 1977). Thomas was an enthusiastic improvisational performer on Jones's piano.
8. *South Wales Daily Post*, 7 July, 11 August 1914.
9. Deirdre Beddoe, *Discovering Women's History: A Practical Manual* (London: Pandora Press, 1983), pp. 206–20.
10. *South Wales Daily Post*, 7 September 1915.
11. *South Wales Daily Post*, 14, 25 September 1915.
12. See *www.joes-icecream.com/our story.html*. Accessed 4 August 2016.
13. *South Wales Daily Post*, 15 August 1921.
14. *South Wales Daily Post*, 18, 20 May 1918.

15 *South Wales Daily Post*, 9 October, 16 November 1915.
16 *South Wales Daily Post*, 15 February 1916.
17 *South Wales Daily Post*, 18 March 1916.
18 Douglas F. Warner, 'The Warner Family History' (Swansea, unpublished, c.2003).
19 John Mullen, *The Show Must Go On: Popular Song in Britain During the First World War* (Farnham: Ashgate Publishing, 2015), pp. 99–101.
20 See *www.irvingberlin.com*.
21 A history of the Warner family can be found at 'Our Story', *www.homepage.ntlworld.com/d.f.warner/story*, accessed 15 September 2015.
22 *South Wales Daily Post*, 31 October 1916.
23 Frank Cullen, *Vaudeville Old and New, An Encyclopedia of Variety Performers in America Volume 1* (New York: Routledge, Taylor and Francis Group, 2007), pp. xi, 163–4.
24 *South Wales Daily Post*, 31 October 1916, 1 January 1917.
25 *South Wales Daily Post*, 13, 27 February, 22 May 1917.
26 *South Wales Daily Post*, 5 June 1917.
27 *South Wales Daily Post*, 3 July 1917.
28 *South Wales Daily Post*, 21 August 1917. See also *https://www.cecilbdemille.com*, accessed 28 March 2017.
29 *South Wales Daily Post*, 4 September 1917.
30 *South Wales Daily Post*, 25 September 1917. An approximation of a plantation dance/ring shout, 'Raise a Ruckus Tonight' (PBS Learning Media/KET Arts 2013), can be accessed at *www.pbslearningmedia.org/dance.plantation/african-american-culture*, accessed 11 July 2016.
31 *South Wales Daily Post*, 23, 30 October 1917.
32 *South Wales Daily Post*, 13 November, 1, 4 December 1917.
33 *South Wales Daily Post*, 5 February 1918.
34 Tim Brooks, *Lost Sounds: Blacks and the Birth of the Recording Industry, 1890–1919* (Urbana and Chicago: University of Illinois Press, 2005), p. 307.
35 Brooks, *Lost Sounds*, pp. 308–9.
36 Howard Rye, 'Fearsome Means of Discord: Early Encounters with Black Jazz', in Paul Oliver (ed.), *Black Music in Britain, Essays on the Afro-Asian Contribution to Popular Music* (Milton Keynes: Open University Press, 1990), p. 46.
37 A recording of Callahan and Roberts's 'Smiles', played by Joseph P. Smith's Orchestra of 1918, is available on YouTube, accessed 16 September 2015.
38 *South Wales Daily Post*, 19 March 1918. See also Don Tyler, *Music of the First World War* (Santa Barbara, CA: Greenwood, an imprint of ABC-CLIO, LLC, 2016), pp. 148–9.
39 *South Wales Daily Post*, 16 April 1918.
40 *South Wales Daily Post*, 20 April 1918.

41 *South Wales Daily Post*, 18, 27, 28 June, 9, 16 July, 6 August, 3, 10 September 1918.
42 *South Wales Daily Post*, 5 November 1918.
43 *South Wales Daily Post*, 16 October, 24 December 1918.
44 *South Wales Daily Post*, 11 November 1918.
45 *South Wales Daily Post*, 26, 30 November 1918.
46 *South Wales Daily Post*, 17, 24 December 1918, 7 January 1919. Carrie Tubb lived long enough to be on *Desert Island Discs* in 1970 and reached her century (1876–1976). She was a regular performer at the BBC Proms.
47 *South Wales Daily Post*, 18, 25 January 1919.
48 *South Wales Daily Post*, 4 February 1919.
49 The *Dancing Times* (September 1919), 544, in 'The Evolving Image of Jazz in Britain in Sheet Music', in Catherine Parsonage, *The Evolution of Jazz in Britain* (Aldershot: Ashgate Publishing, 2005), pp. 14, 21.
50 Rye, 'Fearsome Means of Discord', in Oliver (ed.), *Black Music in Britain*, p. 47.
51 *South Wales Daily Post*, 15 February, 10 July, 25 March 1919.
52 *South Wales Daily Post*, 12 December 1919, 6 March 1920, 31 January, 5 February, 13 April 1921, 11 March 1922, 10 February 1923.
53 *South Wales Daily Post*, 12 December, 1 August, 28 July 1919.
54 *South Wales Daily Post*, 18 August 1919.
55 *South Wales Daily Post*, 13 December 1919.
56 *South Wales Daily Post*, 15 November 1919.
57 *South Wales Daily Post*, 10 March, 25 September 1919, 14 January 1920.
58 *The Cambrian Daily Leader*, 24 September 1919.
59 *South Wales Daily Post*, 12 December 1925.
60 *South Wales Daily Post*, 26 September 1919. For additional information on the role of women in community actions in Wales see Rosemary Jones, 'Sociability, solidarity, and social exclusion: women's activism in the South Wales coalfield 1830–1939', in Laurie Mercier and Jaclyn J. Gier (eds), *Mining Women: Gender in the Development of a Global Industry, 1670–2000* (New York: Palgrave Macmillan, 2006).
61 The author was trained in this manner at Swansea Secondary Technical School for Girls 1958–60.
62 *South Wales Daily Post*, 20 August, 30 October, 3 December 1919, 23 March 1923. Deirdre Beddoe, *Back to Home and Duty: Women Between the Wars 1918–1939* (London: Pandora Press, 1989), p. 136. 'Feminism split in the 1920s into two camps. There were those who were "old feminists" like Lady Rhondda and Winifred Holtby, who regarded feminism as being about equal rights and were therefore opposed to any form of special protective legislation for women in the workplace. The "new feminists" such as Eleanor Rathbone,

Mary Stocks and Maude Royden concentrated on the special position of women and mothers; their platform was primarily the welfare of women at home and the main aim of the new feminists was to being about "family endowment", or family allowances. Once women had the vote and had achieved their single dominant aim a host of choices lay before them with regard to ways and means of bringing about a better world for women.'

63 Neil Evans, 'The South Wales Race Riots of 1919', in *Llafur*, 3 (1980), 5–29.
64 *South Wales Daily Post*, September 1920. See also S. Bourne, *Black Poppies: Britain's Black Community and the Great War* (Stroud: History Press, 2014), pp. 74–6, 140–1. Bourne quotes Beatrice Sinclair (formerly Headley, daughter of Augustus Headley from Barbados and a 'lass from Lancashire', Agnes) describing Cardiff's Tiger Bay as 'just like a little village, about a mile, and everybody knew everyone else. We were very very happy'. Beatrice felt that the Cardiff riots had been instigated by white men returning from the forces who found there was no work for them and that 'some black men had married white women'. Tensions exploded. There was a Swansea sequel to the Cardiff riots in July 1919, when nine 'Negroes' appeared at Swansea Assizes accused of shooting at a crowd. However, the 'crowd' had set fire to premises and the accused had been defending themselves. The nine prisoners were found not guilty and were discharged on 16 July 1919. Bourne cites many distressing stories of attitudes to black servicemen at this time; a sad instance was the shooting of Herbert Morris of Jamaica for desertion, aged just 16 when he volunteered for war service with the 6th Battalion of the British West Indies Regiment. 'The shell-shocked youngster fled from the trenches . . . desertion lowered the morale of the troops'. Herbert was executed by firing squad on 20 September 1917. Private Herbert Morris was pardoned in 2006. See also Neil Sinclair, *The Tiger Bay Story* (Cardiff: Butetown History and Arts Project, 1993).
65 *South Wales Daily Post*, 27 September, 8, 15 November 1919.
66 *South Wales Daily Post*, 30 January, 6 February, 23 March 1920.
67 *South Wales Daily Post*, 14 February, 30 March, 3 April 1920.
68 Grant Clarke (lyrics), Milton Ager and Geo. W. Meyer (composers), 'Everything is Peaches Down in Georgia' (sheet music) (New York: Leo. Feist, Inc., 1918).
69 *South Wales Daily Post*, 10, 17 April, 1 May 1920.
70 *South Wales Daily Post*, 3, 10, 17 April 1920, 10 November 1921.
71 *South Wales Daily Post*, 17 April 1920.
72 *South Wales Daily Post*, 26 May 1920.
73 Beddoe, *Discovering Women's History*, pp. 114–15.
74 *South Wales Daily Post*, 26, 27 May, 8, 23 June, 7 July, 9 December 1920.
75 Irving Berlin (composer), 'Everybody's Doing It' (New York: Ted Snyder Co., 1911).

76 *South Wales Daily Post*, 24 September, 4 December 1920.
77 *South Wales Daily Post*, 23 March 1921.
78 *South Wales Daily Post*, 28 September, 2 November 1925.
79 *South Wales Daily Post*, 27 April, 5 December 1921, 3 May, 11 July 1922, 26 May, 2 June, 11 July 1923.
80 *South Wales Daily Post*, 10 February 1925. For further reading on the south Wales coalfields, see Hywel Francis and Dai Smith, *The Fed: History of the South Wales Miners in the Twentieth Century* (London: Lawrence and Wishart, 1980).
81 *South Wales Daily Post*, 10 June 1920.
82 *South Wales Daily Post*, 14 May, 12, 24 July 1920, 13 May, 11 July 1921, 8 May 1924, 16 February, 10 August 1925.
83 *South Wales Daily Post*, 19 March 1921, 5 June, 7 July 1925. Further reading on the 'Tea Shop Kings', plus list of cafes, holdings and business ventures, is available at *https://elwyjones.wordpress.com/r-r-jones-ltd-1923-1962/*, accessed 24 March 2015.
84 *South Wales Daily Post*, 17 December 1921, 7 August 1922, 6 April, 28 July, 31 October 1923, 22 January, 20 February, 27 March, 22 September 1924, 15 January 1926.
85 *Melody Maker*, 11/85 (5 January 1935).
86 The Kardomah was bombed during the Second World War, reopening in 1957 at Morris Buildings, Portland Street, Swansea, where it continues to serve patrons today in its original 1950s interior . . . but with no live music.

Chapter Seven

1 Catherine Parsonage, *The Evolution of Jazz in Britain, 1880–1935* (Aldershot: Ashgate Publishing, 2005), pp. 35–43.
2 *South Wales Daily Post*, 11 September 1923.
3 Arna Bontemps (ed.), *W. C. Handy (1873–1958) Father of the Blues, An Autobiography*, foreword by Abbe Niles (New York: Da Capo Press, 1941), p. 122.
4 Ray Allen Billington (ed.), *The Journal of Charlotte L. Forten: A young black woman's reactions to the white world of the Civil War era* (New York: Dryden Press, 1953), p. 165.
5 Paul Oliver, *The Story of the Blues* (London: Penguin Books, 1969), p. 8.
6 *South Wales Daily Post*, 7 September 1922, 7 September 1923, 27 March 1924.
7 *South Wales Daily Post*, 13 April, 29 September, 13, 19, 31 October, 19 November, 1, 10 December 1921, 5 January, 6, 9 May, 4 November 1922, 11 May 1923.
8 *South Wales Daily Post*, 11 January, 2, 12 November, 19, 24, 31 December 1925, 14 January, 7, 10 April 1926.
9 Parsonage, *The Evolution of Jazz in Britain 1880–1935*, p. 192.

10 *Melody Maker*, 3/26, February 1928.
11 *Melody Maker*, 10/72, October 1934.
12 *South Wales Daily Post*, 3 April 1925.
13 *South Wales Daily Post*, 18 January 1926.
14 R. M. W. Dixon and John Godrich, *Blues & Gospel Records 1902–1943* (Essex: Storyville Publications, 1982), p. 15. John Godrich, co-writer of this world-renowned volume, was a Swansea man. For further reading on discographies, see Brian Rust, *Jazz Records 1897–1942* (Essex: Storyville Publications, 1969).
15 H. R. Schleman, *Rhythm on Record* (London: *Melody Maker*, 1936), p. 127. *South Wales Daily Post*, 19 December 1923, 20 February 1924. See Elsie Carlisle depicted on a Wills Cigarettes radio celebrities card, 1934, at *http://www.elsiecarlisle.com*.
16 M. Jempson, *Centenary Celebration: An Illustrated History of the Musicians' Union* (London: Musicians' Union, 1993), p. 15.
17 *South Wales Daily Post*, 9, 12 September 1921.
18 *South Wales Daily Post*, 11 November 1919.
19 *South Wales Daily Post*, 6 May 1922.
20 *South Wales Daily Post*, 14 January, 20, 28 March, 18, 28 December 1920, 16 October 1924.
21 *South Wales Daily Post*, 21, 24, 28, 31 January, 1, 5 February 1921.
22 *South Wales Daily Post*, 10 February 1921.
23 *South Wales Daily Post*, 7, 23 March, 1 April 1921.
24 Jane Aaron, 'Finding a voice in two tongues: gender and colonization', in *Our Sisters' Land: The Changing Identities of Women in Wales* (Cardiff: University of Wales Press, 1994), pp. 188–9.
25 *South Wales Daily Post*, 4 January 1921.
26 *South Wales Daily Post*, 21, 24 January 1921.
27 *South Wales Daily Post*, 12 August, 8, 11 October 1921. Abbie Mitchell (1884–1960) and her Harmonic Quartette are mentioned in Cary Wintz and Paul Finkelman (eds), *Encyclopedia of the Harlem Renaissance Volume 1 and Volume 2 A–Z* (New York: Routledge, 2004). Abbie Mitchell 'appeared in leading roles with Williams and Walker's company . . . she continued to sing parlor songs, ragtime numbers, and early jazz pieces'.
28 *South Wales Daily Post*, 17 May 1921.
29 *South Wales Daily Post*, 8, 11 October 1921.
30 Howard Rye, 'Fearsome Means of Discord: Early Encounters with Black Jazz', in Paul Oliver (ed.), *Black Music in Britain: Essays on the Afro-Asian Contribution to Popular Music* (Milton Keynes: Open University Press, 1990), pp. 48–50.
31 *South Wales Daily Post*, 17 May, 8, 31 October 1921. See also Julian Joseph discussing the music of the Southern Syncopated Orchestra at *http://www.londonlive.co.uk/rememberingthelondonjazzpioneers*, accessed 22 February 2017.
32 *South Wales Daily Post*, 25 January, 7 February 1921.

33 *South Wales Daily Post*, 18 April, 18 July, 12 August 1921.
34 *South Wales Daily Post*, 14 February 1923.
35 *South Wales Daily Post*, 15 February 1923.
36 *South Wales Daily Post*, 16, 19 February 1923.
37 *South Wales Daily Post*, 12 April 1923.
38 *South Wales Daily Post*, 18, 27 February 1924. Swansea is now a city, but 'dividend and money' still rule over culture and heritage. Gone is the Mumbles railway. The city neglected any interest in Dylan Thomas's old house at 5 Cwmdonkin Drive, now run by structural engineer Geoff Haden. A large part of the Dylan Thomas Centre is now leased to the University of Wales as a business centre for creative industries, the council saying it could no longer afford to run the centre opened by former US President Jimmy Carter in 1995. SWAG (Swansea Writers and Artists Group) had lobbied for a Centre for Literature and Writing from the early 1990s under the chairmanship of Nigel Jenkins. However, jazz has managed to survive in these times of austerity with the successful Swansea Jazzland, 'Wales' Premier Live Jazz Club', and the fledgling Swansea International Jazz Festival, inaugurated in 2014 by Dave Cottle with Arts Council of Wales support.
39 *South Wales Evening Post*, 27 March 1924.
40 *South Wales Daily Post*, 23 May, 7 September 1922.
41 *South Wales Daily Post*, 2 November 1923. See also www.footlightnotes.tumble.com and the Behind The Lines production *All The Nice Girls* at www.brightonfringe.org.
42 *South Wales Daily Post*, 18 September 1925.
43 See Stanford University Libraries, http://riverwalkjazz.stanford.edu.program/running-wild-biography-james-p-johnson, accessed 24 July 2016.
44 *South Wales Daily Post*, 23 September, 15 October 1924.
45 *South Wales Daily Post*, 18 March 1925.
46 Hywel Francis, *Miners Against Facism: Wales and the Spanish Civil War* (London: Lawrence and Wishart, 1984), p. 119. Pollitt writes: 'I never was so moved as on Sunday night when, at the conclusion of a wonderful unity demonstration, Glyn Jones, on behalf of the Rhondda and District Committee of the CP, handed me over £60. This money has been collected in pennies and half-pennies through street collections in the Rhondda on behalf of the International Brigades.'
47 *South Wales Daily Post*, 2, 6 February, 24 March, 8 April 1926. See also Henry R. Winkler, *British Labour Seeks a Foreign Policy 1900–1940* (New Jersey: Transaction Publishers, 2005), p. 73. For further reading on the General Strike and its implications for the south Wales coalfields, see Sue Bruley, *The Women and Men of 1926* (Cardiff: University of Wales Press, 2010), and Hywel Francis and David Smith, *The Fed: The History of the South Wales Miners in the Twentieth Century* (London: Lawrence and Wishart, 1980).
48 *South Wales Daily Post*, 10 December 1925.

49 *South Wales Daily Post*, 7 April 1926.
50 *South Wales Daily Post*, 10 April 1926.
51 *South Wales Daily Post*, 16 April 1926.
52 *South Wales Daily Post*, 2 April, 23 November, 10 December 1925, 27 January, 6 February, 31 March, 7, 8, 16 April, 14 May 1926.
53 *Melody Maker*, 2/21, September 1927.
54 bell hooks, *Ain't I A Woman: Black Women and Feminism* (London: Pluto Press, 1981), p. 33.
55 *Melody Maker*, 6, December 1931; 30, December 1933.
56 Howard Rye, 'Visiting Firemen: 2. Louis Armstrong' (Louis Armstrong UK tours 1933–4), *Storyville*, 89 (June–July 1980), ed. Laurie Wright, 187. This was a British jazz magazine that ran from 1965 to 2003, featuring jazz history and discography; available at National Jazz Archive, https://archive.nationaljazzarchive.co.uk/archive/journals/storyville/storyville-089.
57 Read more at http://www.southwales-eveningpost.co.uk/woman-serenaded-louis-armstrong-18th-birthday/story-20034986-detail/story.html#rV1iRydYa12SGdeX.99, 5 Nov 2013, accessed 27 February 2017.
58 Max Jones and John Chilton (eds), *Salute to Satchmo* (London: IPC/Melody Maker, 1970), p. 99.
59 *Melody Maker*, 8/33, January 1934.
60 *Melody Maker*, 10/68, 8 August 1934.
61 *Melody Maker*, 10/76, 3 November 1934.
62 *Melody Maker*, 11/89, February 1935.
63 *Melody Maker*, 11/106, 1 June 1935.
64 *Melody Maker*, 11/105, 25 May 1935.
65 *Melody Maker*, 11/114, 27 July 1935.
66 *Melody Maker*, 11/121, 14 September 1935.
67 *Melody Maker*, 11/133, 7 December 1935; 11/135, 21 December 1935.
68 *Melody Maker*, 13/140, 25 January 1936.
69 *Melody Maker*, 12/148, 21 March 1936.
70 *Melody Maker*, 12/152, 18 April 1936; 12/160, 13 June 1936.
71 *Melody Maker*, 12/178, 17 October 1936.
72 See henrybebop.co.uk/parry/htm, accessed 13 April 2018. See also Harry Parry, yba.llgc.org.uk/en/s2PARR-HEN-1912.htm.
73 *The New York Times*, 26 June 1984, p. 8.
74 *Melody Maker*, 12/180, 31 October 1936. The BBC building is now part of the department of music and technology at UWTSD.
75 *Melody Maker*, 12/182, 14 November 1936.
76 *Melody Maker*, 12/189, 2 January 1937.
77 *Melody Maker*, 13/195, 13 February 1937.
78 *Melody Maker*, 13/197, 27 February 1937.

79 *Melody Maker*, 13/200, 20 March 1937.
80 *Melody Maker*, 13/210, 29 May 1937.
81 Val Wilmer, 'Obituary of Clare Deniz', *Guardian*, 3 January 2003. Val Wilmer is a highly regarded jazz photographer and oral historian of black music and musicians.
82 *Melody Maker*, 13/233, 28 August 1937.
83 *Melody Maker*, 13/232, 30 October 1937.
84 *Melody Maker*, 13/223, August 1937; 14/264, June 1938.
85 *Melody Maker*, 14/255, 9 April 1938.
86 *Melody Maker*, 14/264, 11 June 1938.
87 *Melody Maker*, 15/304, 18 March 1939.
88 *Melody Maker*, 15/299, 18 February 1939; 15/306, 1 April 1939.
89 *Melody Maker*, 15/313, 20 May 1939.
90 *Melody Maker*, 15/314, 27 May 1939.
91 *Melody Maker*, 15/329, 9 September 1939.
92 *Melody Maker*, 15/331, 3 November 1939
93 *Melody Maker*, 15/333, 9 December 1939.
94 *Melody Maker*, 15/334, 16 December 1939.
95 Margaret Plumber, née Carlson, interviewed for *Back of the Front Line*, VHS documentary (Swansea Women's History Group, 1984). Deposited with Women's Archive of Wales at West Glamorgan Archives Service, Swansea.
96 Elton Box, Sonny Cox and Lewis Ilda (composers), 'Choc'late Soldier from the USA' (London: Irwin Dash Music, 1944), in Sheet Music Collection, Jazz Heritage Wales.
97 Jen Wilson (ed.), *Those Saturday Nights: The Story of Swansea's Tower Ballroom* (Swansea: Jazz Heritage Wales, 2013), p. 5.
98 Jenna Bailey, '"Play Like a Man and Look Like a Woman", Exploring the Role of Gender in Ivy Benson's All Girl Band', in Wolfram Knauer (ed.), *Gender and Identity in Jazz* (Darmstadt: Jazzinstitut, 2016), pp. 179–94.
99 Wilson (ed.), *Those Saturday Nights: The Story of Swansea's Tower Ballroom*, p.13.
100 Wilson (ed.), *Those Saturday Nights: The Story of Swansea's Tower Ballroom*, p. 14.
101 Wilson (ed.), *Those Saturday Nights: The Story of Swansea's Tower Ballroom*, pp. 28–9.
102 Derek Gabriel, *Photographic Memories of Jazz in Swansea* (Llandysul: Derek Gabriel/Gomer, 2014).

Chapter Eight

1 Patricia Adkins Chiti (ed.), *Women in Jazz . . . Donne in Jazz* (Italy: Fondazione Adkins Chiti, 2007), pp. 12–13.

2 Jenna Bailey, '"Play Like a Man and Look Like a Woman": Exploring the Role of Gender in Ivy Benson's All Girl Band', in Wolfram Knauer (ed.), *Gender and Identity in Jazz* (Darmstadt: Jazzinstitut Darmstadt, 2016), pp. 184, 191.
3 Catherine Parsonage and Kathy Dyson, 'The History of Women in Jazz in Britain', in *Women in Jazz . . . Donne in Jazz* (Italy: Fondazione Adkins Chiti, 2007), pp. 129–40.
4 Paula Gardiner, interviewed by Joel McIver, *Bass Guitar Magazine* (17 December 2015). Available at *www.bassguitarmagazine.com/interviews/all-that-jazz-paula-gardiner*, accessed 4 March 2017.
5 Paula Gardiner, interviewed by Jen Wilson (Jazz Heritage Wales Oral History Collection, 1988). The Paula Gardiner suite *In Pursuit of Venus* was commissioned by the Women's Jazz Archive for the UK Year of Literature and Writing 1995, celebrating 1,000 years of women's poetry, and performed at the Taliesin Theatre, 2 November 1995, funded by Arts Council of Wales. Paula Gardiner is also the double bassist on Jen Wilson's *The Dylan Thomas Jazz Suite 'Twelve Poems'* commissioned by the Dylan Thomas Centre, and recorded on CD in celebration of Wilson's fifty years in jazz, funded by Arts Council of Wales.
6 Eva Rieger, '"Dolce Semplice"? On the Changing Role of Women in Music', in Gisela Ecker (ed.), *Feminist Aesthetics* (London: Women's Press, 1985), pp. 135–49.
7 Maria Jane Williams, *Ancient National Airs of Gwent and Morgannwg (A Facsimile of the 1844 Edition with Introduction and Notes on the songs by Daniel Huws)* (Aberystwyth: The Welsh Folk Song Society, 1988, repr. 1994); 'Williams, Maria Jane (Llinos; 1795?–1873), musician', *Dictionary of Welsh Biography*, National Library of Wales. Available at *http://yba.llgc.org.uk/en/s-WILL-JAN-1795.html*, accessed 18 March 2018.
8 David Edward Pike, 'Morfydd Llwyn Owen of Trefforest' (19 September 2014). Available at *http://daibach-welldigger.blogspot.com/#!/2014/09/morfydd-owen.html*, accessed 19 March 2018.
9 'Owen, Morfydd Llwyn (1891–1918), composer, singer, and pianist', *Dictionary of Welsh Biography*, National Library of Wales. Available at *yba.llgc.org/uk/en/s-OWEN-LLW-1891.html*, accessed 27 May 2015. See also Morfydd Owen Archive, Cardiff University, *www.cardiff.ac.uk/insrv/libraries/scolar/special/morfyddowen.html*, accessed 27 May 2015. An original 1905 Edison phonograph cylinder recording machine resides in Jazz Heritage Wales, similar to that used for recording purposes by Morfydd Owen.
10 See *http://www.sweetshoprevolution.com/production/i-loved-you-and-i-loved-you*, accessed 17 February 2017.
11 See *http://www.elinmanahanthomas.org/news/portrait-of-a-lost-icon*, accessed 27 February 2017.
12 See *www.TyCerdd.org/welshcomposers/grace-williams/grace-in-her-own-words*, reproduced in Tŷ Cerdd by kind permission of BBC Cymru Wales.

13. Alan Lomax, *The Land Where the Blues Began* (London: Methuen, 1993), Preface, pp. x–xi.
14. *Melody Maker*, June 1928, 643.
15. *Melody Maker*, 6, August 1931.
16. *Reports of the Commissioners of Inquiry into The State of Education in Wales* (London: Her Majesty's Stationery Office, 1847).
17. Spike Hughes, *Second Movement* (London: Museum Press, 1951), p. 111.
18. Hughes, *Second Movement*, pp. 124, 163, 165.
19. Hughes, *Second Movement*, pp. 112–15.
20. *Melody Maker*, 3/28, April 1928.
21. Dave Harker, *One For The Money: Politics and Popular Song* (London: Hutchinson, 1980), pp. 66–7.
22. *Melody Maker*, 3/28, April 1928.
23. Matthew Riley (ed.), *British Music and Modernism 1895–1960* (Aldershot: Ashgate Publishing, 2010), pp. 204–5; Catherine Parsonage, *The Evolution of Jazz in Britain, 1880–1935* (Aldershot: Ashgate Publishing, 2005).
24. *Melody Maker*, 3/29, May 1928.
25. *Melody Maker*, 3/30, June 1928.
26. *Melody Maker*, 3/30, June 1928.
27. *Melody Maker*, 3/32, August 1928.
28. National Jazz Archive, *The Story of British Jazz: Dance Band Diaries Volume 2 1927*.
29. *Melody Maker*, May 1928.
30. Hughes, *Second Movement*, p. 128.
31. *Melody Maker*, 10/71, September 1929.
32. *Melody Maker*, 2/24, November/December 1929.
33. *Melody Maker*, 2/18, June 1927, and many other examples.
34. *Melody Maker*, 7, July, August 1932.
35. *Melody Maker*, 2/18, June 1927.
36. *Melody Maker*, 6, July 1931.
37. *Melody Maker*, 2/17, May 1927.
38. *Melody Maker*, 2/21, September 1927.
39. *Melody Maker*, 2, Nov/Dec 1927.
40. *Melody Maker*, 3/26, February 1928.
41. *Melody Maker*, 3/36, December 1928.
42. *Melody Maker*, 6, May 1931.
43. *Melody Maker*, 4, 1929.
44. *Melody Maker*, 26 August, 7 October 1933.
45. *Melody Maker*, 11 November 1933.
46. *Melody Maker*, 9/11, August 1933; 9/28, December 1933.
47. *Melody Maker*, 10/69, September 1934.
48. *Melody Maker*, 9/28, December 1933.

⁴⁹ *Melody Maker*, 9/28, 2 December 1933; 10/71, 1934.
⁵⁰ Leonard Feather, *Jazz Years: Earwitness to an Era* (London, Sydney and Auckland: Pan, 1986), p. 164.
⁵¹ *Melody Maker*, 13/236, 27 November 1937.
⁵² *Melody Maker*, 10/64, August 1934.
⁵³ *Melody Maker*, 20 October 1934.
⁵⁴ *Melody Maker*, 11/108, 15 June; 11/115, 3 August 1935.
⁵⁵ Katherine Williams, '"Alright for a Girl", and Other Jazz Myths', in Wolfram Knauer (ed.), *Gender and Identity in Jazz* (Darmstadt: Jazzinstitut Darmstadt, 2016), p. 57.
⁵⁶ Williams, '"Alright for a Girl", and Other Jazz Myths', p. 68.
⁵⁷ *Melody Maker*, 15/312, 13 May 1939.
⁵⁸ *Melody Maker*, 15/316, 10 June 1939.
⁵⁹ *Melody Maker*, 17/345, 2 March 1940.
⁶⁰ *Melody Maker*, 16/359, 8 June 1940.
⁶¹ Ivy Benson does not feature in any of these acknowledged authorities on big bands: George T. Simon, *The Big Bands, Revised Edition* (Collier Books, Macmillan, 1974), Albert McCarthy, *The Dance Band Era* (London: Hamlyn, 1974), Chris Way, *The Big Bands Go To War* (Edinburgh: Mainstream Publishing, 1991), Sid Colin, *And The Bands Played On: An Informal History of British Dance Bands* (London: Elm Tree Books, 1977). There is also no entry for Ivy Benson in Ian Carr, Digby Fairweather and Brian Priestley, *Jazz: The Essential Companion* (London: Paladin, 1988), the jazz dictionary of who's who.
⁶² 'Airtimes 1950', in *The Dance Band Music Annual* (London: John Dilworth, 1951).
⁶³ *Melody Maker*, 16/343, 17 February 1940.
⁶⁴ *Melody Maker*, incorporating *Rhythm*, 27 April 1946.
⁶⁵ 'Jazz double bass player Paula Gardiner talks to BASCA', BASCA (18 August 2015). Available at *https://basca.org.uk/2015/08/18/paula-gardiner/*, accessed 14 July 2018.

Conclusion

¹ W. E. B. Du Bois, *The Souls of Black Folk* (Chicago: A. C. McClurg and Co., 1903; repr. New York: Fawcett Publications, Inc., Fawcett World Library, 1961), p. vi.
² Du Bois, *The Souls of Black Folk*, p. 182.

Bibliography

Aaron, Jane, et al. (eds), *Our Sisters' Land: The Changing Identities of Women in Wales*, (Cardiff: University of Wales Press, 1994).
Aaron, Jane, and Masson, Ursula (eds), *The Very Salt of Life: Welsh Women's Political Writings from Chartism to Suffrage* (Dinas Powys: Honno Welsh Women's Classics, 2007).
Abbott, Lynn, and Seroff, Doug, *Out of Sight: The Rise of African American Popular Music 1889–1895* (Jackson, MS: University Press of Mississippi, 2002).
Abbott, Lynn, and Seroff, Doug, *To Do This, You Must Know How: Music Pedagogy in the Black Gospel Quartet Tradition* (Jackson, MS: University Press of Mississippi, 2013).
Abbott, Lynn, '"Do Thyself a' no Harm": The Jubilee Singing Phenomenon and the "Only Original New Orleans University Singers"', *American Music Research Center Journal* (2013), available at *www.colorado.edu/amrc/node/277/attachment*, accessed 20 January 2016.
Albertson, Chris, *Bessie: Empress of the Blues* (London: Sphere Books, 1975).
Andrews, Elizabeth, *A Woman's Work is Never Done*, ed. Ursula Masson (Dinas Powys: Honno Welsh Women's Classics, 2006).
Bailey, Jenna, '"Play Like a Man and Look Like a Woman", Exploring the Role of Gender in Ivy Benson's All Girl Band', in Wolfram Knauer (ed.), *Gender and Identity in Jazz* (Darmstadt: Jazzinstitut, 2016).
Balliett, Whitney, *American Musicians: 56 Portraits in Jazz* (Oxford: Oxford University Press, 1986).

Beddoe, Deirdre, *Back to Home and Duty: Women Between the Wars 1918–1939* (London: Pandora Press, 1989).
Beddoe, Deirdre, *Discovering Women's History: A Practical Manual* (London: Pandora Press, 1983).
Beddoe, Deirdre, 'Fur Coats and Widows' Weeds: The Great War, 1914–1918', in Deirdre Beddoe, *Out of the Shadows: A History of Women in Twentieth-Century Wales* (Cardiff: University of Wales Press, 2000).
Berlin, Irving (composer), *Watch Your Step* (1914), recreated by American Classics (2000), *www.americanclassicsmusic.org/watch-your-step*, accessed 18 May 2016.
Billington, Ray Allen (ed.), *The Journal of Charlotte L. Forten: A young black woman's reactions to the white world of the Civil War era* (New York: Dryden Press, 1953).
'Black Past Remembered and Reclaimed: The Online Reference Guide to African American History', *www.blackpast.org*.
Bontemps, Arna, *W. C. Handy (1873–1958), Father of the Blues, An Autobiography*, Foreword by Abbe Niles (New York: Da Capo Press, 1941).
Boulton, Derek, *Jazz in Britain* (London: W. H. Allen, 1959).
Bourke, Joanna, *Gender, Class and Ethnicity: Working-class Cultures in Britain 1890–1960* (London: Routledge, 1994).
Bourne, Stephen, 'Sophisticated Lady: a Celebration of Adelaide Hall' (London: ECOHP [Ethnic Communities Oral History Project], 2001).
Bourne, Stephen, *Black Poppies: Britain's Black Community and the Great War* (Stroud: History Press, 2014).
Bratton, Jacqueline S. (ed.), *Music Hall: Performance and Style* (Milton Keynes: Open University Press, 1986).
Brooks, Tim, *Lost Sounds: Blacks and The Birth of The Recording Industry 1890–1919* (Urbana and Chicago: University of Illinois Press, 2005).
Burroughs, Nannie Helen, Speech given at the National Baptist Church Twentieth Annual Session of the Women's Convention (1920).
Butetown History and Arts Centre, Cardiff, 'Oral History Collection' (1986–2016).
Callahan, J. Will (lyricist), and Roberts, Lee S. (composer), 'Smiles', performed by Joseph C. Smith's Orchestra of 1918, *https://www.youtube.com/watch?v=gHf4UL41UNc*, accessed 16 September 2015.
Cambrensis, Giraldus/Gerald of Wales, *The Journey Through Wales/The Description of Wales*, trans. Lewis Thorpe (Harmondsworth and New York: Penguin Books, 1978).
Carney Smith, Jessie (ed.), *Notable Black American Women: Book II* (Detroit, MI: Gale Research, 1996).
Chapman, Maria Weston, *Songs of the Free and Hymns of Christian Freedom* (Washington Street, Boston: Isaac Knapp, MDCCCXXXVI (1836)), in John A. Collins, *The Anti-Slavery Picknick – A Collection of Speeches, Poems, Dialogues and Songs: Intended for Use in Schools and Anti-Slavery Meetings* (Ithaca, NY: Cornell University Library, copyrighted material, 1 January 1842).

Chase, Gilbert, *America's Music: From the Pilgrims to the Present* (Urbana and Chicago: University of Illinois Press, 1987, rev. 3rd edn).
Clarkson, Thomas, 'Tour on Behalf of the Anti-Slavery Society', NLW MS14984A.
Colin, Sid, *And The Bands Played On: An Informal History of British Dance Bands* (London: Elm Tree Books, 1977).
Cooper, Richard, and Jackson, Dr Eric R., *Cincinnati's Underground Railroad* (Charleston, SC: Arcadia Publishing, 2014).
Crenshaw, Kimberle, 'Demarginalizing the Intersection of Race and Sex: A Black Feminist Critique of Antidiscrimination Doctrine, Feminist Theory and Antiracist Policies', *University of Chicago Legal Forum*, 1 (1989).
Cullen, Frank, *Vaudeville Old & New. An Encyclopedia of Variety Performers in America: Volume 1* (New York: Routledge, 2007).
Dahl, Linda, *Stormy Weather: The Music and Lives of a Century of Jazzwomen* (London: Quartet Books, 1984).
Davis, Angela, *Women, Race and Class* (London: Women's Press, 1982).
Dee, Luana, and Katell, Keineg (eds), *Women in Wales* (Cardiff: Womenwrite Press, 1987).
Dixon, Robert M. W., and Godrich, John, *Blues & Gospel Records 1902–1943* (Essex: Storyville Publications, 1982).
Delany, Martin, and Levine, Robert S., *Frederick Douglass, and the Politics of Representative Identity* (Chapel Hill: University of North Carolina Press, 1997).
Donaldson, Mrs Richard Alexander, IV (researched and compiled), *Donaldson: A history of the William Donaldson family of St. Andrews, Fife, Scotland, the province of New Jersey, North America, and London, England, with a record of his descendants in the United States of America . . .*, with Preface and Addenda compiled by Pat Donaldson (Georgetown, OH: Donaldson, June 1978).
Douglass, Frederick, *Narrative of the Life of Frederick Douglass* (New York and Oxford: Oxford University Press, Oxford World's Classics, 1999).
Du Bois, W. E. B., *The Souls of Black Folk: Essays and Sketches* (Chicago: A. C. McClurg and Co., 1903; repr. New York: Fawcett Publications, Inc., Fawcett World Library, 1961).
Ecker, Gisela (ed.), *Feminist Aesthetics* (London: Women's Press, 1985).
Ehrlich, Cyril, *The Piano: A History* (London: J. M. Dent, 1976).
Elkins, Stanley, and McKitrick, Eric, *The Age of Federalism: The Early American Republic, 1788–1800* (New York and Oxford: Oxford University Press, 1992).
Ellis, Osian, *The Story of the Harp in Wales* (Cardiff: University of Wales Press, 1991).
'Elwy-Jones', *https://elwyjones.wordpress.com/r-e-jones-ltd-1923-1962/*, blog about R. E. Jones Ltd, the 'Tea Shop Kings', including lists of cafes, holdings and business ventures, accessed 12 July 2016.

Evans, Chris, *Slave Wales: The Welsh and Atlantic Slavery, 1660–1850* (Cardiff: University of Wales Press, 2010).
Evans, Neil, 'The South Wales Race Riots of 1919', in *Llafur*, 3/1 (1980).
Fanon, Frantz, *Black Skin, White Masks*, trans. Charles Lam Markmann (London: Pluto Press, 1986).
Fawcett, Millicent Garrett, *Women's Suffrage: A Short History of a Great Movement* (London and Edinburgh: T. C. and C. Jack, 1911).
Feather, Leonard, *Jazz Years: Earwitness to an Era* (London and Sydney, Auckland: Pan, 1986).
Ferris, Paul (ed.), *The Collected Letters of Dylan Thomas* (London: J. M. Dent, first pub. 1985; new edn 2000).
Francis, Hywel, and Smith, Dai, *The Fed: History of the South Wales Miners in the Twentieth Century* (London: Lawrence and Wishart, 1980).
Francis, Hywel, *Miners Against Facism: Wales and the Spanish Civil War* (London: Lawrence and Wishart, 1984).
Franklin, John Hope, and Schweninger, Loren, *Runaway Slaves, Rebels on the Plantation* (New York: Oxford University Press, 1999).
Gammond, Peter, *Scott Joplin and the Ragtime Era* (London: Sphere Books, 1975).
Gates, Henry Louis Jr, and Higginbotham, Evelyn Brooks (eds), *African American Lives* (New York and Oxford: Oxford University Press, 2004).
Gibbs, W. J., *Negro Spirituals, or The Songs of the Jubilee Singers* (Bromley, Kent, and Ambleside, Clacton-on-Sea: W. J. Gibbs, *c*.1900).
Graham, Sandra, 'On the Road to Freedom: The Contracts of the Fisk Jubilee Singers', *American Music*, 24/1 (Spring 2006).
Green, Jeffrey, 'Afro-American Symphony: Popular Black Concert Hall Performers 1900–1940', in Paul Oliver (ed.), *Black Music in Britain: Essays on the Afro-Asian Contribution to Popular Music* (Milton Keynes: Open University Press, 1990).
Green, Jeffrey, 'The Jamaican Native Choir in Britain 1906–1908', *Black Music Research Journal*, 13/1 (Spring 1993).
Hamm, Charles, *Irving Berlin, Songs from the Melting Pot: The Formative Years, 1907–1914* (New York: Oxford University Press, 1997).
Harding, Rosamond E. M., *The Piano Forte: Its History Traced to the Great Exhibition of 1851* (Cambridge: Cambridge University Press, 1933).
Harding, Sandra (ed.), *Feminism and Methodology: Social Science Issues* (Bloomington, IN: Indiana University Press, 1987).
Harker, Dave, *One For The Money: Politics and Popular Song* (London: Hutchinson, 1980).
Higginbotham, Evelyn Brooks, *Righteous Discontent: The Women's Movement in the Black Baptist Church 1880–1920* (Cambridge, MA: Harvard University Press, 1993).
Hobsbawm, Eric, *The Jazz Scene* (London: Faber & Faber, 1959; repr. 2015).
hooks, bell, *Ain't I A Woman: Black Women and Feminism* (London: Pluto Press, 1981).

Hughes, Spike, *Second Movement* (London: Museum Press, 1951).
Hulonce, Lesley, 'Angels in the House?' Women's Work in the Workhouse' (paper for Women's Archive Wales conference, 10 October 2015).
Hulonce, Lesley, 'Workhouse Tales', *https://lesleyhulonce.wordpress.com*, accessed 12 July 2016.
Hurmence, Belinda (ed.), *Before Freedom: When I Just Can Remember. Personal Accounts of Slavery in South Carolina* (Winston-Salem, NC: John F. Blair, 1989; from the Penn School Collection, Penn Center, Library of Congress, 1966).
Jamison, Philip, *Hoedowns, Reels and Frolics: Roots and Branches of Southern Appalachian Dance* (Urbana and Chicago: University of Illinois Press, 2015).
Jempson, Mike, *The Musicians' Union: A Centenary Celebration* (London: Musicians' Union, 1993).
Jenkins, Nigel, *Gwalia in Khasia: The Biggest Overseas Venture Ever Sustained by the Welsh* (Llandeilo: Gomer Press, 1995).
Jones, Daniel, *My Friend Dylan Thomas* (Worthing, W. Sussex: Littlehampton Book Services,1977).
Jones, Evan ['Ieuan Gwynedd'] (ed.), *Y Gymraes*, established 1850–2; revived 1896–1934, editor Alice Gray Jones.
Kent, Greta, *A View from the Bandstand* (London: Sheba Feminist Publishers, 1983).
Knauer, Wolfram (ed.), *Gender and Identity in Jazz*, Darmstadt Studies in Jazz Research, vol. 14 (Darmstadt: Jazzinstitut Darmstadt, 2016).
Ladner, Joyce, 'Introduction to *Tomorrow's Tomorrow: The Black Woman*', in Sandra Harding (ed.), *Feminism and Methodology: Social Science Issues* (Bloomington, IN: Indiana University Press, 1987).
Levin, Floyd, *Classic Jazz: A Personal View of the Music and the Musicians* (Berkeley, Los Angeles, and London: University of California Press, 2000).
Levine, Robert S., *Martin Delany, Frederick Douglass and the Politics of Representative Identity* (Chapel Hill and London: University of North Carolina Press, 1997).
Lewis, Bernard *Swansea and the Workhouse: The Poor Law in 19th Century Swansea* (West Glamorgan Archive Service, 2003).
Lewis, David Levering, *W. E. B. Du Bois: Biography of a Race, 1868–1919* (New York: Owl Books, 1994).
Lewis, David Levering, *W. E. B. Du Bois: The Fight for Equality and the American Century 1916–1923* (New York: Owl Books, 2001).
Llwyd, Alan, *Cymru Ddu/Black Wales: A History* (Cardiff: Butetown History and Arts Centre/Hughes and Son, 2005).
Loesser, Arthur, *Men, Women and Pianos: A Social History* (New York: Dover Publications, 1990).
Lomax, Alan, *The Land Where the Blues Began* (London: Methuen, 1993).
Lorde, Audre, 'The Master's Tools will Never Dismantle the Master's House', comments at 'The Personal and the Political' panel (*The Second*

Sex conference, 29 October 1979); also in Audre Lorde, *Sister Outsider: Essays and Speeches* (Berkeley, CA: Crossing Press, 1984).

Mackenzie, John (ed.), *Imperialism and Popular Culture* (Manchester: Manchester University Press, 1986).

Marsh, J. B. T., and Loudin, F. J., *The Story of the Jubilee Singers, with Supplement by F. J. Loudin* (London: Hodder and Stoughton, 1901), with notation.

Masson, Ursula, 'The Swansea Suffragettes' (for Swansea Women's History Group), in Luana Dee and Keineg Katell (eds), *Women in Wales* (Cardiff: Womenwrite Press, 1987).

Masson, Ursula, *For Women, For Wales and For Liberalism: Women in Liberal Politics in Wales, 1880–1914* (Cardiff: University of Wales Press, 2010).

Mercier, Laurie, and Gier, Jaclyn J. (eds), *Mining Women: Gender in the Development of a Global Industry, 1670–2000* (New York: Palgrave Macmillan, 2006).

Mullen, John, *The Show Must Go On! Popular Song in Britain During the First World War* (Farnham: Ashgate Publishing, 2015).

National Jazz Archive, 'Dance Band Diaries from the *Melody Maker*. Volume 2 – 1927'. Available at *https://archive.nationaljazzarchive.co.uk/archive/journals/the-dance-band-diaries/volume-2-1927?*, accessed 12 July 2016.

Northup, Solomon, *12 Years a Slave* (London: Penguin Books, 2012).

National Library of Wales, *Dictionary of Welsh Biography*, 'Owen, Morfydd Llwyn (1891–1918), composer, singer, and pianist', *http://wbo.llgc.org.uk/en/s-OWEN-LLW-1891.html*, accessed 12 July 2016.

O'Connell, Sid, 'Women in Ragtime', in *Women in Music* newsletter (July 1992).

Oliver, Paul, *Songsters and Saints: Vocal Traditions on Race Records* (Cambridge: Cambridge University Press, 1984).

Oliver, Paul, *The Story of The Blues* (London: Penguin Books, 1978).

Oliver, Paul (ed.), *Black Music in Britain: Essays on the Afro-Asian Contribution to Popular Music* (Milton Keynes: Open University Press, 1990).

Painting, David, *Amy Dillwyn* (Cardiff: University of Wales Press, 2013).

Parsonage, Catherine, *The Evolution of Jazz in Britain, 1880–1935* (Aldershot: Ashgate Publishing, 2005).

Parsonage, Catherine, 'In Dahomey: a Negro musical comedy', in C. Parsonage, *The Evolution of Jazz in Britain 1880–1935* (Aldershot: Ashgate Publishing, 2005).

Parsonage, Catherine, and Dyson, Kathy, 'The History of Women in Jazz in Britain', in Patricia Adkins Chiti, *Women in Jazz/Donne in Jazz* (Italy: Fondazione Adkins Chiti, 2007).

Pickering, Michael, 'White Skin, Black Masks: "Nigger" Minstrelsy in Victorian England', in J. S. Bratton (ed.), *Music Hall: Performance and Style* (Milton Keynes: Open University Press, 1986).

Pickering, Michael, 'Jet Ornament to Society: Black Music in Nineteenth Century Britain', in Len Platt, Tobias Backer and David Linton (eds), *Popular Musical Theatre in London and Berlin 1890–1939* (Cambridge: Cambridge University Press, 2014).

'Plantation dance/ring shout: "Raise a Ruckus Tonight"' (PBS Learning Media/KET Arts 2013), http://www.pbslearningmedia.org/resource/afriam. arts.dance.plantation/africanafrican-american-culture-plantation-dancering-shout/, an approximation of a plantation dance/ring shout, accessed 11 July 2016.

Rappaport, Helen, *Queen Victoria: A Biographical Companion* (Santa Barbara, CA: ABC-CLIO, 2003).

Reports of the Commissioners of Inquiry into the State of Education in Wales, Appointed by the Committee of Council on Education (London: HMSO, 1848).

Reynolds, Harry, *Minstrel Memories: The Story of Burnt Cork Minstrels in Great Britain 1836–1927* (London: Alston Rivers, 1928).

Rieger, Eva, '"Dolce Semplice"? On the Changing Role of Women in Music', in Gisela Ecker (ed.), *Feminist Aesthetics* (London: Women's Press, 1985).

Rowbotham, Sheila, *Hidden From History: 300 Years of Women's Oppression and the Fight Against It* (London: Pluto Press, 1973).

Rust, Brian, *Jazz Records 1897–1942* (England: Storyville Publications, 1969).

Rutling, Tom, *Tom* (Torrington, Devon: Thomas J. Dyer, 1910).

Sankey, Ira D., *Sacred Songs and Solos and New Hymns and Solos 888 Pieces* (London: Morgan and Scott, c.1872).

Schleman, Hilton R., *Rhythm on Record* (London: Melody Maker, 1936).

Silverman, Jerry, *Ballads & Songs of the Civil War* (Pacific, MO: Mel Bay Publications, 1993).

Sinclair, Neil, *The Tiger Bay Story* (Cardiff: Butetown History and Arts Project, 1993).

Škvorecký, Josef, *The Bass Saxophone* (London: Picador, 1980).

Slout, William L., *Burnt Cork and Tambourines: A Source Book for Negro Minstrelsy* (San Bernadino, CA: 2007).

Stanford University Libraries Riverwalk Jazz Collection, http://rwj-a.stanford.edu/home, accessed 12 July 2016.

Stanford University Libraries, 'James P. Johnson, Composer of the Charleston', http://rwj-a.stanford.edu/program/runnin-wild-biography-james-p-johnson, accessed 12 July 2016.

Stennett, Stan, with Grandin, Terry, *Fully Booked* (Skipton: Vertical Editions, 2010).

Summerfield, Penelope, 'Patriotism and Empire: Music-Hall Entertainment 1870–1914', in John MacKenzie (ed.), *Imperialism and Popular Culture* (Manchester: Manchester University Press, 1986).

Sutcliffe, Andrea (ed.), *Mighty Rough Times, I Tell You: Personal Accounts of Slavery in Tennessee* (Winston-Salem, NC: John F. Blair, 2000).

Toynbee, Jayson, Tackley, Catherine, and Doffman, Mark (eds), *Black British Jazz: Routes, Ownership and Performance* (Farnham: Ashgate, 2014).

Traies, Jane, 'Jones and the Working Girl: Class Marginality in Music Hall Song 1860–1900', in Jacqueline S. Bratton (ed.), *Music Hall: Performance and Style* (Milton Keynes: Open University Press, 1986).

Tweedie, William, *Running a Thousand Miles for Freedom; or, The Escape of William and Ellen Craft from Slavery* (London: William Tweedie, 337 Strand, 1860).
Vincent, Ted, *Keep Cool: The Black Activists Who Built the Jazz Age* (London: Pluto Press 1995).
Von Eschen, Penny M., *Satchmo Blows up The World: Jazz Ambassadors Play the Cold War* (Cambridge, MA: Harvard University Press, 2006).
Washington, Booker T., *Up From Slavery* (London: Penguin Books, 1986; first pub. New York: Doubleday, Page and Co., 1901).
West, Cornel, *The Cornel West Reader* (New York: Civitas Books, 1999).
Williams, Daniel G., *Black Skin, Blue Books: African Americans and Wales 1845–1945* (Cardiff: University of Wales Press, 2012).
Williams, Daniel G., 'Frederick Douglass, Abolitionism and Victorian Wales', in Daniel G. Williams, *Black Skin, Blue Books: African Americans and Wales 1845–1945* (Cardiff: University of Wales Press, 2012).
Williams, Daniel G., *Wales Unchained: Literature, Politics and Identity in the American Century* (Cardiff: University of Wales Press, 2015).
Williams, Sian Rhiannon, 'The True "Cymraes": Images of Women in Women's Nineteenth-Century Welsh Periodicals', in Angela V. John (ed.), *Our Mother's Land: Chapters in Welsh Women's History 1830–1939* (Cardiff: University of Wales Press, 1991).
Wilson, Jen, 'Devil's Music', *Planet: The Welsh Internationalist*, 132 (1998/9).
Wilson, Jen, 'Jessie Donaldson, 1799–1889, Swansea Abolitionist', in *Minerva, The Journal of Swansea History*, Transactions of the Royal Institution of South Wales, 12 (2004), 41–50.
Wilson, Jen, 'Doing the Walkaround Skedaddle', *Planet: The Welsh Internationalist*, 177 (2006).
Wilson, Jen, 'Looking for Bessie Smith', *Planet: The Welsh Internationalist*, 195 (2009).
Wilson, Jen (ed.), *Those Saturday Nights: The Story of Swansea's Tower Ballroom* (Swansea: Jazz Heritage Wales, 2013).
Wilson, Jen, 'The Devil's Music in Wales: feminists, fascists, fashion and some o' that Old Time Religion', presentation to NAASWCH [North American Association for the Study of Welsh Culture and History] conference, Bangor (2012).
Wilson, Jen, 'Before Freedom: The Story of Willis the Runaway Slave', schools resource pack (Swansea: Jazz Heritage Wales, 2010).
Winkler, Henry R., *British Labour Seeks a Foreign Policy 1900–1940* (New Jersey: Transaction Publishers, 2005).
Wintz, Cary, and Finkelman, Paul (eds), *Encyclopedia of the Harlem Renaissance Volume 1 and Volume 2 A–Z* (New York: Routledge, 2004).
Zwerin, Mike, *Swing Under the Nazis: Jazz as a Metaphor for Freedom* (New York: Cooper Square Press, 2000).

Archives

Wilson, Jen, 'Swansea Women's History Group Oral History Collection' (1980–92), housed at West Glamorgan Archive Service, Swansea Civic Centre.

Wilson, Jen, 'Jazz Heritage Wales Oral History Collection' (1986–2016), housed at Jazz Heritage Wales, University of Wales Trinity St David, Townhill Campus Library, Swansea.

Women's Archive Wales, *https://www.womensarchivewales.org/en/* (held in county archive services, the National Library and National Museum of Wales, university archives and other repositories).

Newspapers

The Cambrian, 1830–1900, accessed at the Cambrian indexing project, City and County of Swansea Library Service, via microfiche.

The Cambrian Daily Leader, accessed at the Cambrian indexing project, City and County of Swansea Library Service, via microfiche.

Melody Maker, 1926–37, accessed at National Jazz Archive, Loughton, Essex, in original format.

South Wales Daily Post, 1894–1939, accessed at the Cambrian indexing project, City and County of Swansea Library Service, via microfiche.

Index

Aaron, Jane
  feminist historian 1
aerodrome, Swansea (1919) 170
Aberystwyth, dance protest 209
abolition, Britain 58
abolitionists 15, 16
  Clarkson, Thomas 19–20
  Quakers, Unitarians 15
abolitionists, Cincinnati
  Coffin, Levi and Catherine 33
  Craft, Ellen and William 33, 38–40
  Douglass, Frederick 33–8
  Garrison, William Lloyd 32
  Rankin, Rev. John 34–6
  Stowe, Harriet Beecher 32–3
abolitionist newspapers
  The Philanthropist 23–6
  The Liberator 34
Abbott, Lynn
  black pride, Fisk Jubilee Singers 94–5
  black women's cultural identity 93
African American GIs, Swansea 218

African American identity
  attitudes to, Welsh 96
African American performers 206–8
  respected in Wales 206–7
Alabama Sam 61, 62
Ammanford 200
Amman Valley 171
anti-semitism and jazz 197–201
anti-Slavery Movement, Wales 38
anti-Slavery Society
  Cincinnati 1, 25
  Ohio 26
  Swansea 14, 18
anti-Slavery Society, Wales 58
Appalachian music
  rooted in West Virginia 5
ap Huw, Robert (1580–1665)
  harpist, composer 3
ap Huw manuscript (1613) 3
Armstrong, Louis 208–9
  Harlem Hot Rhythm Band (1934) 208–9
  Swansea (1934) 208–9
Arnold, Betsy (age 104 in 1919) 152
  end of war celebratory dance, Abergavenny 152

Ashwell, Lena 145
  frontline touring shows 145
Bailey, Jenna 223
  author, feminist 223
  women musicians 'unskilled' 223
banjo 75
BBC Radio 213–14
  BBC Jazz Club 213–14
  BBC studio, Swansea 214
  dance band racket, monopolies 214
  monopoly 235
Beattie and Babs 141–2
  All Women Revue 142
  press report 141–2
'Beauty Chorus' 163
  Razzle Dazzle 60
  women 163
Beard, Chrissie 241
  drummer, Society Ladies Quartet 241
Bechet, Sydney 196
Beddoe, Deirdre
  challenge to gendered roles 132, 138
  feminist historian, film-maker 1
  on feminism 112
  women's work 172
Benson, Ivy 219–20, **220**
  All Girl Orchestra 219
  BBC discrimination 248
  invisibility in publications 248
  Musicians' Union and equal pay 248
  performs in Swansea 219
Berlin, Irving 121
  'Alexander's Ragtime Band' 122
  Hullo Ragtime! 121
  Lyrics and culture 160
  Watch Your Step 141
blackface 52, 57
Black and White Minstrel Show, BBC 30–1

Black Patti 113
Black Swan Records 154
  Harlem 154
Black Swan Trio 64, 75, 76
  Bohee Bros. 75
  Cushman, Carlene 64, 75–6
  Height, Amy 75
  Rivers, Rosie 75
black women music teachers 94
  Negro delineators 56
  Welsh performers 59, 60, 61, 63, 80
Blaney and Farrar 202
  female duo, English 202
  Running Wild, 202
Blaney, Nora 202
  pianist 202
Blondinette Melodists 66–7
  troupe, female 66–7
Blue Books (1847) 38
Blues 184
  'Blues' scale 184
  dancing 184
Bob'd Uns, female 4-piece band 240
  belittling review, *Melody Maker* 240
Bohee Bros.
  Swansea tours 75–6
Boulton, David 138
  dance teachers 138
Bourke, J. 148
  women's post-war income 148
boxing kangaroos 79
Brader's Musical Emporium 113, 145
Bridgend Munitions Factory 217–18
  women workers 217–18
Brown, Colin
  popularity of Fisk Jubilee Singers 91
Brown, Lonzo 121
  black Welsh performer, Swansea 121
burlesque 61, 63, 161
  Cullen, Frank 161

Burman, Maurice 207
'Hot Music, Is It Negroid or Hebrew' (1931) 207
Burroughs, Nannie Helen
stereotypes 97
Butetown History and Arts Centre
Howard, May 161
oral and photographic resources 5
South Wales 162

café culture, South Wales 150–1
women managers and entrepreneurs 150
'Café life' 157
review 157
café performers 157
cafés Swansea 153–82
Baltic Lounge 157, 176, 179, 181
Carlton 157, 158–9, 167, 181
Castle Restaurant 181
Chantant, Mackworth Hotel 157, 159, 167, 168, 170, 173–5, 181
Cascarini's 158
Continental 157–9, 163–6
Cutglass Temperance Bar 179
Exchange 157
Kardomah 156, 181, 182
Lovells 179, 181
Metropole 157, 168, 175
Mumbles Pier 157, 167
Patti Pavilion 179
Regent 179
R. E. Jones Ltd., Tea Shop Kings 158, 169, 180
Café Society, Swansea 154
new cultural awareness 156
cake walk 111
competitions 121, 192
parody 113
Canlish, Wil 79
Carlton Café, Swansea 158–9
advertisement Cartoon **159**

Carr, Laura A.
Fisk Jubilee Trio singer, 84, 107
Caluza, Thola'Kele 212
origins of jazz 212
Zulu musician 212
Carmarthen rugby scrum dances 205
Cartwright, Deirdre 224
guitarist, BBC TV *Rockschool* 224
Castle, Vernon and Irene, dancers 141
CCC Christy Minstrels 60
newspaper review 69–70
Plantation Walkaround Skedaddle 60
Chapman, Maria Weston
ideas of freedom 46–7
Charleston 186, 202, 203
description of 202
short dresses, flappers 202
Johnson, James P. 202
Chase, Salmon P.
Orphan Asylum 26
Cheetham, Arthur, film pioneer Wales 79
'Choc'late Soldier' 218–19
lyrics, racist 218–19
'Chocolate Coloured Coon' 123, 139
G. H. Elliott 123
impersonation of 139
Church politics 194, 198
Aberystwyth, dance protest 209
dangers of hot music 211
immorality and dancing 194, 198
Cincinnati
abolitionists, Cincinnati 32–40
Anti-Slavery Society 1, 25
History Museum 31
Quaker Slave Owners 32
Steamboat, Queen City of the West 32
Union Society of Colored Persons 25
Colored Orphan Society, Cincinnati 26

Cincinnati Riots (1836)
'Abolitionists Beware' Notice **23**, 24
Birney, James G. 23–4
Donaldson(s) 22–6
The Philanthropist 23–6
sailing of escaped slaves 32
Cincinnati safe houses, Welsh
Frandon 17
Penmaen 28
Clermont 28
cinema music, role of women 242–3
positive view of women musicians 242–3
cinemas, Swansea 189–90
Albert Hall 189
Carlton 189
Elysium 189
Shaftesbury 189
Tower Cinema 219
Ciro's Supper Club, London 165
touring revue 165
Clarke, May
Swansea tour 78
Clarkson, Thomas
tour of Wales (1824) 19–20
'black cattle' 19
Clayton, Jenkins and Jasper 79
class, culture and jazz 130
Pickering, Michael 130
Clermont County
Donaldson(s) 24
Colin, Sid 138
dance teaching 138
ragtime dances 114
Collins, Harry, Minstrels **51**
Colored Orphan Society, Cincinnati 26
Coonie, Harrie 164, 173–4
dancer and singer, African American 164
'Come Let Us All Go Down'
Fisk Jubilee Songbook 101

competition, cafés 158, 159, 162, 163, 179
Cardiff vs. Swansea 158
Cook, Wil Marion 116, 118–19
Cora, Madame 53
Craft, Ellen and William
Boston 39
escape plan 39
letter to Garrison 38–9
Swansea, Mount Pleasant Chapel 40
Walking a Thousand Miles for Freedom (1860) 38
Woodville Co-operative Farm School 40
Craig, Edith 132, 134
Women's Freedom League 132
Craig-y-Nos Castle, 78
Cullen, Frank 161
Burlesque and vaudeville 161
Cushman, Carlene 64, 75–6
Black Swan Trio 64, 75–6
equality 64
Cuyler, Dr Theo L. 86
description of Fisk Jubilee Singers music 86
Cwmamman 201

dance competition 138
Grand Theatre 138
dances 57–8
Louisiana Toe and Heel 57
ragtime 132
Tennessee Double Shuffle 57
Virginny Breakdown 57
war dances 58
dances, department stores, Swansea 190
Ben Evans 190
Woolworth Ballroom 190
dances, immorality 136
dances, jazz origins of 129
flatfootin' 130
patting, plantation breakdown 130

popularity in Wales 132
dance teachers 138, 139
  Imperial Society of Dance
    Teachers 114
  Langdon, Miss, Swansea 139
  Madame Jessie 190, **191**
  Welch, Egerton 138
  Davies, Jessie 171
  Treharne, Miss 171
  Swansea 190, **191**
dance troupes 136–7
dances, new 186
  Apache 186
  Charleston 186, 202
  Chicago Maze 192
  Dazzle Foxtrot 192
  Jitterbug 217
  Marina Saunter 192
  Polo Trot 186
dances, open air 192
Darktown Circus 79
David Evans department store 125
Davis, Angela
  black feminism 97
Davis, Bella 124
  Cracker Jacks, and her 124
Davies, David, Editor *South Wales Daly Post*
  racist account of 'Negro Funeral Service' 44
Davies, Francis 30
Dawson, Gladys 139
  Elysium 139
  Star Theatre 139
  Swansea's Historic Playhouse 139
  'Tipperary' 139
Dawson, Glyn 30
Dean, Dora 119–21
  song by Bert Williams 121
'Deep in the Mine'
  Jude, W. H., composed by 104–5
'Degenerate' behaviour, Wales 194–5
  Carmarthen 205

dances as rugby scrums 205
Davies, Walford, Director of
  Music in Wales 197, 200–1
Jews blamed 197
Jones, Morgan Rev. 196
Magistrates' comments 197
Negroes blamed 194–5
Patti Pavilion 197
Phillips, Rev. 197
De Ham Fat Man 62, 63
Dell, Peggy 188
  piano player 188
department store, Swansea 125
  Castle Follies 125
  David Evans 125
Deniz, Clare 214–15
  black pianist, Cardiff 214–15
  performs in London 215
Despard, Charlotte 133–4
  anti-war campaigner 133
  as 'Florence Nightingale', *South Wales Daily Post* report 133
  South Wales Daily Post report 133–4
  Women's Freedom League 133
Dillwyn, Amy
  feminist, entrepreneur, writer 106–7
Dilward, Thomas 63
  performer 63
  equality, women 65, 68, 69
  hooks, bell 65
Dixie songs 160
  Mullen, John 160
  'Night Time Down in Dixieland' lyrics 160
Donaldson, Anna Margaretta
  Cincinnati 16, 22–6
  Cincinnati Riots 24
  safe house 20
  obituary 27–8
Donaldson, Francis
  death of (1873) 46
  first Swansea visit 27

310 ❧ Index

marriage 27
return to Swansea 46
Donaldson, Jessie 13–49, **33**
  death of (1889) 46
  family 14, 15, 18
  marriage 27
  National Underground Railroad Freedom Center 49
  obituary 13
  school 16–27
Dormer, Daisy 122
  Oh-I-O Girls 122
Douglass, Frederick 33, 36–8, 72
  abolitionist 33, 36–8
  disagreement with Garrison 36
  escape from slavery 37
  Life of Frederick Douglass 37
  'The Fugitive's Song' 38
  The North Star 38
  Wrexham visit 38
  UK tour 72
Dramatic Art, School of, Swansea 171
  Gleaves, Evelyn 171
  Hutten, Muriel 171
Dresses, dance 185–6
Du Bois, W. E. B. (1868–1963)
  historian, civil rights activist 6
  Souls of Black Folk 154
Durk, Millie 184
  dance teacher, Wales 184
Dyson, Katherine 224
  British women in jazz 224

Edwards, Bettie 207–8
  history of jazz 207–8
Elliott, G. H. 123
  Carlton, Swansea 123
  Chocolate Coloured Coon 123
Ellis, Osian
  harpist, composer, author 3
Ellison, Ralfe 153
  Swansea 153

emancipation of slaves 47
  America 47
  Britain 47
emancipation of women 132, 136, 146
  campaign for 132
  changes in clothing 136
  'Joan' journalist, Swansea 136
escaped USA slaves in Britain
  Brown, Henry 'Box', lectured in Swansea 48
  Henson, Josiah, lectured in Swansea 41
  Johnson, Rev., lectured in Swansea 48
  Rigby, Thomas, lived in Llanelli 48
  Thompson, James, lectured in Swansea 48
  Willis, lived in Swansea 47–8
Ethiopian 53
  Female Serenaders Originals 57
Europe, Jim 150
  Harlem Hell Fighters 150
  New York Clef Club 150
'Everybody Loves a "Jass" Band' 1917 130, **131**
  lyrics 130
  sheet music **131**
'Everything is Peaches Down in Georgia' 174
  John, Gretta, production 174
  lyrics, Ager, Milton and Meyer, Geo. W. 174

fabrics, dance dresses 185–6
fair treatment for women performers 249
  in newspapers 249
Fannon, Franz
  black culture, discussion of 55
Farrar, Gwen 202
  cellist 202

fascists, Swansea 203–4
  Pollitt, Harry, assault on 204
  fundraising dance (1926) 204
fashion, changes in twentieth
    century 170
  morals, dancewear 170
  trouseritis 170
fashion, and dance 136
  Flexmore, Lily 137
  'Joan', journalist, Swansea 136
fashion and jazz 185
  dance floor fashions 185
  men's fashions 186
  short skirts 186
'Father of the Blues' 184
  Handy, autobiography (ed.) 184
Female Serenaders 53
  Ethiopian 53, 54,
  Original American 53
Feather, Leonard 207, 243–5
  colour question (1933) 207
  women in jazz 243–5
Finch, Catrin 250–1
  culture, jazz, international 250–1
Fisk Jubilee Singers 83–110, **84**
  advertisement (1874), *The Cambrian* **88**
  black women's cultural identity 93
  Craddock Street, Swansea Music Hall, 46
  Cincinnati newspaper report 85
  cultural expectations, 85, 89, 96, 107
  early days 110
  Free Trade Hall, Manchester 92
  fundraising tour 83, **84**
  gender identity, attitudes to, Welsh 96
  Greenock, Scotland 93
  Hull 92
  images **84**
  in Wales 83–109
  popularity 91, 101, 102, **103**
  pride in culture 92
  Sankey and Moody 90
  Scarborough 92
  songbooks, for sale 89, 92
  songs, sheet music 91, 92, 101, 102, **103**
  stereotypes of African American performers 107
  Swansea Music Hall 86, 87
Fisk Jubilee Singers, female 85, 107
  Carr, Laura A. 85, 107
  Jackson, Jennie, 85
  Mocara, Emma 85, 107
  Shepherd, Ella, 83, 85
  Tate, Maggie 85
  Walker, Eliza 85
Fisk Jubilee Singers, tour of Wales 86, 95, 102–3 109
  Newport, Cardiff, Merthyr Tydfil 102
  Swansea (1874) 86, 95
  Swansea (1889) 102–3
  Aberavon, Clydach, Morriston, Pontardawe, Ystalyfera, Pontardulais, 109
Fisk Jubilee Trio (1907) 106–7
  fundraising, Swansea 106, 107
  cultural expectations 107
Fisk University
  education of Freed Slaves 83
  Nashville, Tenn. 83
Flappers 185
  fashion and jazz 185
'Follow the Drinking Gourd' 21
Forten, Charlotte 184
  African American teacher, writer 184–5
  Oliver, Paul 185
  'The Blues' 184
Foster, Stephen Collins
  ballads 29
  'Old Folks at Home' 31
  plantation songs 29
  river boats 29–30
  re-enactment, Ashley Ford 31
  sentimentality 29–30

Francis, Dai 30
Frandon, safe house 17
Freedom
   Booker T. Washington 18
   Fugitive Slave Act 1850
   bounty hunters 32

Gardiner, Paula 224–5, 250
   Course Director RWCMD 224
   culture and jazz, international 250
Garland, Wil 117–19
   Musical productions 119
   A Trip to Coontown (1906) 119
   Coloured Lights (1927) 119
   Coloured Society (1917) 119
Garrison, William Lloyd
   anti-slavery campaigning 32, 34–5
   disagreements with Douglass 36
   letter to wife Helen 35
   lyrics 34
   The Liberator 34
gendered roles 132
   Beddoe Dierdre 132
   challenge to 132
George Mitchell Singers 30
Giraldus Cambrensis, Gerald of Wales (1146–1223)
   author, diarist, traveller 2
   harpists, young women 2
'Going Back to Dixie' 125–6
   lyrics 126
Goodman, Leon 246
   'No More Women Movement', article *Melody Maker* 246
gospel music 188
Graham, Sandra
   Fisk Jubilee Choir, life on the road 110
Gramaphone advertisement, Swansea (1919) **133**
   Oxford Music Stores 133
'Gram-o-Phone' 113

Green, Jeffrey
   black women music teachers 94
   Jamaican Native Choir 106
Greenbaum, Hyam 239
   Decca Records, director 239
   friend, Spike Hughes 239
Gwynedd, Ieuan
   Y Gymraes, morals 100

Haggar, William, film pioneer
   Wales 79
Hague, Sam, Minstrels 72–3
   Reynolds, H. 73
   Swansea tour 73
Haines, Cris
   trumpet, flugelhorn, composer 3
Hall, Stuart 154
   Du Bois, W. E. B. 154
Hamilton, Cicely 132
   Women's Freedom League 132
Handy, W. C. 84
   'Father of the Blues' 184
   'St Louis Blues' 184
Harding, Rosamond, E. M. 148
   pianos 'respectable' for women 148
Harlem Hell Fighters 150
   Ragtime band, American 150
   Europe, Jim 150
harmonium 60
Harker, Dave 235
   Victor Silvester monopoly 235
Harries, Emmy 124
Hayes, Chris 248
   Melody Maker memories 248
   Spike Hughes outed 248
Heineken, Samuel
   Adventures of, in *The Cambrian* 45
   in American Civil War 45
Henson, Josiah
   A Life of Josiah Henson 41
   escape from slavery 42
   leaflet, Beecher Stowe House 41–2
   lectures in London 41

Index 313

Swansea article 41
Welsh translation 41
'He's the Lily of the Valley' 101
Fisk Jubilee Songbook 101
Higginbotham, Evelyn Brooks
   stereotypes 97
Hobsbawm, Eric, Marxist historian
   (1917–2012) 5
   on the music of protest and
   rebellion 5
hooks, bell 65
   women's equality 65
hospital dance, Swansea 204–5
   dance as rugby scrum 205–6
   hot music 187
Hughes, David
   Poet, writer, 14
   'Rescuers' 15
Hughes, Spike 232, **233**, 249
   BBC monopoly 235
   jazz columnist *Melody Maker*
   232–49
   sexism against women 232–49
Hullo Ragtime! (1913) 121–2
   Irving Berlin 121
Hutchinson and Tayleure 63
   Slave Troupe, Great American
   63–4
hwyl
   translates as a 'state of being or
   condition' 90, 210
   Melody Maker article (1934) **210**
Hylton, Jack 141, 186
   Watch Your Step 141
   Drill Hall, Swansea 186

In Dahomey **115**, 116
   cake walk dance **116**
   sheet music **115**
   Williams and Walker **115**
   improvisation 187
   hot music 187
   Parsonage, Catherine 187
Italian cafés, Wales 158
   Joe's Ice Cream Parlour 158

Jackson, Jennie
   Fisk Jubilee singer 85
James, Miss 204–5
   organiser of peace
   demonstration, Swansea to
   London 204–5
Jamaican Native Choir
Jones, Alfred Lewis aka 'Banana'
   Jones 105–6
   Swansea 105, 106
Jamison, Phillip 129
   origins of jazz 129
jass 129
jazz age, first 130
jazz band instruments, sale of
   151
jazz, development of 188
   challenging conformity 193–4
   'Jazz It' advertisement **155**
jazz in chapels, Swansea 201
   Jeffreys, Pastor 201
   Mount Zion Chapel 201–2
   Wesleyan Chapel, 201
jazz, origins of 129, 151
   Jamison, Philip 129
   Patterson, Ottilie 129
   South Wales advertisement
   (1919) **151**
   Welsh jigs and reels 129
Jazz Wallahs, Miss Loxton's 127,
   198–9
   workhouse dance 127
Jeffreys, Pastor 201
   Jazz music in chapels 201
   Llanelli 201
   Mount Zion Chapel, Swansea
   201
   ragtime hymns 201
Jenkins and Jasper, 79
Jewish Association Football Club,
   Swansea 204
   dance with jazz band 204
Jewish musicians 211
   banning of 211
   Coward, Henry, anti-Jewish 211

John, Angela
   feminist historian 1
John, Gretta, producer, 163, 166–8, 173, 174
Jones, Dill (Dillwyn) 213
   BBC Jazz Club 213
   pianist, composer, Newcastle Emlyn 213
   New York 213
Jones, Mae 214
Johnson, Charles E. and Dean, Dora 119, **120**
   pianist, composer, bandleader 214
   cake walk competition, Swansea 121
   sheet music, 'Cause I'se in Society Now' **120**
   Tour of Europe and Russia (1907) 121
Joseph, Julian 196
   pianist, composer, broadcaster 196
   Southern Syncopated Orchestra 196
Juba, Master 57
   dancer 57
Jubilee Singers, Swansea's tribute choir
   performance 102
Jude, W. H.
   composer 'Deep in the Mine' (1882) 104

Kardomah Exhibition Salon 156
   ladies welcome 156
Kildare, Dan 165
   pianist, orchestra leader, African-American 165
Kilvey Coloured Minstrels 59, 60
Kipling, Rudyard, 10
Kit Kat Club, Swansea 186

Ladner, J.
   black feminism 96, 97
lady drummers 146

lady drummers, ten 112
lady syncopators 187
   Millar, Jennie 187
   Ward, Hilda, and Lady Syncopators 187
Lane, Williams Henry 57
   Master Juba 57
Leigh, Kate 137
   Musicians' Union 137
Lemke, Sieglinde
   primitivism 89
licences, for music and dancing 169
   local authorities 169
   cafés 169
   committee dispute 201
   Jeffreys, Pastor 201
   Llandudno, Payne's Café 213
   Neath, curfew 206
   magistrates, anti-semitism 197–8
magistrates, immorality 197

Livermore Bros. 65–6
Llandudno, Payne's Café 213
Llanelli 201
Lloyd George, David 135
   arson attack on house 135
Loesser, A. 147
   pianos 147
Lorde, Audre 55
Loudin, F. J. **84**
   death of (1904) 110
   'Deep in the Mine', performance of 104
   manager and bass singer, Fisk Jubilee Singers 85
Loxton, Amy 127, 128, 142
   Jazz Wallahs 127
   ragtime pianist 128
   pianist and bandleader 142
   jazz pioneer, Wales 142
Lynne, Maisie 139
   Little Miss Ragtime 139

Mandolin band, women 52
   Tregaron **53**

Manhattan Syncopated Orchestra 127
marching songs
  'John Brown's Body' (adaption) 45–6
Marsh, J. B. T. and Loudin, F. J.
  Fisk Jubilee Singers, diary of tour 83
  popularity of Fisk Jubilee Singers 91, 101–2
Masson, Ursula (1945–2008) 135
  feminist historian, film-maker, founder, Women's Archive of Wales/ Archif Menywod Cymru 13
  suffragettes, Welsh 135
McAdoo, Eugene
  comparing Welsh and English audiences 107–8
  Fisk Jubilee Trio singer 107–9
McDowell, Deborah, E.
  Frederick Douglass 37
McNulty Sisters 79
Melody Maker 206
  anti-Welsh 211–13
  list of bands (1937) 214–15
  list of bands (1939) 216–17
  origins of jazz 207
  published (1926) 206
  racist article (1927) 207
  'South Wales Notes' 213
messages, quilts 21
message songs 21–2
  'Follow the Drinking Gourd' 21
  music business, Cincinnati 34
  'Old Folks at Home' 31
  'Roll Jordan Roll' 22
Minstrel(s) 52, 54
  'Negro' 54
  Pickering, Michael 55
  show 52
Minstrels, British
  Queen's Minstrels Troupe 96
  Royal Caledonian 95
  Tute's Minstrels 95

Minstrels female 70, 71
  Butterworth 70
  Christy 71
  Happy Ashantees (blackface) 71
Minstrelsy, Irish 65
  troupes 65
Minstrels, Miscellaneous
  Crown 79
  Kentucky Am-Euro Original Coloured Operatic 79
  Midget 79
Minstrels, Wales, amateur
  Aberavon 73
  Blackface 73
  Mumbles, 71, 73
  Pontardawe 76–7
  Port Talbot 77
  Swansea 78
Mississippi, floods 67
Mitchell, Abbie 195
  African American singer 195
Mitchell, Lewis, drummer 169
  bringing jazz to Britain 169
Mocara, Emma
  Fisk Jubilee Trio singer 107
modernism 183
  Parsonage, Catherine 183
morals, opinions on Welsh behaviour 74, 136, 170–1, 177, 187, 192–222
  Amman Valley 171
  Blue Books 99–100
  Carmarthen 205
  class distinction 171
  dancewear 170
  dancing 136
  domestic servants 136
  hot music 187, 211
  Neath 171
  Pontardawe 171
  Rawlings, Dr 136, 187, 194, 197, 199
  'rugby scrum' dances 205
  scullery maids 170
  Swansea 171, 205–6

trouseritis 170
Welsh press 74
Y Gymraes, 100
morals, debate, 125, 126, 127
Morris, Margaret **218**
   piano demonstrator 218
movies, silent 189
   piano players, live music 189
Mullen, John 160
   singing 'Dixie' 160
Munition Girls Concert Party (1917) **143**
   advertisement, *South Wales Daily Post* (1917) **143**
music hall 113
music teachers 145
Musicians' Union 137, 189
   Leigh, Kate 137
   women members 189
   women musicians 137
Myles, Ynet 240
   All Woman Band 240
   London competition winners 240

National Underground Railroad Freedom Center 49
   Jessie Donaldson 49
Neath 171
Neath, curfew for dances 206

O'Connell, Joanne
   Stephen Collins Foster 29–30
O'Connell, Sid 114
   bawdy houses 114
Octoroon Comic Ballet 70–1
Oh-I-O Girls 122
   Daisy Dormer 122
Ohio River, as 'River Jordan' 17, 21
'Old Folks at Home' 31
Oliver, Paul 103–4, 112, 116, 185
   Black Music in Britain 103–4
   Forten, Charlotte 185
   'In Dahomey' 116
   sheet music 112
   'The Blues' 185

Owen, Morfydd 226, 229
   pianist, composer, singer, collector, Treforest 226

Page, Doris, 163, 164, 168, 173
Pankhurst, Sylvia 134–5
   Star Theatre, Swansea 134
parody 58
   African American culture 58
   by Welsh performers 59
Parry, Harry 213
   BBC Jazz Club 213
   clarinettist, Bangor 213
   Payne's Café, Llandudno 213
Parry, Joseph 60
   musician 60
Parsonage, Catherine, musicologist, author 118–19, 168, 183, 187, 224
   British women in jazz 224
   'hot' music 187
   jazz, connotations 168
   modernism 183
   primitivism 183
Patterson, Ottilie, blues singer 129
   origins of jazz 129
Patti, Madame Adelina, singer, Craig-y-Nos Castle 78
Pauline and her Madcap Dancers 123
   Empire, Swansea 123
   tram conductress (1914) 124
Peace demonstration, London 204–5
   300 Swansea women 204–5
Pearl, Molly 236
   women in jazz 236
'Penmaen'
   Donaldson, Thomas 28
   safe house 28
Penrhyn Castle, slave owners 18
Phillips, Philip
   music business, Cincinnati 34
pianos, cheap in Wales 146–7
   Dell, Peggy, Woolworths, demonstrator in 188

hire purchase 147–8
women demonstrators 187, 218
Piccadilly Playtime Girls in Gower 180
silent film 180
Pickford, Emily 145
frontline touring shows 145
music teacher 145
Pickering, Michael 55, 73, 74, 89, 94, 109–10, 130
assimilation 74
black performers settling inBritain 94, 109–10
class, culture and jazz 130
minstrelsy 55
plantation songs 18, 29
plantation walkaround 63
Pocket Pierrots 159
Jones, Sybil 159
Warner, Freddie (blackface) 159, 161
Pollard, Hughes 141
aka Black Lightning, drummer 141
Pontardawe 171, 200
Price May(e) 142, 163, 167–8
pioneer of jazz, Wales 142
Professor Payne 140–1, 159
American Ragtime Orchestra 140–1
Primitivism 183
jazz music 183
Parsonage, Catherine

race records 188
Dinwiddie Colored Quartet 188
Monarch Label 188
race riots, Cardiff (1919) 172
Evans, Neil 172
Bourne, Stephen 172–3
ragtime (raggedy) 111–28
ragtime composers
Aufderheide, May Frances 114

Berlin, Irving 121–2
Joplin, Scott 114
Koninski, Sadie 114
Shepherd, Adeline 114
ragtime dances 114
Boston 114
cake walk 114
Charleston 114
grizzly bear 114
ramble 114
shimmy 114
tango 114
three-step 114
ragtime songs 114, 122, 125
'Alexander's Ragtime Band' 122
'Dusty Rag' 114
'Eli Green's Cakewalk' 114
'Going Back to Dixie' 125
'Maple Leaf Rag' 114
'Pickles and Peppers' 114
ragtime trenches 140
front line entertainment 140
Read, Ivy 241
Ladies Band 241
record labels, early 189
HMV 202
Monarch 188
recording, women, Britain 188
Zeitlin, Louisa 188–9
revue 74
competition with minstrelsy 74
Rhondda, Lady 135
political activist 135–6
Rhythm Clubs 244
Riddell, Fern
black regiment in American Civil War 45
Rieger, Eva 225
jazz, women and culture 225
river boats
slave workers 22
Foster, Stephen Collins 29
Robeson, Paul 153
south Wales 153

Rogers, Edna 237–8
   bandleader, Welsh parentage 237–8
   multi-instrumentalist 238
   Musical Dolls 238–9
   response to Spike Hughes 237–8
   prejudice against women 238
'Roll Jordan Roll', message song 22
Royal Theatre, Swansea 144
   advertisement, *South Wales Daily Post* (1918) **144**
   'rugby scrum' dances 205
   Carmarthen 205
   Swansea 205–6
Rye, Howard 196
   Southern Syncopated Orchestra 196

safe houses, Welsh, Cincinnati
   Frandon 17
   Penmaen 28
   Clermont 28
Sankey and Moody 90
Savage South Africa
   performance troupe 104
Second World War 183–222
   beginning of 216
   jazz bands 216
   women entrepreneurs 190
   women's work 187
Shepherd, Ella **84**
   Fisk Jubilee Singer, piano, harmonium 83, **84**
Silvester, Victor 114
Silvester, Victor 235
   bandleader, strict tempo 235
   BBC monopoly 235
Sims, Sergeant 79
skedaddle, plantation walkaround 60
slave ship, capture of 68
Slave Troupe, Great American 63–4

slave songs 129
   and jass or jazz 129
   popularity in Wales 131
   resonances with Welsh communities 101, 102
   'Song of the Little Negro'/'Cân y Negro Bach', Price, Benjamin 28
slave owners, Wales
   De La Beche 19
   Pennant, Penrhyn Castle 19–20
   Eaton, Thomas 19
Snell and Sons, Swansea, record store and recording studio **147**, 173
Smiles Broadway musical 166
   Lyrics 166
songbooks 57
   Fisk Jubilee Songbook 91–3, 101
   refined Negro music 57
songs, jazz or jass 130
   'Everybody Loves a "Jass" Band' (1917) 130
   'That Funny Jas Band from Dixieland' (1916) 130
song collectors 229–30, **230**
   Lomax, USA 229
   Owen Morfydd 226–9
   uncredited photograph, Llandysul (1911) **230**
   Williams, Maria Jane 226
Souls of Black Folk 154
Southern Syncopated Orchestra 195
   African American musicians, tour in Britain 195
   Bechet, Sydney 196
   tragedy 196
south Wales valley's immorality 200
   Ammanford 200
   Cwmamman 201
   Open air concerts 200
   Pontardawe 200
   Ynysmeudw 200
spirituals and slave songs 17–18, 29, 188

Stennett, Stan 30
Stevens, Jerry, Miss, trumpet, 241
St Johns, Herbert and Lily, dancers 123
   exhibition tango 123
   Martin, Miss, pianist 123
   Mumbles 123
'St Louis Blues' 184
Stowe, Harriet Beecher
   Beecher Stowe House 40
   Cincinnati 32–33, 40
   Douglass, Garrison 36–7
   letter to editor 40
   romantic racialism 30
   Secret Passage tour 40
   slave auction 41
   Uncle Tom's Cabin 36, 40
   Welsh ancestor 40
Stuart, Sylvia 215
   European tour 215
   vocalist, Swansea 215
suffragettes, Wales 134
   Swansea 134
   Llanelli 134
   Barratt, Miss 134
Summerfield, Penny 112
   revues 112
Sutcliffe, Andrea, oral history, slavery 97–9
Swansea, Anti-Slavery Society 14
Swansea, Brader's Musical Emporium 113
Swansea (1874), description of, newspaper report, *The Cambrian* 86–7
Swansea School of Dramatic Art 171
syncopation 183, 187

Tate, Maggie
   Fisk Jubilee Singer 85
Tea Shop Kings 158, 180
   R. E. Jones 158
   musical teas 158, 161
Texerkansas, Mlle.
   Swansea tour 78–9

Thomas, Dylan, poet 156
   Kardomah boys 156
Thomas, Elin Manahan 228
   singer 228
Traies, Jane 113
   class 113
Tregaron Mandolin Band 52, **53**
Trocaderians 188–9
Zeitlin, Louisa 188–9
Truth, Sojourner 64–5
   'Ain't I A Woman' speech 64–5
Uncle Tom's Cabin
   Swansea Star Theatre 42 Theatre Royal 42–3
   Kilvey Music Hall 42
   Theatre Royal advert **43**
   Welsh translation 43–4
Up From Slavery, Washington, Booker T. 18

variety 111
Venues, Swansea
   Albert Hall 132, 140, 145
   Assembly Rooms 52, 53, 57, 186
   Baltic Lounge 186
   Bioscope Theatre, Morriston 121
   Carlton 123
   Conservative Club 186
   Drill Hall 79, 186
   Elysium 139
   Empire 121, 123, 187, 145–6, 192, 195, 208
   Exchange Restaurant 149
   Gloucester Arms 67
   Grand Theatre 105, 114, 138, 140
   Langland Bay Hotel 217
   Mackworth Hotel 140–1, 149
   Metropole 186, 190
   Mumbles Assembly Rooms 71, 73
   Mumbles Pier Pavilion 123, 137, 146, 212
   Music Hall (Albert Hall) 59, 61, 65, 70, 76, 86, 87, 95, 106

Palace Theatre 121
Patti Pavilion 186, 192–4, 217
Pierrot Pavilion, Swansea Sands 137
Sketty Schoolroom 61
Shaftesbury 121
Star Theatre 63, 70, 73, 134, 139
Swansea Empire 76
Theatre Royal 70
Thomas's Café 204
Tower Ballroom 219
YMCA 67
Venues, Wales
   Capitol, Cardiff 217
   Carlton, Cardiff 217
   Cold Knap, Barry 216
   Coney Beach Restaurant, Porthcawl 211
   Gwyn Hall, Neath 194
   Loughor Schoolroom 60
   Marina, Penarth 216
   Merthyr Temperance Hall 60
Payne's Café, Llandudno 213
Vincent, Ted 154
   Black Swan Records 154
votes for women 132
   'pageant of famous women' (1910) 132

Wales, Nationalism 59
war dances 58
Ward, Hilda 187, 206
   All Woman Band 187
   saxophonist, band leader 187
   Ten Lady Syncopators 241
Walkaround, plantation 55
   Pickering, Michael 55, 56
Walker, Aida Overton **116**, 117
Walker, Eliza
   Fisk Jubilee Singer 85
Walker, George 116–18
   In Dahomey **115**, 117
Warner, Larry 159–60
   stage manager 160

Watch Your Step 141
   Berlin, Irving 141
   Hylton, Jack 141
Washington, Booker T. 18
   freedom 18
   Up From Slavery 18
Way Down South 173
   all black orchestra 173
   Coonie, Harry, newspaper review 173–4
   plantation dancing 173
Welsh jigs and reels 129
   jazz 129
Welsh miners 129
   Appalachian coalfields 129
Welsh Music, harmonies
   Dr Rimbault, English organist, article 95
White Eyed Coons 126
   minstrel troupe, Welsh 126
Wild Men of Africa 58
Williams and Walker **115**–119
   cake walk competition 117
   Cook, Wil Marion 116, 118–19
   expectations 119
   Garland, Wil 117
   Hart, Stella, lead singer 116
   humour, *South Wales Daily Post* 117
   In Dahomey 116
   Kipling, Rudyard, comments 117–18
   Parsonage, Catherine, significance of 118–19
   respect for performers 119
   In Dahomey **116**, 117
Williams, Bert **115**, 116, 117
   Dora Dean's song 121
   In Dahomey 116–18
Williams, D. (1829) 16–17
   journey home 16–17
Williams, Daniel G. 38, 72, 153
   anti-slavery movement, Wales 38
   Blue Books 100

Index ❦ 321

Frederick Douglass 38, 72
transatlantic discussion 153
Williams, Grace 228–9
   composer, influenced by jazz
     228–9
Williams, Gweneth 149
   and Her Jazz Orchestra 149
Williams, Gwyn Alf (1925–95)
   historian 1
Williams, Katherine 247
   gender and identity in jazz
     247
Williams, Maria Jane 225–7, **227**
   guitarist, harpist, Welsh 225
   song collector 226
Williams, Sian Rhiannon
   Our Mothers' Land, women in
     nineteenth century Wales
     100
Winstone, Eric 249
   diatribe against womenvocalists,
     Melody Maker 249
women bandleaders, south Wales
   180
   Aplin, Miss 180
   Burman, Rhys, Mrs 180
   Five Drummer Girls 181
   Gwynne, Mrs 180
   Jones, E. Miss 180
   Live Wires, with Daisy, Mavis
     and Dolly 181
   Oxton's Orchestra, Miss 181
   Scannel, Winnie 181
   Shearson, Lena 180
   Talbot, Winnie 181
   Williams, Gilbert, Mrs 180
women, demeaning of 134
   Bad Girl of the Family 134
   theatre shows 134
women's Freedom League 132,
   139
   Hamilton, Cicely 132
women's Institute 211
   dance licence, Pontardawe 211
womens' meeting place 157, 163

daytime cafés 157, 163
women musicians 137, 146, 150
   All Women Revue 141–2
   Etherington, Win, piano 137
   Kramer, Maude, banjo 137
   Leigh, Kate 137
   Musicians' Union 137
   Ten Dixie Girls 137
women, musicians, discrimination
   against 230–1, 243, 244
   physical ability, musician ability
     245
   traditional culture, Wales 232
   visual appearance 230–1
   women's 'lackability', writer
     New Yorker 245
'women, pageant of famous' 132
   South Wales Daily Post report
     133–4
   suffragette production, Swansea
     132
women pianists, Swansea 142–79
   Branson, Alice 146, 167
   Davey, Florence 146, 167
   Evelyn, Dorothy 167
   Framer, Amy 179
   Jackson, Cissie 146, 167
   Laurie, Betty 146, 167
   Loxton, Amy 142
   Thomas, Mabel 149
women performers 122
   regarded as second class 122
   wartime revues 124
women producers, floorshows
   163–4, 175
   John, Gretta 163, 166–8, 173,
     174
   Laura, Emm 163
   Page, Doris 163, 164, 168, 173
   Price May(e) 163, 167, 168
women's suffrage societies, Wales
   135
   Masson, Ursula 135
women's touring productions
   141–2

All Women Revue 141–2
Kodak Girl 142
Woman Power 142
women's work 171–2, 175–6, 178
   married teachers 171
   office work 172
   domestic work 172, 178
   strike action 175–6
   refusal of unemployment benefit 178
   entrepreneurs 190
   musicians 187, 218
   on tour 190
   piano demonstrators 187, 218
   Second World War 217–18
Workhouse, Swansea Union 124
   concerts 124, 127
   dances 125
   moral debate 125, 126, 127
   old Kentucky plantation décor 126
   variety acts 125
Wrexham
   Frederick Douglass visit 38
Wrexham, mine disaster (1934) 209
   jazz band fundraiser 209

Ynysmeudw 200

'Zulu' 58, 212
   Caluza, Thola'Kele, Zulu jazz musician 212
   origins of jazz 212
   performance 58